Daniel J. Hynan, PhD

Parenting PLANS

Meeting the Challenges with Facts and Analysis

Defending Liberty Pursuing Justice
SECTION OF FAMILY LAW

Cover design by Tahiti Spears/ABA Design.

Printed in the United States of America.

22 21 20 19 18   5 4 3 2 1

Library of Congress Cataloging-in-Publication Data

Names: Hynan, Daniel J., author. | American Bar Association. Section of Family Law, sponsoring body.
Title: Parenting plans / Daniel J. Hynan.
Description: First edition. | Chicago : American Bar Association, 2018. | Includes index.
Identifiers: LCCN 2017061335 | ISBN 9781641051033 (print) | ISBN 9781641051040 (epub)
Subjects: LCSH: Custody of children—United States—Psychological aspects. | Parenting, Part-time—United States—Psychological aspects. | Children of divorced parents—Legal status, laws, etc.—United States—Psychological aspects.
Classification: LCC KF547 .H97 2018 | DDC 346.7301/7—dc23
LC record available at https://lccn.loc.gov/2017061335

Discounts are available for books ordered in bulk. Special consideration is given to state bars, CLE programs, and other bar-related organizations. Inquire at Book Publishing, ABA Publishing, American Bar Association, 321 N. Clark Street, Chicago, Illinois 60654-7598.

www.shopABA.org

Table of Contents

About the Author vii

Preface ix

Chapter 1: Introduction 1

Chapter 2: Parenting Plan Controversies 5

Prominent Controversies 5

Chapter 3: The Foundation for Building a Good Parenting Plan 11

Methods to Improve Reasoning 20

Chapter 4: Scientific Evidence Regarding Children of Divorce 25

Research 25

What Influences Children's Well-Being? 28

Children of Divorce 32

Shared/Joint Parenting 34

Parenting Plan Considerations 39

Chapter 5: Very Young Children 45

Attachment 46

Research on Overnight Visits for Very Young Children 49

Criticisms, Commentaries, and Progress toward Consensus 54

Additional Parenting Plan Considerations 61

Trying to Make Sense of Complex Case Information 68

Chapter 6: Domestic Violence 73
Domestic Violence 74
Assessment 78
Parenting Plan Considerations 80

Chapter 7: Other Marital Conflict 85
Marital Conflict 86
Protecting Children from Conflict and Promoting Healthy Contact with Parents 89
Parenting Plan Considerations 96

Chapter 8: Children's Mental Health and Special Needs 109
General Principles 112
ADHD 115
Conduct Disorders 118
Depressive and Anxiety Disorders 119
Specific Learning Disorders 122
Autism Spectrum Disorders (ASD) 123
Court-Involved Therapy 125

Chapter 9: Parental Mental Health and Related Problems 131
Common Adult Mental Health Problems 131
Assessment 135
Parenting Plan Applications 138

Chapter 10: Parental Alienation and Gatekeeping 147
Overview of Parental Alienation 147
Research 151
Intervention Research 153
Gatekeeping 158
Parenting Plan Applications 160

Chapter 11: Relocation **167**

Relocation Factors 167

Practicalities of Residential Moves 169

Research 173

Additional Parenting Plan Considerations 175

Chapter 12: Nontraditional Families **181**

Gay and Lesbian Parents 182

Never-Married Parents 183

Implications for Parenting Plans 189

Chapter 13: Child Abuse and Neglect **193**

Child Abuse Investigations 195

Heterogeneity of Abuse and Neglect, Recidivism, and Rehabilitation 197

Parenting Plan Applications 202

Chapter 14: Practical Considerations **209**

Reports of Parenting History 209

Remarriage 210

Decision Making 212

Child Safety 214

Children Going between Households 217

Child-Focused Calendars 223

Communication between Parents 224

Interviewing Children 225

Individual and Family Therapy 227

Parenting Plan Components 228

Chapter 15: Schedule-Focused Practical Considerations **233**

Prepared Schedule Templates 234

Family Circumstances 235

How Much to Share and Exchange Children 237
Restrictions on Parenting Time 238
Integrating Basic, Holiday, and Vacation Schedules 238
Provisions for Future Parenting Plans 240

Chapter 16: Age-Appropriate Parenting Schedules 243
Child Age, Development, and Individual Factors 244
Parenting Schedule Examples 246
Very Young Children 246
Middle Childhood 250
Adolescents 256

Appendix A: Assertion/Information Worksheet 261

Appendix B: Airplane Travel for Unaccompanied Children 263
Newspaper Article 263
Safety Tips 263
A Number of Airline Policies 263
U.S. Department of Transportation Brochure "When Kids Fly Alone" 263

Appendix C: Parenting Plan Legal Criteria 265

Index 375

About the Author

Daniel J. Hynan, PhD, ABAP, is a clinical and forensic psychologist in independent practice. For decades, he has had a specialty in working with children and families of divorce. He has extensive experience conducting evaluations of parenting time, decision making, child custody, visitation, relocation, and individual functioning relevant to parenting. He also carries out work product reviews and trial consultations.

Soon after he began to specialize in work with children of divorce in the early 1990s, he recognized the need to increase the scientific foundations of evaluations and integrate such knowledge with professional practice principles. Consequently, he wrote the first peer-reviewed journal article on interviewing children in custody evaluations. Not long afterward, he wrote the first peer-reviewed journal article on observing parent–child interactions within the context of such evaluations. Also, he wrote the first such journal article on child physical health and safety in custody evaluations.

As an outgrowth of Dr. Hynan's combined focus on professional practice and scientific knowledge, he identified that a psychological test used by a significant proportion of custody evaluators had a gender bias. He published an article in a prominent journal describing that gender bias and how it could have a very negative impact on women undergoing custody evaluations. Afterward, the test publisher changed aspects of the test construction and eliminated the gender bias.

Dr. Hynan's work has focused on advancing the field in other ways, also. For example, his article on others' research regarding overnight visits for young children helped to shed light on the importance of prior patterns of parent–child and interparental relationships.

A multi-year project strengthened the scientific foundations of a number of psychological tests used in parenting plan evaluations. Dr. Hynan wrote journal articles that included psychological test data specific to custody evaluation parents regarding the Personality

Assessment Inventory and the Parent–Child Relationship Inventory, and he published supplementary information on these tests in his previous book. Also, he published Minnesota Multiphasic Personality Inventory-2 results in his prior book that had the largest psychological testing sample in the custody evaluation field, thereby improving the scientific foundation for the use of that measure.

That earlier book, *Child Custody Evaluation: New Theoretical Applications and Research*, was published in 2014 and covered a broad array of crucial content areas for divorce professionals. It was the number one bestseller in its Amazon category very soon after its publication.

Dr. Hynan received his BA from the University of Notre Dame in 1977 and his PhD from Northern Illinois University in 1982. He is board certified by the American Board of Assessment Psychology.

His website is drhynan.com. He can be contacted by email at drdanhynan@gmail.com.

Preface

In the latter part of 2015, I received a message from Steven Peskind that encouraged me to submit a book proposal to the American Bar Association Family Law Section. At the time, I was not thinking about writing another book, and it had not been long since my previous one had been published. However, it helped that I had seen very high-level work by Steven, including as a trial attorney (in part, conducting an excellent and very challenging cross-examination of an expert, namely me) and having written a superb law review article and book. Therefore, I was open to his encouragement to submit a proposal.

We communicated back and forth about a number of possible book topics. Eventually we arrived at the topic of parenting plans, about which I thought I could make a substantive contribution to benefit children of divorce.

My main concern in writing such a book was that the main readers would be legal professionals. Other than having been a second author on a law review article, my earlier articles and book had been aimed primarily at psychologists and other mental health professionals. It helped that parenting plan and best-interest-of-the-child legal criteria overlap a good deal with results of psychosocial research about what influences children of divorce; therefore, a considerable amount of the book contents are relevant both for legal and mental health professionals.

I wish to thank attorney Lynne Ustach, co-chair of the ABA Family Law Section Publications Board, for her time and effort reviewing the book manuscript, and especially for her excellent feedback that contributed to substantial improvements in it. Thanks also go to the Hon. Edward Newman for his review of the manuscript. I have a great deal of appreciation for Jeff Salyards, executive editor of the American Bar Association Publishing, who has guided me through the course of many months of work on this book.

I am grateful for the assistance and input of a number of other individuals. My administrative assistant, Marzena Powala, carried out her usual, consistently high level of work helping me in a number of phases as I was writing. I appreciate the responses and input of a number of colleagues and friends, including those on the Best Interest listserv. Periodically, I placed inquiries on the listserv when I was having difficulty finding quality published resources about one of the content areas covered. In particular, I wish to thank Bud Dale for providing multiple leads about parenting plan statutes that served as excellent cross checks for the online searches that Marzena and I conducted.

Most importantly, I am grateful for the support and encouragement of my family, including my wife and children, as well as my deceased parents. Among many other wonderful qualities, my parents were great models of how to work and interact with others, and their lessons live on.

CHAPTER 1
INTRODUCTION

This book covers a broad range of content relevant to parenting plans, from ongoing controversies to empirical research to practical yet crucial considerations in the day-to-day lives of families. My goal is to facilitate the creation of high-quality parenting plans for children of separation and divorce. The primary audience is family law professionals, including attorneys for parents or children, judges, mediators, arbitrators, parenting coordinators, and those involved in the process of collaborative family law. An additional main audience includes professionals with mental health backgrounds who are serving as evaluators, mediators, therapists, or parenting coordinators. Because this book integrates considerable research, theory, and scholarly debate, it is also useful for those involved in scholarship related to parenting plans.

There are a number of different ways to use this book. It can be used as a type of toolbox or, alternately, as a general source of comprehensive knowledge highly relevant for parenting plans. For example, if attorneys or other professionals have a case that involves very young children, they might choose to go directly to Chapter 5. If there are allegations of parental alienation, the reader might decide that it is most productive to go directly to Chapter 10. There may be case-relevant questions about primarily practical, circumstantial factors or about how to consider child age and stage of development, and such information can be found in Chapters 14 through 16. In contrast, if a reader wishes to gain a more thorough understanding of what has an impact on children of divorce and how to apply that knowledge to parenting plans, it would be best for that individual to start at the beginning and read the entire book. Many readers of scholarly or professional books begin by looking at specific sections that seem most relevant for pressing questions or concerns, and they later return to consume larger chunks of related information.

Throughout the book, there is an integration of practical considerations about parenting plans with scientifically based and professional information. After a fairly concise description in Chapter 2 of a number of the main controversies in the parenting plan arena, Chapter 3 summarizes crucial, foundational information about the cognitive processing of complex material as previously described by a Nobel Prize winner and his colleagues. An overview of scientific, factual information about what is important for children of separation and divorce is found in Chapter 4. A large proportion of difficult parenting plan cases have strong elements of concern about very young children, domestic violence, and/or other family conflict; they are covered in Chapters 5 through 7. In a number of challenging cases, there are questions or concerns about child mental health and/or special needs, covered in Chapter 8. Questions and issues about parental mental health and related problems are covered in Chapter 9. Although parenting plan cases that involve allegations of parental alienation or possible relocation occur a minority of the time, each such case tends to present with highly challenging and perplexing elements. Those content areas are covered in Chapters 10 and 11. The numbers of gay and lesbian parents, as well as never married parents, have grown considerably in recent years, and relevant parenting plan concerns are covered in Chapter 12. Considerations about parenting plans when there are concerns about child abuse and/or neglect are found in Chapter 13.

Of course, a significant proportion of cases do not have problems or areas of controversy, such as high conflict, mental health difficulties, or parental alienation, and yet there are practical circumstantial factors and children's ages and stages of development that need to be considered. As noted earlier, those content areas are found in Chapters 14 and 15. Perhaps obviously, real family law cases often present with a mix of issues that cover a number of these areas of concern. Consequently, there are a number of parenting plan case descriptions that include real-life complexities and related efforts to develop time-sharing calendars that promote what is best for the children. That material, including calendars for each case, is covered in Chapter 16. Although the case examples are very representative of problems faced in reality, the privacy and confidentiality of actual parenting plan or custody dispute cases are completely maintained in this book.

Before proceeding further, it is crucial to define central terms and concepts that frequently occur in family law and that are used repeatedly throughout this book. As I described previously,[1] the terminology

1. Daniel J. Hynan, Child Custody Evaluation: New Theoretical Applications and Research 10 (2014) [hereinafter Evaluation].

often used to describe parenting schedules and aspects of legal custody such as decision making can be quite confusing. The phrase shared parenting frequently is not clearly defined in the writing and speech of family law or mental health professionals. Similarly, research reports have often operationally defined shared parenting in divergent ways. Among researchers, shared parenting has generally described parenting schedules in which a child spends considerable time with each parent. In many cases, under the category of shared parenting, a child spends two or three times as many days with one parent as with the other. However, there are also instances of shared parenting in which a child is with each parent an equal amount of time.

Even though both 70–30 percent and 50–50 percent arrangements can be referred to as shared parenting, the realities of life are very different for families in which the child is with one parent a solid majority of time versus when the time is split equally. The many important differences in family life between these dissimilar arrangements have contributed to the periodic use of the term equally shared parenting, in which each parent has the child approximately an equal amount of time.

For purposes of clarity, in this book, unless indicated otherwise, equally shared parenting is used to describe children being with each parent an equal amount of time, with only very minimal variation, such as a 52 to 48 percent split. In contrast, the term shared parenting generally represents a time-sharing arrangement in which the parent with the lesser residential time has the children an average of at least two overnights each seven days, or 29 percent, consistent with studies that followed children and families of divorce over a number of years.[2] Therefore, the term shared parenting is used here when the parent with the lesser residential time has between approximately 29 and 47 percent of the parenting time. An exception is that a number of research studies I summarize only make a general distinction between shared parenting and sole custody.

Also, in this book, terms such as children of divorce and divorced families are used as a type of shorthand for children and families who have gone through a permanent separation or divorce. In recent decades, a greatly increased proportion of families with children have formed outside the structure of marriage and go through the legal

2. Eleanor E. Maccoby & Robert W. Mnookin, Dividing the Child: Social and Legal Dilemmas of Custody 72 (1992) [hereinafter Dividing; authors use the phrase dual residence]; Richard Cloutier & Christian Jacques, *Evolution of Residential Custody Arrangements in Separated Families: A Longitudinal Study*, 28 J. Divorce & Remarriage 17 (1997).

system when the parents split up. The contents of this book pertain as much to those families as to others in which marriage has taken place.

As described earlier, this book can be considered a toolbox and each chapter a different type of tool. However, a number of the best workers in any occupation or profession combine specialization skills with a thorough understanding of the overall task at hand. In terms of parenting plans, the more professionals are unaware of important facts about children of divorce, the more they are subject to the WYSIATI (What You See Is All There Is) phenomenon described in Chapter 3, which powerfully limits their ability to grasp the big picture.

Parenting plans are interventions. They are not just any type of intervention; they are usually legally binding interventions into the complex functioning of family systems. In fact, because families are splitting up or have already done so, parenting plans are characteristically legal interventions into two rather separate but interconnected family systems.

The best interventions are based on highly competent assessments. Interventions without good assessments are like a marksman who fires without having taken careful aim. Any professional who improves his or her understanding of this broad realm of children of divorce has a better chance of assessing the big picture of each family and being able to use that knowledge to intervene helpfully and productively.

A competent assessment of what is needed in parenting plans relies both on scientific evidence and on the experiences that professionals, including myself, have had over decades in working with children and families of divorce. A good deal of this scientifically informed experiential wisdom has been available for decades,[3] and recent work has reinforced and expanded its usefulness.[4]

Children of divorce are at a much higher risk of experiencing significant problems in life than children in general, and responsible use of the contents of this book, whether relatively specific or comprehensive, is likely to be beneficial. Any reader who makes the effort to go through especially the foundational material found in the early chapters, as well as the later ones, will very likely increase her or his capacity to devise parenting plans that have a good chance to facilitate positive lives for these high-risk children.

3. *E.g.*, ISOLINA RICCI, MOM'S HOUSE, DAD'S HOUSE: MAKING TWO HOMES FOR YOUR CHILD (1997).

4. *E.g.*, ROBERT E. EMERY, TWO HOMES, ONE CHILDHOOD: A PARENTING PLAN TO LAST A LIFETIME (2016); ISOLINA RICCI, THE COPARENTING TOOLKIT: THE ESSENTIAL SUPPLEMENT FOR MOM'S HOUSE, DAD'S HOUSE (2012).

CHAPTER 2
PARENTING PLAN CONTROVERSIES

Many parenting plan controversies are fueled by the increased consideration given to children spending a good deal of time with each of their parents. Over time, the term shared parenting has supplanted phrases such as joint custody and dual residences, which have been used as shorthand to describe parenting schedules in which children spend a lot of time with each parent. Especially as it pertains to very young children, shared parenting has been described as a potential danger[5] and, in contrast, as an arrangement that encourages positive child development.[6]

This chapter briefly summarizes important controversies related to parenting plans. Each of these content areas is described in greater detail in later chapters. Relevant scholarly and professional citations are found in the later sections of this book where more detailed descriptions of these controversies are found.

Prominent Controversies

A conspicuous controversy involves the question of overnight visits for very young children, including infants and toddlers. A number of scholars and professionals have energetically argued that overnight visits for very young children interfere with emotional attachment to the primary caregiver, who is, of course, characteristically the mother. Those authorities maintain that, consequently, such overnight visits

5. *E.g.*, Jennifer E. McIntosh, *Guest Editor's Introduction to Special Issue on Attachment Theory, Separation, and Divorce: Forging Coherent Understandings for the Law*, 49 FAM. CT. REV. 418 (2011).

6. *E.g.*, Michael E. Lamb, *Placing Children's Interests First: Developmentally Appropriate Parenting Plans,* 10 VA. J. SOC. POL'Y & L. 98, 118 (2002).

have a negative impact on very young children. A belief that overnight visits are bad for very young children tends to be associated with a perspective that emotional attachment in this age group occurs primarily with just one parent. Other scholars and professionals maintain that attachment can and often does take place with both parents at the same time. Accordingly, such authorities assert that overnight visits by very young children promote positive relationships with both parents, and they therefore facilitate healthy child development.

The vigor of this controversy is represented by multiple series of articles on the topic in the multidisciplinary *Family Court Review*. A special issue in 2011 included an initial series of articles, including excerpted interviews with a number of attachment scholars. In 2012, a set of *Family Court Review* commentary articles by scholars and professionals focused on the 2011 special issue. Later, in 2014, as a result of collaboration between leading scholars, including a number who had disparate views on the topic, articles appeared that strove to integrate findings and recommendations regarding overnight visits for very young children. More detailed coverage of this area is found in Chapter 5.

Children of all ages are included in the controversy over what criteria or guidelines should be used to determine parenting schedules and parental decision making. For decades, most U.S. statutes primarily have relied on criteria intended to focus on what is in the best interest of children. In about the last 15 years, a number of authorities have argued that such qualitative criteria are counterproductive and contribute toward negative outcomes for children and families of divorce. Such individuals have proposed an alternative that relies on reported histories of how much each parent has provided care for the children prior to the separation. This quantitative alternative primarily relies on self-reports of the extent to which each parent has carried out preseparation decision making regarding the children.

The proponents of relying on preseparation parental behavior assert that it can be accurately recalled by parents and communicated to the court. Those proponents also maintain that parents generally give honest reports that are consistent with one another, and contend the court is better equipped to successfully engage in fact finding about quantitative matters than to effectively weigh the traditional qualitative best interest principles. Others assert that the amount of time a child has spent with a parent does not determine relationship quality, such as attachment security; in addition, critics argue that parents in contested child custody cases rarely agree about the amount of past caretaking done by each parent, and that reliance on such quantitative information makes things worse for families because it leads parents to fight over who does what for and with the children.

Although there is a general consensus that, in most circumstances, children should have regular contact and positive relationships with both parents, there are controversies about particular elements of such arrangements, even above and beyond disagreements about overnight visits for very young children. Controversial aspects include practical matters such as the potential stresses and challenges of children largely splitting time between two homes instead of having a primary home base.

Another type of dilemma involves decision making. Specifically, in many cases, there are questions about the extent to which major decisions about children should be made jointly by parents versus having one parent be the decision-maker about one or more decision categories.

Although there are a number of research studies that show children of divorce generally function better when they are from families whose parents have joint custody versus one parent having sole custody, there are ongoing debates about the meaning of those findings. It is possible that the results indicate joint custody or shared parenting is the cause of better child adjustment, but it is practically impossible to conduct research that proves such causation. It could also be the case that families who had better parent–child relationships and/or interparental cooperation before the separation frequently were able to obtain shared parenting, and all these factors together facilitated better child adjustment.

There are questions about the stability of shared parenting versus arrangements in which children are predominantly with one parent, such as 70 percent of the time or more. A number of studies found that shared parenting or joint custody was less stable than sole custody in that children were more likely to change their place of residence in the former type of arrangement than the latter. However, a lower level of stability in shared parenting families has not been found in all research.

A major controversy has involved the role of conflict between parents as a central factor in determining whether shared parenting or equally shared parenting is likely to be carried out successfully. Similarly, there are major questions about interparental conflict and its impact on the ability of parents to successfully share decision making regarding children. An aspect of this controversy that has received too little attention involves the type, intensity, and duration of interparental conflict insofar as it has an impact on the children. Conflict between parents can range from relatively modest verbal arguments, which periodically take place in essentially all marriages, to injury-producing physical domestic violence.

There have been many debates about domestic violence in the context of divorce and child custody disputes. Although there is essentially universal agreement that domestic violence is bad, there are different points of view about what types and intensities of domestic violence usually take place within families of divorce. There are frequent reports of domestic violence in child custody disputes, and there have been numerous allegations that many such charges of domestic violence are false or at least significantly distorted, ostensibly so that the accuser can try to gain a legal advantage. In an effort to try to address dilemmas associated with domestic violence in the divorce context, a number of scholars and professionals have worked to identify typologies of domestic violence. There have also been recommendations for managing child and parent actions based on the type, intensity, and danger potential associated with domestic violence.

The frequency of marriage in the United States has been decreasing, and the percentage of children born outside of marriage has increased a great deal in recent decades. For the large proportion of the population that is outside higher socioeconomic groups, having a child outside of marriage is quite common. In certain cases, there are dilemmas about the best parenting plans, given that never-married couples tend to have lower rates of family stability than do married or remarried couples.

Gay marriage is fully legally approved in the United States. However, some individuals wonder about how well children fare being raised by gay or lesbian parents as compared to heterosexual ones.

Considerations about parenting plans typically take place when both parents wish to have a good deal of contact with the child or children, and often both parents want the major portion of the residential time. However, there are also circumstances in which there is a history or risk of very little to no contact between the child and a parent, characteristically the father. At times, such parents have not had much opportunity for child contact or face great barriers to child contact because they have been incarcerated. In other instances, there is no clear reason why there has been such little father–child contact.

It happens more frequently when the parents have not been married to one another and perhaps never even lived together. Such largely absent parents also tend to be relatively young and from lower socioeconomic groups. It is not known to what extent such parents simply drop away from contact on their own volition, versus to what extent the caretaking parent has carried out action that makes it very difficult to see the child. There are also concerns that the serious difficulties associated with being involved in the family law system discourage a significant number of parents from making and/or maintaining contact with their child, to the child's detriment. There have been recent efforts to identify how best to encourage potential or actual dropout parents to be positively involved with their children.

Family law is supposed to be gender neutral. However, a number of individuals, especially parents who have had difficult, unhappy involvements in the legal system assert that family law is biased in a direction contrary to their own interests. Such disgruntled individuals often believe that their own gender brings uniquely beneficial characteristics to the parent–child relationship. Mothers and fathers often manifest somewhat different parenting styles, and there are individuals of one gender who believe the other gender does not sufficiently understand the great value that they bring to parenting. Also, there are parents of each gender who believe that they, or perhaps loved ones, have been mistreated within the legal system by a parent of the other gender.

For example, the Protective Mothers' Alliance International (PMAI) states that its main focus is advocating for abused mothers and their children who have been the recipients of injustice in the family court system. It is noteworthy that PMAI acknowledges that women at times can also be perpetrators of abuse.[7] The American Coalition for Fathers and Children (ACFC) describes that they are a shared parenting organization and maintains that some of the organization's main opponents are groups that are focused on domestic violence. At the same time, the ACFC indicates that victims of domestic violence deserve protection and assistance.[8]

This brief summary of controversies related to parenting plans is by no means complete or exhaustive. It merely highlights a number of

---

7. PROTECTIVE MOTHERS' ALLIANCE INTERNATIONAL, https://protectivemothersallianceinternational.org.

8. *ACFC Is America's Shared Parenting Organization, "Children Need Both Parents,"* AMERICAN COALITION FOR FATHERS & CHILDREN, www.acfc.org.

the main serious challenges confronted when families split up and children are involved. It also establishes a foundation for why it is crucial to closely examine and try to understand complexities associated with efforts to establish parenting plans that are likely to facilitate healthy child development.

The complexities involved in working with children and families are far more daunting than many people recognize. Sending a rocket to the moon has been described as a complicated problem, but it involves processes that can be replicated and largely perfected over time with other rockets. In contrast, raising a child is a more complex problem because every child is unique;[9] furthermore, family relationships are at an even higher level of complexity because they involve interactions between multiple people. The likelihood of a child developing into a healthy and successful adult increases with a solid understanding of the factors that contribute to positive human development.

9. Atul Gawande, The Checklist Manifesto: How to Get Things Right 49 (2011).

CHAPTER 3
THE FOUNDATION FOR BUILDING A GOOD PARENTING PLAN

How does one determine what a good parenting plan is? Almost everyone grows up in a family, and shouldn't that give us a good understanding of how family should operate? A considerable proportion of professionals in family law and related fields are parents. Doesn't that personal experience give us enough knowledge to craft good parenting plans? Many of us feel we have good insight about human nature—shouldn't that be sufficient to allow us to carry out this task well? The best answer to these last three questions is no.

More specifically, it's possible that these personal background experiences and characteristics may help at times to put together good parenting plans. However, it is more likely that such experiences contribute to professional intuition that is just as likely to be entirely off target as it is to hit the bull's-eye.

My goal in this chapter is to describe a conceptual foundation for the development of good parenting plans. A good parenting plan is one that facilitates healthy child development and family functioning. Perhaps obviously, there is no evidence that only a single, specific parenting plan would be a good one for a certain family. Instead, it is more useful to conceptualize that there is a range or cluster of parenting plans that would be likely to be a good fit for specified child and family characteristics.

I rely extensively in this chapter on the work of Nobel laureate Daniel Kahneman[10] and his colleagues, who have spent decades

---

10. *E.g.*, Daniel Kahneman, Thinking, Fast and Slow (2011) [hereinafter Thinking].

researching and developing a body of knowledge about judgment under conditions of uncertainty. As described at the end of Chapter 2, matters that pertain to children and families have high levels of complexity, and there is essentially always a degree of uncertainty about relevant child and family functioning. Of course, there is also a great deal of uncertainty about future child and family outcomes, especially because we rarely learn anything useful about future functioning once the legal case is closed. The degree and importance of this uncertainty is most pronounced in difficult cases that involve serious concerns about an individual or about the family generally.

Kahneman[11] has demonstrated the cognitive processes carried out by even highly knowledgeable individuals who make judgment errors. Those mistakes frequently are apparent because they are quantitative in nature, and mathematical proofs show the differences between the mistakes and the correct answers. Clearly, there are no right answers that can be demonstrated mathematically in the realm of parenting plans. However, many of the cognitive processes and principles used by Kahneman are applicable to the uncertainty intrinsic in parenting planning.

In this chapter, I first describe the fundamental differences between the two types of thinking, intuition and reasoning. Second, I explain the importance of categories of intuitive errors, namely heuristics and biases. Third, I endeavor to illustrate how an understanding of such cognitive processes is highly relevant for parenting planning. Fourth, I offer examples of how to inject greater reasoning and deliberation into the parenting plan process.

Distinctions about different types of thinking have been identified going back to the philosopher Aristotle.[12] The difference between intuition and reasoning is central to the comprehension of judgment under conditions of uncertainty. Perhaps as a means of clarifying the distinctions between the two types of thinking, intuition has been described as System 1 and reasoning as System 2.[13] In brief, intuition is relatively effortless, quick, automatic, and often tied to emotion. Internal

---

11. Daniel Kahneman, *A Perspective on Judgment and Choice: Mapping Bounded Rationality*, 58 Am. Psychologist 697 (2003).

12. Steven A. Sloman, *The Empirical Case for Two Systems of Reasoning*, 119 Psychol. Bull. 3 (1996).

13. Keith E. Stanovich & Richard F. West, *Individual Differences in Reasoning: Implications for the Rationality Debate*, *in* Heuristics and Biases 421 (Thomas Gilovich et al. eds., 2002).

processes in perception and intuition are very similar. Reasoning, in contrast, is effortful, slow, controlled, and emotionally neutral. As can be seen in Figure 3.1, although the thinking *processes* of intuition and reasoning are very different, the thought *contents* are essentially the same. That is, both intuition and reasoning include conceptual representations and considerations of past and future, in contrast to perception, which is tied to current stimuli.

Within the context of parenting planning, a highly relevant and important difference between the two types of thinking is that reasoning, or System 2, is able to monitor cognitive processes, such as intuition, or System 1. However, such self-monitoring is difficult and occurs all too rarely.

As described in more detail later, especially in circumstances of complexity and uncertainty, System 2 generally holds greater promise than System 1 in terms of deriving reasonable judgment.[14] However, it

14. THINKING, *supra* note 10, at 417.

FIGURE 3.1 Process and Content in Two Cognitive Systems

	PERCEPTION	INTUITION System 1	REASONING System 2
PROCESS	Fast (Perception and Intuition)		Slow
	Parallel		Serial
	Automatic		Controlled
	Effortless		Effortful
	Associative		Rule-governed
	Slow-learning		Flexible
	Emotional		Neutral
CONTEST	Percepts	Conceptual representations (Intuition and Reasoning)	
	Current stimulation	Past, present, and future	
	Stimulus bond	Can be evoked by language	

Reprinted from Kahneman, note 11, at 698.

is noteworthy that System 1 can be accurate. For intuition to be consistently accurate, there need to be numerous opportunities for extensive practice and learning in environments that give clear feedback as to the accuracy of judgments.[15] In the realm of parenting planning, there is no environment that gives clear feedback as to the accuracy of judgment, in part because professionals almost never learn comprehensive information about family outcomes. Therefore, in order to maximize the likelihood of producing parenting plans that foster healthy child and family functioning, relevant family specialists need to learn about System 1 errors and methods to engage System 2. For purposes of parenting planning, one of the most important reasons for engaging System 2 is to identify relevant aspects of evidence about what is most important for children of divorce, and to deliberate about how to apply that information given the facts and circumstances of each family case.

Biases and heuristics are both types of System 1 thinking, and understanding them has a great deal of relevance for parenting plans. There are numerous well-known types of biases, including those based on gender, race, socioeconomic status, cultural background, and physical attractiveness. In addition to biases for or against certain types of people, there are also biases that involve cognitive processes.

The confirmatory bias involves looking for, remembering, and making use of information that confirms a preexisting point of view. The confirmatory bias also encompasses discounting, criticizing, and/or ignoring information that is contrary to a favored point of view or belief.[16] This very powerful human tendency has been recognized since ancient times.[17]

Heuristics are cognitive shortcuts that represent relatively simple thinking processes instead of more careful deliberation or reasoning.[18] Kahneman gives a more expanded description of a heuristic:

> A judgment is said to be mediated by a heuristic when the individual assesses a specified *target attribute* of a judgment object by substituting a related *heuristic*

15. *Id.* at 234.

16. P.C. Wason, *On the Failure to Eliminate Hypotheses in a Conceptual Task*, 12 Q. J. Experimental Psychol. 129 (1960).

17. Thucydides, The Peloponnesian War, at 4.108.4, *available at* http://www.perseus.tufts.edu/hopper/text?doc=Perseus:text:1999.01.0200:book=4:chapter=108:section=4.

18. Amos Tversky & Daniel Kahneman, *Judgment under Uncertainty: Heuristics and Biases*, 185 Sci. 1124 (1974).

> *attribute* that comes more readily to mind. This definition elaborates a theme of the early research, namely, that people who are confronted with a difficult question sometimes answer an easier one instead. The word *heuristic* is used in two senses in the new definition. The noun refers to the cognitive process, and the adjective in *heuristic attribute* specifies the attribute that is substituted in a particular judgment.[19]

The judgment, for the specific purposes of this book, is represented by the parenting plan. The target attribute is the well-being of the child. There are partially different perspectives from child development and legal standpoints regarding the well-being of the child.

From a child development standpoint, what is of utmost importance is the body of knowledge primarily derived from high-quality research about what influences the well-being of children of divorce. In family law, the well-being and best interest of the child is characteristically defined by relevant statutes. In a number of crucial areas, there is considerable overlap between statutory factors and relevant research findings. For more detail about the common ground between scientific evidence and relevant statutes, see Chapter 4.

There are numerous types of heuristics, though no finite list.[20] A number of common heuristics are described here, accompanied by hypothetical examples related to the task of putting together parenting plans.

The affect heuristic is defined by an individual's emotions exerting a dominant influence on judgment processes. A relevant example involves a professional, working to construct a parenting plan, who had a very unhappy experience as a child when living in an apartment. That professional is dealing with a case in which one parent will be residing in an apartment and the other in a house. The highly negative emotions associated with the memories of living in an apartment leads that professional to focus excessively on the features of the residential circumstances, associated with a well-intended wish to arrange a plan that would minimize child distress. Accordingly, there is too little focus on numerous other individual, interpersonal, legal, and practical factors that should be given serious consideration in the parenting plan.

---

19. THINKING, *supra* note 10, at 707.
20. *Id.* at 710.

The representativeness heuristic involves judgment based on superficial matters such as outward appearances. A hypothetical example involves a mediator working to try to get a separating couple to arrive at a parenting plan agreement. Both parents consistently and energetically assert they should have primary residential care of their 12-year-old son, and the mediator has the impression that neither one would tolerate the other having most of the residential time. The mediator has briefly interviewed the son to establish rapport with him and sizes him up to be a "tough kid." The mediator is aware that there can be a number of challenges associated with spending an equal amount of time between two homes, especially because these parents have very different parenting styles from one another, and they plan to live about a 45-minute drive from one another. The mediator makes a decision to press hard for an equally shared custody arrangement, and there are considerable efforts at persuasion directed to the parents that the son is ostensibly tough enough to cope with it, even though there is only a shallow understanding of him.

When the availability heuristic is relied upon, a decision is made based on the ease with which certain attributes come to mind. A hypothetical case pertains to an ongoing evaluation. The evaluator has recently completed a full-day continuing education seminar on post-traumatic stress disorder. Since that training, the evaluator has decided that the father in the evaluation case suffers from that condition. Accordingly, the evaluator has been pondering how to create and propose a parenting plan that adequately considers the parent who supposedly has that disorder. However, the evaluator has not carefully examined the extent to which the father actually manifests the diagnostic criteria of post-traumatic stress disorder. Similarly, there has not been consideration given to the possible presence of other mental health conditions and to whether the father may simply be experiencing transient stress that frequently accompanies divorce and litigation.

In these examples, the hypothetical professional engaged in intuition that relied upon the heuristic attributes of emotion associated with childhood experiences, the superficial appraisal of a 12-year-old boy, and easily recalled information from a continuing education class. In each case, the hypothetical professional failed to engage in deliberative reasoning that closely considered relevant statutory factors and the considerable body of research-based facts relevant to children of divorce.

Anchoring is a common cognitive process that is not always categorized as a heuristic because it can involve aspects of both System 1 and System 2.[21] Examples of anchoring primarily involve quantitative data. Therefore, it is especially applicable for matters such as negotiations about the relative proportions of parenting time for the mother and father. As a hypothetical example of anchoring, in an opening move in negotiations, the attorney for a parent asserts that the parent should have the child all the time except alternate Saturdays and Sundays. That time-sharing proposal becomes an anchor (System 1) in the negotiations and is likely to have a significant impact on the final parenting plan unless the other side can engage in a countermaneuver to significantly change it.[22] The anchor is very likely to exert a strong influence on other proposals, though adjustments (System 2) are often made as a result of the alternate propositions.

Individuals engaged in planning for parenting time schedules need to also be aware of many other factors that can impede or facilitate productive judgment processes. All individuals, including experts, tend to have considerable overconfidence in their own decisions.[23] As can be seen in Figure 3.1, intuition is effortless. In fact, the ease of associative, effortless System 1 thinking is associated with being in a positive mood. Being in a good mood tends to be an internal signal that all is well and diligence is not needed. Accordingly, excessive self-confidence in one's own judgment is associated with a superficial appearance of the details of the judgment contents fitting easily together into a coherent package. Also, the ease with which a decision comes to mind, which is characteristically related to quick and superficial cognitive processing as well as positive mood, contributes to overconfidence.

Too often, a decision is made easily and seems thoroughly coherent when we have not bothered to consider, collect, and examine an adequate amount and variety of relevant information. Similarly, an illusion of coherence can be present when we have not thought sufficiently to retrieve adequate information from memory.

There is a profoundly important danger for professionals of all disciplines in potentially relying primarily on their own family experiences as they engage in judgments relevant to parenting plans. With very rare exceptions, all of us grew up in families. Similarly, many of

21. THINKING, *supra* note 10, at 119.

22. *Id.* at 126.

23. *Id.* at 255; Hillel J. Einhorn & Robin M. Hogarth, *Confidence in Judgment: Persistence of the Illusion of Validity*, 85 PSYCHOL. REV. 395 (1978).

us formed our own families as adults and may have children of our own. These experiences are the primary sources of intuition about children and families. Although the intuitions about our own family experiences may at times provide for reasonably accurate judgments about other children and families, reliance on such intuition risks ignoring extremely important factual and legal factors when we have responsibility in terms of input or decisions about others in the family law arena.

Simply put, there can be vast differences between our own families and others in terms of individual characteristics, interpersonal behaviors, and innumerable circumstantial factors. What may seem obviously correct to each of us in terms of our own families carries a great risk of jumping to inaccurate conclusions regarding children and families who may be very different from our own reference points and are at an extremely challenging time of life.

When we rely primarily on our own experiences, we ignore a vast amount of other relevant information and evidence. Because there is no possibility of cognitively processing information and evidence that is ignored or not collected, we figuratively wear blinders and cannot engage in higher-level reasoning. Kahneman has emphasized that the failure to consider comprehensive information is central to many types of intuitive errors, and he has labeled it What You See Is All There Is, or WYSIATI. He maintains that WYSIATI plays a central role in judgment overconfidence and reliance on numerous heuristics and biases.[24]

There are numerous factors that can lead individuals to fail to engage in deliberative reasoning. Some are very common in the lives of busy professionals, such as excessive time pressure, which in part can reduce even the motivation to adequately collect and consider appropriately comprehensive information. For example, researchers found that when individuals have strong motivation to make a correct decision and adequate time to focus on relevant information, they tend to make reasonable decisions based on the information provided to them. However, when there are time pressures combined with relatively low motivation, the relevant information provided tends not to be adequately considered and individuals make decisions intuitively, based on general attitude.[25]

---

24. THINKING, *supra* note 10, at 85.

25. David M. Sanbonmatsu & Russell H. Fazio, *The Role of Attitudes in Memory-based Decision-Making*, 59 J. PERSONALITY & SOC. PSYCHOL. 664 (1990).

How an attorney, judge, mediator, or evaluator perceives the psychological functioning of a parent can play an important and relevant role, as parental psychological functioning that has an impact on parent-child interaction is a significant factor in children's well-being.[26] For example, anxiety on the part of a parent at times can be raised as a concern in terms of the well-being of the children and parenting plans. Cognitive distractions, such as attending to other information, can lead relevant professionals to fail to consider whether the anxiety is an ongoing problem or just a transient situational reaction.[27] In order to adequately investigate the parental anxiety, an evaluator would need to collect and examine important information such as the extent to which the anxiety has been present at times and in situations other than the divorce and contested child custody, the intensity of the anxiety, parental strengths and skills, and the extent to which the anxiety has had an impact on parent–child interactions.[28]

As noted earlier, interpersonal biases such as those based on race or physical attractiveness can play a role in almost any decision-making context. A number of racial biases are associated with cultural stereotypes, and individuals who are inclined not to engage in racial bias tend to use System 2 reasoning to decrease the impact of those stereotypes. When an individual is not able to adequately engage System 2 to monitor the more emotional System 1 cognitive processes associated with racial stereotypes, those stereotypes are more likely to have an impact on judgment.[29] Somewhat similarly, individuals low in physical attractiveness are often believed to have fewer positive personality characteristics than those who are high in physical attractiveness. The influence of this stereotype is diminished when there is greater information provided about an individual, especially about relevant characteristics such as empathy and integrity.[30]

---

26. Paul Amato, *Children's Adjustment to Divorce: Theories, Hypotheses and Empirical Support*, 55 J. Marriage & Fam. 55 (1993).

27. Daniel T. Gilbert & Randall E. Osborne, *Thinking Backward: Some Curable and Incurable Consequences of Cognitive Busyness*, 57 J. Personality & Soc. Psychol. 904 (1989).

28. Evaluation, *supra* note 1, at 49.

29. Patricia G. Devine, *Stereotypes and Prejudice: Their Automatic and Controlled Components*, 56 J. Personality & Soc. Psychol. 5 (1989).

30. Alice H. Eagly et al., *What Is Beautiful Is Good, But . . .: A Meta-Analytic Review of Research on the Physical Attractiveness Stereotype*, 110 Psychol. Bull. 109 (1991).

Methods to Improve Reasoning

In order to improve deliberation and reasoning, Kahneman has emphasized that a considerable amount of consistent effort is necessary. First, it is necessary to pause and recognize that one is in a situation that requires System 2 thinking. Kahneman refers to such a circumstance as a cognitive minefield. As described earlier, the process of constructing parenting plans is complex, and such complexity constitutes a type of cognitive minefield. A next step is to self-monitor the type and amount of information that has been collected and that needs to be gathered. For example, as noted previously, it is necessary to consider relevant scientific findings[31] in content areas that pertain to parenting plans.

In a number of complex areas, the amount of information that is available can overwhelm the ability of individuals to process it productively; therefore, specific but relatively simple mechanisms can be extremely useful in promoting adequate yet efficient System 2 thinking. The use of well-designed checklists has been found to improve performance in high-risk, complex arenas such as surgery, other areas of medical practice, construction, and venture capital.[32]

Checklists and similar forms have been used in evaluations of child custody or allocation of parental responsibility in order to improve deliberation about areas of focus pertaining to the interactions between children and parents.[33] Checklists have also been used to promote System 2 reasoning in custody evaluations about matters such as research findings, practice considerations, ethics, and report writing.[34] An alternative is a decision tree format used to facilitate deliberative reasoning in the evaluative process.[35] The bullet point material that is found at the end of this and subsequent chapters serves a similar function as a checklist.

A principal benefit of using checklists is that they prompt us to consider information that we otherwise might tend to ignore; without

31. Howard N. Garb, Studying the Clinician: Judgment Research and Psychological Assessment 234 (1998).

32. Gawande, *supra* note 9.

33. Daniel J. Hynan, *Forensic Child Evaluations*, *in* Innovations in Clinical Practice: Focus on Children and Families 63, 79 (Leon VandeCreek & Thomas L. Jackson eds., 2003).

34. Evaluation, *supra* note 1, at start of each chapter.

35. Leslie M. Drozd et al., Parenting Plan and Child Custody Evaluations: Using Decision Trees to Increase Evaluator Competence and Avoid Preventable Errors (2013).

such methods, we tend to make quick, emotional, and easy judgments. Information that is first noticed has a tendency to override later substantive information. Similarly, close consideration of subsequent or unanticipated information that does not fit easily with our earlier impressions is often accompanied by a sense of cognitive strain and a decrease in positive mood. Therefore, we need to put systems in effect to carefully think about data that are contrary to our initial impressions and preferred hypotheses.[36]

A procedure recommended by Kahneman and a colleague for deliberating about counterintuitive possibilities in the business realm is called the premortem. Its use has been suggested for new business endeavors of any type, which are often viewed very optimistically by the individuals who initiate them. The premortem starts with an assumption that the endeavor has failed, and it requires individuals to identify what are likely to be the main characteristics that contributed to the failure. The utility of this procedure is to identify the potential weak points of the proposed enterprise and to strengthen them so as to have a greater likelihood of success.[37]

The premortem approach could be used as a parenting plan is considered and put into tentatively final form. The procedure would prod the creator of the plan and others who might be involved in its formation to think about what might have the greatest chance of going wrong, and accordingly, facilitate reflection about possible improvements.

Another practical, highly productive technique focused on improving deliberation is to list information that supports and refutes the main assertions of the parents relevant to parenting planning. For example, a hypothetical parent asserts that he or she has greater availability to be with the child, has greater ability to attend to the child's special needs, and has a track record of facilitating the child's involvement with the other parent. That parent also maintains that the other parent has difficulties with impulse control that affects parenting. A list would be completed that indicates what evidence there is for and against each such assertion, with the most objective evidence being clearly highlighted. The same procedures would occur regarding relevant contentions made by the other parent.

In addition, the professional involved in the parent planning process might generate hypotheses independent of those proposed by the

36. THINKING, *supra* note 10, at 80.

37. *Id.* at 264.

parents. For instance, the professional might have concerns about positive social opportunities available to the child in each parental home and would create a list relevant to each residence regarding factors that would promote or interfere with good peer interactions.

A simple yet effective format for listing information that supports or contradicts a parental assertion or a hypothesis generated by a parenting plan professional is found in Appendix A. The material at the bottom of the form prompts the user to collect and consider information from various sources, including relevant documents, collaterals, legal factors, parent interviews, child interviews, and observations of parent–child interactions. It is important to highlight on the form relatively objective information.

It is important to strive to make independent judgments about different aspects of a complex situation. Otherwise, individuals tend to be strongly influenced by a halo effect in which they view a subject of judgment in a generally positive or negative light. Therefore, when considering data that bolster or contradict the assertions of a parent, System 2 is more likely to be put into effect if each of the parental assertions is deliberated upon separately, thereby working to decorrelate error associated with the halo effect.[38]

Of course, professionals of all disciplines need to carefully consider whether their training, experience, and licensure provide them with adequate ability to engage in parent planning, depending upon the specifics of each case. If there is a case that involves parenting planning, and there is a primary focus on legal and financial matters, it may require the involvement of an individual from a legal background. In contrast, cases that include an emphasis on matters such as child development, parent–child interactions, psychological functioning, and/or interparental conflict are likely to necessitate a central role for an individual with appropriate mental health training and experience.

In summary, to establish a foundation for creating a good parenting plan, crucial factors to keep in mind include the following:

- The main goal of a good parenting plan is to facilitate positive child development and functioning.
- It is an error to rely primarily on one's own personal and family experiences.

38. *Id.* at 84.

- Intuition (System 1) is automatic, fast, effortless, and tied to emotion.
- Reasoning (System 2) is deliberative, relatively slow, effortful, and rule-governed.
- Recognize that parenting planning is a cognitive minefield and engage System 2.
- Stay aware of the influence of the confirmatory bias and use methods to enhance impartiality.
- Remain cognizant of other biases and heuristics.
- Self-confidence in judgment is not associated with judgment accuracy.
- Keep WYSIATI firmly in mind and collect relevant, comprehensive information.
- Maintain a consistent main focus on relevant legal factors integrated with scientific evidence about children of divorce.
- System 2 deliberation needs to include close attention to information supportive of *and* contradictory to the assertions or hypotheses.
- Avoid involvement where System 2 may be ineffective, such as cases with undue time pressures, those in which you might have inadequate expertise, and those in which there may be limitations in the ability to be objective.

CHAPTER 4
SCIENTIFIC EVIDENCE REGARDING CHILDREN OF DIVORCE

Because effective parenting plans increase the likelihood of positive life outcomes for children, professionals need to have solid grasps of what factors contribute toward such beneficial results. Accordingly, this chapter focuses on summarizing scientific evidence about what promotes positive functioning in children, especially those who experience parental separation or divorce.

First, I describe brief background information about the strengths and limitations of scientific research on children of divorce and its appropriate use in parenting planning. Second, I briefly summarize empirical findings about what influences children's well-being generally. Third, research findings about children of divorce are reviewed. Fourth, I describe research focused on shared or joint parenting (though more detailed summaries about very young children and interparental conflict are covered in Chapters 5 through 7). Fifth, parenting plan considerations that emerge from scientific evidence are summarized.

Research

Facts about children of divorce are based on scientific evidence. Scientific evidence about children of divorce is obtained through research. High-quality research is the best source of objective information about children of divorce. At the same time, it is important to be aware that all research has its limitations. Therefore, in this section I include a brief summary of research limitations and one regarding how research is typically conducted.

The worst limitation is that research is sometimes conducted fraudulently,[39] which is presumably rare. Other less egregious shortcomings include the file drawer problem, which involves publication of only positive results and not negative findings, the latter of which are literally or figuratively just placed in a file drawer. Not publishing negative findings can contribute to an impression that scientific effects are more robust than they are in reality.[40] In other instances, authors of research papers have changed the outcome measures they used during the course of the investigation, or have reported results only about statistically significant outcome measures while not mentioning certain findings that failed to be significant. Such limitations have contributed to concern about the reproducibility of scientific findings. However, other than cases of blatant scientific fraud, most of these problems can be well addressed by a burgeoning movement to preregister research plans.[41] Also, although there are areas of controversy about research regarding children of divorce, there does not appear to be concern that there has been fraud.

Well-conducted research yields scientific evidence that is highly relevant for creating parenting plans. Especially when there are findings from different scientific sources that show results consistent with one another, there is very sound reason for reliance on the conclusions.[42]

The divorce field does not lend itself to controlled laboratory experiments. Generally, in a basic experiment, a researcher assigns individuals, at times randomly, to one of a number of conditions, called independent variables, and examines differences between those conditions on designated outcome or dependent variables. However, it is not possible to assign individuals randomly to conditions of having lived in divorced versus intact families. Similarly, it is not realistic to use experimental assignment of families to different postseparation parenting plans; consequently, there is no causal empirical evidence about

---

39. *E.g.*, Siri Carpenter, *Harvard Psychology Researcher Committed Fraud, U.S. Investigation Concludes*, SCIENCE (Sept. 6, 2012, 4:57 PM), http://www.sciencemag.org/news/2012/09/harvard-psychology-researcher-committed-fraud-us-investigation-concludes.

40. *E.g.*, Irving Kirsch et al., *Initial Severity and Antidepressant Benefit: A Meta-Analysis of Data Submitted to the Food and Drug Administration*, 5(2) PLoS MED (Feb. 26, 2008), https://doi.org/10.1371/journal.pmed.0050045.

41. Don A. Moore, *Preregister If You Want To*, 71 AM. PSYCHOLOGIST 238 (2016).

42. Michael E. Lamb, *Mothers, Fathers, Families, and Circumstances: Factors Affecting Children's Adjustment*, 16 APPLIED DEVELOPMENTAL SCI. 98, 106 (2012).

the benefits or risks of specified parenting plans.[43] Therefore, almost all research in the divorce field is essentially correlational in nature in that it is able to examine associations between important variables but is not able to establish causation with certainty.

In a brief but highly relevant example, there are studies that have found children who were in joint custody arrangements to have generally better outcomes than those who were in sole custody arrangements,[44] but it cannot be concluded that joint custody is the reason for the superior outcome in child adjustment. It may be that another factor is primarily responsible for the superior life consequences in the joint custody group. For example, divorcing families who experience greater cooperation between parents are more likely to receive joint custody, and it may be that cooperation and related positive relationships factors lead the children to manifest better outcomes.

Despite the limitations of not being able to routinely rely on random assignment of individuals to experimental conditions, a great deal of highly relevant information about children of divorce has been learned from the appropriate use of scientific methods. For example, multiple quasi-experimental and other research designs are available for such purposes.[45]

In the legal field, as in other realms of life, such as politics, the anecdote can be a powerful tool for persuasion. An anecdote in family law typically involves a child/family case argued to be relevant for the matter at hand. It is crucial to keep in mind that the available body of research on children of divorce covers tens of thousands of individual stories with the most important material characteristically extracted and presented statistically. Although statistics do not carry the dramatic punch of a well-told story, when carried out appropriately, they convey a tremendously greater amount of useful information.

The statistical presentation of these important data is almost always done in terms of comparisons between relevant groups. Such

---

43. Michael E. Lamb, *Critical Analysis of Research on Parenting Plans and Children's Well-Being, in* PARENTING PLAN EVALUATIONS: APPLIED RESEARCH FOR THE FAMILY COURT, 2d ed. 170, 182 (Leslie Drozd et al. eds., 2016).

44. Robert Bauserman, *Child Adjustment in Joint-Custody versus Sole-Custody Arrangements: A Meta-Analytic Review*, 16 J. FAM. PSYCHOL. 91 (2002).

45. *E.g.*, W. LAWRENCE NEUMAN, BASICS OF SOCIAL RESEARCH: QUALITATIVE AND QUANTITATIVE APPROACHES (2d ed. 2007).

group-level data are frequently highly informative for the dilemmas faced by individual children and families and therefore need to be considered in parenting plans. At the same time, professionals need to apply that group-level information to the individual facts and circumstances of each family case.

If individuals involved in parenting planning rely just on their own personal experiences and informal observations of family life, perhaps augmented by having heard a few relevant anecdotes, they are engaged only in System 1 intuition (see Chapter 3) and are at a high risk of overlooking important considerations. If those professionals consider only relevant scientific findings that are available in terms of group-level differences, they have engaged System 2 reasoning, but are doing so in a partial, inadequate manner that can be described as blind empiricism. In these situations, good quality System 2 reasoning includes both close attention to relevant empirical data *and* serious consideration given to the facts and circumstances of the individual family case.

Therefore, professionals involved in parenting planning need to keep a balanced perspective about the strengths and limitations of relevant research. There are limits as to what can be accurately stated about the applicability of relevant empirical findings to each case, though there are tremendous numbers of routinely made decisions that could be improved as a result of a solid grasp of the relevant knowledge base.[46] The crucial, balanced perspective required in parenting planning includes adequate self-knowledge about one's own limitations in adequately understanding the scientific evidence and knowing when and how to involve a professional who has such expertise.

What Influences Children's Well-Being?

There has been very extensive research on what generally has an effect on relevant life outcomes for children. Qualitative and quantitative reviews of relevant research frequently discuss such life outcomes in terms of child adjustment. Child adjustment is a general term that covers areas such as psychological functioning, academic performance, and interpersonal relationships. In some cases, children may be

46. Bruce M. Smyth et al., *Shared-Time Parenting: Evaluating the Evidence of Risks and Benefits to Children, in* PARENTING PLAN EVALUATIONS: APPLIED RESEARCH FOR THE FAMILY COURT, 2d ed. 118, 157 (Leslie Drozd et al. eds., 2016).

followed long term into adulthood, and then measures of adjustment can include areas such as work and marital functioning.[47]

Even before there was substantial research on children of divorce, the legal community at times relied on theoretical work by mental health professionals and others. For example, an influential theory posited that each child has a "psychological parent" who plays the most important role, and that individual should have all control, even to the point of eliminating visitation by the other parent.[48] The term "psychological parent" is a legal one, is not used as a central concept in psychosocial research, and the original theory has no scientific support. However, currently that term is periodically employed to make reference to consideration of parental rights for individuals who have had a very substantial relationship with a child but who are not legal or biological parents.[49]

In general, the quality of the relationship between the child and the parents is a crucial factor that affects child adjustment. Another crucial consideration in child adjustment is the quality of the relationship between the parents. In particular, exposure to interparental conflict has been found to have a negative effect on child adjustment, whereas positive interactions between parents facilitate good child functioning. Also, adequate financial, physical, and social resources facilitate positive child functioning, in contrast to poverty and a lack of positive social opportunities, which are associated with child maladjustment.[50]

Numerous researchers have investigated what aspects of parent–child relationship quality are most important in influencing child development and adjustment. Diana Baumrind[51] posited categories of parenting style identified as authoritative, authoritarian, and permissive. Authoritative parenting is characterized by parents holding the executive role through child supervision and management, while also being supportive and open to child psychological autonomy and input. In contrast, the authoritarian style involves more intensely strict

47. *E.g.*, Paul R. Amato, *Children of Divorce in the 1990s: An Update of the Amato and Keith (1991) Meta-Analysis*, 15 J. FAM. PSYCHOL. 355 (2001). *See also* Lamb, *supra* note 42, at 99.

48. JOSEPH GOLDSTEIN ET AL., BEYOND THE BEST INTEREST OF THE CHILD (1973).

49. Mary Jean Dolan & Daniel J. Hynan, *Fighting over Bedtime Stories: An Empirical Study of the Risks of Valuing Quantity over Quality in Child Custody Decisions*, 38 LAW & PSYCHOL. REV., 2013–14, at 45, 75.

50. Lamb, *supra* note 42.

51. Diana Baumrind, *Effects of Authoritative Parental Control on Child Behavior*, 37 CHILD DEV. 887 (1966).

parenting with very little acceptance of child input and psychological autonomy. Permissive parenting features very little supervision and a great deal of child freedom.

Other academicians modified this model and proposed that parenting was best conceptualized as varying along two dimensions identified as responsiveness and demandingness. In this revised version, permissive parenting was divided into two separate styles, indulgent and neglectful.[52] In general, the authoritative parenting style has been found to be superior to others,[53] though exceptions have been identified.[54]

These parenting style categories are broad in that they potentially include many different types of parenting behaviors. In that regard, parenting style most productively represents an important context for more specific parenting behaviors.[55] For example, a parent who provides direction to a child about interactions with peers is likely to engage in such communication quite differently when using an authoritative style versus an authoritarian one.

Parent–child interactions, when viewed at a more specific behavioral level, can rapidly generate such large amounts of information in brief time periods that they can appear indistinct and confusing. Therefore, it is useful that research has focused on relatively specific types of parent–child interactions characteristically seen in healthy versus dysfunctional families. Such research has found that competent parents tend to show strong levels of positive reinforcement, informal education, sensitivity to child distress, appropriate limit setting, and reasonable reciprocity in parent–child interactions. In contrast, dysfunctional families, such as those having been identified as abusive or neglectful, more frequently manifest negative

---

52. Eleanor E. Maccoby & John A. Martin, *Socialization in the Context of the Family: Parent-Child Interaction*, *in* HANDBOOK OF CHILD PSYCHOLOGY, 4th ed., Vol. 4, 1 (Paul H. Mussen & E. Mavis Hetherington, eds., 1983).

53. *E.g.*, Laurence Steinberg et al., *Impact of Parenting Practices on Adolescence Achievement: Authoritative Parenting, School Involvement, and Encouragement to Succeed*, 63 CHILD DEV. 1266 (1993).

54. Diana Baumrind, *An Exploratory Study of Socialization Effects on Black Children: Some Black-White Comparisons*, 43 CHILD DEV. 261 (1972); Fernando Garcia & Enrique Gracia, *Is Always Authoritative the Optimum Parenting Style? Evidence from Spanish Families*, 44 ADOLESCENCE 101 (2009).

55. Nancy Darling & Laurence Steinberg, *Parenting Style as Context: An Integrative Model*, 113 PSYCHOL. BULL. 487 (1993).

emotionality, chaotic interactions, lower levels of organization, fewer instances of positive reinforcement and support, less reasoning, and more frequent inappropriate parental responses to positive child behaviors.[56]

In the vast majority of cases, children of divorce have heterosexual parents, and therefore it is very relevant to examine the role of gender differences in parenting behavior and child adjustment. In general, unsurprisingly, mothers spend more time than fathers engaged in parenting. However, neither gender has a greater capacity to engage in good quality parenting. Parenting skill tends to improve with experience, and is characterized by a blend of warmth, engagement, and maintaining an authoritative role.[57]

Despite the fact that mothers in the United States generally spend more time with infants than do fathers, infants tend to form attachments, which are a type of close human connection, with both parents at about the same time, during the middle of their first year.[58] The style of attachment formed by mothers and fathers tends to manifest a number of differences. Mothers tend to be more comforting and soothing, whereas fathers tend to be more playful, adventurous, and engaging of the external world.[59] However, general parental stylistic differences with infants and later in life do not describe all mothers and fathers, and there are numerous cultural differences.[60]

Even though such gender differences in parenting style are frequently found, they generally do not result in differences in child development and functioning. A study compared a large number of single-parent households and included those headed by fathers as well as by mothers. Results indicated that there were no substantial differences in child adjustment when children were raised by single mothers

---

56. *E.g.*, Karen S. Budd et al., Evaluation of Parenting Capacity in Child Protection (2011); Daniel J. Hynan, *Parent-Child Observations in Custody Evaluations*, 41 Fam. Ct. Rev. 214 (2003); Steven R. Wilson et al., *Comparing Physically Abusive, Neglectful, and Non-Maltreating Parents during Interactions with Their Children: A Meta-Analysis of Observational Studies*, 32 Child Abuse & Neglect 897 (2008).

57. Lamb, *supra* note 42, at 101.

58. Lamb, *supra* note 6, at 109.

59. Marc H. Bornstein, *Parenting Infants,* Handbook of Parenting, 2d ed., Vol. 1, 3 (Mark H. Bornstein ed., 2002); Kyle Pruett & Marsha Kline Pruett, Partnership Parenting 15 (2009).

60. Lamb, *supra* note 42, at 103.

as compared to single fathers.[61] Furthermore, there is an absence of evidence that being raised in a single-parent household by a parent of the same gender is superior to being raised in a single-parent household by the opposite-gender parent.[62]

Children of Divorce

Overall, approximately 20 to 25 percent of children of divorce have been found to suffer significant adjustment problems, in comparison to about 10 to 12 percent of the general child population.[63] To consider these facts in a comprehensive and balanced manner, it is necessary to keep in mind that separation and divorce substantially increase the risk of child adjustment problems, but it is also the case that most children of divorce do not experience serious problems in life functioning.

An early quantitative research review examined three hypotheses about the reasons that children of divorce show generally lower well-being than children from intact families: family conflict, parental absence, and financial disadvantage. Although there was statistical support for all three reasons, the most robust finding was for family conflict.[64] An additional research review investigated the same three hypotheses and two others: the effects of parental psychological maladjustment and general life stress. Each of the five hypotheses received a degree of support, though at different levels. The strongest support was found for interparental conflict and parental psychological adjustment. The study emphasized that there are important areas of overlap between each of the five hypotheses, and it is crucial to consider numerous factors simultaneously in attempts to adequately consider what has an impact on children of divorce.[65] More recent research reviews have reported similar findings about what has an impact on

---

61. Douglas B. Downey et al., *Sex of Parenting and Children's Well-Being in Single-Parent Households,* 60 J. MARRIAGE & FAM. 878 (1998).

62. Brian Powell & Douglas B. Downey, *Living in Single-Parent Households: An Investigation of the Same-Sex Hypothesis*, 62 AM. SOC. REV. 521 (1997).

63. Joan B. Kelly, *Risk and Protective Factors Associated with Child and Adolescent Adjustment Following Separation and Divorce: Social Science Applications, in* PARENTING PLAN EVALUATIONS: APPLIED RESEARCH FOR THE FAMILY COURT 49 (Kathryn Kuehnle & Leslie Drozd eds., 2012); Lamb, *supra* note 42, at 102.

64. Paul R. Amato & Bruce Keith, *Parental Divorce and the Well-Being of Children: A Meta-analysis*, 111 PSYCHOL. BULL. 256 (1992).

65. Amato, *supra* note 26.

children of divorce and the importance of simultaneously attending to multiple causal factors.[66]

There is a good deal of congruence between empirical evidence about children of divorce and many of the state statutes that must be taken into consideration when devising parenting plans.[67] Many states have adopted aspects of the Uniform Marriage and Divorce Act (UMDA),[68] which indicates that the primary legal principle is the best interest of the child and describes factors to be considered.[69] The UMDA factors include the wishes of the parents; the wishes of the child; the interactions of the child with the parents, siblings, and other relevant individuals; the child's adjustment to home, school, and community; the mental and physical health of all relevant individuals; and other criteria that may be relevant in individual cases. A number of state statutes include additional factors such as domestic violence, child abuse, and parental behavior that facilitates a positive relationship between the child and the other parent.

Separation and divorce are most productively viewed as processes instead of discrete events, especially in terms of their impact on children. In practice, it is commonly seen that parents manifest numerous problems simultaneously, which can affect one another in complicated ways. For example, a parent with a significant mood disorder may rely in part on alcohol and/or other substances to try to feel better, but the substance use may lead to increased anger and open conflict with the other parent, thereby having multiple negative effects on the children. In another instance, interparental conflict might lead one or both parents to become less active in terms of support and management directed toward the children, and such withdrawal from parental functioning places the children at risk of worsened outcomes. In that regard, a number of the factors described here that influence outcomes for children may have been present, at least in some families, before the divorce process started or was even contemplated. The multifaceted challenges of the divorce process can certainly heighten preexisting

66. Paul R. Amato, *Research on Divorce: Continuing Trends and New Developments*, 72 J. Marriage & Fam. 650 (2010); Jennifer E. Lansford, *Parental Divorce and Children's Adjustment*, 4 Perspectives on Psychol. Sci. 140 (2009).

67. Evaluation, *supra* note 1.

68. National Conference of Commissioners on Uniform State Laws, Uniform Marriage and Divorce Act (1979).

69. Linda D. Elrod & Milfred D. Dale, *Paradigm Shifts and Pendulum Swings in Child Custody: The Interests of Children in the Balance,* 42 Fam. L.Q. 381 (2008–09).

problems; however, in other families, problems such as interparental conflict, economic strain, and parental psychological dysfunction arise only when the course of the divorce has begun.

The importance of conceptualizing divorce as a process that affects children extends to the time after the divorce itself has taken place. For example, an investigation of adolescents whose parents had divorced reported that positive adolescent adjustment was predicted by parent-child closeness and active parental management and control.[70] In a separate research review, not specific to children of divorce, conflict between parents was found to lead to a decrease in parental acceptance of the children as well as less appropriate discipline.[71] Also outside the specific realm of divorce, though including such families, an extensive program of research has pointed to decreased emotional security as a main pathway by which interparental conflict leads to a generally negative impact on children's well-being.[72]

Shared/Joint Parenting

In general, active and positive parental involvement tends to have a beneficial effect on children's well-being. In that regard, research tends to focus on father involvement because fathers are less likely than mothers to be actively involved with the children. For instance, a study that relied on the National Longitudinal Study of Youth investigated the role of father involvement in adolescent well-being. A good deal of the difference in adolescent adjustment between divorced and two-parent homes could be explained by the active role of the father.[73] Somewhat similarly, in low-income families, active father involvement was found to be associated with decreased delinquency in adolescence.[74]

However, when the focus is on families of divorce, there has been a somewhat mixed picture in terms of the impact of the type of custody on child adjustment. A number of studies have not found consistently

70. Christy M. Buchanan et al., Adolescents after Divorce 92 (1996).

71. Ambika Krishnakumar & Cheryl Buehler, *Interparental Conflict and Parenting Behavior: A Meta-Analytic Review*, 49 Fam. Rel. 25 (2000).

72. E. Mark Cummings & Patrick T. Davies, Marital Conflict and Children: An Emotional Security Perspective (2010).

73. Marcia J. Carlson, *Family Structure, Father Involvement, and Adolescent Behavioral Outcomes*, 68 J. Marriage & Fam. 137 (2006).

74. Rebekah Levine Coley & Bethany Medeiros, *Reciprocal Longitudinal Relations between Nonresident Father Involvement and Adolescent Delinquency*, 78 Child Dev. 132 (2007).

significant differences in child adjustment based on the type of custody arrangement.[75]

In contrast, other research has found an association between the type of custody and child adjustment. Boys who were six through 11 years of age in joint custody were found to have better behavioral functioning than those whose mothers had sole custody.[76] A study of both girls and boys reported that children in joint custody described having had a greater number of positive experiences and manifested higher self-esteem than those in sole maternal custody.[77]

A different pattern of results was found by a research project that studied primarily high-conflict families who litigated about children over a period of one to four years. It found that the type of custody designated by the courts was not associated with the level of child adjustment. However, higher levels of actual child access by the nonresidential parents were associated with increased child adjustment problems.[78]

As noted earlier, a meta-analysis investigated the differences in child outcome between sole and joint custody families. However, the report had a number of limitations associated with the available research that was reviewed, including partial reliance on numerous nonpublished dissertations, which comprised the majority of the studies analyzed, and combining different types of joint custody families. Specifically, joint custody based on time sharing and joint custody based on decision making were combined into one category in that meta-analysis. Overall, the review found that joint custody families manifested better child adjustment than sole custody families, though the size of the effect was small.[79]

More recently, William Fabricius and his colleagues reported on the experiences of university students whose parents had divorced. The

---

75. *E.g.*, BUCHANAN et al., *supra* note 70, at 288; Marsha Kline et al., *Children's Adjustment in Joint in Sole Physical Custody Families*, 23 DEV. PSYCHOL. 430 (1989); Jessica Pearson & Nancy Thoennes, *Custody after Divorce: Demographic and Attitudinal Patterns*, 60 AM. J. ORTHOPSYCHIATRY 223 (1990).

76. Virginia M. Shiller, *Joint versus Maternal Custody for Families with Latency Age Boys: Parent Characteristics and Child Adjustment*, 56 AM. J. ORTHOPSYCHIATRY 486 (1986).

77. Sharlene A. Wolchik et al., *Maternal versus Joint Custody: Children's Postseparation Experiences and Adjustment*, 14 J. CLINICAL CHILD PSYCHOL. 5 (1985).

78. Janet Johnston et al., *Ongoing Postdivorce Conflict: Effects on Children of Joint Custody and Frequent Access*, 59 AM. J. ORTHOPSYCHIATRY 576 (1989).

79. Bauserman, *supra* note 44.

behaviors investigated included histories of living arrangements with each parent, relationship quality with the father, and physical health. Greater amount of time with the father was associated with both a positive relationship quality with him and better physical health.[80]

Other findings from that research group were that there was a significant positive correlation between the percentage of time the student spent with their fathers, up through 50 percent, and emotional security experienced with the fathers, with no loss of emotional security with the mother. An examination of the data indicated that the strongest portion of the correlation was the portion between having spent zero days with the father and one through three days with him in a 28-day period. The next strongest portion of that association was between one through three days with the father and four through six days with him.[81] Additional data received from Fabricius indicated that approximately 18 percent of those students had not been seeing their father at all and 38 percent saw their fathers less than once per week. As a result, it seems that the highest magnitude of the positive correlation between contact time with the father and emotional security with him could be attributed to the understandably low emotional security of individuals who had no or relatively meager contact with the father. It seems likely that a significant proportion of the zero-contact fathers had left their children, or that there was such a negative father–child relationship that a no-contact pattern developed. It is also possible that conflict between the parents contributed toward the father having been absent or having a relatively minor role in the child's life.[82]

There is limited published research evidence available regarding how unusual it is that such a large proportion of the Fabricius sample saw their fathers so little. That limited evidence included a much earlier research report that described, two years after having started that study, children younger than college-age had an average of only four days of contact with the father per month when there was sole maternal custody, though under conditions of joint custody there were 10

---

80. William V. Fabricius & Linda J. Luecken, *Postdivorce Living Arrangements, Parental Conflict, and Long-Term Physical Health Correlates for Children of Divorce*, 21 J. FAM. PSYCHOL. 195 (2007).

81. William V. Fabricius et al., *Parenting Time, Parent Conflict, Parent-Child Relationships, and Children's Physical Health, in* PARENTING PLAN EVALUATIONS: APPLIED RESEARCH FOR THE FAMILY COURT 188, 195 (Kathryn Kuehnle & Leslie Drozd eds., 2012).

82. EVALUATION, *supra* note 1, at 65.

contact days per month.[83] A more recent report estimated that approximately one-quarter to one-third of nonresident fathers maintain little to no contact with their children.[84]

The research findings briefly summarized here tend to present shared parenting in a generally positive light, and it may be that such parenting plans, for appropriate families, encourage healthy development and functioning for children of divorce. However, the generally positive outcomes for shared parenting are also likely to reflect, at least in part, beneficial individual and family characteristics that were in place before the divorce and that contributed to the shared parenting arrangements.[85] It is noteworthy that a scholar whose work frequently describes the benefits of father involvement has noted, along with others, that if parents manifest long-standing conflict with one another without a history of successful cooperation in parenting, children may be unlikely to benefit from shared parenting.[86]

There is vigorous controversy about the interface between interparental conflict and considerations of shared or joint custody, and it has been focused upon a great deal as it pertains to very young children.[87] That debate is manifested both in scholarly work and family law practice. Chapter 5 concentrates on controversies regarding time sharing for very young children. Dilemmas related to conflict, including domestic violence, and time sharing, beyond the realm of very young children, are focused upon in more depth in Chapters 6 and 7.

In general, stability in family life is valued, and there are concerns about whether shared parenting may have a higher risk for residential changes than custody primarily with one parent, which is typically characterized by that parent having the child approximately 70

---

83. Kline et al., *supra* note 75, at 434.

84. Paul R. Amato & Julie M. Sobolewski, *The Effects of Divorce on Fathers and Children: Nonresidential Fathers and Stepfathers*, *in* THE ROLE OF THE FATHER IN CHILD DEVELOPMENT, 4th ed., 341, 348 (Michael E. Lamb ed., 2004).

85. Lamb, *supra* note 42, at 189; Smyth et al., *supra* note 46, at 157.

86. Lamb, *supra* note 42, at 192.

87. *E.g.*, Jennifer E. McIntosh et al., *Responding to Concerns about a Study of Infant Overnight Care Postseparation, with Comments on Consensus: Reply to Warshak*, 21 PSYCHOL., PUB. POL'Y, & LAW 111 (2015); Marsha Kline Pruett et al., *Parental Separation and Overnight Care of Young Children, Part I: Consensus through Theoretical and Empirical Integration*, 52 FAM. CT. REV. 240 (2014); Richard A. Warshak, *Social Science and Parenting Plans for Young Children: A Consensus Report*, 20 PSYCHOL., PUB. POL'Y, & LAW 46 (2014).

percent of the time or more.[88] Relatively early research projects that retrospectively examined residential changes found that they occurred somewhat more frequently in joint custody as compared to sole custody families,[89] though one report noted that residential changes in joint custody families tended to take the form of a different type of joint custody arrangement and not a change to sole custody.[90] A 1992 longitudinal study reported that children who resided in a shared parenting arrangement about six months after the marital separation were much more likely to have made a residential change, to sole custody, about three years later than were those who lived mainly either with the mother or with the father.[91] As described in a later report, children who were living in a shared parenting arrangement about six years after the separation were also more likely to have made a subsequent residential change than those who had been living mostly with the mother or with the father.[92]

A much more recent Australian study that used a high-conflict mediation sample manifested the same general pattern. The authors collected information over four years after mediation and reported that the shared parenting children experienced less residential stability than did those who had been in sole custody. As a highly relevant example of the necessity of examining specific family characteristics when devising parenting plans, the shared custody parents who exhibited relatively good cooperation with one another also manifested a greater likelihood of successfully maintaining shared care over time than did the parents who were not able to attain adequate cooperation and decreased conflict.[93]

A 2008 study based on a sizable Wisconsin sample found a different pattern from the one just described. It compared children in shared parenting arrangements with those in sole maternal custody over about three years following the divorce. Overall, the residential stability was

88. *E.g.*, DIVIDING, *supra* note 2.

89. Kline et al., *supra* note 75; Pearson & Thoennes, *supra* note 75.

90. Pearson & Thoennes, *supra* note 75.

91. DIVIDING, *supra* note 2.

92. Cloutier & Jacques, *supra* note 2.

93. Jennifer McIntosh et al., *Post-Separation Parenting Arrangements and Developmental Outcomes for Infants and Children. Collected Reports. Study I: Longitudinal Study of School-Age Children in High Conflict Separation*, FAM. TRANSITIONS, N. CARLTON, AUSTL. (2010), https://www.ag.gov.au/FamiliesAndMarriage/Families/FamilyLawSystem/Documents/Postseparationparentingarrangementsanddevelopmentaloutcomesforinfantsandchildrencollectedreports.PDF.

equally high for the shared parenting, equally shared parenting, and sole maternal custody groups.[94] Although this study is an outlier, it may represent a gradual shift toward shared parenting taking place more frequently.

Overall, however, most of the evidence indicates that equally shared parenting occurs in a modest proportion of cases, and that there is somewhat less residential stability for shared parenting children generally. It is absolutely necessary that the characteristics and circumstances of each family need to be considered in parenting planning, and there is a great deal of reason for caution about potentially relying on a default or anchor position of plans that require equally shared parenting.

A related concern pertains to residential stability and consequent child outcomes in different types of households, such as married versus cohabiting parents. That topic is covered in Chapter 12.

Parenting Plan Considerations

Scientific evidence frequently provides highly useful information for parenting plans. In particular, scientific findings provide potential guidelines and general directions that need to be seriously considered when devising specific parenting plans. For example, as described earlier, the following family characteristics have consistently been found to be associated with worsened outcomes for children: exposure to interparental conflict, parental mental health problems that have an effect on parent–child relationships, and excessive levels of stress. Consequently, individuals involved in creating parent plans should generally strive to devise plans that minimize exposure to conflict between parents and unwarranted stress. Similarly, in families in which one parent has significantly better psychological health (in ways that affect parenting) than the other, if there are no other overriding considerations, parenting plans should try to establish schedules so that the children are primarily with the healthier parent and are shielded from the other parent's inappropriate behaviors.

However, parenting plan considerations that rely on scientific evidence are not able to provide the answers for every family about parenting schedules and decision making. Numerous other factors must

94. Lawrence M. Berger et al., *The Stability of Child Physical Placement Following Divorce: Descriptive Evidence from Wisconsin*, 70 J. MARRIAGE & FAM. 273 (2008).

be taken into consideration. Such factors include parental availability, histories of relationships between each child and each parent, child age and stage of development, and multiple other considerations that can differ greatly between families.

Scientific evidence, by itself, is limited in terms of being able to provide clear input for parenting plans when there are cases with complicated family circumstances that may point in contradictory directions. For example, a parent who has performed very well consistently attending to and providing care for a special needs child might also manifest limited empathy toward and engagement with the other child at home. In a different case, a parent who has shown strong emotional support for the children and routinely helps a great deal with homework might also have a serious drinking problem; unfortunately, a teenager at home may have also been found to be getting intoxicated regularly. In these cases, a main challenge for those involved in trying to come up with a parenting plan is to weigh and compare the relative strengths and weaknesses of the parents described here, while also considering relevant information about the other parent, as well as multiple other child, parent, and family-level factors. Scientific evidence might be able to help in ascertaining the positive and negative effects of each of the relevant factors, but in most instances, it is not able to provide information about how to weigh those factors. At the same time, taking steps to maximize active deliberation (as described in Chapter 3) about the complicated and somewhat contradictory case information is of crucial importance.

In addition, research findings are not always crystal clear. Scholars and professionals can disagree about research methodology, interpretation of results, and the relevance of findings. Competent understanding of research characteristically requires an individual to have had training and experience in conducting it, including carrying out statistical analyses. In the divorce field, it is crucial to have a strong grasp of research methodologies that permit interpretations of correlation versus causation. Individuals in all walks of life, whether or not they are trained and have conducted research, can have strongly preferred viewpoints; consequently, they can skip deliberation, engage in intuitive thinking, and be at risk of carrying out confirmatory bias.

Therefore, a competent research background must be integrated with purposeful, unbiased deliberation about research findings in order to provide productive input into parenting plans. Under such conditions, when combined with adequate judgment about each family's relevant characteristics, it is likely that parenting plans will increase the chances of positive life functioning for children.

However, in the parenting plan process, it is also necessary to focus on important matters like the feelings and beliefs of each parent in addition to scientific findings and cognitive processes. When thinking about the possible success of shared parenting or equally shared parenting, for example, it is necessary to consider each parent's experiences and attitudes toward the other. In particular, parental expectations and beliefs about the other parent are central regarding trustworthiness, the likelihood of cooperating consistently about the child, parenting competency, the ability to place the child's needs first, and the history of child interactions with that parent.

A number of parents may have clear and strong attitudes about these characteristics of the other parent, whereas others are unsure of how they feel and think about them. Certain parents may have had positive experiences observing the child together with the other parent, and yet they also worry whether that parent will be adequately cooperative over a number of years into the future.

Perhaps obviously, positive and realistic expectations by both parents point in the direction that some type of shared parenting will work out well. In contrast, if both parents anticipate that future interactions about the child will be a virtual train wreck, shared decision making is very unlikely to succeed, and it makes sense to work toward a parenting plan that will balance an appropriate amount of time for each parent with a schedule that endeavors to avoid stress and interparental conflict.

There are a number of parenting plan provisions to consider in efforts to limit interparental conflict. As described in more detail in Chapter 7, they include reliance on electronic instead of direct or phone communication, structuring child transitions to minimize parents' contact with one another, and professional services aimed at helping each individual carefully plan their communications to promote civility and effectiveness.

To the extent that one or both parents have considerable uncertainty about what to expect from the other in the future, it is best for attorneys, mediators, and/or other professionals to examine past patterns of interactions between the parents regarding matters relevant to the child. In brief, no one can predict the future, but the best predictor of future actions is past behavior.

Circumstantial factors need to be investigated when deliberating about the relevance of past interaction patterns. For example, if the parents have been separated for a considerable amount of time before the parenting plan efforts started, that time may provide very relevant information about their child-relevant interactions with one another, assuming the parents can largely agree on their behavioral patterns with one another or there is another source of objective information. However, there may be other circumstances that lead the past to not be a good predictor of future interaction patterns. Prior to the initiation of divorce proceedings, parents may have had a positive and cooperative pattern with one another regarding the child, but a parent learning about the other's extramarital affair could lead to greatly heightened resentment and anger, thereby replacing the positive interparental behavior with high levels of marital conflict to which the child is frequently exposed.

At times, there is a lot of uncertainty over how long the ill will parents hold toward one another will persist. In most cases, the intensely negative feelings tend to dissipate especially after the divorce is final and each parent may be busy reconstructing their personal lives. However, in a number of cases the negative emotion does not wane and might even intensify—such an unfortunate life trajectory is most likely to occur if a parent experiences seriously adverse events that he or she attributes to the other parent. For example, if a parent experiences unexpectedly harmful economic consequences or the relationships with the children get substantially worse, that parent would be at risk of acting in a far more conflictual and less cooperative way than her or his past behavior would have suggested.

To the extent that this type of information is available to the professionals who are trying to devise a parenting plan, there needs to be close deliberation about it. Such careful deliberation affords the best likelihood of creating an effective plan in the face of the frequently inevitable uncertainty.

Essential points to keep in mind about research on children and families of divorce include the following:

- All individuals involved in parenting plans need to know what facilitates positive child outcomes.
- While scientific evidence does not provide all answers for each case, the information is often highly relevant and far superior to reliance on personal experience and/or anecdotes.
- Parenting plan considerations require foundations based on scientific evidence, relevant legal factors, and the facts and circumstances of each case.

- There should be considerable caution about relying on one type or category of parenting plan as an anchor or default option.
- Neither gender manifests superiority in parenting.
- An authoritative parenting style (characterized by supportiveness, openness to child psychological autonomy and input, and active supervision and management) has generally been found to be optimal.
- Beneficial parenting behaviors include
  - positive reinforcement,
  - informal education,
  - sensitivity to child distress,
  - clear communication,
  - appropriate limit setting,
  - explanations for negative consequences,
  - reasonable reciprocity in parent–child interaction, and
  - being able to provide for basic physical needs.
- Highly dysfunctional families tend to manifest
  - lower degrees of positive reinforcement and informal education,
  - relatively high levels of negative emotionality,
  - chaotic interactions,
  - lower levels of reasoning and organization, and
  - inappropriate responses to positive child behaviors.
- Research on children of divorce has found a number of factors to have a negative influence on child well-being, due to a harmful impact on parent–child relationships and/or resources available for healthy child development, including
  - interparental conflict,
  - parental psychological maladjustment that affects parenting behavior,
  - loss of contact with a parent,
  - financial insecurity, and
  - stress.
- There is considerable overlap between scientific findings on the well-being of children of divorce and common statutory factors regarding the best interest of the child.

- Shared parenting may provide very positive circumstances for children of divorce as long as both parents have consistent histories of parenting safely and competently, have been able to coparent with one another reasonably well, and do not expose the children to excessive conflict.
- In order for shared parenting to be successful, each parent needs to have primarily positive beliefs and expectations about the other parent, particularly in terms of
  - caregiving competency,
  - the relationships between the children and that parent,
  - trustworthiness,
  - motivation to be positively involved with the children,
  - placing the children's needs ahead of one's own, and
  - future cooperation.
- Shared parenting may be risky for children if one or both parents do not have histories of competent and safe caregiving, there is unduly high interparental conflict, or a history of parents cooperating poorly with one another.
- Parenting plans can include provisions to minimize conflict between parents.
- It may be necessary to obtain deliberative, unbiased input from an individual with research competency in order to clarify how to apply scientific findings to a family case.
- The more complicated the family, the more important it is to have close deliberation about each relevant aspect of child, parent, and family functioning.

CHAPTER 5
VERY YOUNG CHILDREN

There has been particularly heated and ongoing controversy about appropriate parenting plans for very young children. The heat is highest regarding the issue of whether overnight visits are good or bad for this age group.

In the historically predominant American family structure, prior to many women entering the workforce, the mother stayed home with the children while the father was employed full-time, and she was almost exclusively the parent to provide the tremendous amount of care required by infants, toddlers, and slightly older children. The tender years legal doctrine indicated that, in general, children up through about age 5 belonged with the mother, though it was supplanted by the best-interest-of-the-child standard. A number of critics of family law, including a number of fathers' rights groups, have maintained that the legal system has persisted with an informal bias toward mothers in child custody and parenting plans.

In recent decades, associated with concerns about time sharing that extend to children of all ages, scholars and professionals have increased focus on the mixed research findings and theoretical positions pertaining to parenting plans for very young children. In this chapter, I focus on summarizing the research and related theory. First, I explain the concept of emotional attachment of very young children to caregivers and briefly summarize two of the main methods of attempting to measure emotional attachment. Second, I focus on competing views regarding the impact of overnight visits on emotional security. Third, I describe how Australia has dealt legally with shared parenting for very young children, as that nation's legal policy had been influenced by supporters of shared parenting and, in turn, motivated and provided the circumstances for certain relevant research. Fourth, I summarize the main research studies that investigated overnight visits for very young children. Fifth, I discuss controversies associated with the research on overnights with very young children, including efforts to construct a consensus. I conclude with multiple considerations regarding parenting plans.

Attachment

Attachment in a child is a close interpersonal connection with a parent or other caregiver that establishes a secure base for further development and functioning.[95] Although in the past, a number of legal scholars have referred to the *strength* of attachment, represented in the amount of time a child has spent with a parent, as crucial in potentially determining child custody,[96] what is actually important is attachment *security*, and it is the quality of the parent–child relationship, not the extent of contact, that affects attachment security.[97] A number of authorities in the attachment field argue that it is crucial for a child to have a primary attachment figure,[98] whereas others assert that children routinely form healthy and secure attachments with more than one person at a time,[99] and that a primary attachment figure is neither necessary nor routine.

The most frequently used research method to assess attachment security is called the Strange Situation procedure, and it has primarily been used with very young children over one year of age.[100] It occurs in a laboratory setting and involves a number of steps, including the caregiver and child being in a room together, a stranger coming into the room, and the caregiver leaving the child in the room. There is a focus on a number of child behaviors, including the child's proximity

---

95. John Bowlby, A Secure Base: Parent-Child Attachment and Healthy Human Development (1988).

96. *E.g.*, Elizabeth S. Scott, *Pluralism, Parental Preference and Child Custody*, 80 Cal. L. Rev. 616 (1992); American Law Institute, Principles of the Law of Family Dissolution: Analysis and Recommendations (2002).

97. Shelley A. Riggs, *Is the Approximation Rule in the Child's Best Interest? A Critique from the Perspective of Attachment Theory*, 43 Fam. Ct. Rev. 481 (2005); Alan Sroufe & Jennifer E. McIntosh, *Divorce and Attachment Relationships: The Longitudinal Journey*, 49 Fam. Ct. Rev. 464, 472 (2011); Everett Waters & Jennifer E. McIntosh, *Are We Asking the Right Questions about Attachment?*, 49 Fam. Ct. Rev. 474, 478 (2011).

98. McIntosh, *supra* note 5; Mary Main et al., *Attachment Theory and Research: Overview with Suggested Applications to Child Custody*, 49 Fam. Ct. Rev. 426, 427 (2011).

99. Lamb, *supra* note 6, at 109; Waters & McIntosh, *supra* note 97, at 480.

100. Mary D.S. Ainsworth et al., Patterns of Attachment: A Psychological Study of the Strange Situation (1978).

to and seeking contact with the caregiver, child avoidance of contact and proximity, and child resistance.

Another research method of assessing child attachment security is the Attachment Q Sort.[101] It involves making ratings of a broad variety of child behaviors, a number of which are focused on the caregiver, though other rated child activities include interactions with individuals other than the caregiver and how the child uses objects such as toys. The Attachment Q Sort is typically used outside a laboratory setting, such as at home, and may be used with children somewhat older than those characteristically assessed with the Strange Situation procedure, though in its standard version it takes much more time to complete.

Both assessment procedures are focused on the extent to which a child may have a secure emotional attachment with the caregiver. There are other attachment categories that are relatively dysfunctional, such as ambivalent, avoidant, or disorganized. When the Attachment Q Sort is carried out by a trained observer, it has been found to have a moderate correlation with attachment classifications obtained through the Strange Situation procedure.[102]

In brief, a number of authorities have emphasized the point of view that very young children, especially infants and toddlers, are better able to achieve good attachment security, and consequently healthier functioning in many realms of life, when they have parenting plans that do not include overnight visits away from the parent who is providing most of the care. Such authorities emphasize that it is crucial not to interrupt the attachment process and maintain that there are signs of child distress when interruptions take place.[103]

In contrast, other scholars and professionals maintain that children benefit from close and active relationships with both parents, starting at the very earliest ages. These authorities emphasize that attachment routinely takes place with both parents and that there is no empirical evidence that a child benefits from having just one primary attachment figure. They note that there are often stylistic differences

---

101. Everett Waters & Kathleen E. Deane, *Defining and Assessing Individual Differences in Attachment Relationships: Q-Methodology and the Organization of Behavior in Infancy and Early Childhood*, *in* 50 Nos. 1–2 Monographs of the Society for Research in Child Development 41 (Inge Bretherton & Everett Waters eds., 1985).

102. Marinus H. van IJzendoorn et al., *Assessing Attachment Security with the Attachment Q Sort: Meta-Analytic Evidence for the Validity of the Observer AQS*, 75 Child Dev. 1188 (2004).

103. McIntosh, *supra* note 5; Main, *supra* note 98; Sroufe & McIntosh, *supra* note 97.

between mothers and fathers in terms of the types of parental behaviors involved in the attachment process, though the entire range of those parental behaviors is important for children to experience.[104]

It is important to note that these different viewpoints are not entirely diametrically opposed to one another in all instances, as there has been a degree of convergence toward at least a partial consensus in recent years. Later in this chapter, this development is described in greater detail.

The controversy about overnight visits was fueled in part by legislative developments in Australia. Specifically, the Family Law Amendment (Shared Parental Responsibility) Act 2006[105] initiated a series of reforms that had a major impact on children and families of separation or divorce, and relevant authorities in other parts of the globe, including the United States, have taken considerable interest in it. As summarized at somewhat greater length elsewhere,[106] that amendment required the judiciary to consider establishing orders that included parenting plans with equally shared parenting, or at least a substantial amount of time with each parent. Similarly, other professionals involved with such families in the legal system were obliged to educate parents that they could consider parenting plans with equally shared parenting or at least a significant amount of time with each parent, if such plans appeared to be in the best interest of the children. Although the legislation reportedly was influenced to some extent by research about the potential benefits of shared parenting, there was also concern by a number of authorities about the effects of such parenting plans especially on very young children, particularly within the context of shared parenting that was not agreed upon by both parents, but instead ordered by court even when the parents may have had a history of limited cooperation or significant conflict with one another.

---

104. Joan B. Kelly & Michael E. Lamb, *Using Child Development Research to Make Appropriate Custody and Access Decisions*. 38 FAM. & CONCILIATION CT. REV. 297 (2000); Lamb, *supra* note 6; Pruett & Pruett, *supra* note 59.

105. https://www.legislation.gov.au/Details/C2006A00046.

106. Lamb, *supra* note 43, at 186; Jennifer McIntosh et al., *Post-Separation Parenting Arrangements and Developmental Outcomes for Infants and Children. Collected Reports. Study II: Overnight Care Patterns and Psycho-emotional Development in Infants and Young Children*. FAMILY TRANSITIONS, N. CARLTON, AUSTL., at 89 (2010), https://www.ag.gov.au/FamiliesAndMarriage/Families/FamilyLawSystem/Documents/Postseparationparentingarrangementsanddevelopmentaloutcomesforinfantsandchildrencollectedreports.PDF.

Research on Overnight Visits for Very Young Children

Controversies continue in many courtrooms about parenting plans for very young children, especially about the question of overnights. Parents, attorneys, and other professionals at times make blanket statements about what the research allegedly shows regarding overnight visits, although many such statements can be inaccurate or at least vast overgeneralizations. Therefore, in this section, I endeavor to provide summaries of each of the main, pertinent research studies, with a focus on relevant and statistically significant differences that were identified. Summaries inevitably leave out details, but it would not be practically useful for readers of this book if I described each and every aspect of the research, and any individuals who are interested in more specific information can delve into the original articles through the citations listed here.

The main research studies are summarized in order of their dates of publication. The section that follows the research summaries includes commentaries by multiple authors about the strengths and weaknesses of the studies, as well as a number of findings that appear to emerge consistently in the literature. I also summarize the work to develop a consensus about overnight visits for very young children.

In the first such research project, the focus was on attachment. There were 145 children, ages 12 months through 20 months. Three groups were compared. In two of the groups, the parents were separated, and in general, the interactions between the separated parents were remarkably negative. For example, over 90 percent of these fathers were subject to restraining orders, and parental separation occurred when the infants were an average of four to five months of age, which is prior to when attachment behavior is characteristically seen. In about 20 percent of the cases, the parents had separated prior to the birth of the child. Infants who had overnight visits with the father (though the frequency of overnights could be as low as one per month) comprised one of the groups, and another consisted of infants who had daytime only visits (again, a minimum of one visit per month). Therefore, there was not an adequate opportunity for attachment security to develop with fathers prior to the separation, and many of the separated fathers had never been meaningfully involved in the care of the child. The third group consisted of infants from intact families. The Strange Situation procedure was used to measure child attachment with the parent, and additional data consisted of ratings from mothers.

There was not a significant difference in attachment classification between the separated parents group who had no overnight visits and those who had overnights, though that difference approached the conventional level of statistical significance. Infants whose parents were married were significantly more frequently classified as securely attached than those who had overnights with their fathers. In addition, for those children with overnight visits, disorganized attachment to the mothers was correlated with low levels of interparental communication and high levels of conflict.[107]

A follow-up assessment of these infants and mothers took place one year later, though because the children were older, the Strange Situation procedure could not be used.[108] Instead, the researchers investigated child behavior during structured tasks with the mother. There were no differences between the overnight and no-overnight groups on the child task-related behaviors. However, in an additional statistical analysis that took place after the main results had been collected, the overnight group showed somewhat more frequent emotional breakdowns with the mothers than did the no-overnight children.

A later research project[109] investigated differences in general child functioning between children who had at least one overnight visit per week and those who did not have overnights. It used a well-validated measure of child functioning and did not assess attachment security. The 132 children ranged in age from a few months through six years at the initial time of the study, with the majority in the older portion of that age range. The second assessment of functioning took place 15 to 18 months after the initial assessment. The parents in this study were profoundly different in terms of their relationship histories than those in the research report described previously. Specifically, the parents were all recruited from a research project focused on collaborative divorce, and 77 percent of the couples had been married for an average of eight years. There were 31 unmarried couples, but only three had never lived with one another. Before they started participating in

---

107. Judith Solomon & Carol George, *The Development of Attachment in Separated and Divorced Families: Effects of Overnight Visitation, Parent and Couple Variables*, 1 Attachment & Human Dev. 2 (1999).

108. Judith Solomon & Carol George, *The Effects on Attachment of Overnight Visitation in Divorced and Separated Families: A Longitudinal Follow-Up*, *in* Attachment Disorganization 243 (Judith Solomon & Carol George eds., 1999).

109. Marsha Kline Pruett et al., *Critical Aspects of Parenting Plans for Young Children: Interjecting Data into the Debate about Overnights*, 42 Fam. Ct. Rev. 39 (2004).

the study, 75 percent of the couples had been carrying out overnight visits, and the average frequency was more than once per week. Both mothers and fathers completed ratings that were reported in the study. Parents who had histories of domestic violence, child abuse, or substance abuse were not permitted to participate in the research.

In children through three years of age, there was no overall difference in functioning between the overnight and no-overnight groups. However, among the girls in this age group, those who had overnight visits were less withdrawn than girls in the no-overnight group. In children ages four through six, those who had overnights scored better on a number of areas of functioning.

The third main research study took place in Australia and was focused on investigating how different overnight care patterns were associated with a number of types of functioning in very young children[110] who had been included in the large Longitudinal Study of Australian Children. The investigators compared children in three age ranges: under two years of age, two to three years old, and four to five years old. There were three main residential arrangements in separated families, though the specifics of those categorizations differed for the different age ranges. Specifically, for the youngest group, children were classified as having had either one or more overnights per week (categorized as shared care), one overnight per month up to just under once per week (categorized as primary care), or less than one overnight per year (categorized as rare overnights). For the older two groups, rare overnights were categorized the same way as for children under two years old. However, for the older two groups, the classification of primary care was defined as at least one overnight visit per month but less than five in a two-week period. The categorization of shared care for the older two groups was defined as five or more overnights in each two-week period.

The numbers of children studied were much larger than the earlier research reports just described, but the specifics vary depending upon the age range. For example, in the youngest age group there were 468 children, whereas in the oldest there were 1,115.

The relationships between the parents were in stark contrast to those in the study just described. In general, small proportions of the parents had ever been married to one another, though the percentages were larger for the older child age groups. For example, for the youngest child age group, the proportion of primary parents who had ever been married to

110. McIntosh et al., *supra* note 106.

the nonresidential parent ranged from 9 through 12 percent, depending upon the frequency of child overnights. For the group of four- to five-year-old children, those proportions ranged from 27 to 52 percent. The proportions of primary parents who had histories of cohabitation with the parent living elsewhere were significantly higher than the proportions who had been married to the other parent, but the research report did not provide data about how long parents either had been married to one another or had cohabitated with one another.

To place the parental relationship histories in appropriate context, it is noteworthy that the rates of cohabitation have generally been higher in Australia than in the United States. However, the proportion of parents who had histories of cohabitation in this study was lower than those who had cohabitated in the research report described previously.

There were a number of different measures of child functioning used, including a number of well-validated ones. There was no direct assessment of attachment classification, though there were a few specific measures believed to conceptually reflect features of attachment, including one regarding infant visual monitoring of the mother. Ratings of child functioning generally were made only by the mother.

The ambitious goals of this study led to a relatively complicated array of independent and dependent variables, as well as efforts to examine moderating variables (i.e., to determine how factors such as socioeconomic status, parenting, and coparenting quality influenced the statistical association between the independent and dependent variables). Consequently, it is challenging to clearly and simply summarize the results. However, in general, the authors reported that, for the youngest age group, those who had one or more overnights per week (shared care) showed greater visual monitoring of the primary parent than those who had rare overnights when the moderating variables were included in the statistical analyses. The study authors maintained that child visual monitoring of the parent represented attachment insecurity. Also, in the youngest age group, on a measure of health defined as "illness with wheezing," children who had rare overnights had better scores than those who had shared care, though the effects were primarily only marginally significant statistically and were less notable when the moderator variables were included.

In the two- to three-year-old group, the main significant finding was that the rare overnight care children showed greater persistence than those in shared care. Also, the primary care group showed greater persistence than those in the shared care group, though only when all moderator variables were included in the statistical analysis.

In the four- to five-year-old group, the shared care group manifested somewhat lower conflict with teachers and caregivers than did the rare overnights group. However, the strength of that statistical association decreased when moderator variables were included.

The most recent of the main studies described here investigated a large sample of very young children from separated families. These families were drawn from the Fragile Families and Child Wellbeing Study conducted in the United States,[111] which involved primarily financially disadvantaged families. Only about 25 percent of families in Fragile Families were married, and approximately 50 percent of the parents lived apart from one another.

There was a primary focus on two age groups: one-year-olds and three-year-olds. For the one-year-old group, there were three residential categories: daytime only visits, children who had one to 51 overnight visits during the first year (some overnights category), and those who stayed overnight with their fathers between 52 and 256 times during the first year (frequent overnights). For the three-year-old children, there were four residential categories: daytime only visits, overnights between one and 12 times per year (rare overnights), 13 to 127 overnights per year (some overnights), and 128 to 256 overnights per year (frequent overnights). Perhaps obviously, the frequent overnights categories included children who actually spent the majority of overnights (through 70 percent) with their fathers.

The researchers looked at attachment security by using an abbreviated form of the Attachment Q Sort that was completed by the mother instead of the usual trained observer. There were also ratings of child adjustment using a well-validated measure.

Results for attachment security showed that, for one-year-olds, those who had frequent overnights had higher proportions of insecure attachment than those with some overnights. However, there was not a statistically significant difference between infants with frequent overnights and those with daytime visits only. For the three-year-olds, there were significant differences in attachment security between the four residential groups, but there was not a significant difference found between the frequent overnights group and any of the other three groups.

111. Samantha L. Tornello et al., *Overnight Custody Arrangements, Attachment, and Adjustment among Very Young Children,* 75 J. Marriage & Fam. 871 (2013).

The measurement of child adjustment took place at ages three and five. The only statistically significant finding was that children who had frequent overnights when they were three years old showed more positive behaviors when they were five years old than the daytime-only group and the rare overnights group.

Criticisms, Commentaries, and Progress toward Consensus

The research studies briefly summarized here all have significant limitations. It is inevitable that at least aspects of such shortcomings exist, in part because it is a challenge to find separated families in relevant circumstances, such as children in the relevant age ranges. It is also extremely time-consuming and expensive to track families and take relevant measurements over time, as was done in these research projects.

As an example of a noteworthy research limitation, in the study that found favorable results for overnights in the four- to six-year-old age group, the children tended to be on the older side[112] and there was not a very large sample of the younger group. There was also a small number of children in the youngest age group in the Australian study.[113] Numerous limitations have been pointed out about a number of the other studies summarized earlier, including (but not limited to) that data was collected only from mothers, in a significant proportion of cases parents had limited and/or negative relationships with one another, and certain outcome measures lacked acceptable evidence of reliability and validity.[114] Readers who are interested in detailed and critical analyses of these studies are strongly encouraged to examine relevant literature[115] and should also read the original research papers.

---

112. Marsha Kline Pruett et al., *Parental Separation and Overnight Care of Young Children, Part I: Consensus through Theoretical and Empirical Integration,* 52 Fam. Ct. Rev. 240 (2014).

113. Warshak, *supra* note 87.

114. *E.g.*, *id.*; Lamb, *supra* note 42.

115. *E.g.*, McIntosh *supra* note 87; Jennifer E. McIntosh et al., *Shared-Time Parenting and Risk: An Evidence-Based Matrix, in* Parenting Plan Evaluations: Applied Research for the Family Court 155 (Katherine Kuehnle & Leslie Drozd eds., 2012); Marsha Kline Pruett et al., *Supporting Father Involvement in the Context of Separation and Divorce, in* Parenting Plan Evaluations: Applied Research for the Family Court 123 (Katherine Kuehnle & Leslie Drozd eds., 2012); Warshak, *supra* note 87.

Despite the divergent findings and limitations of the research, there are consistencies that emerge in the results. When parents had a good deal of preseparation experience providing care for the children, and when they had significant histories of positive coparenting, the outcomes for children with overnight visits were neutral to positive compared to those with no overnights. In contrast, when parents had not established a healthy caretaking relationship with the child, and/or there was an absence of positive coparenting, such outcomes tended to be negative.[116]

Although demographic characteristics alone should not be used as a basis for judgment about parenting plans, it is instructive that such features appear to play a role in child outcomes in the studies. For example, when comparing the Macintosh[117] Australian study and Tornello report[118] with the Pruett[119] research, distinct differences can be noted. In the Australian study, for the child group under two years of age, the vast majority of the parents were primarily reliant on government aid. That proportion was lower, though generally greater than 50 percent, in the four- to five-year-old group. The Tornello subjects were drawn from a database of lower socioeconomic status individuals. Although the Pruett study did not report the percentage of individuals who primarily relied on government support, it described that parents were from financially diverse backgrounds, and that the average parents were approximately middle class. It may be that parents who have greater financial resources and who manifest more self-reliance experience less overall stress and have generally higher levels of personal resources. Consequently, these types of characteristics may help provide a foundation for positive coparenting and the ability to successfully carry out overnight visits.[120]

Clearly, child attachment has been a primary focus of the controversies associated with the studies summarized in this chapter. Of the five research reports, two used attachment measures as outcome variables, and a third used at least one measure (child visual monitoring of

116. *E.g.*, Daniel J. Hynan, *Young Children, Attachment Security, and Parenting Schedules*, 50 FAM. CT. REV. 471 (2012); Michael E. Lamb, *A Wasted Opportunity to Engage with the Literature on the Implications of Attachment Research for Family Court Professionals,* 50 FAM. CT. REV. 481 (2012).

117. McIntosh et al., *supra* note 106.

118. Tornello et al., *supra* note 111.

119. Pruett et al., *supra* note 112.

120. Hynan, *supra* note 116.

the primary parent) that the authors conceptualized as representative of attachment. One of the reports did not use an attachment measure only because the children were involved in a follow-up and were too old for the Strange Situations procedure.

A great deal of the focus of attachment research has been on infants and toddlers. However, in recent years, there has been a shift to consider attachment from a longer-term developmental standpoint, covering a greater portion of the age span.[121] In a very relevant example, a longitudinal study over 20 years reported that a significant minority of individuals experienced changes in attachment security, and for those who manifested such changes, a considerable proportion had gone through a parental divorce. That study noted numerous other life experiences were also associated with changes in attachment status.[122] The primary author of that study indicated that "attachment development runs the entire lifespan."[123] Somewhat similarly, other longitudinal research reported that infant attachment is able to predict only a very modest proportion of early adult functioning, but when broader experiences such as parental support, home environment, and peer interactions are included, a much higher percentage of adult functioning can be predicted.[124]

The relatively comprehensive consideration of numerous child and parent experiences beyond just attachment is consistent with a family systems perspective on development.[125] Given especially the scientific evidence that there are numerous factors that influence functioning as an adult, attachment is best conceptualized as an important emotional and interpersonal factor, but one that is not exclusively or even predominantly predictive of overall health and life adjustment.[126]

A number of leading scholars and practitioners have worked to achieve at least a partial consensus about overnight visits for very young children, up through and including three years of age. One

---

121. *Id.*; Pamela S. Ludolph, *The Special Issue on Attachment: Overreaching Theory and Data*, 50 FAM. CT. REV. 486 (2012).

122. Everett Waters et al., *Attachment Security in Infancy and Early Adulthood: A Twenty-Year Longitudinal Study*, 71 CHILD DEV. (2000).

123. Waters & McIntosh, *supra* note 97, at 476.

124. L. ALAN SROUFE ET AL., THE DEVELOPMENT OF THE PERSON: THE MINNESOTA STUDY OF RISK AND ADAPTATION FROM BIRTH TO ADULTHOOD (2005).

125. Philip A. Cowan, *Beyond Meta-Analysis: A Plea for a Family Systems View of Attachment*, 68 CHILD DEV. 601 (1997).

126. Pamela S. Ludolph & Milfred D. Dale, *Attachment in Child Custody: An Additive Factor, Not a Determinative One*, 46 FAM. L.Q. 1 (2012).

important part of that consensus has focused on integrating information from the attachment perspective, the joint parental involvement point of view, and relevant research findings.[127] A central area of broad consensus is that the relationships between the child and others, especially caregivers, is extremely important in healthy development and functioning in infancy and later in life. There is a great deal of consensus that it is beneficial for an infant to develop positive attachment relationships with both parents. Having an attachment with at least one adult is crucial, though there does not appear to be empirical evidence comparing outcomes of children with one versus two positive attachment relationships. In families where fathers are active caregivers, there are more similarities than differences between mothers and fathers in terms of their attachment-relevant behaviors. There is a lack of solid evidence that infants have gender preferences in attachments. Instead, regardless of gender, babies appear to respond well to predictably good quality care.

Research on parental involvement has mainly pertained to fathers because of the reality that they are most likely to have low or no involvement with the child. There are crucially beneficial effects of father involvement across multiple areas of child and adult functioning, and there are heightened risks of significant child problems when fathers are little involved or absent. Numerous factors have been identified that are associated with inadequate father involvement. In terms of parenting planning, the most directly relevant behaviors are those that can be assessed on an individual basis.

Specifically, a number of fathers face understandable barriers to involvement with their children when they have had little to no prior involvement and, therefore, may be unlikely to manifest good parenting skills. Similarly, there are barriers to a father's involvement when he shows limited ability to be available and to cooperate with the other parent in terms of time-sharing and reasonable consistency in caregiving. A father might also display problems with mental health, substance abuse, and/or aggressive behavior, though such features, obviously, can also be present in a mother.

For parenting planning, interpersonal patterns between the parents need to be assessed for each family. A pattern of highly conflictual interactions between parents can provide a barrier to parental

127. Marsha Kline Pruett et al., *Parental Separation and Overnight Care of Young Children, Part I: Consensus through Theoretical and Empirical Integration*, 52 Fam. Ct. Rev. 240 (2014).

involvement, though in many difficult family cases, there are vigorous disputes about details such as the specific conflictual behaviors that have taken place and who has been the main perpetrator (focused upon in the next chapter). In certain cases, restrictive maternal gatekeeping can lead to barriers to father involvement—it is necessary on a case-by-case basis to ascertain the extent to which the gatekeeping hinders or fosters positive child development.[128]

In addition, there is consensus that the research on overnights for very young children is highly informative, but it is not able to provide definitive answers relevant to parenting plans. In particular, the research studies that involve parents who have had relatively little involvement with one another, and thereby include a parent with very limited prior contact with the child, have limited generalizability to a sizable proportion of disputed cases seen in family court. However, when there are cases with such features, a number of aspects of that research may be instructive.[129] Overall, to adequately consider the best interest of the very young child in parenting planning, both the attachment point of view and the joint parental involvement perspective need to be actively considered.

A crucial part of the consensus regarding overnights for very young children focuses on practical applications.[130] Much of the main contents of that report are summarized next, with commentary about a number of the practical challenges of applying the consensus considerations.

In particular, in parenting plan work, consistent with the research described previously, it is important to closely examine what has been the pattern of child–parent interaction, especially regarding direct caregiving. It is also necessary to carefully consider histories of interparental conflict and cooperation. Substantial caution is needed regarding potential overnight visits during the first three years of life if a child does not appear to have a secure and safe relationship with the visiting parent. For instance, when a child and parent have interacted so little that a relationship between the two has not been established, and especially when there is sound reason for concern that adequate parenting skills may be lacking, overnight visits would not be recommended. At the same time, in the vast majority of such cases there would be reason

128. *Id.*

129. *Id.*

130. Jennifer E. McIntosh et al., *Parental Separation and Overnight Care of Young Children, Part II: Putting Theory into Practice*, 52 FAM. CT. REV. 256 (2014).

to initially set up relatively short duration daytime visits, so that the child can develop an adequately secure interaction pattern with the nonresident parent. If that parent has little or no experience in providing care for a young child, it would likely be necessary to require a support person who has such expertise, such as a grandparent, to be present to provide relevant teaching and supervision.

After the child develops a sense of emotional security and the parent gains adequate competency in caregiving, consideration can be given to gradually adding in overnight stays. Perhaps obviously, the central factor is the quality of the parent–child interaction pattern, including parenting competency.

If there is consistently positive and ongoing care by a nonresident parent, it is cause for optimism that overnight visits would be successful. An important sign that a child has a secure relationship with a nonresident parent is that parent being able to soothe the child. Another is that the child looks to the parent for comfort. Also, a positive sign is the child looking to that parent for support when they explore or try something new. There may be parents who have not lived together who have each had considerable experience providing good quality care for the child, and under such circumstances, overnights may be successful. Somewhat similarly, a history of good parental cooperation regarding a child is cause for optimism regarding overnights, whereas a child having been exposed to considerable conflict between the parents leads to a reason for caution.

Multiple child, family, and circumstantial features need to be taken into account and examined in each parenting plan case in order to carry out adequate deliberation about what would be in the child's best interest. For example, a child may have unusual medical, mental health, and/or developmental challenges (see Chapter 8). In such cases, close attention needs to paid to whether both parents have adequate abilities and resources to competently attend to those challenges when they have parenting time. The more each parent demonstrates clear parenting competency and can provide a good environment for the child, the greater there is reason for confidence that overnight visits would be a safe and healthy option.

A parenting plan that provides adequate security and support for a child is likely to contribute to a relative absence of significant problem behaviors. However, for a number of reasons, it is often difficult to assess such matters. One reason is that young children of different ages have different likelihoods of exhibiting certain challenging behaviors. Also, there are often differences in temperament between children that need to be considered as potential problem behaviors are being assessed.

A critical practical consideration is that separated parents in contested cases frequently give very different reports about the child's behavior. There have been numerous cases in which a primary residential parent asserted that the child had displayed significant problems since the nonresident parent's time started or expanded, whereas the nonresident parent consistently maintained that the child had been perfectly fine during his or her parenting time. A further complication involves transitions. It is common that a young child becomes fussy at such times, and a parent may understandably worry that such distress shows there is something wrong with the caregiving by the other parent. However, in many such instances the fussiness dissipates rapidly after the transition has been completed.

It is crucial to keep such complications in mind and to be cognizant of the limitations in obtaining an accurate assessment of such matters. There are a broad range of behaviors a child might manifest that can be representative of stresses associated with overnight visits. As noted earlier, a child may seem fussy, irritable, tearful, or show other signs of distress. Alternately, or concurrently, a child might manifest regression from their eating, elimination, and/or sleeping baseline behaviors. Other relevant problem behaviors can include physical aggression toward others or oneself and/or sluggishness or low persistence in play and related behaviors. It is extremely important to keep in mind that young children can go through brief periods of time of showing such difficult behaviors without any evident cause. Many tend to resolve by themselves or are significantly helped by relatively minor parental interventions. Child problem behaviors as described here are more likely to be clinically significant if they have persisted about three weeks or more.

Of course, in certain cases, parents also suffer from significant mental health problems that have a negative influence on their parenting (it is possible that a parental medical problem has an undesirable impact on parenting, though in practice it is found quite rarely). The most commonly occurring adult psychological problems are anxiety, depressive, and substance misuse disorders; therefore, it is reasonable to assume that they are the most frequently seen types of dysfunction when parenting plans are contested.

Although all categories of mental health problems can have a negative impact on parenting, many parents may have such a disorder without there being any adverse effect on the relationships with their children. Parents may manage their mental health difficulties in a variety of ways, including professional treatment, support groups, and self-help. If concern about parental mental health has been raised, the key points are to assess the extent of such difficulties and determine to what degree, if any, they impact the children in an undesirable way. The less that mental health concerns have a deleterious effect on children, there is greater reason for optimism that a good frequency of overnight visits would be successful (see Chapter 9).

In a number of cases, there is overlap between the presence of a significant mental health problem in one or both parents and the extent to which they can cooperatively coparent without exposing the children to excessive conflict. However, low levels of cooperation and high degrees of conflict between parents can certainly occur without the presence of any parental psychological dysfunction at all.

Additional Parenting Plan Considerations

Multiple practical day-to-day realities of coparenting are essential to consider. For example, in infants, good coordination between households in feeding and sleeping schedules can be very beneficial for a child. Even for slightly older children, approximately similar routines and expectations in both households can be very positive; in contrast, major differences between parents in how they interact with and manage very young children increase risks of child confusion and frustration. In a large proportion of cases, both parents are employed, and they experience hectic lives between parenting, work, and other activities. A very frazzled parent is less likely to have the time, focus, and energy to interact with a very young child in such a manner that promotes secure attachment. Strong cooperation between parents helps make both of their lives more calm and predictable, and therefore leaves them with more internal resources to carry out the demanding challenges of parenting a very young child.

In that regard, numerous ways in which parents interact need to be considered. Positive parental behaviors include a degree of selflessness in many circumstances: a parent needs to consider the needs of the child more than their own adult preferences, and a parent needs to levelheadedly value the child's relationship with the other parent. Other interparental behaviors beneficial for very young children include communicating clearly about all aspects of the parenting plan, including potential alterations; working to facilitate smooth child exchanges; and managing conflict with one another civilly, including not exposing the child to it. The more these types of positive coparenting are consistently present, the greater reason there is for optimism that overnight visits will be successful.

Exposure to high levels of conflict potentially can be damaging for very young children, as well as older children. However, there is a great deal of controversy about this matter. In particular, there are disagreements about the relative benefits and risks of shielding children from interparental conflict versus promoting healthy contact with both parents. This debate is covered in more depth in Chapters 6 and 7.

In addition, multiple other circumstances of both emotional and practical importance need to be assessed in making determinations about overnights. A basic yet central factor is the extent to which each parent is directly available to be with the child. A crucial priority is that a parenting plan should generally try to maximize the amount of time a child can be directly with a parent. Somewhat similarly, at times, a very young child being able to be together with siblings is an important consideration. An issue that presents itself in a number of cases is the geographical distance between the parents and the resulting amount of travel required to carry out a child transition.

Especially as both parents are frequently employed, concern about childcare can be a challenge in parenting planning. When neither parent is available, in certain circumstances there may be another family member, such as a grandparent, who is available to take care of the child. When there has been a positive relationship between that family member and the child, a high-quality parenting plan may prioritize caregiving by the family member.

The practice-oriented consensus report[131] also described that, in certain cases, conflict between parents emanates primarily from just one of them. For example, one parent, often the one with the majority of parenting time, may work to unreasonably restrict or even entirely block contact between the child and the other parent. Allegations of parental alienation and/or restrictive gatekeeping often emerge under these circumstances and necessitate an in-depth assessment. When there is evidence that the nonresident parent has had a history of positive interactions with the child, accompanied by a lack of evidence of abuse or other highly inappropriate behavior by that parent,

131. *Id.*

parenting plans need to include that individual in all aspects of caring for the child.

In cases that include complications, such as concerns about child health, parental mental health, interparental cooperation and conflict, and the quality of interactions between the child and parent, it is crucial that appropriately trained and experienced professionals are involved in assessing and providing relevant information in the parenting plan process. Such concerns are likely to require input from mental health professionals who have the relevant expertise. Questions about child physical health may require direct medical examination, perhaps from a specialist. If the child's physical condition has already been competently evaluated, obtaining medical records may be sufficient.

An extremely important, though frequently overlooked reality is that parents of very young children are often at a very emotionally challenging stage of life, even if they are not going through a separation or divorce. Many such parents have an infant or toddler for the first time and are making multiple life adjustments. In addition to normal anxiety and worry about appropriately caring for a very vulnerable young child, parents tend to routinely be low on sleep and often have not eaten well. Frequently, there are multiple stresses associated with having had a young child, including issues around money, work, home, social life, and the child's and/or one's own health. Time management characteristically becomes a greater concern, associated with transitions, employment requirements of both parents, unpredictable traffic or public transportation availability, and child eating and sleeping schedules. The time management challenges are usually magnified if there is a considerable distance between the two homes.

All these factors lead to a very high risk that parents regularly experience difficulties staying calm and cooperating with one another. Attorneys often have to assist their clients with both the practical realities and the emotional consequences of such stressful circumstances. They may tend to look at whether negotiations are likely to help the case progress adequately and/or whether to pursue remedies in court.

Professionals such as parenting coordinators, mediators, and coparenting counselors at times are involved to try to help the parents make progress in their interactions with one another. Such professionals tend to use a variety of problem-solving techniques, a number of which are focused on working with parents to try different communication approaches with one another. Other aspects of problem solving can be directed to each individual, with the goal of helping them manage their emotions and thoughts in such a way as to increase the likelihood of at least adequate interactions with the other parent. In working with each individual, it can be effective to try to at least briefly address the continuing emotional distress that remains from the prior romantic relationship, described well by the term negative intimacy.[132]

If parents have had regular arguments, instances of avoiding talking with one another, and/or other forms of negative communication between them, they need to make substantial improvements in order to promote the well-being of their children. Constructive communication is very important for all parents, regardless of the ages of the children, but it is particularly crucial when children are very young. The younger the children, the more they are reliant on the physical care of parents or other caregivers to stay alive and healthy. When an infant is involved, there is information about feeding, elimination, sleeping, bathing, and related matters that needs to be regularly exchanged between parents. Both physical and psychological care are necessary for slightly older children, with certain variations depending upon child age and stage of development.

When parents have a great deal of difficulty talking with one another to exchange essential child information, an important problem-solving step involves the routine use of written communication such as e-mail or text. It can be easier for parents to stay away from arguments or disparaging remarks when these methods are used, but it is also the case that unnecessary battles can be fought using such electronic communication. As a result, even when using such methods, parents need to focus on being civil with one another and on effectively conveying child-related reports.

Two general principles are applicable and potentially very helpful in keeping parents on a productive communication pathway with one another. The first principle is to keep one's focus, both in thought and communication, on what is best for the child or children. The second is to consistently strive to communicate with the other parent in a calm, matter-of-fact, and businesslike manner.

A leading author recommends that parents work to achieve a productive communication style by reminding themselves of "CCD"; that is, to be calm, courteous, and diplomatic with the other parent.[133] The more there has been an argumentative and nonproductive behavior

132. Ricci, *supra* note 4, at 48.
133. *Id.* at 11.

pattern with the other parent, the more important it is to take the time and effort to construct useful communications. It takes consistent efforts by both parties to build a reasonable degree of trust that the other person has positive intentions to treat the children's well-being as a priority. Mutual trust is likely to be enhanced by each parent engaging in communication that is child focused, respectful, and productive.

In that regard, useful tips for parents include the necessity of giving advanced thought to how to construct a child-oriented e-mail or text, keeping it brief and focused, carefully reading the message prior to sending it to ensure that it is useful and not provocative, and also making an effort to try to make sure that it will be clear to the recipient. Especially with very young children, there are a number of content areas of child functioning that often need to be summarized for the other parent shortly before the transition to that individual. Accordingly, an e-mail or text can routinely be prepared in advance for the parent who is to receive the child that summarizes relevant child functioning and anything else of importance that might have happened since the prior transition. If there are very infrequent transitions, a weekly summary can be very useful in promoting a good communication pattern with the other parent.[134]

Transitions of many types can be stressful for very young children and their parents, even when there is not an exchange between parents. Almost all parents have made comments about how difficult it was to get their child ready and out the door. If child transitions between parents have repeatedly been a source of difficulty, a number of problem-solving efforts can be considered. In some cases, parents may be able to work out agreements for transition routines by relying upon their attorneys. In other cases, they may need assistance from a parenting coordinator or mediator.

At times, it is helpful to remind parents that young children cannot be relied upon to consistently cooperate in a timely manner, and that exchanges require especially large doses of patience and planning, including building in adequate time. Infants might require feeding and/or a diaper change prior to being ready to go to the other parent. Three-year-old children are unlikely to quickly and easily change from an activity they enjoy in order to go with the other parent. Attempting to carry out such a transition under a major time pressure is a prescription for everyone to experience a great deal of stress. Similarly, the parent

134. *Id.* at 70.

who receives the child needs to build adequate time into her or his preparation for the exchange. Despite the best of intentions, it is almost inevitable that, at times, someone will run late, and there needs to be an agreed-upon routine to notify the other parent, typically with a polite text or phone call. Also, in advance, there needs to be clear agreement on who will be providing transportation for each exchange, with clear arrangements for materials such as car seats, diaper bags, and/or the child's clothing and belongings.

It is beneficial for each parent to routinely convey, prior to the exchange, to the child that he or she has a good deal to look forward to when the other parent takes over. That is especially the case if the child has expressed distress about past transitions, assuming there is no indication that anything significantly wrong has actually taken place with the other parent.

It is routinely helpful to provide the child with a well-liked object such as a stuffed animal or toy to bring to the home of the other parent. Such items have periodically been referred to as transitional objects by mental health professionals. If a child seems particularly upset in advance of the transition even with such an object in his or her possession, it can be worth a try to add an additional "special" one.

For many children, it can be comforting for the parent to remind her or him that they will be with one another again, presumably after just a few days. Also, a parental comment that the child can talk to the parent by phone or see them through FaceTime or Skype can help to ease transient distress.

If there has been regular conflict in the past between parents during exchanges, a reasonable objective would be to devise a plan for transitions that do not require the parents to speak with one another. One or both parents may benefit from having a relative or close friend present who is able to consistently be civil toward the other parent. Also, it is essential that any such individual never makes any negative comment about the other parent to or in front of the child.

When professionals such as parenting coordinators or counselors engage in productive problem-solving efforts with individual parents, whether about transitions or any other topic, they tend to focus on helping individuals gain greater insight into their own patterns of emotion and thought. Professionals also help individuals use that understanding to facilitate actions that keep an appropriate focus on the needs of the child. That increased understanding can also be used to help guide more productive communication and related interactions with the other parent. For example, such efforts might include assisting a parent to cope with stress in a healthier manner and/or modify thought patterns in such a way as to better control anger and reduce the likelihood of argumentativeness.

There are certain cases in which a parent desires to increase the extent of involvement with the child. In the majority of circumstances, that parent is a father. He may have had essentially no contact with the child and wishes to initiate it. In other instances, the father may have had relatively limited involvement with the child and has a desire to become a much more engaged parent. Considerations about parenting plans in such step-up cases[135] overlap to a significant degree with what has been covered previously in this chapter.

For example, consistently safe and secure parenting has to be a priority in order to facilitate the child's well-being. When the father does not have appropriate experience and expertise in caring for the child, he often needs to receive relevant training and supervision. In order for a step up to occur, it needs to be clear that there will not be child maltreatment or domestic violence of any type, and that both parents will be able to interact at least adequately with one another. There is reason for very significant concern if the step-up parent shows indications of substance misuse, mental health problems, or the potential to expose the child to other negative influences. Overall, there needs to be a close assessment of the step-up parent and his social and physical environments when considering increasing his involvement with the child. At the same time, there are cases in which one parent has restricted contact between the child and the other parent, and a close assessment reveals there is a lack of evidence to support a parenting restriction. That content area will be covered in more depth in Chapter 10 on parental alienation and gatekeeping.

In general, individuals carrying out parenting planning in such potential step-up cases need to stay strongly cognizant both of the importance of safety and that children benefit from positive, active relationships with both parents. Often, when step-up parenting has started, there are concerns about how it will proceed. Therefore, relevant parenting plans need to build in processes for monitoring, including getting feedback from both parents and any other individual who

135. Marcia Kline Pruett et al., *Considerations for Step-up Parenting: When and How to Determine the "Right" Time*, *in* PARENTING PLAN EVALUATIONS: APPLIED RESEARCH FOR THE FAMILY COURT, 2d ed., 535 (Leslie Drozd et al. eds., 2016).

might be in a supervisory or observing role. Perhaps obviously, the degree of progress would dictate whether there should be ongoing expansions of parenting time for the father, or whether difficulties or lack of progress necessitate a change in the direction of the step up.

Trying to Make Sense of Complex Case Information

Many cases involving very young children include a great deal of information covering a number of factors about the child, family, and related circumstances. The easiest and quickest approach to deal with this information is to rely on one's own intuition and develop a feel for what kind of parenting plan should be put in effect. However, as summarized in Chapter 3, there is a major risk of missing or not adequately considering relevant information when a professional approaches case information in that manner.

A number of the main methods to promote adequate deliberation about complex matters in and of themselves are relatively simple, but they are powerful in terms of prodding us to consider the big picture—not only the information that fits easily with our quick, automatic thinking, but also crucial considerations that may be contrary to it. It is more time-consuming and in a number of ways less enjoyable to process information in this deliberative manner, but children of divorce deserve the extra time and effort.

A few practical methods to promote deliberation are described in Chapter 3. One way is to generally check that adequate information has been collected and that knowledge about children of divorce is appropriately applied to the specific case. The checklists at the end of these chapters can be useful in that regard.

In cases with disputes about overnights for very young children, high-quality parenting plans need to strongly consider the extent to which each parent has had adequate experience and possesses a good level of competency in providing care for the child. The use of a pro–con list to record evidence that supports and contradicts that each parent has sufficient caregiving competency greatly increases the odds that there will be sufficient deliberation about this matter.

Because there needs to be reasonable cooperation between parents of very young children and little to no serious conflict (especially of the type that would risk child and/or parental safety), the same type of procedure would routinely be needed about this area of concern.

Specifically, professionals are much more likely to engage in thorough reasoning by using a pro–con format that records evidence for and against parents having adequate histories of coparenting with one another and little to no serious conflict.

Crucial points from this chapter include the following:

- Emotional attachment is a psychological connection, typically with a parent.
- *Security* of attachment is important for healthy child development, but the *strength* of the attachment is not relevant.
- Children can and often do form secure attachments to both parents, though it is crucial to have at least one secure attachment.
- There are a number of insecure types of attachment, and it is possible for a child not to have any emotional attachment to a parent.
- Controversy about overnight visits for very young children is partially based on concern regarding whether the overnights interfere with secure attachments.
- Controversy about overnight visits is also partially based on findings that children develop and function better when there are good levels of healthy involvement with both parents.
- Research on very young children and overnight stays is limited to a few studies that have mixed results.
- The limited research findings about overnights for very young children suggest that outcomes can be neutral to positive when parents have had histories of positive child caretaking and good coparenting. Negative child outcomes are associated with inadequate or nonexistent prior caretaking by the nonresident parent and lack of an adequate prior coparenting relationship.
- Attachment occurs across the lifespan and can change in later years, such as when older individuals experience parental divorce. Attachment security in very early childhood predicts only a small amount of adult functioning. Other factors such as parental support, home environment, and peer relationships also influence adult functioning.
- In practice, it is crucial to examine each case individually, including (but not limited to)
  - patterns of parent-child interaction,

  - the extent to which the child has a safe and secure relationship with each parent,
  - the history of positive coparenting, if any,
  - the history of interparental conflict, if any,
  - whether interparental conflict is mainly due to one parent,
  - child medical or developmental special needs, if any, and
  - parental dysfunction, including mental health difficulties that interfere with parenting competence.
- Parents of very young children often face multiple stresses and practical challenges that can increase the risk of decreased cooperation and heightened conflict with one another, all of which are relevant for parenting plans.
- In many cases that include substantial interparental conflict, there are questions about whether it will be relatively temporary or persist long-term.
  - Most divorce-related interparental conflict dissipates within a year or two after the divorce is final.
  - Depending upon multiple specific factors, including parental experiences during the divorce process and after it, in a number of cases high conflict and poor cooperation continues for years.
  - There needs to be primary consideration given to how much the children are exposed to interparental conflict, independent of its eventual duration.
- In cases where parents have had substantial problems talking with one another calmly and productively, consideration should be given to communicating about the children only through written methods such as e-mail or text.
- Even with reliance on e-mail or text, parents may need professional assistance to communicate with one another in effective, nonaggressive ways.
- Interventions such as parenting coordination, mediation, or coparenting counseling may be helpful in facilitating communication between the parents that is consistently effective and civil.
- Step-up parenting considerations need to include an assessment of individual, family, social, and environmental factors; monitoring of the progress of step-up efforts is also a necessity.

- When there are concerns about child mental health and development, parental mental health, or related matters, professionals with relevant expertise will need to be involved in the parenting plan process.
- In order to promote case-specific deliberation about the well-being of children, it is essential to use practical methods such as lists of evidence supporting and contradicting the main assertions of each parent, with highlighted focus on relatively objective evidence.

CHAPTER 6
DOMESTIC VIOLENCE

Domestic violence occurs in a significant proportion of marriages and other close relationships. In numerous cases, domestic violence has been happening for months or years and contributes to a decision to divorce. In other families, when couples get to the point of considering separation, psychological and verbal marital conflict can worsen and result in physical aggression or other types of domestic violence, as well as divorce. In many cases, causation is more complex and circular than these two brief examples. For years, there have been major controversies about domestic violence within the context of child custody and parenting plan disputes.[136]

This chapter covers information about domestic violence that is relevant to parenting planning. First, there is a summary regarding domestic violence in the context of divorce, including prevalence, gender comparisons, and typologies. It is essential that the reader be aware that a thorough description of facts and findings related to domestic violence would require at least a separate book. As usual, readers are encouraged to go to original sources cited here for greater detail, and other important references can be found in those citations.

Second, I summarize information about domestic violence assessment. Third, I describe parenting plan considerations, which must substantially rely on an assessment of domestic violence and its impact on the children.

As in other content areas relevant for parenting plans, the available group-level research is highly useful for professionals. It is essential that such research be integrated with the individual facts and circumstances of each family case.

---

136. Irwin R. Sandler et al., *Convenient and Inconvenient Truths in Family Law: Preventing Scholar-Advocacy Bias in the Use of Social Science Research for Public Policy: Researchers Roundtable*, 54 FAM. CT. REV. 150 (2016).

Domestic Violence

It is very clear that observing domestic violence has a negative impact on children, significantly increasing the likelihood of experiencing depression, anxiety, aggression, other disruptive behavior, and low self-esteem.[137] Allegations of domestic violence take place in a substantial portion of divorces. Research done in California on 18,000 child custody cases found there were domestic violence allegations regarding 26 percent of fathers and 9 percent of mothers.[138] In a much smaller sample of 120 high-conflict marriages, there were domestic violence allegations against 55 percent of fathers and 30 percent of mothers.[139] A different California research project reported that domestic violence allegations took place in 76 percent of a sample of custody and visitation disputes.[140]

There are frequently vigorous disputes over allegations of domestic violence, and substantiation of such allegations is highly challenging. There are questions about how to conceptualize unsubstantiated cases. It is important to be aware that the unsubstantiated cases have not necessarily been disproven. There are controversies about whether it is more reasonable to categorize them as allegations that did not have sufficient objective evidence, as examples of false accusations, or a combination of the two. Clearly, in many unsubstantiated cases of domestic abuse, it will never be known with certainty what actually took place. In the sample of high-conflict couples described earlier, allegations that the father was the perpetrator of domestic violence were substantiated 41 percent of the time and those regarding the mother 15 percent of the time.[141]

In the view of many people, domestic violence is predominately carried out by men, who are seen as more aggressive than women by nature, and who are usually the physically stronger partner. However,

---

137. *E.g.*, Cummings & Davies, *supra* note 72; John H. Grych et al., *Patterns of Adjustment among Children of Battered Women*, 68 J. Consulting & Clinical Psychol. 84 (2000); Peter G. Jaffe et al., Protecting Children from Domestic Violence: Strategies for Community Interventions (2004).

138. Janet R. Johnston et al., *Allegations and Substantiations of Abuse in Custody-Disputing Families*, 2005 Fam. Ct. Rev. 43 (2005).

139. *Id.*

140. Joan B. Kelly & Michael P. Johnson, *Differentiating Types of Intimate Partner Violence: Research Update and Implications for Interventions*, 2008 Fam. Ct. Rev. 46 (2008).

141. Johnston et al., *supra* note 138.

it is relevant to consider research on gender differences in aggression. While such research, which extends beyond the divorce field, generally finds males to display more physical aggression than females, that tendency is modified by the presence of provocation. Specifically, there is evidence that if provocation is experienced, the difference between men and women in physical aggression is significantly less than if no provocation has taken place.[142]

Research on gender differences in domestic violence has found a range of results. Those findings vary a good deal largely according to the source of data. Research information collected from law enforcement sources and female victims shows that men are by far the most common perpetrators of physical aggression. Other research drawn from married, cohabitating, and dating couples results in findings of approximately equal frequencies of aggression by women and men.[143]

A comprehensive statistical review of previously conducted research on gender comparisons between heterosexual romantic partners included married and unmarried couples living together, but also couples who were only dating; other research subjects included individuals living in women's shelters and people in counseling for marital violence. The controversial findings of that review were that there was a small difference in terms of women having been found to be more frequently aggressive than men. However, when measurement focused on physical injuries, the pattern of results was quite different. When physical injuries occurred, the woman was the victim 65 percent of the time. When the focus was on relatively serious injuries that required medical treatment, in 71 percent of the cases the victim was a woman. Similarly, when only couples with marital problems were investigated in the research, 83 percent of those who needed medical treatment were female.

Also, in that same statistical review of existing research, comparisons were made between couples who were just dating versus those who were married or cohabitating. There was a tendency for a higher frequency of overall aggressive acts by women to have occurred in the dating sample, whereas in the married/cohabiting couples there was no difference in the frequency of aggressive acts between men and women. When the focus was on violence that resulted in injury, the

142. *E.g.*, B. Ann Bettencourt & Norman Miller, *Gender Differences in Aggression as a Function of Provocation: A Meta-Analysis*, 119 PSYCHOL. BULL. 422 (1996).

143. John Archer, *Sex Differences in Aggression between Heterosexual Partners: A Meta-Analytic Review*, 126 PSYCHOL. BULL. 651 (2000); Kelly & Johnson, *supra* note 140.

married/cohabiting group showed a larger percentage of males having been the perpetrators of aggression than the dating group.[144]

A follow-up statistical analysis conducted a separate comparison for each of the specific physically aggressive acts included in the research outcome measure. That study reported that there was an overall small gender difference in that males tended to be the perpetrators of relatively severe aggressive acts, whereas more minor ones tended to be carried out by women. The largest difference was that men were more likely to carry out choking or strangling of their partner than were women.[145]

Typologies of domestic violence have emerged over time. Relatively early understanding of domestic violence was that it was essentially all carried out by men and was typically called battering or wife beating. Traditional intervention programs were based on this perspective, and were often referred to as the Duluth model, which included the Power and Control Wheel as a means of understanding and teaching about domestic violence.[146]

Over time, individuals from academic, family court, and related professional backgrounds reported perspectives of types of domestic violence different from the classic male battering focused upon by the Duluth model.[147] For example, a group of researchers classified domestically violent males in terms of those who engaged in planned, controlling violence versus others who appeared to be more reactive in their aggressive behavior.[148] A separate empirical study classified domestically violent males into those who were violent only within the family, those who were generally violent and antisocial, and a third group who appeared to have mood difficulties and features of borderline personality disorder.[149]

The divergent points of view and accumulated empirical evidence contributed to the Wingspread Conference on Domestic Violence and Family Courts, cosponsored by the National Council of Juvenile and

144. Archer, *supra* note 143.

145. John Archer, *Sex Differences in Physically Aggressive Acts between Heterosexual Partners: A Meta-Analytic Review*, 7 AGGRESSION & VIOLENT BEHAV. 213 (2002).

146. ELLEN PENCE & MICHAEL PAYMAR, EDUCATION GROUPS FOR MEN WHO BATTER: THE DULUTH MODEL (1993).

147. Sandler et al., *supra* note 136.

148. Kenneth A. Chase et al., *Categorizing Partner-Violent Men within the Reactive-Proactive Typology Model*, 69 J. CONSULTING & CLINICAL PSYCHOL. 567 (2001).

149. Amy Holtzworth-Monroe & Gregory L. Stuart, *Typologies of Male Batterers: Three Subtypes and the Differences among Them*, 116 PSYCHOL. BULL. 476 (1994).

Family Court Judges and the Association of Family and Conciliation Courts in 2007. One of the work products of that conference relevant to parenting plans was a conceptualization of domestic violence relevant to the divorce field that could serve to assist in assessment and intervention efforts.

In particular, a relevant typology of domestic violence was proposed with four main categories.[150] It encompasses, in the Coercive Controlling Violence classification, the traditional view of physical aggression toward a partner that includes intimidation, oppression, and an objective of robbing the victim of personal power and control. In contrast, Situational Couples Violence represents a pattern of interactions, not primarily characterized by efforts at power and control, that typically progresses from heated arguments to physical aggression.

Separation-Instigated Violence is a category that represents aggressive behavior that first emerges during the separation. In that regard, it tends to last a shorter period of time than the other types of domestic violence, and if it does persist relatively longer, it needs to be reclassified, characteristically as either Coercive Controlling or Situational Couples Violence. The fourth category is called Violent Resistance, and it represents efforts to defend oneself and to stop Coercive Controlling Violence. In the past, a number of individuals who have been advocates for female victims of domestic violence have maintained that such resistance is the only type of violence carried out by women.[151]

This categorization potentially is very helpful, but it is not perfect and should not be considered the last word. For example, in some cases, Situational Couples Violence can increase in scope and include efforts at intimidating force and control, and under such circumstances this intensified violent behavior should be reclassified as Coercive Couples Violence.[152]

Gender differences have been noted regarding this classification format, in addition to what was described previously regarding Violent Resistance. Coercive Controlling Violence involves higher levels of physical force and severity than do other categories of domestic violence, and it is mainly carried out by men. Research from community samples suggests that Situational Couples Violence involves relatively lower levels of physical aggression, takes place most frequently, and has a relatively even gender balance. Research that has collected data

150. Kelly & Johnson, *supra* note 140.

151. *E.g.*, LENORE WALKER, THE BATTERED WOMAN SYNDROME (1984).

152. Kelly & Johnson, *supra* note 140.

from domestic violence shelters, police records, and hospitals has found high frequencies of Coercive Controlling Violence.[153]

Assessment

The process of developing parenting plans needs to routinely include assessment of domestic violence. That concern leads to efforts to prioritize child and parental safety into assessments about time sharing and decision making in the parenting plan process.[154]

There should be screening for domestic violence,[155] even if there has been no allegation that it has occurred because a number of victims may never have disclosed that it took place, and all such relevant information is crucial. If information emerges that domestic violence may have occurred, either through screening or a different avenue, there needs to be a closer assessment that includes methods such as individual interviews, efforts to collect relatively objective information such as police records, and talking with collaterals, though other methods may also be required depending upon the circumstances. There are very frequent challenges in carrying out such assessments, many of which are associated with the reality that parental reports about each person's behaviors during an incident are routinely contradictory. Information from collaterals needs to be considered within the context of the objectivity of each such individual.[156] Although there routinely needs to be attention given to whether any child abuse may

153. Michael P. Johnson, *Conflict and Control: Gender Symmetry and Asymmetry in Domestic Violence*, 12 Violence Against Women 1003 (2006).

154. *E.g.*, Peter G. Jaffe et al., *Custody Disputes Involving Allegations of Domestic Violence: Toward a Differentiated Approach to Parenting Plans*, 46 Fam. Ct. Rev. 500 (2008); AFCC, *Guidelines for Examining Intimate Partner Violence: A Supplement to the AFCC Model Standards of Practice for Child Custody Evaluation*, 54 Fam. Ct. Rev. 674 (2016).

155. *E.g.*, American Bar Association Commission on Domestic Violence, Tool for Attorneys to Screen for Domestic Violence, https://www.americanbar.org/content/dam/aba/administrative/domestic_violence1/20110419_cdv_screeningtool.authcheckdam.pdf; Desmond Ellis & Noreen Stuckless, *Domestic Violence, Dove, and Divorce Mediation*, 44 Fam. Ct. Rev. 658 (2006).

156. *Id.*; William G. Austin, *Guidelines for Utilizing Collateral Sources of Information in Child Custody Evaluations*, 40 Fam. Ct. Rev. 177 (2002); William G. Austin & Leslie M. Drozd, *Judge's Bench Book for the Application of the Integrated Framework for the Assessment of Intimate Partner Violence in Child Custody Disputes*, 10 J. Child Custody 99 (2013).

have occurred, that possibility deserves heightened focus if it is determined that there has been aggression between parents.

Assessment of domestic violence and other interparental conflict needs to consider multiple factors, including the potency, frequency, pattern, and whether one or both parents have been the initiator(s) or perpetrator(s). The examination needs to extend beyond instances of physical aggression to verbal/psychological aggression; sexually aggressive behavior; and means of coercion such as threats, intimidation, isolation, and financial oppression. Efforts should be made to ascertain the emotional reactions of all individuals involved, including children, as well as coping or problem-solving behaviors that have been considered or carried out.[157] All professionals who carry out this type of assessment or screening require substantial education and training.

Especially because parents routinely give such contradictory information about domestic violence incidents, and also due to the fact that there is often very limited objective information, it is essential that assessments make use of decision aids such as pro–con worksheets to assist in the deliberation about what may have taken place in actuality. In addition, such decision aids can facilitate careful reasoning by considering the potential advantages and drawbacks of a number of potential parenting plan features.

Perhaps obviously, if it has been determined that significant abuse has occurred, especially of a coercive and high potency type, and there is a lack of evidence that the perpetrator has undergone sufficient rehabilitation that resulted in a recent absence of such behaviors, there needs to be strong consideration given to allowing only supervised visits or perhaps even suspending visitation. Because Situational Couples Violence appears to be the most frequent type when there are contested child matters, parenting plans more often are likely to consider structural modifications that are less restrictive than supervised or suspended visits.

However, even at the end of a long divorce process, with close examination of allegations about domestic violence and other serious conflict, it often occurs that there is a lack of definitive evidence or agreement about whether any serious conflict or domestic violence took place, what were the patterns and intensities of the interactions, and who (if anyone) was the main initiator or perpetrator. Even in the cases that have gone to trial because of a domestic battery or related charge, an individual who has pled or has been found guilty may still

157. Jaffe et al., *supra* note 154; AFCC, *supra* note 154.

insist they are innocent. In certain instances, legally guilty individuals acknowledged they participated in a physical altercation but assert that the other parent was the actual perpetrator.

Parenting Plan Considerations

Therefore, parenting plans frequently are devised under conditions of considerable uncertainty regarding interparental conflict, including domestic violence. Consequently, especially when dealing with the pressure to arrive at an agreement, individuals involved in creating parenting plans should attempt to both provide for safety and, when the conditions are right, allow for regular, positive child access to both parents.

If the conflict that occurred appeared to be Situational Couples Violence or a similar type that involves relatively minor physical aggression, a number of provisions can be put into place to decrease the likelihood of a safety risk. Similarly, such provisions can be effective in shielding a child from exposure to conflict between the parents.

For example, the parenting plan can include measures to minimize parental need to have contact with one another when the child is exchanged. A number of jurisdictions have a neutral exchange site where a parent can bring a child to supervisory staff members and the other parent can pick them up at that location, at a slightly different time or in a different part of the building. Depending upon circumstances such as parental availability and the child being in school or daycare, on designated days the parent who has had the children can drop them off at the facility, and the other parent can pick them up at the end of the day. In some instances, especially for very young children, the transition may be able to be carried out by neutral, calm relatives or friends instead of the parents. Somewhat similarly, with very young children, parents may be accompanied by such a relative or friend during the transition. Then, the relative or friend gets out of the vehicle with the child and carries out the final part of the exchange. It is essential that any relative or friend who is involved in transitions always be polite and civil—if they are unlikely to be, then they should have no involvement. In some instances, these types of transitions occur in public places such as a parking lot, the lobby of a community center or library, or a fast food restaurant.

In cases where there has been Coercive Controlling Violence, professionals need to be exceptionally careful to protect child and parent safety. It is important to be cognizant that Coercive Controlling

Violence can take place even in the absence of actual physical aggression. For example, one parent might have glared menacingly at the other while holding their hand to mimic a gun firing, thereby silently conveying a death threat without any physical contact or verbal interaction at all. It would be entirely understandable for the recipient of such actions to be extremely fearful about any interactions with the other parent. Living under such fear would be an ongoing, extreme emotional challenge for the parent. Such a parent would naturally be frightened not only for themselves but for the children as well. As described earlier, in a significant proportion of households in which domestic violence has taken place, there has also been child abuse.

If a child reports to a parent what sounds like it could be abusive or neglectful behavior in the household of the other parent, that individual needs to act to protect child safety as a priority, while also remaining reasonably calm and making an effort to think through what the next best step would be. Often, a parent quickly obtaining consultation with her or his family law attorney is the next best step. If there is serious concern about abuse or neglect, a call to the local child protective services hotline will be necessary, and the police may need to be involved.

Even when there has been severe domestic violence, after the separation, a child may spend significant time with each parent, and consequently, the parents need to communicate with one another about the child. In many such cases, arguments can develop even in telephone conversations, and there can be considerable worry and fear that verbal disputes might expand into potential physical aggression. When these circumstances permeate parental interactions, it is frequently necessary to limit parental communications to written forms such as e-mails, texts, or letters. An exception is routinely necessary for legitimate health-related emergencies.

However, even written communications can disintegrate into forums for conflict, arguments, and even threats. As a result, parents need to learn how to write and send written communications that are routinely businesslike, civil, child focused, and productive. This topic is discussed in greater detail in the following chapter.

When there has been Coercive Controlling Violence, parenting plan professionals need to remain highly cognizant that aspects of shared parenting carry a substantial risk for the victim parent, and there is also potential hazard for children observing more conflict between parents. Assuming there is no risk for the child directly interacting with either parent, a sound general strategy is to develop a parenting plan that encourages parents to disengage from one another and carry out parallel parenting.

Even in parenting time arrangements that have the child with each parent a considerable proportion of the time, parents can remain largely disengaged from one another. However, the closer the parenting time is to equal, the higher the risk that parents have regular contact with one another, especially when there are schedules with relatively frequent transitions.

The greater risk occurs when there has been significant domestic violence and yet parents share decision making. Such a decision-making requirement forces parents into contact with one another, at least intermittently. It increases the risk that children may be exposed to significant conflict between parents. It is well-established that exposure to interparental conflict is a significant risk for child distress and negative life outcomes.

In the interests of getting a difficult case settled, there is often serious consideration given to shared parenting, including about decisions, as the main avenue to a possible agreement. However, there are very few persistently high conflict parents who transform themselves into cooperative ones who can successfully carry out shared parenting. The less successful ones tend to remain in high conflict with one another, and the more successful disengage and carry out parallel parenting.[158]

Also, parents with higher intensities and durations of interparental conflict often require very detailed parenting plans. The detail is likely to be especially productive about areas that have been sources of past conflict. For example, if there have been repeated disputes about what each parent says to the children and regarding transitions, a great deal of detail about those topics in the parenting plan can potentially prevent at least some instances of potential future conflict (see the next chapter for more examples).

When domestic violence has been in a relatively modest range of intensity and frequency, including most instances of Situational Couples Violence, there tends to be uncertainty in terms of parental responsibility for initiating and maintaining it. Also, there are often more gray areas in terms of planning both for parenting time and decision-making. In each case, regardless of the extent or type of domestic violence, individual and interpersonal family information needs to be closely considered, together with relevant life circumstances.

158. DIVIDING, *supra* note 2, at 234.

Especially in cases of relatively severe domestic violence, assessment needs to include parental mental health functioning, as a significant proportion of perpetrators manifest mood or impulse control problems, substance misuse, and/or severe personality disorders. Therefore, well-trained and experienced mental health practitioners need to be routinely involved in the assessment process and have input into parenting plan development.

Depending upon the specifics of the case, it may be productive to make use of professionals such as parenting coordinators or mediators. However, if there has been significant domestic violence that has led to fear in a parent or a power imbalance, no sessions should take place with both parents together.

Crucial points contained in this chapter include the following:

- Allegations of domestic violence frequently are accompanied by vigorous disputes between parents about the facts of what actually occurred.
- A constructive typology proposed the following categories of domestic violence:
  - Coercive Controlling Violence,
  - Situational Couples Violence (most frequent type),
  - Separation-Instigated Violence, and
  - Violent Resistance.
- Domestic violence that results in injury is carried out more frequently by men than women, though females and males appear to be roughly equal in terms of initiating relatively minor physical aggression.
- Children suffer from exposure to domestic violence.
- Child abuse takes place in a substantial proportion of families with domestic violence.
- Parenting plans need to try to balance the generally positive benefits of parent–child interactions with providing for child and parental safety and security.
- Routine screening for domestic violence needs to occur.
- When there is reason for concern that domestic violence may have taken place, there needs to be a more in-depth assessment, including individual methods such as interviews.

- Empirically informed interview methods need to be used by competent child interviewers to obtain information about possible child maltreatment, domestic violence, and other parental conflict.
- High-conflict parents tend not to develop into a pattern of cooperative coparenting; instead, they tend to become disengaged from one another or remain in high conflict.
- High-conflict families are often very different from one another, and each case needs to be assessed and considered individually.
- Assessment of domestic violence needs to include information about the intensity, pattern, and main perpetrator. It needs to involve areas of focus beyond only physical violence, and include evaluation of possible verbal/psychological aggression; sexual aggression; and coercion such as threats of harm, isolation, and depleted finances.
- Parenting plans need to prioritize safety for children and parents.
- When relatively minor domestic violence has occurred, parenting plans may be able to combine methods to provide for safety (e.g., regarding child transitions and parental communication) while allowing considerable child contact with both parents.
- It is essential to use decision aids, such as pro–con formats, to fully enumerate evidence that supports and contradicts assertions regarding domestic violence and/or other conflict, while also considering benefits and drawbacks of relevant timesharing schedules.
- When a couple has consistently been engaged in high conflict interactions, beyond the time surrounding the separation and divorce, shared decision-making has a risk of creating a foundation for parents to persist in open conflict with one another and thereby negatively influence their children.
- It may be necessary to directly examine additional domestic violence and conflict resources[159] in the parenting plan process.

159. *E.g.*, Jaffe et al., *supra* note 154, AFCC, *supra* note 154; ABA Commission on Domestic Violence, *supra* note 155; Ellis & Stuckless, *supra* note 155; Austin, *supra* note 156; Austin & Drozd, *supra* note 156.

CHAPTER 7
OTHER MARITAL CONFLICT

Controversies over marital conflict overlap a good deal with concerns about domestic violence within the context of parenting planning. However, there are many important aspects of marital conflict that do not include domestic violence.

Conflict occurs, at least to some extent, in all marriages and other close relationships. To some degree, the frequency and intensity of conflict depends on the definition used. One group of prominent researchers and theoreticians has defined marital conflict, for purposes of their research, as "any major or minor interparental interaction that involved a difference of opinion, whether it was mostly negative or even mostly positive."[160] On a practical basis, professionals working with families about parenting plans are not going to be very concerned about minor or positive differences of opinion, but this definition illustrates that conflict is ubiquitous, and there is a wide range in its intensity.

At the same time, for most families, the level of interparental conflict is low. A longitudinal study covering hundreds of children found that three-quarters of the families had negligible to mild levels of conflict, and for most of them, the divorce was uncontested and without substantial disagreement about parenting plans. In that study, less than 4 percent went to trial, and most of those cases settled during the trial.[161]

When there is substantial conflict during the course of the divorce, in most cases it tends to fade out over a period of time that can last from a few months to two or three years. Cases in which a high level of conflict is ongoing over a number of years consume a disproportionate amount of court time. Those cases tend to be highly challenging for

160. Cummings & Davies, *supra* note 72, at 6.
161. Dividing, *supra* note 2, at 137.

all professionals involved and can result in parents spending a vast proportion of their financial assets, as well as children being exposed to relentless long-term hostility between parents.

An important objective for those involved in parenting planning is to be able to ascertain what are the types or characteristics of marital conflict that are harmful for children and which parents are at particular risk of carrying out such actions. It is also critical to be cognizant that there are parental actions that can provide at least partial repair of exposure to marital conflict in the psychological lives of children.

This chapter covers information about marital conflict and its impact on children that is relevant to parenting planning. It is important to note that relevant research at times has examined the effects on children of exposure to domestic violence as well as conflict that does not reach the threshold of violence. The summary here first focuses on both the effects of direct exposure to conflict and the more complex set of interactions among multiple related factors. Those factors include parental mood dysfunction, parental substance abuse, parenting behaviors outside the realm of marital conflict, children's psychological processes, and other aspects of family systems functioning. Also, within the overall context of the effects of marital conflict on children, there are descriptions of especially destructive or constructive parental actions and statements.

Second, I summarize practical and scientific considerations associated with the challenges of both protecting children from exposure to interparental conflict and promoting healthy child relationships with both parents. Third, I describe parenting plan considerations.

Findings of relevant group-level research are often highly useful for professionals. It is essential that such research be integrated with the individual facts and circumstances of each family case.

Marital Conflict

Because children's exposure to marital conflict that is less extreme than domestic violence can also have an exceedingly negative impact on their well-being, it is essential to be aware of the relevant facts when considering parenting plans. At times, in family court cases, arguments have been made that there is no need to worry about the impact of conflict on the children simply because there has been no domestic violence. Those arguments ignore the harmful effects on children of exposure to other serious conflict.

Domestic violence can be seen as a subset of marital conflict, and researchers who focus on this area have typically investigated partner physical aggression, verbal aggression, nonverbal hostility, and at times, even nonhostile disagreements. Also, it is important to be aware that child abuse occurs in a significant proportion of families with intimate partner violence.[162]

In general, exposure to intimate partner physical aggression and verbal aggression, such as yelling, name-calling, and swearing, have both been found to have a significantly negative impact on child adjustment.[163] Not surprisingly, there is evidence that exposure to physical violence tends to have a larger negative impact on children than does witnessing verbal aggression only.[164]

Also, child exposure to nonverbal expressions of conflict that do not include physical aggression, such as facial expression, body language, and/or a spouse not speaking to the other parent, also has a negative impact on child well-being. Fear plays a central role. In particular, child perceptions of fear in a parent lead to considerable distress. Parental threats to leave the relationship elicit child reactions similar to responses when viewing physical violence.[165]

There are complex factors that contribute to the negative effects on children of exposure to parental aggression and violence. For example, when a child believes he or she has some involvement in the interparental conflict, such as the parents arguing about child-related matters, it tends to result in increased likelihood that the child will attempt to be an informal mediator between the parents. Children who blame themselves for the conflict and those who become involved in it tend to experience especially negative emotional effects.[166]

---

162. Anne Appel & George W. Holden, *The Co-occurrence of Spouse and Physical Abuse: A Review and Appraisal*, 12 J. FAM. PSYCHOL. 578 (1998).

163. CUMMINGS & DAVIES, *supra* note 72; John H. Grych & Frank D. Fincham, *Marital Conflict and Children's Adjustment: A Cognitive-Contextual Framework*, 108 PSYCHOL. BULL. 267 (1990); Ernest N. Jouriles et al., *Physical Violence and Other Forms of Marital Aggression: Links with Children's Behavior Problems*, 10 J. FAM. PSYCHOL. 223 (1996); McDonald et al., *Violence toward a Family Member, Angry Adult Conflict, and Child Adjustment Difficulties: Relations and Families with 1- to 3-Year-Old Children,* 21 J. FAM. PSYCHOL. 176 (2007).

164. Grych & Fincham, *supra* note 164; Katherine M. Kitzmann et al., *Child Witnesses to Domestic Violence: A Meta-Analytic Review*, 71 J. CONSULTING & CLINICAL PSYCHOL. 339 (2003).

165. CUMMINGS & DAVIES, *supra* note 72, at 65.

166. *Id.*; Jennifer C. Ablow et al., *Linking Marital Conflict and Children's Adjustment: The Role of Young Children's Perceptions*, 23 J. FAM. PSYCHOL. 485 (2009).

Parental statements and actions after the conflict has ended also have an impact. Negative parental emotion tends to lead to considerable child distress. In contrast, indications of positive feelings by parents are experienced as comforting to children even when they have not observed parents resolve their conflict. Exhibits of parental support for the other parent and parental compromise have consistently positive influences on children. Parental efforts at problem-solving are viewed as at least modestly constructive by children.

The effects of parental apology to the other parent differ depending upon accompanying statements and behaviors. Apology accompanied by positive parental emotions is experienced as reassuring to children. However, parental apology accompanied by negative emotions and/or submission by the other parent can be seen as one parent winning and the other one losing, which is characteristically upsetting for children.[167]

Numerous other individual and interpersonal factors also play a role in the association between exposure to interparental conflict and child maladjustment. A holistic family systems conceptualization is necessary in order to understand the multiple processes and causal pathways that are involved. It is not possible to briefly summarize the many individual child, parent, interpersonal, family-level, and circumstantial factors that influence the effects on children of exposure to marital conflict, but a number of the main factors relevant to parenting plans are noted here.

For example, child temperament factors, such as propensities for emotional distress, misbehavior, or resilience can have an influence on how children are affected by exposure to marital conflict. Also, child actions can at times precipitate marital conflict, such as when there are serious parental disagreements about how to best respond to child oppositional behavior. At times, children play a role in trying to prevent or lessen interparental conflict and may be more afraid of the disintegration of the family than of physical and verbal aggression. When there are repeated exposures over time to serious interparental conflict, children may experience a sensitization effect that involves an increased intensity of emotional distress. Parental mood and/or impulse control problems, including substance abuse, can increase the risk for marital conflict; in turn, incidents of open conflict often worsen the individual psychological condition of each parent and the degree of security each of them have about their marital relationship.

---

167. CUMMINGS & DAVIES, *supra* note 72, at 64.

At times, parents with significant psychological problems and/or considerable insecurity within their marriages are less effective in carrying out positive parenting behaviors such as support, informal education, monitoring, and limit setting.[168] In cases in which there has been considerable family conflict, it is crucial for there to be a professional involved who has relevant mental health training and experience.

Protecting Children from Conflict and Promoting Healthy Contact with Parents

A family law attorney asserts that his client should have equally shared parenting and decision making because there is no history of domestic violence in the marriage. Another family law attorney in a different case maintains that her client should have the vast majority of parenting time and sole decision-making ability, and bases that argument on the view that it is a high-conflict marriage, as evidenced by the fact that the parents are litigating the matter and have not arrived at an agreement. A custody evaluator routinely recommends for shared parenting, including decision making, and contends that position is based on research showing that children of divorce who grew up with joint custody function better than sole custody children.

All of the professionals referred to in the preceding paragraph are hypothetical and do not exist in reality. These scenarios are very real (though altered to protect privacy) and exemplify professionals' perspectives based on selected and limited information, without consideration of a sufficiently broad picture. They are also examples of the hypothetical professionals engaging in WYSIATI (What You See Is All There Is),[169] as described in Chapter 3.

Of course, it is important to facilitate a child having a good relationship with both parents. However, considerable caution is needed when there is a risk that a child may be exposed to significant conflict between the parents. Each case must be considered individually, and there are always multiple factors that need to be considered when looking closely at the reality of each family.

In general, there is agreement in the field that children should be protected from domestic violence and other forms of interparental conflict. Also, there is general agreement that regular contact and

168. Cummings & Davies, *supra* note 72, at 24; Grych & Fincham, *supra* note 164.
169. Thinking, *supra* note 10.

meaningful involvement with both parents is good for children in the solid majority of cases. However, in a considerable proportion of cases that take a disproportionate amount of court time, there are disputes about the specifics of interparental conflict and the consistent appropriateness of parenting.

As described earlier,[170] there is considerable research demonstrating that children exposed to conflict between parents generally experience a negative effect. That research is not limited to children of divorce, though some of the specific studies have involved such samples. It is important and relevant that this body of research includes both field studies of conflictual families and laboratory analog experiments. The reliability of these studies is further demonstrated by the fact that the data have been collected and analyzed by different groups of researchers.

There are also studies focused specifically on how interparental conflict affects children of divorce while concurrently measuring the level of child contact with the nonresident parent. A number of these research reports have indicated that, when conflict between the parents is high, contact with the nonresident parent increases the likelihood of child adjustment problems in at least some of the children. Other research studies have described that the level of conflict between parents does not impact child adjustment or does not outweigh the reported benefits of greater contact with the nonresidential parent. Because high-conflict cases are often extremely challenging, I briefly summarize a number of relevant studies here.

For example, when a general measure of child behavioral problems was used, under conditions of high interparental conflict, increased contact between boys and their nonresident fathers was associated with heightened child behavior problems. However, there was not a similar effect for girls, and when interparental conflict was not high, increased contact with the nonresident father was associated with better child behavioral functioning.[171]

Another study specifically examined depressive symptoms in children. It was found that interparental conflict after the divorce generally increased child depressive symptoms. The interparental conflict led to particularly high levels of depressive signs when there was greater

---

170. *E.g.*, CUMMINGS & DAVIES, *supra* note 72.

171. Paul R. Amato & Sandra J. Rezac, *Contact with the Nonresident Parents, Interparental Conflict, and Children's Behavior*, 15 J. FAM. ISSUES 191 (1994).

contact between boys and the nonresident father. Similar to the prior study, there was no similar effect for girls.[172]

Two longitudinal studies found that child exposure to interparental conflict had a negative impact on life adjustment into adulthood. In a 17-year longitudinal study that covered two generations, it was found that children of divorce experienced lower levels of psychological well-being in adulthood. In addition, it looked at the impact of parental marital discord, which included direct marital conflict as well as related indications of marital problems. The results indicated that exposure to marital discord also predicted lower levels of psychological well-being in adulthood, and it appeared to do so at least in part by eroding the relationships between the children and the parents.

A second longitudinal study looked at adolescents whose parents had divorced six to eight years earlier. Based on adolescent ratings of discord between the parents and the adolescent–father relationships, the divorced families were classified into one of three main groups: Moderate Involvement (with fathers)/Low Conflict, Low Involvement/Moderate Conflict, and High Involvement/High Conflict. Nine years later, when the study subjects were young adults, academic achievement and psychological adjustment were measured. Individuals in the Moderate Involvement/Low Conflict group had higher levels of educational achievement than those in the other two groups. Also, the Moderate Involvement/Low Conflict group showed fewer externalizing problems (e.g., impulsivity) than did the Low Involvement/Moderate Conflict group. There were no differences between the three groups on internalizing problems (e.g., depression). Follow-up analyses also indicated that individuals in the Moderate Involvement/Low Conflict group had higher levels of academic achievement and lower levels of externalizing behaviors when compared to those whose fathers had no contact with them.[173]

In contrast, a meta-analysis of studies that compared children in joint physical or legal custody with those in sole custody reported

---

172. Matthijs Kalmijn, *Father-Child Contact, Interparental Conflict, and Depressive Symptoms among Children of Divorced Parents*, 32 European Soc. Rev. 68 (2016).

173. Paul R. Amato & Juliana M. Sobolewski, *The Effects of Divorce and Marital Discord on Adult Children's Psychological Well-Being*, 66 Am. Soc. Rev. 900 (2001); Kathryn Lynn Modecki et al., *Latent Profiles of Nonresidential Father Engagement Six Years after Divorce Predict Long-Term Offspring Outcomes*, 44 J. Clinical Child & Adolescent Psychol. 123 (2015).

better child adjustment for those in joint custody, and did not find that the level of interparental conflict predicted adjustment. However, that article also noted that there were only five studies in the meta-analysis that provided adequate data about past marital conflict, and therefore limited conclusions could be reached. In addition, the meta-analysis primarily looked at research studies that had not been published, and therefore, they were likely of lower quality than studies characteristically examined in most meta-analyses.[174]

A more recent study investigated divorcing families who manifested a high level of legal conflict, as identified by judges assigned to the cases. The article describes that no standard criteria were given to the judges to make this identification, though one judge described that "they can't agree that the sky is blue." The authors investigated factors that predicted child mental health problems. They reported that parenting quality and the number of overnights with the parents were positively associated with child mental health, but that the level of interparental conflict did not have an impact. A particular limitation of this study is the inclusion only of high-conflict families, which statistically leads to a restricted range of conflict scores and thereby decreases the likelihood of finding a significant correlation between interparental conflict and child mental health.[175]

In addition, a study that collected retrospective data from university students reported that higher levels of time spent with nonresident fathers was correlated with more positive relationships with those fathers and better health. Interparental conflict, both prior to the divorce and up to five years after it, was associated with a less positive relationship with the father and more apparent physical health symptoms. However, the authors concluded that increased post-divorce time with the father was beneficial regardless of the level of interparental conflict,[176] in contrast to a number of the studies summarized earlier.[177]

A large longitudinal study measured parents' perceptions of their own involvement in child rearing as well as parental perspectives on child rearing done by the other parent. When both parents tended to agree about their respective contributions to child rearing, the average

---

174. Bauserman, *supra* note 44.

175. Irwin N. Sandler, *Relations of Parenting Quality, Interparental Conflict, and Overnights with Mental Health Problems of Children in Divorcing Families with High Legal Conflict*, 27 J. FAM. PSYCHOL. 915 (2013).

176. Fabricius & Luecken, *supra* note 80.

177. *E.g., supra* notes 171–73.

amount of legal conflict was low, but when there were large differences of opinion regarding involvement with the children, the amount of legal conflict was relatively high. Similarly, when a parent described having little worry about the child's welfare in the household of the other parent, the level of legal conflict tended to be low, but parental expressions of serious concern about child welfare in the other home were associated with higher levels of legal conflict.[178]

These research studies are useful and relevant when considering the role of interparental conflict in devising parenting plans. However, a significant limitation is that they typically have used brief, general measures of marital conflict. When professionals involved in parenting planning are working with families in which interparental conflict has been an area of controversy, it is crucial that there be a much closer examination of the allegations and factual details of the conflict. That is especially true regarding the impact of conflict on the children. A number of these research studies regarding divorced families had brief measures of conflict completed only by parents and did not obtain children's perspectives.

When there is reason for concern that children may be harmed by exposure to conflict, an adequate case investigation would require pursuing and closely reviewing all relevant data. A relevant parallel in mental health research is the LEAD (Longitudinal, Expert, All Data) criteria, a method of attempting to identify a gold standard for sufficient information.[179] Sensitive, competent child interviewers who routinely use empirically informed interview techniques should be used to collect relevant evidence.[180]

High-conflict families have often been seen as largely the same as one another, perhaps because that classification is a useful shorthand for many family cases that are very demanding and take an outsized proportion of court time. However, high-conflict families come in many different shapes and sizes, figuratively speaking, with respect to the characteristics that lead them to be so very challenging.

The reasons and motivations for ongoing levels of high conflict are multiple and often interrelated. In certain families, a parent has experienced the spouse manifesting multiple serious problems over years or decades, such as spousal and/or child abuse, addiction, financial irresponsibility, infidelity, and poor child rearing. As a result, the

178. DIVIDING, *supra* note 2, at 145.

179. GARB, *supra* note 31, at 48.

180. *E.g.*, EVALUATION, *supra* note 1, at 99.

parent may have concluded that the spouse is incompetent as a parent and should have little contact with the children, which in turn leads to highly contentious and lengthy litigation. In other families, a parent may have severe personality dysfunction, and the stress associated with the separation and divorce leads that parent to become increasingly belligerent and suspicious, to the serious detriment of the children and the other parent. The profound mistrust that accompanies the disordered personality features, perhaps combined with a horrified response by the other parent, can also provide fuel for enduring interparental conflict. Divorce litigation can take many forms, but in a number of instances it can significantly worsen and extend conflict between parents. For example, attorneys may accept the vigorous claims of their clients that they are excellent parents, and that the spouses are highly deficient and perhaps even dangerous in terms of their relationships with the children.[181]

In some cases, professionals in the family law system can take an approach of trying to maintain a balance of neutrality between parents, and therefore attribute to each parent an equal degree of responsibility for the high level of ongoing conflict. However, there are a significant proportion of cases in which one parent provides the vast majority of the fuel that keeps the fires of conflict burning. That parent might engage in such disruptive and challenging behaviors as making multiple, unsubstantiated complaints of child abuse against the other parent or making repeated calls to the police without good reason.[182]

Not surprisingly, patterns of conflict and cooperation between parents tend to show stability over time. In a relatively comprehensive long-term study, parents who had high levels of conflict with one another at one and a half years after separation tended to remain either conflicted (36 percent) or disengaged (carrying out parallel parenting) from one another (33 percent) two years later. Unfortunately, in 19 percent of that high-conflict group, the nonresident parent was no longer seeing the child at all. In the group of parents who had high levels of cooperation at one and one-half years after separation, almost half remained cooperative and 28 percent had become disengaged from one another two years later. A much smaller proportion of the formerly

---

181. Joan B. Kelly, *Parents with Enduring Child Disputes: Multiple Pathways to Enduring Disputes*, 9 J. FAM. STUDIES 37 (2003).

182. *Id.*; Michael Friedman, *The So-Called High-Conflict Couple: A Closer Look*, 32 AM. J. FAM. THERAPY 101 (2004).

cooperative nonresident parents, about 8 percent, were no longer visiting the child.[183]

For individuals working to devise parenting plans, these research findings mean that, when working with families who have had substantial marital conflict, there is a potential risk for children if the plan includes considerable joint decision making. At the same time, in many such cases, parenting plans can be created that schedule a good deal of contact with both parents while minimizing or even largely eliminating the likelihood of a child witnessing parents in conflict with one another.

In addition, the research described earlier demonstrates that it is naïve to expect high-conflict couples to regularly evolve into cooperative couples. However, a significant proportion may improve to the point of no longer being in conflict with one another, while also not actively cooperating with one another. Only a very small proportion of intense conflict parents will successfully make the big leap to successful coparenting.

At the same time, it is important to recognize the frequently grim realities involved in high-conflict parents moving through the legal system. They tend to find multiple areas for dispute, remain active in the legal system for years and spend large amounts of money for legal and other professional services. Children are exposed to sustained conflict and are at significant risk of worsened functioning. Families who have very deep pockets can, at times, serve as a type of informal annuity for the law firms they hire. Much more frequently, family finances become depleted, and all involved individuals eventually get exhausted and impatient.

Under such circumstances, the court, families, and attorneys are all looking for a way to get the case completed. Because there frequently is insufficient money for a trial, settlement is the only option. For many, the only realistic way to get the parents to agree to settle is for there to be shared parenting, and in many such instances equally shared parenting is the only option that has any chance of leading to an agreement.

A prominent concern of individuals focused on trying to prevent domestic violence and other serious interparental conflict is that a parent who has been victimized by an ex-spouse will be forced into dangerous circumstances. That apprehension is particularly acute if shared

---

183. DIVIDING, *supra* note 2, at 234.

parenting is the legal outcome or there are other legal provisions that potentially increase the risk of harm.

Parenting Plan Considerations

Unfortunately, because parents with enduring levels of high conflict with one another are the least likely to successfully carry out equally shared parenting, especially shared decision making, the best that can be hoped for is that the parents will learn to disengage from one another, have very little contact beyond what is necessary for the child, and carry out parallel parenting that is at least adequate in both households. Certain parents may be relatively successful proceeding down that pathway, and others will continue to be frequent fliers in court, especially if and when decisions need to be made about matters such as health care, school, and extracurricular activities.

So, it is an all too frequent dilemma. On the one hand, consistently high-conflict parents tend not to develop into cooperative ones who are likely to be able to succeed at shared parenting while shielding their children from exposure to conflict. On the other hand, there are often practical pressures to get the case settled, and shared parenting seems to be the most likely pathway to an agreement. Of course, in addition to these conflicting realities, parents and their attorneys frequently perceive relevant matters very differently and disagree vigorously about facts and what would be the best parenting plan.

As a result, parenting plan development efforts frequently take place under conditions of major uncertainty, including what are the facts about interparental conflict. Nevertheless, in many cases, it is possible for parenting plans to reasonably balance safety for children and parents with the promotion of positive parent–child relationships.

For example, each individual parent may do well interacting with a child, but the parents have conflicts when communicating with one another, even over the telephone. In such cases, parenting plans may specify that routine communication takes place only by text, e-mail, or by exchanging a notebook.

Of course, arguments and insults can be easily transmitted by e-mail or text, and it is critical that parents strive to all extents possible to consistently carry out nonaggressive, effective communication with one another. They may require professional help to do so, described in more detail later in the chapter.

In order for productive communication to take place consistently, parents need to accept two main general principles and actively work to put them into practice. In a number of cases, to put these principles into effect, parents will need the assistance of parenting coordinators, mediators, or counselors to make required changes. Other families may be able to accept these ideas and increase the effectiveness of their communications through work with their attorneys.

First, parents need to accept, in all aspects of their thinking and action, that the best interest of their children is the priority, above all other aspects of their interactions with the other parent. Second, parents need to take individual responsibility to try to ensure that their own communications are civil and businesslike.

If parents are able to make progress in establishing a pattern of productive and nonaggressive communication with one another, at least about the children, they begin to build trust with one another that the other parent means well about child-related matters. In turn, as this foundation of trust expands, it promotes the likelihood that effective communication will become more consistent.

It takes time and effort to carry out beneficial communication about the child, even with each specific e-mail, text, or note. In advance of starting to type an e-mail, for example, a parent needs to think about what it is that he or she wishes to convey and how to do so in a way that is both clear and unlikely to lead to a negative reaction by the other parent. It is vital to keep any such communication focused on the child. Keeping it brief is important as long as relevant information about the child is conveyed. Because messages are effective only when they do not add to disputes, it is better not to use abbreviations or other items that might be misunderstood by the parent on the receiving end. Parents should routinely check an e-mail or text before sending it to make sure it is child focused, businesslike, and does not include irrelevant information or anything that the recipient is likely to find offensive. It can be useful and at times even necessary to include all these points in a parenting plan.

Very difficult relationships can include communication that is at times openly aggressive and at other times avoidant or passive-aggressive. Consequently, parenting plans may need to include specific provisions for emergency communication. Emergencies require a phone call or text because they are more likely to be received quickly. Emergency communication should be able to occur at any time.

In high-conflict cases, for nonemergency matters, there may need to be parenting plan provisions for how long it should take for a parent to reply to an e-mail or text, assuming that a reply is needed.[184] There is no magic number that works in all cases, but reasonable options include 24 or 48 hours. If there has been a past dispute about whether an e-mail or text was actually sent, with a parent asserting that she or he had never received it, there should be a parenting plan provision that the recipient should send a brief reply acknowledging receipt, preferably with a positive tone, such as "got it, thanks."

In cases with ongoing, substantial conflict, there are often additional factors for consideration regarding parenting plans. In a number of these cases, there may be relatively few transitions and a relatively long period of time when the child is with just one parent. Accordingly, it is wise for the parent who has had the child for a relatively long stretch of time to send regular, brief e-mail updates, such as on a weekly basis. They need to be brief, clear, and informative. Even if there is no new information that would be essential for the other parent, it can help build or maintain a civil interaction pattern just to convey that there is no news, even if it is only an e-mail that states "nothing new—Josh is fine."

Stuff happens—more specifically, there are likely to be times that difficult incidents occur, even when parents are both working sincerely to try to communicate productively. For example, a child in high school might have been absent due to illness and needs to make up a few missed tests, but the only time to do so is after school during what has been dad's parenting time. In another hypothetical case, a child has repeatedly forgotten to bring her track shoes, needed for daily practice, to dad's home, and it has just happened again. There are an almost unlimited number of possible scenarios that can occur to challenge parental patience and that place parents at risk of arguing with one another, especially if they have an entrenched history of doing so. Therefore, it is often very important for parents to carefully word their messages to the other parent about such matters.

In that regard, it is typically counterproductive to describe one's own negative emotional reactions and to make statements that can be interpreted as accusatory, such as "I am fed up with those shoes not getting to my house—you're a parent and should be doing something about it." A potentially more effective alternative would be "I noticed

184. Ricci, *supra* note 4, at 70.

Sara did not bring her track shoes again. Since it keeps happening I wonder if we can try different ways to remind her, or maybe just pack the shoes ourselves." The alternative wording eliminates the accusation, includes a connotation that both parents can calmly coordinate their efforts, and raises possible problem-solving options instead of making a hostile and controlling statement to the other parent.[185]

Parents can often make excellent investments in their working relationship with the other parent, regardless of whether or not there is any type of shared parenting, by finding opportunities to make positive statements about the interactions between the child and the other parent.[186] Although it may feel emotionally very challenging in the short run for a parent to give the other parent such a compliment, over the long run it can contribute to a mutual sense of trust and facilitate the child's well-being.

Unfortunately, low trust and high conflict are often present. An essential component for parenting plans when there has been a high level of conflict is to take all steps necessary to keep the children out of the middle of the battle; this principle has a very solid foundation in research[187] and is an important piece of advice given to parents.[188] Because it is much easier said than done, multiple factors deserve a closer look.

At times, parents rely on an intuitive but counterproductive sense of honesty and feel comfortable saying negative things about the other parents to the children. Other parents may know that doing so tends to have a negative effect on children, but when angry or otherwise upset can talk themselves into believing that such statements are acceptable. In general, making any kind of negative communication to the child about the other parent, including in facial expression and/or tone of voice, is to be strenuously avoided.

Almost any parent going through a separation or divorce is likely to be talking about it with their family and friends. Fortunately, a large proportion of the family and friends are understanding and supportive. Unfortunately, that understanding and support can, depending on what is said, fuel the fires of the anger their loved ones have toward the other parent. Even more unfortunately, loved ones might openly convey their disdain for the other parent to the child or children. Any professionals,

185. *Id.* at 75.

186. *Id.* at 76.

187. Amato, *supra* note 66; Cummings & Davies, *supra* note 72.

188. Ricci, *supra* notes 3 & 4; Emery, *supra* note 4.

in any discipline, need to inform parents that, while it is important to talk with and gather support from loved ones, those individuals need to be firmly and perhaps repeatedly instructed that there should be no negative communication about the other parent to or in front of the children.

It is all too easy for parents to assume that children do not hear their arguments. Similarly, parents can be very unaware that children, even those just engaged in normal snooping in the house, can see material critical of the other parent on a computer or stumble across court-related paperwork. Children routinely eavesdrop and snoop, and having parents in the process of separation or divorce may increase their motivation to do so. Accordingly, parents need to be very disciplined to prevent accidentally exposing children to substantive marital conflict.

It can be tempting for parents to have children pass along messages or other information to the other parent living in a different household. The assumption that doing so will not be a problem is often based on a preseparation background of occasionally having a child deliver innocuous information to the other parent, such as "tell dad his laundry is done and I need the dryer." However, once parents begin the process of splitting up, there is characteristically increased tension that the children notice, and very few messages are likely to be completely innocent. It is much more likely that messages delivered between parents by children are going to include at least aspects of critical or otherwise unhappy communications. As described earlier in this chapter, children's exposures to conflict between parents have an especially strong negative impact when children experience themselves as being in the middle or somehow responsible for the discord. For example, children can experience worry and anxiety about delivering parental messages accurately. In addition, they can feel responsible and unhappy if the parent who receives the message becomes upset about it. Consequently, parents need to not rely on children to deliver information to the other parent, and they need to develop effective routines of communicating directly.

When a child has returned from time spent with the other parent, it is reasonable for a parent to express general interest by asking questions such as "how was your weekend," and "what did you do?" These types of questions would be no different from those asked if a child was returning from a sleepover at a friend's house. However, parental efforts to extract more detailed information about a visit with the other parent can cause a child to feel pressured and caught in the middle. For example, questions such as "did that guy Sam come over your mom's house" or "how much time did you and dad just play video games" convey clear, if indirect, disapproval of the other parent and place the child in a role of being a virtual spy in the other home. As a result, parental questions to a returning child need to be general and at least neutral in tone regarding the other household. Otherwise, there is a strong risk of those types of questions placing the child in the middle of the conflict and experiencing a harmful psychological effect.

An emotionally and practically challenging circumstance for a parent is when a child initiates a negative remark about the other parent. For example, a young child might report "mom doesn't make me use the car seat," or "dad is always sleeping." Of course, to a parent who has a negative view of the other parent, such statements are easy to believe, and might initiate longer, critical conversations with the child about the other parent. It can be very challenging to know how to handle these kinds of child comments productively.

Somewhat similarly, a child might make statements about the other parent that are not directly critical, but they are alarming for other reasons. For instance, a child says to her mother, "dad says we're going to go to a football game on Thanksgiving weekend," but she believes that is her parenting time. Alternately, a child comments to his father that "mom went out Saturday night and the babysitter was mean."

For high-conflict parents, an initial impulse might be to call up and berate the other parent. However, it is essential for any parent who hears one of these types of child comments to remain calm and think carefully about how to respond. Although children can and often do report events accurately, they may not know or relate the big picture accurately. In families where a parent has made critical statements about the other parent, a child might be motivated to also make negative statements. The child's derogatory comments could be an imitation of the parent.

There are often multiple stubborn, persistent challenges for parents when there has been a history of substantial interparental conflict. Difficulties about decision making are frequently prominent when such parents are ordered to equally share in the process or there is a desire for equally shared decisions. When parents have unsuccessfully attempted over time to devise a parenting plan with agreements about major decisions, they tend to be frustrated and veer into increased arguments with one another. However, there are problem-solving avenues to consider that increase the odds of being able to get through such an impasse.

When anger and arguments dominate parents' interactions, as described earlier, a change to communicate by e-mail and text, at least temporarily, increases the likelihood of productive exchanges of ideas. However, parents would need to put in effect the steps described earlier intended to make the e-mails and text communications calm and businesslike.

Then, to work toward a possible solution, one or both parents can propose a number of options to deal with the impasse, perhaps accompanied by that individual's thoughts about the strengths and weaknesses of each of the options. For example, in a hypothetical case, the Johnsons have an eight-year-old girl, Destiny, who has had repeated respiratory problems. The couple has separated, is in the divorce process, and there is no agreement or order in place that pertains to decisions about the children. The pediatrician has attributed these problems to common viruses, but the father, who has a family history of asthma, voices that their daughter may suffer from it. The mother sees no reason to believe that the pediatrician is incorrect in her diagnosis, and is concerned that the father is just attempting to convince the court that he is thoroughly involved in their daughter's life. They have argued repeatedly about that matter as well as others and decided to communicate by e-mail or text.

In an e-mail, the mother submits three options for how to possibly deal with the asthma question: first, wait and see if Destiny has any further respiratory problems over the next three months, and if she does, make a decision about health care at that time; second, make an appointment with the pediatrician and ask for a more specific assessment about asthma; and third, ask the pediatrician for a referral to an asthma specialist. The father has expressed a dislike for the pediatrician and proposes two options: first, his preferred option is to see a specialist who has provided care for a number of his family members; second, he and the mother would check online and each identify at least three other asthma specialists, and they would decide on one based on insurance coverage and location. Each of the parents identifies potential pros and cons of each of their options.

It is certainly possible that the Johnsons could take the time and effort to construct and exchange such civil e-mails with one another and put together a good compromise about how to proceed. It is also possible that any of a variety of emotional, interpersonal, or situational factors could arise and figuratively toss a hand grenade into these problem-solving efforts. However, such steps provide a potential route for productively pursuing the child's best interest and increase the likelihood of a good outcome. A number of parents may be able to carry out such procedures on their own, others may benefit from guidance from their attorneys, and still others might require working with parenting coordinators or mediators.

In contrast, if there is consistent evidence that parents are unlikely to be able to make decisions together, other parenting plan options are worth considering in the interests of arriving at an agreement. Whether or not these parenting plan options would be successful depends a great deal on the details of each case. In certain cases, a decision is made by the parents or the court to divide up the major decisions in terms of having one parent have sole authority over one or more areas while the other parent has sole decision-making ability about one or more of the other areas. Such an arrangement is worth considering especially if each parent has a particularly strong concern and/or expertise in a certain decision-making area and the other parent has substantial concern or expertise in a separate area. For example, Parent A has been an educator and is given sole decision-making ability about schooling, whereas Parent B has been a physician and is awarded sole decision-making about health care; however, the limitations of such a potential solution include the realities that educators are very seldom expert about all aspects of school matters, and physicians are rarely skilled in assessing and treating all illnesses. In other cases, it might be possible to formulate a parenting plan compromise that involves Parent A obtaining sole decision-making ability about a certain area while Parent B is given additional parenting time.

In a number of cases, all the best efforts by parents and professionals are not going to result in parents being able to make decisions together effectively. While no one can predict the future with certainty, professionals can look to a number of factors to assess whether or not shared decision-making might be successful. One important factor is the couple's decision-making history, especially about the children. The more parents have had long-standing disputes about child-related decisions, including ones that preceded the separation or divorce action, the less likely it is that they will be able to effectively and consistently arrive at shared decisions.

The greater the overall intensity of conflict between the parents and the longer its duration, the less likely it is that shared parenting would be effective. If there has been intense interparental conflict, a requirement for shared parenting carries a substantial safety risk for the parents; similarly, it includes a considerable risk that the children would be further exposed to intense interparental conflict. Also, the more parents have demonstrated vehement and consistent disagreement about certain decision-making areas, the less likely it is that they will successfully share decision-making about those topics, and the greater the risk that the children will suffer because important decisions will not be made or will be excessively delayed. Under the conditions described here, a competent parenting plan would require sole decision making.

As described earlier, there are high-conflict cases in which one parent has been the cause of the vast majority of the discord and related problems. That parent may have engaged in extremely negative and potentially destructive behavior such as false accusations of domestic violence and/or child abuse or efforts to alienate a child from the other parent. Such behaviors seriously risk damaging parent–child relationships, and competent parenting plans will very likely need to have sole decision making in the hands of the parent who has not carried out such actions.

For high-conflict couples, sharing decision making can be even more challenging than sharing parenting time. In certain instances, there is a great deal of overlap between the challenges of decision making and parenting time.

For example, especially when there is a parenting time arrangement that involves a child being with the nonresidential parent about a third of the time or more, many extracurricular activities will fall on the parenting time of both the mother and the father. The fact that many children are involved in more than one extracurricular activity at a time can contribute to the challenges of conflict when parents have different preferences as to specific extracurricular activities. Also, in certain instances, a parent may insist that an extracurricular activity does not impinge on a specific portion of their parenting time.

It is simply not possible to disengage enough when parents share decision making. There may be periods of time when parents are not required to make decisions about the child—consequently, there is calm. While many decisions about extracurriculars can be relatively minor, problems or choices about health and/or school can often provide major difficulties for parents in terms of getting along with one another civilly.

Cases with backgrounds that include considerable conflict tend to have multiple areas of uncertainty, often focused on but not limited to what conflict has occurred. At times, there appear to be indications that significant conflict has occurred, but that there have also been times of relatively good coparenting. In a number of these cases, parental reports about parent–child relationships also differ a great deal. Therefore, the professionals involved in parenting planning need to work to ensure they are engaging in adequate deliberation about these crucial yet uncertain matters.

As described in prior chapters, the use of pro–con types of lists can be very effective in promoting diligent reasoning instead of reliance on quick, automatic, and emotional intuition. For example, in a hypothetical case in which parents disagree about exactly what conflict has occurred, who has been the main initiator of interparental physical aggression, the extent of prior positive coparenting, and the parent–child relationship histories, a number of pro–con lists would be necessary. For each parent separately, there would be lists completed that show parental assertions about what conflict has occurred, with indications about evidence that supports and contradicts each of those assertions. Similarly, there would be forms completed that display parental assertions about who has been the main perpetrator of aggression and evidence for and against what each parent has maintained. Separate lists would carry out the same steps about parental assertions regarding coparenting and parent–child relationship histories. As noted earlier, professionals frequently develop hypotheses about aspects of the case independent of parental claims, and use of the same deliberative format is advisable. On all such forms, it would be essential to highlight any relatively objective evidence.

The creation of parenting plans under the shadow of competing and inconsistent parental allegations is challenging and time-consuming. Especially in the very latest stages of the divorce process, as there are efforts to end the proceedings and put a final agreement in place, it may be tempting to word a parenting plan very generally, both to obtain agreement from both parties and to just get it done. However, the more parents have a track record of multiple conflictual interactions with one another, including getting into arguments about specific details such as times of transitions, items of clothing, and who gets to attend child activities, the more it is crucial to have a very specific parenting plan that clearly spells out relevant details as much as possible. An important general principle is the higher the level of conflict between the couple and the longer its duration, the greater is the need for a highly detailed parenting plan.

There is no finite list of topics that potentially could be important to include in parenting plans. However, parenting plans for high-conflict couples frequently need more detail about specific dates, times, and locations of exchanges, as well as regarding transportation. For example, a provision for alternate weekends should include specific starting and ending days and times. Such specifics should be included about weekday visits, also. Including a statement of the specific weekend that the schedule begins can help to eliminate later confusion, such as "the alternate weekends are to begin with the mother having all children the weekend of October 20–22, 2018." Because holidays, birthdays, and other special occasions frequently alternate year-to-year, it is often necessary to specify when the mother and father have them, respectively, according to even and odd years; again, it is frequently essential to identify starting and ending times.

Parenting plans for high-conflict couples should be further informed by details that address the types of disputes that have previously taken place. For example, there may have been disputes about clothing, car seats, and/or sports equipment accompanying the child to each household. When the families have the financial capacity to purchase duplicates of such items, it can eliminate such arguments, but when money is tight, other problem-solving avenues need to be explored. These are only a few examples of the many content areas that can require very detailed attention in the parenting plans of high-conflict couples.

In developing parenting plans, it is important to remain cognizant that parenting time and decision making can be considered as entirely separate from one another. If it is clear that parents cannot cooperate with one another well enough to share decision making, but each functions well with the children, one parent can have sole decision-making ability while the other parent still has a very substantial proportion of time with the children. Although intuition might suggest that assigning sole decision making to one parent should be accompanied by a very high proportion of parenting time, more careful judgment indicates that, for many families, there is not a rational basis for such a correlation. If there is a concern that parents may quarrel with one another during exchanges, it may be possible to create a transition structure that minimizes their direct contact with one another. Also, depending upon other factors such as child age and stage of development, it may be possible to create a sound parenting schedule with relatively few exchanges.

Important factors in this chapter include the following:

- The small proportion of high-conflict cases often have multiple challenges and take up a disproportionate amount of professional and court time.
- Children suffer from exposure to nonphysical aggression (e.g., yelling, arguments, etc.) and domestic violence.
- Children tend to be especially harmed by exposure to conflict that leads to fear, worries about parental breakups, and indications that the children play a role in the conflict.
- Children tend to be comforted by post-conflict evidence of positive parental emotions, parental support for the other parent, and parental compromise.
- Child involvement with both parents generally promotes child well-being.
- Empirically informed interview methods need to be used by competent child interviewers to obtain information about interparental conflict.
- High-conflict parents tend not to develop into a pattern of cooperation with one another; instead, they tend to remain in high conflict or become disengaged from one another.
- The continued exposure of children to interparental conflict extends the risk of a negative impact on child well-being.
- High-conflict families are often very different from one another, and each case needs to be assessed and considered individually.
- In cases where shared decision making is being considered for high-conflict parents, it is crucial to use decision aids to promote careful reasoning by considering the potential advantages and shortcomings of shared versus sole decision making regarding each relevant content area.
- Parenting plan efforts with families that have consistent patterns of child-related argument or other conflict need to consider the use of
  - careful planning of communications to make them calm, businesslike, and not provocative.

  - e-mail and text communication instead of in person and telephone (except emergencies), and they need to be
    - › focused only on child matters,
    - › brief, and
    - › clear.
  - transitions structured to eliminate or minimize direct parental contact.
  - compliments to the other parent regarding that individual's positive interactions with and about the child.
  - highly detailed parenting plans regarding matters such as
    - › transition dates and times;
    - › transition locations;
    - › holidays and other special occasions;
    - › clarifications about potential conflicts between routine schedules, holidays, and vacations; and
    - › other factors about which there have been past conflicts.
  - professional assistance from parenting coordinators, mediators, or counselors.
- Parenting plan should specify that parents do not have a child convey messages for them to the other parent.

CHAPTER 8
CHILDREN'S MENTAL HEALTH AND SPECIAL NEEDS

Mental disorders are common in children across the world. The term special needs is used especially in educational settings, and mental health difficulties are one major category of special needs. In this chapter, there is particular attention given to those child characteristics that often are relevant for the parenting plan process.

There are a number of categories used to describe how frequently these types of disorders occur. One common method is to look at how frequently individuals have experienced one or more disorders within the last year, called the 12-month prevalence. Another main way is to count how frequently individuals have experienced one or more disorders at any point during their lifetime, called lifetime prevalence. Certain research studies obtain measures of both the 12-month and lifetime prevalence, whereas others use just one of those two.[189]

A recent study found that the 12-month prevalence of any mental health disorder for 8- to 15-year-olds was 13 percent. A separate study found that, in 13- to 18-year-olds, the lifetime prevalence of any mental health disorder was 46 percent. In that same age group, the lifetime prevalence of a severe mental health disorder was 21 percent.[190] Because these disorders occur in a sizable minority of the general population, they are likely to take place at about the same frequency in children of divorce.

---

189. *E.g.*, NAT'L INST. OF MENTAL HEALTH, *Any Disorder among Children*, https://nimh.nih.gov/health/statistics/prevalence/any-disorder-among-children.shtml.

190. *Id.*

Across different research reports, the most frequently found child and adolescent mental health problem areas include attention deficit hyperactivity disorders (ADHD), anxiety disorders, depressive disorders, and conduct disorders.[191] Therefore, this chapter will focus on those disorders plus two other categories: Autism Spectrum Disorders (ASD) and learning disorders. ASD have been increasing in frequency in recent years and provide parents with challenges that range from very substantial to profound. Learning disabilities or disorders also provide a great deal of difficulty for parents, and there are considerable areas of co-occurrence or comorbidity between learning disorders and other commonly occurring child and adolescent problem areas.

First, I provide an overview of these mental health or special needs areas. The main purpose is to present basic information along with features of each type of disorder that are most important for parenting considerations. Second, I describe a general approach to relevant parenting plans focused on the extent of child functional difficulties and comparing them to strengths and limitations in parenting capabilities. Third, I summarize practical yet emotionally challenging features associated with each of these mental health or special needs problem areas, including more specific parenting plan factors. Fourth, I discuss court-involved therapy.

ADHD is characterized by significant problems with cognitive functioning such as excessive distractibility and difficulty paying attention, behavioral features such as overly high motor activity and/or impulsive behavior, or impairments covering both of those categories. Estimates of the prevalence of ADHD have varied between research studies, but recent statistics from the U.S. National Institute of Mental Health indicate that its 12-month prevalence for children ages 8 through 15 years is over 8 percent.[192] It is consistently found more frequently in males than females, especially in the type of ADHD that includes hyperactivity.

Depressive disorders, including the relatively severe form of major depression, reportedly affect just under 4 percent of youths in the 8- to 15-year-old age group.[193] It is found more frequently in females than males both in child and adult samples. Depression prevalence is higher among older teenagers. Serious concerns associated with depression

191. *Id.*; Kathleen Ries Merikangas et al., *Epidemiology of Mental Disorders in Children and Adolescents*, 11 Dialogues Clinical Neuroscience 7 (2009).

192. *Id.*

193. *Id.*

include suicide and nonsuicidal self-injury. For both children and adults, females make more suicide attempts but males complete more suicides, associated with the methods of the suicide attempts. Males tend to choose more lethal methods such as firearms whereas females are more likely to overdose. In recent decades, nonsuicidal self-injury has been reported with increased frequency. About 13 percent of teenagers reported such behavior in a recent study.[194]

There are a number of types of anxiety disorders, including generalized anxiety, social anxiety, and panic disorders. In the United States, estimates of the 12-month prevalence of any type of anxiety disorder in children range from about 7 through 10 percent.[195]

Conduct disorders often refer to a category of specific childhood problems characteristically manifested by impulsive, oppositional, and/or potentially dangerous behaviors. Recent 3- to 12-month prevalence rates average about 7 percent.[196]

There are a number of specific learning disorders, more commonly called learning disabilities. A learning disorder is diagnosed when an individual manifests a particular academic deficit that is not commensurate with his or her general cognitive abilities and is not due to an underlying medical factor such as a brain injury. The specific learning disorders are mainly characterized as those that pertain to reading, written expression, or mathematics.[197] The prevalence of one of these types of specific learning disorders among school-age children is in the range of 5 to 15 percent.

ASD first presents itself in early childhood and is characterized by ongoing impairments in social communication and interaction, as well as restricted and often repetitive patterns of activity and interests. There is a broad range of functioning that can be present. On the mild end of the spectrum, children may manifest decreased interest in social interactions and inflexible behaviors. On the most severe end of the spectrum, there may be profound communication deficits, with the use of only a few words. Also, severely autistic individuals may show extreme restrictions and/or repetitions in behavior that have a highly negative impact on all areas of life, can manifest great difficulties

---

194. Shana Ross et al., *Non-Suicidal Self-Injury and Eating Pathology in High School Students*, 79 AM. J. ORTHOPSYCHIATRY 83 (2009).

195. NAT'L INST. OF MENTAL HEALTH, *supra* note 189.

196. *Id.*

197. AMERICAN PSYCHIATRIC ASSOCIATION, DIAGNOSTIC AND STATISTICAL MANUAL OF MENTAL DISORDERS (DSM-5) 69 (5th ed. 2013).

coping with change, and most have at least one other co-occurring mental disorder.[198] As noted earlier, estimates of prevalence have increased considerably in recent years, though it is unclear to what extent that change represents a broadening of the diagnostic criteria and an increased awareness of the condition, or an actual increase in the frequency of the disorder.

It is important to be aware that many children suffer from more than just one disorder. For example, a large proportion of children with ADHD also present with a second disorder: an average of about 25 to 35 percent concurrently suffer from depressive or anxiety disorders, 45 to 55 percent with a conduct disorder, and approximately 10 to 40 percent with a specific learning disorder.[199]

General Principles

There needs to be an individualized assessment for each child who may have significant mental health difficulties or special needs. That assessment needs to be conducted by an individual with appropriate training and expertise in the problem area(s) in question. The assessment should be focused on child functioning as opposed to diagnosis, because within each diagnosis there can be children who demonstrate a wide range of functioning, from only mild limitations to profound impairments. The family-level assessment needs to include a close examination of parental functioning, including parent–child relationships. At the same time, there are a number of general principles that can productively inform each individual assessment.[200]

A crucial component of any such assessment is to obtain thorough information from health care treatment professionals and educational sources. Such relatively objective information needs to be combined with evaluative data collected from the parents, child, and perhaps other family members who have a strong level of familiarity with the case. For children who have been involved with appropriate health care and in an educational setting that has adequate resources and services,

198. *Id.* at 53.

199. RUSSELL A. BARKLEY, ATTENTION-DEFICIT HYPERACTIVITY DISORDER: A HANDBOOK FOR DIAGNOSIS AND TREATMENT, 127, 206 (3d ed. 2006).

200. Rachel Birnbaum et al., *Children with Neurodevelopmental Disorders in Parental Separation and Divorce*, *in* PARENTING PLAN EVALUATIONS: APPLIED RESEARCH FOR THE FAMILY COURT, 2d ed. 205 (Leslie Drozd et al. eds., 2016); Daniel B. Pickar & Robert L. Kaufman, *Parenting Plans for Special Needs Children: Applying a Risk-Assessment Model*, 53 FAM. CT. REV. 113 (2014).

it is likely that there are treatment and school service plans in place. Unless there is sound reason for concern that such plans may be inadequate, they can serve as a foundation for obtaining relatively objective perspectives about child functioning and needed interventions, both within and outside of the home.

Most health care records contain objective and useful information in that they describe a child's clinical condition and response to treatment at the times the services were provided. However, in some cases, records obtained from treatment providers may not provide productive data. For example, in certain cases, when requests have been made to mental health providers for contemporaneously made records about relevant information such as presenting problems, current condition, diagnoses, responses to treatment, and treatment plans, practitioners respond instead with letters of advocacy in favor of whichever parent has initiated and continued the child's services. Treatment providers who send such letters either do not recognize or disregard that they are at risk of violating professional ethics by providing an evaluative opinion when they have not conducted a relevant evaluation. In practice, competent and useful health care records tend to come from settings that have requirements for the contents and the timing of records and correspondence. Relatively large clinical settings, including hospital-based ones, tend to have such requirements.

It is not unusual for parents to disagree about the severity of a child's problems; for example, there is evidence that mothers tend to perceive ADHD children as having more serious problems than do fathers.[201] A crucial foundational component of a good assessment is to have a reasonably clear picture of the severity of the childhood problem. Official health care and school records can contribute substantially toward developing a sound evaluative foundation, and such documents can help to overcome the often-divergent viewpoints of each parent. Although some parenting plan professionals rely largely on telephone conversations with health care professionals and school personnel, there is usually much more productive information to be gained by obtaining written records. If there is a lack of a clear formal assessment or treatment plan, steps need to be taken to have clearly competent professionals carry them out.

An overall strategy for evaluating what is needed to meet the child's best interest in a parenting plan involves comparing thorough

201. BARKLEY, *supra* note 199.

knowledge of the child's individual needs with relevant parenting characteristics. In addition to general parenting competencies, it is crucial to examine how well each parent is able, motivated, and available to do a reasonably good job of meeting the child's needs. In many cases, the child's needs will involve coordinating with treatment and educational personnel. Frequently, it is important to closely examine parental consistency and persistence—a crucial parenting skill is to facilitate child cooperation with matters such as medication, school assignments, and other therapeutic recommendations. Parents often need to communicate well with health care and school personnel, both in terms of responsiveness and in assertively conveying information about a child's needs. Clearly, parents also need to be able to communicate well with one another about the child regarding multiple areas of life. Those requirements, to be carried out adequately, oblige each parent to put aside whatever negative emotions and other disagreements they have with the spouse and place the needs of the child ahead of parental needs.

There are often very significant child safety and health considerations that are central to the assessment of parenting. For example, severely autistic children are at heightened risk for engaging in serious self-injury, and individuals with ADHD have higher than normal rates of automobile accidents, particularly when not taking medication. There are multiple other aspects of child functioning about which parents need to be able to communicate with one another, such as what medication has been prescribed or taken, whether a depressed or anxious child may be upset about an interpersonal or academic matter, and regarding what a child needs to do in school. These are only a few of the practically innumerable topics about which parents need to communicate. While it is very likely that a child will spend regular time at each parental residence, if one parent appears to be considerably more competent than the other in one or more of these areas of concern, a parenting plan will need to reflect that reality.[202]

For other than truly wealthy parents, the total number of hours spent in employment is very likely to rise after the marital separation because of the increased costs of having two households. As a result, especially for a parent who has been the primary caretaker, there will probably be a significant decrease in how much time is available to be directly spent with the children. It may be that the specifics of each

202. Pickar & Kaufman, *supra* note 200.

parent's employment hours are not known until after the separation takes place or the divorce is final. Parenting plans need to use the best available information about parental employment hours and consequent availabilities to be directly with the children. When there is uncertainty about future parental employment hours, there may need to be temporary time-sharing schedules put in effect with an understanding that modifications will take place.

In certain cases, parents may pursue a strategy of trying to win greater parenting time by insisting that their work schedule is highly flexible, and that they can work from home while simultaneously taking care of the child. Depending upon the child's needs and behavior patterns and the type of work in which the parent is engaged, such an assertion may at times be true. However, many types of work that potentially can be done at home also require considerable focus and effort, and they leave very little in the way of meaningful opportunities to engage in interactions with a child. Also, children described in this chapter have special conditions, and many are particularly unlikely to be good candidates for taking care of themselves easily at home with a parent present. The higher the severity of the child problem and the lower the level of functioning, the greater will be the demands on the parent for active engagement, monitoring, and supervision.

ADHD

Most parents of children with ADHD experience considerable difficulties in their marital or partner relationships even prior to a separation or divorce, and they have a divorce rate about twice that of parents without an ADHD child.[203] The parent who has the most extensive direct involvement with the child is most likely to experience the effects of the disorder-related child limitations and therefore the higher level of stress of the two parents. As noted earlier, mothers, being the more frequent primary caretaker than fathers, tend to perceive such children as having more clear dysfunctions.

Therefore, as parents are going through the divorce process, and after it, there is an unfortunately large likelihood of disputes about the extent of the child's problems and what, if anything, should be done about them. If a parent believes there is no ADHD or other mental health difficulties in a child who is manifesting significant problems, and just thinks about it as "boys will be boys," that parent is unlikely

203. *Id.*

to agree to often successful interventions such as medication, family therapy, and/or school accommodations. In such cases, if it is not already clear that the child has ADHD, a formal evaluation of its possible presence and effects on the child would be necessary, and the court may need to order it. If the condition is clearly present, and yet one of the two parents insists that the child does not suffer from it, that reality needs to be strongly considered both in terms of parental decision-making ability and time-sharing. Clearly, a parent who denies the presence of a condition that has been accurately identified should not have decision-making ability about the child's health care. That parent may also need to have a relatively small proportion of parenting time with the child, especially if there is a significant risk that they will not follow through with health care or school interventions.

Even if both parents agree that ADHD is present, consideration needs to be given to how each parent is able to assist the child in many areas that recur on a day-to-day basis. For example, individuals with ADHD frequently forget any of a wide variety of items. For a school-age child, that can include not remembering to bring home assignments or books from school, or forgetting items such as clothes, shoes, phones, and school material when going back and forth between households. Other central deficits highly relevant for school pertain to distraction, planning, and organization. It is very common for ADHD children to have trouble paying attention to class lessons and to miss homework and other assignments that are announced by teachers. ADHD students are frequently overly optimistic about how much time and effort it will take to do well on tests and assignments.

Although medication is often helpful with these types of problems, it tends to be partially successful and children still routinely struggle. Interventions and exhortations directed to the child to simply try harder are routinely ineffective. Similarly, hopes that children will learn entirely from their experiences and self-correct mistakes are not well-grounded in reality. Consequently, parents often need to carry out strategies to assist child limitations in executive functions such as attention, focus, planning, self-awareness, motivation, and organization.

For example, a number of schools now routinely place online both assignments and grades. Associated with their executive functioning deficits, ADHD children are particularly unlikely to make consistent use of those online resources that have the potential to provide great help for them. It is typically up to parents to provide external inputs to try to compensate for the child's internal executive functioning deficits, such as consistently checking online student academic information and using it to guide the child's academic efforts. There are numerous other parental functions potentially aimed at helping a child's focus, motivation, planning, and organization in terms of school work.[204]

The hyperactive ADHD subtype child also tends to manifest impulsive behaviors that may include aggression, defiance, potentially dangerous actions, and related behaviors. As noted earlier, a sizable proportion of ADHD children manifest conduct problems. A frequent main objective of family therapy in such cases focuses on parental management of child misbehavior. That type of management often requires consistent tracking and recording of relevant behaviors and administering relevant positive and negative consequences. It is a very big job for any parent to carry out, and it can have a central role in promoting positive child behavior.[205]

The parenting plan process needs to closely examine relevant parental strengths and deficits in terms of these various types of tasks aimed at managing inattention or impulsive behaviors. In some cases, the parents may be about equal to one another in terms of their respective abilities to carry out such tasks. In other cases, one parent may be considerably stronger than the other. A complicating factor is that ADHD in many cases is largely inherited, and therefore the likelihood is fairly strong that one parent, and possibly even both, may also suffer from the same condition. If that is the case, a parent who has ADHD may have significant limitations in the ability to consistently carry out such tasks to promote the child's executive functioning and self-control, even if that parent has considerable knowledge about ADHD and its treatment.

Parenting plans should also draw on each child's relevant habits. For example, while forgetting belongings is common for ADHD children, they can vary quite a bit in how much they experience it. For children with a track record of frequently forgetting items such as school material and clothing, consideration should be given to a schedule that includes relatively few transitions, thereby reducing the number of opportunities for a child to neglect to bring required materials with him or her. In addition, especially if child and family circumstances are such that a reduced number of exchanges may be counterproductive,

---

204. BARKLEY, *supra* note 199.
205. *Id.*

the parents and child might need to develop a routine, coordinated between households, to check to ensure that identified materials are present with the child before departing on a transition.

Conduct Disorders

The term conduct disorder or behavior disorder is often used as a general category that covers a number of specific diagnoses, although most children with a conduct disorder do not receive professional treatment for it. There is a specific Conduct Disorder diagnosis, and that reality contributes to the rather unclear terminology. Other related specific diagnoses include Oppositional Defiant Disorder and Intermittent Explosive Disorder. Conduct Disorder is characterized by serious misbehavior such as aggression toward individuals, property destruction, theft, truancy, and running away from home. Oppositional Defiant Disorder features negative behaviors toward others, though generally less serious ones than Conduct Disorder, such as defiance of authority figures, purposeful annoyance of others, consistently irritable mood, and instances of vindictiveness. Intermittent Explosive Disorder is characterized by repeated outbursts of physical or verbal aggression that tend to occur quickly, without premeditation, and are not carried out with another objective in mind, such as obtaining control or intimidating others. There is a considerable amount of comorbidity between these three diagnoses, as well as co-occurrence with others problem areas, such as ADHD, mood disorders, and substance misuse disorders. A considerable proportion of individuals diagnosed with Conduct Disorder have a parent who has had the same problem, and other parents of such children have higher than usual rates of severe alcohol use disorders, serious mood disorders, and schizophrenia.[206]

Therefore, in working to create a parenting plan, there are multiple serious challenges in terms of trying to manage child behavior. A number of those challenges involve considering how parental strengths and weaknesses are likely to have an impact on the child within the context of needs for educational and therapeutic interventions. There is a stark reality that each parent, within their respective households, is going to need to carry out child management efforts that take a lot of time, effort, and persistence. Also, parents are going to need to have to try to coordinate so that at least the big picture of parenting is fairly

206. American Psychiatric Association, *supra* note 197, at 462.

similar in both homes. A number of the parenting plan considerations have similarity to what was described previously regarding children with ADHD. However, the severity and potentially disruptive quality of behaviors in conduct disordered children is generally greater than ADHD children who do not have conduct disorders.

More specifically, in order to have a reasonable chance at being successful, parents of conduct disordered children need to consistently carry out parenting behaviors characteristic of authoritative parenting, including vigorous support aimed at reinforcing and encouraging positive actions, monitoring multiple aspects of child behavior, and firmly setting limits including carrying out negative consequences. The tasks required for parents to do so include tracking and often recording specified positive and negative child behaviors, attempting to minimize potentially negative behaviors that occur outside the home, working to replace such negative activities with prosocial or at least neutral ones, and coordinating with relevant services and agencies. There is likely to be a need for regular contact with the school, coordination with health care, and there may be a need for interactions with the juvenile justice system.

It is a very large and often exhausting job for any parent, and it is even more daunting for a parent who has his or her own significant individual problems. The difficulty level expands considerably when considering there needs to be communication between two different households that have parents with enough bad blood between them that they decided to split up.

In a number of these cases, one parent is superior to the other in terms of their abilities to carry out these multiple difficult requirements. If that is the case, the child should be with that parent a significant majority of the time. Also, the greater the severity of child problems, the more important it is for decisions to be made in a timely manner. Therefore, if parents are not able to cooperate well, serious consideration needs to be given to one parent having sole decision-making ability regarding relevant areas of concern.

Depressive and Anxiety Disorders

There are a number of specific anxiety and depressive disorders covering a broad range of severity and duration.[207] As noted previously, self-destructive actions such as suicidal behavior and nonsuicidal

207. AMERICAN PSYCHIATRIC ASSOCIATION, *supra* note 197.

self-injury are frequently associated with depression. A number of types of psychotherapy have shown moderate effectiveness. Medication is also prescribed at times, though the FDA issued a serious "black box" warning on antidepressant use with children and adolescents, and it has been in effect about a decade.[208]

Mental health problems such as depression and anxiety are some of the negative effects that can be caused the by children's exposure to marital conflict, as described earlier in this book. In addition, the separation and divorce of parents can be a stressor that increases the risk for depression and anxiety.

In some cases, when the children have not been exposed to much marital conflict, a child is more likely to become psychologically distressed as a result of the loss of the intact family. In other instances, when children have experienced considerable emotional distress as a result of the conflict in the home, the separation or divorce can be experienced as somewhat of a relief as there is decreased exposure to the fighting, though there may be a continuing sense of loss that the family is no longer all residing together.

The more serious the depression or anxiety experienced by the child, the more important it is for each parent to be attentive, attuned, and positively involved with the child in a way that includes both considerable support and a reasonable comfort level functioning as an authority figure. Parents characteristically are meaningfully involved in therapeutic efforts. Treatment personnel often provide educational information to parents about therapeutic efforts. In many cases, parents play an important role in the treatment process, including separate meetings with the therapist or joint sessions with the child present, and overseeing therapeutic homework assignments, while also allowing reasonable child or adolescent autonomy, given the clinical circumstances.

When there is reason for concern that a child or teenager may be thinking about suicide or self-injury, there is a need for a high level of parental monitoring and supervision. Even when there is not a risk of dangerousness, at a basic level, parents typically set up treatment appointments, try to ensure that any prescribed medication is taken

208. U.S. Food & Drug Administration, *Antidepressant Use in Children, Adolescents, and Adults*, https://www.nimh.nih.gov/health/topics/child-and-adolescent-mental-health/antidepressant-medications-for-children-and-adolescents-information-for-parents-and-caregivers.shtml.

appropriately, and may have significant roles at home supporting therapeutic efforts. Depression and anxiety are more likely to be evident in adolescents than in younger children. Effective treatment for depression often includes facilitating the patient to engage in activities that give him or her a sense of accomplishment or enjoyment. Successful therapy also frequently involves work on interpersonal relationships and modification of cognitions to include more realistically positive thoughts. Parents can play a role in these therapeutic efforts in a number of ways.

For example, depression often includes a low level of energy and pessimism, and therefore depressed children or adolescents may feel that it is noxious to go to school or to do homework. Other than severe cases where a child may need to be out of a regular school setting for a while, attending school and making efforts to do homework can lead to an understandable sense of accomplishment and therefore contribute toward improvements in depression. A parent may need to coordinate between treatment personnel, school, and the child or adolescent to encourage ongoing school participation.

A good balance of interpersonal skills is needed by parents to promote a beneficial parent–adolescent relationship, as well as to try to facilitate healthy teen involvement with peers. Although a parent is unlikely to be engaged in direct exploration of an adolescent's cognitive processes, that adult can potentially promote the youth to engage in realistically positive thoughts about oneself in the future by making reinforcing comments about her or his constructive or helpful actions. Similarly, a parent can point out good reasons for positive expectations regarding the future. Any parent needs to maintain appropriate limit setting, but she or he also needs to try to make many more positive comments than critical ones. For a child or adolescent who primarily suffers from anxiety, a parent may need to act as a bridge between therapeutic personnel and the patient by encouraging and prompting the use of healthy coping techniques.

The statements made in the preceding sections regarding the need for parents to communicate reasonably well with one another hold very true for depressed and anxious children, also. As also noted previously, if one parent seems superior to the other in terms of their ability, availability, and motivation to regularly carry out these important parental behaviors, that information needs to be strongly considered in devising parenting plans. Appropriate treatment plans need to be followed, and if a parent is motivated not to do so, that parent should not have decision-making ability regarding health care. At the same time, it is crucial to keep in mind that loss of contact with a parent in childhood is a risk factor for depression, so even if a parent seems to have significant limitations in their individual parenting behavior and/or communication with the other parent, strong efforts should be made to construct a parenting plan that encourages regular positive contact with both parents.

Specific Learning Disorders

When focused on specific learning disabilities in reading, writing, or mathematics, many of the parenting plan considerations pertain to education. At the same time, as noted previously, a significant proportion of children with such learning disorders also have other mental health problems, such as ADHD, ASD, conduct problems, or mood disorders. When one or more of these other comorbid conditions are also present, the parenting plan efforts need to consider those realities.

Characteristically, a child with a specific learning disorder will have an individual education plan (IEP) or 504 plan. Individual education plans are based on state statutes or regulations. In contrast, section 504 of the Rehabilitation Act of 1973 is a federal law that protects the rights of individuals with disabilities who are in programs that receive funding from the U.S. Department of Education.[209] If there is reason to believe that a child may have such a disability but has not been evaluated for it, the parents need to be prompted and perhaps educated to pursue such an assessment with the school district. There are a variety of educational interventions for such disabilities. However, a common feature of many special educational efforts involves work at home with parents that builds in additional practice and repetition. For example, individuals with reading disabilities frequently are assigned additional specified reading at home, usually at least monitored by a parent.[210]

Parenting plans need to consider the availability, motivation, and ability of each parent to do reasonably well in monitoring such

---

209. U.S. Department of Education, *Protecting Students with Disabilities*, https://ed.gov/about/offices/list/ocr/504faq.html.

210. David J. Chard et al., *A Synthesis of Research on Effective Interventions for Building Reading Fluency with Elementary Students with Learning Disabilities*, 35 J. Learning Disabilities 386 (2002).

specialized work at home, as well as to have productive communication with the school about such matters. As with other areas of concern, the relative abilities of each parent to communicate well with the other parent about this area of child functioning and progress is important both for time-sharing and decision-making responsibilities.

Autism Spectrum Disorders (ASD)

For many ASD children and adolescents, except those on the relatively mild end of the spectrum, the level of impairment is so high that a great deal of close monitoring and supervision is needed. For some, 24-hour-a-day supervision is required. ASD children can be physically aggressive, in some instances toward themselves, and have heightened risks for potentially dangerous accidents. Therefore, basic physical safety is a consistent concern, and strong consideration needs to be given to which parent may best be able to provide it.

Many ASD children benefit from an intensive form of behavior modification focused on positive reinforcement for targeted behaviors. Because these therapeutic efforts best start when the child is very young and require time that can equal that of a full-time job, they typically take place at home and add to the profoundly extensive parental responsibilities. The more severe the child deficit, the greater is the parental burden. An additional crucial consideration for ASD children is that their frequent needs to engage in a very restricted range of repetitive activities and for unchanging physical surroundings lead many exchanges between parents and residences to be exceptionally difficult. The severity of ASD problem behaviors and the frequently extensive, painful sensitivity to environmental changes place requirements on both parents to be fully educated and involved in therapeutic efforts, as well as to be able to communicate with one another well about such matters. Very clearly, all these factors need to be front and center in any considerations about parenting plans.[211]

Likely due in large part to the extensive demands on parental time and energy, parents of ASD children exhibit unusually high rates of problems. Mothers are more likely to be the main caregivers for ASD children, and they display worse psychological and physical health than do other mothers with children of the same ages who do not have

211. Pickar & Kaufman, *supra* note 200.

ASD. Parents of ASD children have rates of divorce that are close to twice that of other parents.[212]

Children who have relatively mild ASD often function well enough to attend regular public schools. However, schools and school districts can vary a great deal in terms of being able to carry out such educational efforts, and higher functioning ASD children are not all the same in terms of their educational needs. As a result, there needs to be close examination of educational matters during the parenting plan process. When a child has already been involved in school, there needs to be close attention paid to educational needs and progress, including gathering relevant information from school records such as 504 or individual education plans, and collecting teacher and parent perspectives about what has gone well and not so well. If there are questions about what school an ASD child will attend, there needs to be a careful assessment of the respective abilities of each of the schools to provide a good quality education. Some schools or school districts, depending upon the specific educational functioning of the child, may be able to provide a good level of education within the regular school setting, whereas others may need to place a child in a different school within the district, or make arrangements for a child to attend a specialized school outside of the geographical area. Because ASD children frequently have related therapeutic needs, there needs to be an examination of available support services within each of the educational options that are being considered.[213]

It is important for those involved in the parenting plan process to be cognizant that parents of higher functioning ASD children can frequently present as wary, anxious, or pushy. To some extent, these characteristics may represent coping strategies by parents who have children with chronic, significant limitations and who have experienced a periodic lack of responsiveness from professionals, such as in education or health care settings. While some of the parents may experience psychological difficulties, such problems can also be due

212. Hiie Allik et al., *Health-Related Quality of Life in Parents of School-Age Children with Asperger Syndrome or High-Functioning Autism*, 4 Health & Quality of Life Outcomes 1 (2006); Sigan L. Hartley et al., *The Relative Risk and Timing of Divorce in Families of Children with an Autism Spectrum Disorder*, 24 J. Fam. Psychol. 449 (2010).

213. Sol R. Rappaport et al., *Special Considerations in Child Custody Evaluations for Children with High-Functioning Autism Spectrum Disorder*, 54 Fam. Ct. Rev. 81 (2016).

at least in part to the ongoing stresses associated with caring for their children. Having such knowledge about the frequent prior experiences of parents can help those involved in parenting plans work productively with parents and not dismiss them as unreasonable or hostile.[214]

Court-Involved Therapy

Children who have mental health disorders generally have a good likelihood of benefitting from therapy. A competent therapist who is experienced both with the relevant clinical conditions and the realities of working within the context of a parenting plan dispute will pursue equally positive alliances with both parents. Also, that individual will keep adequate treatment records for each date of service.

However, there is a relatively small proportion of therapists who are both clinically competent and adequately experienced in working within the world of often complicated family law circumstances. In many cases, when a therapist is first contacted to set up an appointment for a child, that practitioner is not given any information about the current or potential court involvement. Because of parental employment circumstances, it is not unusual for just one parent to bring a child to a therapist for an initial appointment. That parent may not offer any substantive information about the other parent. At times, a parent may only note that there has been a separation or divorce or state that the other parent is frequently busy with work, not very engaged with the child, or is unavailable to participate in the therapy. In certain cases, it is only because of subsequent developments that the therapist is brought into the legal process. In other cases, a parent may initiate the therapy with a primary motive to make use of it in order to gain a possible advantage in court by having a therapist be his or her ally against the other parent. In that regard, some therapists may be aware from the beginning of services that it is likely to include court involvement.

In these complicated cases, a therapist needs to be fully aware of the crucial distinction between being in a therapeutic role and a forensic one. In the traditional therapeutic role, there is an assumption that the client, or another important individual such as a parent, is being fully truthful, and the therapist is working to help improve the client's health and life functioning. In contrast, the forensic role requires a stance of active questioning about relevant facts and circumstances, routine consideration of hypotheses and perspectives beyond those

214. *Id.*

supplied by the client and family, and considerable understanding of how to integrate an appropriate clinical focus on the client with competently responding to the realities of what the court may require. For decades, it has been recognized that the therapeutic and forensic roles are in many ways incompatible with one another, and that a therapist should not offer opinions on psycho-legal questions such as parenting plans or child custody.[215]

In a number of these cases, the parent who initiates treatment for the child states that there is a significant problem in the relationship between the child and the other parent. Frequently, there is repeated and vigorous criticism of the other parent to the therapist. If the therapist fails to insist on establishing equally positive alliances with each parent and maintaining an unbiased role, that individual risks becoming a participant in a process that jeopardizes the well-being of the child. Even in cases where the parent who initiates therapy asserts that the other parent has been abusive or neglectful, the therapist can and should obtain information and opinions from the other parent anyway. The therapist can meet with the other parent individually to collect such information, without the child being present. Of course, if there is sound reason to believe that abusive, neglectful, or otherwise inappropriate parental behavior has been carried out by any parent, that information needs to be taken into consideration in the treatment structure and planning.

Any therapist who does not carry out a competent assessment and treatment process by including appropriate contact and alliances with each parent risks harming the child and worsening the stresses of the legal case by becoming aligned with one parent versus the other. At times, such a therapist often writes a letter that maintains that the child should mainly reside with the parent with whom the therapist is aligned. Others may actually make such a statement in court testimony. There have been a number of these types of cases that have resulted in substantiated professional board complaints against the therapist.

---

215. Lyn R. Greenberg et al., *Is the Child's Therapist Part of the Problem? What Judges, Attorneys and Mental Health Professionals Need to Know about Court-Related Treatment for Children*, 37 FAM. L.Q. 39 (2003); Stuart A. Greenberg & Daniel W. Shuman, *Irreconcilable Conflict between Therapeutic and Forensic Roles*, 28 PROF. PSYCHOL.: RESEARCH & PRACTICE 50 (1997); Aaron Robb, *Therapeutic v. Forensic Roles: Avoiding Nonsexual Boundary Violations with Clients*, NASW SPECIALTY PRACTICE SECTIONS, SOCIAL WORK & THE COURTS, SECTION CONNECTION 4 (Fall 2016), http://www.texascounseling.org/articles/SWC_Fall.pdf.

When therapy is carried out with a strong level of clinical competence and a good level of expertise about working within the context of a family law case, it can be very helpful for a child and family. Unfortunately, a number of legal professionals are not aware that the therapy process can be manipulated in the manner described here, consequently harming a child who was already at increased risk for life adjustment problems due to the parental divorce. Also, unfortunately, a large proportion of mental health providers are simply unaware of the additional expertise required, both clinically and practically, in terms of working with cases within the family law system. Both legal and mental health professionals can substantially improve their understanding of this challenging content area by familiarizing themselves with relevant therapy guidelines.[216]

In certain cases, professionals involved in creating a parenting plan perceive that it is important to include a provision for the child and/or family to have therapy. There is often an understandable general hope that the therapy referral will be successful and the participants will experience significant improvements in life. However, in many cases, a general referral to a local therapist who is covered by insurance will miss the mark. There needs to be referral to a competent clinician with appropriate training and experience, as well as substantial motivation and ability to be involved with the court system while concurrently having the child's health and development as the primary goal.

Important points in this chapter about mental health difficulties and special needs in parenting plans include the following:

- General principles that need to be kept in mind; for example,
  - The need for individualized assessments for each child with a possible mental health difficulty or other special needs concern.
  - These assessments need to be carried out by appropriately trained and experienced professionals.
  - It is crucial to obtain relevant background information directly from health care personnel and those in education.
  - Although health care information can be valuable when it contains clinically relevant data about a child's status and needs, letters or records that contain opinions about allocations of

216. Association of Family and Conciliation Courts, *Guidelines for Court-Involved Therapy* (2010).

parental responsibility from providers who have not conducted appropriate evaluations are counterproductive.

  - It is essential to obtain the perspective of each parent, and where possible, the child.
  - Child needs should be compared to each parent's overall ability, availability, and motivation to do what is necessary to meet those needs. A parent who denies the presence of an accurately identified condition should not have decision-making ability about health care (and possibly education, depending upon the circumstances) and may need to have a relatively small proportion of parenting time.
  - It is critical to consider parental abilities to coordinate with external service providers such as health care and schools.
  - Strong consideration must be given to parental abilities to communicate well with one another about the child's functioning, especially regarding their problem areas.
  - The following child and family characteristics will increase the likelihood of needing a parenting plan that is very different from ones commonly seen in cases without significant child dysfunction:
    - › high severity of child problems,
    - › parent–child relationship difficulties,
    - › mental health or other functional parental impairments,
    - › significant limitations in the parents' abilities to cooperate with one another,
    - › high levels of interparental conflict,
    - › parental denial of an accurately identified child dysfunction, and
    - › concerns about dangerousness and safety.

- Characteristics of ADHD children necessitate consideration of the following:
  - The possibility that there may need to be fewer than usual transitions so as to avoid overwhelming limited organizational abilities and decrease the odds of chronically lost items.
  - The need for parents to provide multiple means of assistance with child executive functions.

  - The ability of the parents to be consistently vigilant in reinforcing positive behaviors and setting limits on negative ones, especially with impulsive/hyperactive ADHD children.
- Parents of conduct disordered children need to actively coordinate with multiple agencies and engage in an integration of reinforcement for positive behaviors and active limit setting.
- Regarding children with depression or anxiety:
  - Close parental monitoring is critical if symptoms include thoughts of self-harm.
  - Parents can encourage and facilitate child engagement in activities that lead to a sense of accomplishment and/or enjoyment.
  - Parents can facilitate and encourage healthy coping and problem-solving techniques.
- Parents of children with learning disabilities need to be able to interact effectively with schools and participate actively in special educational homework assignments.
- Regarding children with ASD:
  - Basic safety is a primary concern given potential physical aggression and accident proneness.
  - Parents frequently need to carry out extensive behavior modification efforts for multiple hours each week.
  - Close examination of educational options is frequently a necessity for higher functioning ASD children.
  - Working with parents of ASD children about parenting plans can be aided by professionals having a good understanding of parental burdens and past experiences.
- Mental health treatment and other health care needs to be carried out by providers who are
  - clinically competent,
  - willing and able to maintain treatment alliances with both parents,
  - cognizant of the differences between therapeutic and forensic roles, and
  - knowledgeable about working with court-related cases.

CHAPTER 9
PARENTAL MENTAL HEALTH AND RELATED PROBLEMS

Parental psychological dysfunction that has an impact on parenting behavior can often have a negative influence on child well-being.[217] However, it is also the case that a large proportion of parents who have mental health difficulties nonetheless function well in their relationships with their children.

Any parental mental health problems that have negative effects on children need to be considered in devising parenting plans. In this chapter, I first summarize information about adult mental health problems that occur with the greatest frequency and are most likely to be seen in separation and divorce cases. Second, I describe a number of common assessment procedures and related considerations. Third, I focus on how professionals involved in parenting plans can apply information about parental mental health problems to promote child well-being.

Common Adult Mental Health Problems

There are close to 44 million adults in the United States who have a mental or behavioral disorder, not including substance misuse and developmental disorders. The 44 million represents 18 percent of adults (12-month prevalence data for U.S. adults are used in this

217. Amato, *supra* note 26.

chapter). Mental health disorders, defined in this manner, are more common among women (22 percent) than men (14 percent).[218]

The most frequent types of mental health problems are anxiety disorders. This category includes panic disorders, agoraphobia, generalized anxiety disorder, social phobia, and specific phobias. The most frequent type is specific phobia, which accounts for over 50 percent of the anxiety disorders category. Specific phobias tend to result in a mild to moderate level of functional impairment and, therefore, may have a low likelihood of significantly influencing parenting behavior. Cases of severe anxiety comprise about 4 percent of the adult population,[219] and such disorders may be more likely than specific phobias to have an impact on parent–child relationships.

Approximately 10 percent of the population has a mood disorder, and just under half of those cases are identified as severe. By far, the most common mood disorder is major depression, found in about 7 percent of the population.[220] There are a number of other types of mood disorders, such as bipolar disorder and dysthymia. A great deal of research shows that parental depression can have a substantially negative impact on children, as summarized later in the chapter.

Substance use disorders are also among the most frequently found, occurring in about 9 percent of the population. Substance dependence is the more severe and debilitating type of substance use disorder, whereas substance abuse is the less severe classification. The diagnoses of alcohol abuse or dependence account for the great majority of substance use disorders, at over 8 percent.

Although most people do not think of cigarette smoking the same way they view alcohol or other drug use, nicotine dependence is actually a disorder. Parental cigarette smoking can have a negative impact on children in a number of ways.

---

218. Nat'l Inst. of Mental Health, *Any Mental Illness (AMI) among U.S. Adults*, https://www.nimh.nih.gov/health/statistics/prevalence/any-mental-illness-ami-among-us-adults.shtml.

219. Bridget F. Grant et al., *Prevalence and Co-Occurrence of Substance Use Disorders and Independent Mood and Anxiety Disorders*, 61 ARCHIVES GEN. PSYCHIATRY 807 (2004); Nat'l Inst. of Mental Health, *Any Anxiety Disorder among Adults*, https://www.nimh.nih.gov/health/statistics/prevalence/any-anxiety-disorder-among-adults.shtml.

220. Grant et al., *supra* note 219; Nat'l Inst. of Mental Health, *Any Mood Disorder among Adults*, https://www.nimh.nih.gov/health/statistics/prevalence/any-mood-disorder-among-adults.shtml.

There is considerable co-occurrence of different disorders, especially mood and substance use disorders. For example, just under 30 percent of individuals who have a substance dependence disorder also suffer from a mood disorder. As a result, a substance dependent person is more than four times as likely to have a mood disorder than an individual who does not suffer from substance dependence.[221]

Of course, the relevance of these data pertains to the impact of the disorders on children and considerations about parenting plans. In that regard, it is important to know that about 25 percent of children in the United States are exposed to alcohol misuse in the family.[222]

What about parental psychopathology leads to child adjustment problems? Research studies have examined different possibilities through relatively complex statistical analyses, and a number of pathways have been identified, though these investigations are ongoing. For example, depressive symptoms in both parents were found to contribute to insecurity in close relationships. Depressive symptoms also contributed to marital conflict, and for wives only, the marital conflict appeared to worsen depression. In turn, interparental conflict was associated with child perceptions that the parents were withdrawn or rejecting, and also with increased child conduct problems.[223] Parental withdrawal that included low levels of affection and nurturance toward children led to an increased risk that they would manifest personality disorders in adulthood. Similarly, overly harsh parenting was associated with offspring manifesting personality disorders as adults.[224]

Alcohol abuse can also worsen the lives of children of divorce even when other problems such as parental depression are not present. Paternal alcohol misuse was found to be linked to destructive marital conflict one year later, and that conflict was associated with decreased affection by the parents, as well as excessive efforts at exerting control

---

221. Grant et al., *supra* note 219.

222. Bridget F. Grant, *Estimates of US Children Exposed to Alcohol Abuse and Dependence in the Family*, 90 AM. J. PUB. HEALTH 112 (2000).

223. Katherine H. Shelton & Gordon T. Harold, *Interparental Conflict, Negative Parenting, and Children's Adjustment: Bridging Links between Parents Depression and Children's Psychological Distress*. 22 J. FAM. PSYCHOL. 712 (2008).

224. Jeffrey G. Johnson et al., *Parenting Behaviors Associated with Risk for Offspring Personality Disorders during Adulthood,* 63 ARCHIVES GEN. PSYCHIATRY 579 (2006).

over the children. Both these types of problematic parenting behaviors were tied to a number of later child adjustment problems.[225]

There frequently is confusion about what constitutes normal versus excessive alcohol use. The Centers for Disease Control and Prevention indicate that the upper level of moderate drinking is two normal-sized drinks for a male and one for a female.[226]

Parental cigarette smoking often creates a risk for children through exposure to environmental tobacco smoke. That exposure can cause or contribute to a number of childhood illnesses, including asthma and other serious illnesses, particularly if a child already has a medical vulnerability. Also, tobacco smoke creates residual carcinogenic contamination that can remain in homes and vehicles long after cigarettes have been extinguished. That carcinogenic residue can have a negative impact on children. The effects of smoking on children are not all physiological. Parental smoking creates an increased risk for cigarette use among teenagers.[227] In recent years, there has been increased use of electronic cigarettes, or e-cigarettes, and smoking them is at times referred to as "vaping." At this time, the effects of secondhand and thirdhand e-cigarette use are unknown, but there have been a number of reports of related risks to children, including those associated with the higher concentration of nicotine.[228]

Families are complex systems, and there are often multiple causes and effects going on simultaneously. Parental depression can certainly negatively influence child behavior, and yet child behavior problems have also been found to exacerbate parental depression. Therefore, it is crucial to consider these complex family causal pathways.[229]

---

225. Peggy S. Keller et al., *Longitudinal Relations between Parental Drinking Problems, Family Functioning, and Child Adjustment*, 20 Dev. & Psychopathology 195 (2008).

226. Centers for Disease Control and Prevention, *Fact Sheets—Alcohol Use and Your Health* (July 25, 2016), https://www.cdc.gov/alcohol/fact-sheets/alcohol-use.htm.

227. Joseph R. DiFranza & Robert A. Lew, *Morbidity and Mortality in Children Associated with the Use of Tobacco Products by Other People*, 97 Pediatrics 560 (1996); William J. Doherty & William Allen, *Family Functioning and Parental Smoking as Predictors of Adolescent Cigarette Use: A Six-Year Prospective Study,* 8 J. Fam. Psychol. 347 (1994); Janet T. Thomas et al., *Thirdhand Tobacco Smoke: A Tobacco-Specific Lung Carcinogen on Surfaces in Smokers' Homes*, 16(1) Nicotine & Tobacco Res. 26 (2014).

228. Elizabeth L. Durmowicz, *The Impact of Electronic Cigarettes on the Paediatric Population*, 23 Tobacco Control ii41 (2014).

229. Daniel M. Bagner et al., *Disentangling the Temporal Relationship between Parental Depressive Symptoms and Early Childhood Behavior Problems: A Transactional Framework*, 42 J. Clinical Child & Adolescent Psychol. 78 (2013).

Good parenting requires motivation, frustration tolerance, and relevant skills, some or all of which might be in limited supply when parents suffer from a mental disorder. For example, for a number of parents, decreased positive expectations and lowered energy associated with depression and heightened impulsivity that results from substance misuse might lead parents to be less likely to engage in adequate monitoring, reinforcement, informal education, and limit setting.

Assessment

The assessment of mental health problems needs to be carried out by appropriately trained and experienced mental health personnel. Procedures include interviews, observations, review of relevant records, and, depending upon the circumstances, psychological testing. Because the main objective of parenting plans is to promote child well-being, it is often essential to obtain children's perspective through skilled interviewing. The interviewing should be carried out by professionals with specific expertise, as it can be easy to stumble into multiple errors when questions are asked the wrong way or have inappropriate content. Such errors can make the impressions gained from the interview profoundly misleading.

In disputed parenting plan cases, parents are often highly motivated to present themselves in the best possible light and may not be forthcoming about mental health problems. When individuals have significant acute symptoms, it is relatively hard to hide the difficulties that are present. However, mental health difficulties that occur at a moderate degree of severity can have a significant impact on parenting, yet can be challenging to identify when individuals are defensive about their psychological functioning. In general, two main types of defensiveness have been identified, though there can be considerable overlap between them. One type of defensiveness involves a parent who clearly recognizes his or her own problems, though that individual makes an active effort to keep that information private and instead tries to present in the healthiest possible light. The other individuals have very limited insight into their own psychological health, which is another type of defensiveness.

In a number of especially difficult parenting plan cases, questions are raised about a parent possibly suffering from a personality disorder. These questions are particularly likely with parents who are suspected of mistreating children or those who may be viewed as troublesome and excessively litigious in the legal system. Individuals who have personality disorders frequently have very limited insight about themselves and regarding how their actions have an impact on their interpersonal lives, including with their children and families. Much of the time, individuals with personality disorders do not manifest acute and clearly observable symptoms, and as noted earlier, they may be highly motivated to display only healthy behaviors. All these factors combine to make it particularly difficult to ascertain whether or not a personality disorder is present. While certain psychometric tests can have utility, when combined with other assessment methods, in trying to assess the possible presence of a personality disorder, there can be uncertainties up through the end of the family law involvement.

When there are allegations of parental substance misuse, a parent may also be very motivated to cover up the problem. A number of people who engage in substance abuse may view his or her own use as essentially normal, and believe that the other parent is either overly sensitive about it or tries to magnify it in order to obtain an advantage in the legal dispute.

In certain cases in which substance misuse is alleged, it may make sense to require physiological testing. Urine testing[230] is most commonly carried out for many substances, in large part because concentrations of drugs and related substances called metabolites tend to be relatively high in the urine.

There are five main categories of drugs that are included in most urine tests, associated with the fact that guidelines for workplace testing by the U.S. Department of Health and Human Services focus on those substances. They are amphetamine, cocaine, opiates, cannabinoids, and phencyclidine. However, other drug testing panels that are more inclusive can characteristically be requested of a laboratory.

Drug screening through urine initially is carried out through immunoassays, which characteristically can be accomplished quickly. However, their disadvantage is the potential for false–positive results. Therefore, positive results from an immunoassay need to be confirmed by a laboratory-based test such as gas chromatography–mass spectrometry. Although it is highly accurate, it is time-consuming and costly, and therefore tends to be used only after a positive immunoassay.

Using these procedures, there are common detection times in which a substance can be identified. Screening for alcohol tends not to

230. Karen E. Moeller et al., *Urine Drug Screening: Practical Guide for Clinicians*, 83 Mayo Clinic Proceedings 66 (2008).

take place using these tests because there is a very narrow window of approximately 7 to 12 hours after ingestion when it can be identified. A very short window of detection also occurs for blood alcohol testing.

There can be urine detection up through about 48 hours for amphetamine and more common opioids such as heroin. Cocaine metabolites can be identified up through about two to four days. Certain potentially misused prescription medications can be detected over a significantly longer time. For example, phenobarbital, which is used as an anti-seizure medication and also at times for insomnia, may be detected up through about three weeks. Relatively longer acting antianxiety medication such as diazepam (Valium) can be detected up through about 30 days.

Marijuana also tends to have longer urine detection times. A single use through use a few times per week may be detected up through approximately three to seven days. Long-term heavy marijuana use may be detected through about 30 to 45 days.[231]

Recently, associated with the limited utility of traditional urine and blood tests for alcohol detection, different types of assessments have been developed and used, called alcohol biomarkers. The ethyl glucuronide (EtG) biomarker urine test has been used in legal and clinical settings. The testing may read as positive after even a small amount of alcohol has been consumed, and can be detected through one to two days. However, there can be false positives due to exposure to common products that contain alcohol, such as hand sanitizers.[232]

Testing can also occur through hair analysis, which became more commonly used associated with a belief that it was more resistant to efforts at alteration than was urine testing. However, it also has limitations. For example, after ingestion of a substance, there needs to be approximately 7 to 10 days for hair to grow sufficiently so that it can be properly cut and analyzed. There are multiple websites that advertise alleged ways to overcome hair analysis, such as "The Hair Drug Test Can Be Beat! Here's How."[233] In addition, just as there may be false positives for any of a variety of reasons in urine testing, it can also occur in hair testing. For example, false positive hair testing results have been found for cannabis as a result only of personal contact with

---

231. *Id.*

232. Substance Abuse and Mental Health Services Administration Advisory, *The Role of Biomarkers in the Treatment of Alcohol Use Disorders*, 2012 Revision, http://store.samhsa.gov/shin/content//SMA12-4686/SMA12-4686.pdf.

233. hairfollicledrugtest.info.

someone who had in fact used cannabis.[234] However, more specific lab testing reportedly can distinguish between actual cannabis intake and a positive result that is a consequence of other types of contact with that substance.[235]

Parenting Plan Applications

Concerns about parental mental health usually are initiated by the complaints of one parent about the other. As described at the beginning of this chapter, many parents experience mental health difficulties and yet have positive relationships with their children—therefore, it is crucial to clarify not only whether a mental health problem exists, but also whether and in what ways such potential parental difficulties have an impact on child well-being.

Clearly, a well-trained and experienced mental health professional is required to investigate such matters. The assessment may be a relatively general one to shed light on what is in the child's best interest, or it may be more specifically focused on whether one or both parents have a mental health dysfunction that has a deleterious impact on parenting behavior. Within this family law context, a significant proportion of parents are motivated to present themselves very positively, and a number may receive coaching from their attorneys or others about how to do so. Therefore, even when such an assessment is competently carried out, there may be somewhat less clarity than is optimal about the specifics of parental mental health functioning and its impact on parenting behaviors.

An assessment of mental health needs to focus on parental functioning instead of whether or not a parent has a relevant diagnosis. A diagnosis itself is of arguable relevance in the parenting plan context, and when not accompanied by sufficient detail about relevant parental functioning, the specifics of the diagnosis can be merely a distracting sideshow, or in terms of what is known about judgment and decision making, a heuristic.[236]

234. Bjoern Moosmann et al., *Finding Cannabinoids in Hair Does Not Prove Cannabis Consumption*, Sci. Rep. (Oct. 7, 2015), http://www.readcube.com/articles/10.1038/srep14906.

235. James A. Bourland, *Hair External Contamination Literature Review*, https://www.samhsa.gov/sites/default/files/meeting/documents/september_2013_bourland_contaimination.pdf.

236. Thinking, *supra* note 10.

Any parental mental health problem that is more than just a temporary divorce-related stress reaction needs to be examined in terms of how relevant behaviors impact parent–child relationships. For example, common characteristics of clinical depression include low energy level, diminished motivation, and negative expectations about one's actions having a beneficial effect. Consequently, a clinically depressed parent might manifest a reduced level of involvement with the children that manifests itself in numerous ways. Such a parent might carry out a general parenting style that includes inadequate levels of child management such as supportiveness, monitoring, and limit setting. A clinically depressed parent also may not make adequate efforts to provide more specific behaviors such as appropriate praise and verbal reinforcement. Somewhat similarly, he or she might not provide much informal education and may have limited communication with the child. In contrast, a clinically depressed parent might function adequately or strongly in all these parenting areas—a separate assessment is required in each case.

A different seriously depressed parent may also have problems with impulse control, including possible substance misuse, all of which can have a significant negative impact on a child. Under such circumstances there are greater risks for exposure to potentially dangerous features such as aggression between parents, abusiveness, or neglect.

When a question has been raised about possible substance misuse in a parenting plan case, individualized assessment of the facts and circumstances is needed. Such an assessment needs to be carried out by a professional with specific substance abuse training and experience. While a number of individuals might have obtained a specific substance abuse certification, others may have acquired sufficient training and experience throughout their careers in a number of different mental health disciplines.

When issues are raised about possible substance misuse, there are often disputes about the amount of use and whether or not it has any impact on the children. There is no general template that fits all possible configurations of substance abuse allegations in families with parenting plan disputes.

In a hypothetical case where questions have been raised about a father's alcohol use, a number of related individual mental health and family matters are frequently relevant and need to be carefully assessed and considered by a well-trained and experienced professional. Characteristically, such an evaluation would involve extensive interviewing of the father; interviewing of the mother; collection of data from other relevant, preferably objective sources; and perhaps the father's completion of one or more alcohol-related self-report measures. Depending upon the circumstances, aspects of child interviews may also need to relate to the father's possible alcohol abuse, though a great deal of care is needed to ensure that the questioning process and the contents of the questions have a proper foundation and are appropriate. Physiological testing for alcohol use might also be considered.

Such an assessment is not completed instantaneously, and the legal system frequently looks for interim parenting plan measures that can be put in effect before evaluation answers are available. For example, parents and attorneys may consider an interim agreement for there to be no alcohol or other intoxicants used by either parent when with the child. Such a stipulation should also include no alcohol use for about 24 hours prior to being with the child—a hangover is actually the latter part of the intoxication process and can negatively affect parenting. Depending upon the circumstances, such as evidence that a parent likely would or would not adhere to a no alcohol use provision, there might be consideration given to parenting time limitations such as no overnights or having a supervisor or monitor present. The individuals involved in creating a parent plan also need to think not only about parental intoxication, but also about the possible modeling of alcohol misuse by a parent in front of the children.

After a competent assessment of the father's alcohol use has been completed, depending upon the conclusions, there should be relevant input into the parenting plan. If the conclusion is that substance abuse has been occurring, there needs to be deliberation about a possible requirement for treatment that has a reasonable likelihood of success.

In a separate hypothetical case, the mother suffers from agoraphobia, an anxiety disorder frequently associated with panic. Agoraphobia is characterized by fear of going out into public places, such as stores, malls, or public transportation, accompanied by an expectation that there is a high risk of an embarrassing episode such as a panic attack.

The mother has positive relationships with the children and generally functions very well at home. She is emotionally supportive, active in the children's education, and sets limits well. The father has no mental health difficulties and has positive relationships with the children. The parents communicate with one another cooperatively.

However, in recent years, as a result of her agoraphobia, the mother has gone out of the house only a few times, always accompanied by someone who stayed physically very close to her. Prior to the separation, her husband had primarily been in that role, and since he is no longer present, she would like her 14-year-old son, the oldest of three, to go out in public with her when she needs to do so. The mother had been in treatment, but due to the fact that she continued to experience significant anxiety when she went out of the home alone, she discontinued it. The father has expressed a good deal of concern about the mother potentially putting too much pressure on their son to accompany her outside. Also, he described a worry that the son may come to accept a number of his mother's catastrophic beliefs associated with fears of going out in public.

Once again, there is no single, clear answer about how to devise a parenting plan that accounts for these facts and circumstances while facilitating the children's best interests. However, there needs to be careful consideration not only about parenting time and decision-making, but deliberation about options to help the mother's household function adequately, including purchasing food and clothing, as well as facilitating social opportunities and providing transportation for the six- and eight-year-old children.

In certain cases, parental mental health problems overlap with other factors to influence children. For example, a parent who suffers from concurrent depression and alcohol abuse may be at risk for angry, impulsive outbursts directed toward the spouse, and the odds are unfortunately strong that the children will be exposed to such actions a considerable portion of the time. As described earlier in this book, exposure to physical or verbal aggression from one parent to the other has a generally negative effect on children.

In such cases, there need to be efforts in parenting plans to limit the direct contact and communications between the parents in order to protect the children from being exposed to it. Such efforts include transition structures and communication limits and guidelines that promote calm interactions between parents and shield the children from excessive conflict.[237]

In general, the greater the intensity and extent of individual parental mental health problems, the higher the risk there is of behavior that has a negative impact on children. It is essential to stay cognizant of the broad range of important parenting behaviors, such as maintaining an authoritative versus an alternate parenting style, as well as more

237. Ricci, *supra* note 4, at 86.

specific action such as the extent to which a parent provides affection, other types of support, informal education, reasonable discipline, adequate monitoring, and sufficiently clear communication.

There need to be requests for mental health care records regarding any parent about whom questions have been raised that pertain to psychological functioning and the possible impact on parent–child relationships. Contemporaneously made records about relevant information such as presenting problems, diagnoses, therapeutic services, progress, and treatment plans can be very useful in certain cases for parenting plan considerations. However, instead of sending such requested, productive information, treatment providers at times send summary letters that essentially advocate for their clients. A number of these types of letters include therapists' opinions about matters that pertain to parenting plans, such as assertions that the client should have the majority of parenting time. Therapists who provide clinical services to a parent do not carry out appropriate evaluations that address the allocation of parental responsibility, and much of the time they have had very little or no contact with the other parent. Also, a provider who has carried out both therapy and a forensic evaluation has inappropriately combined professional roles. Multiple mental health associations have ethical standards or practice guidelines that prohibit giving opinions without having carried out an appropriate assessment or combining incompatible professional roles.[238]

In a number of cases, a parenting plan may include a statement that recommends or requires that a parent receive mental health or substance abuse treatment. Much of the time, that recommendation or requirement is worded very generally, and there is an expectation that the referral to a local practitioner who may be covered by insurance will assist the parent in substantially improving his or her health, and thereby also benefit the child. However, in such court involved cases, there are a number of important details to consider in therapy recommendations or requirements.

It is crucial that the treatment provider has the necessary clinical training and skills. Within the family law context, for example, a number of parents who have had difficulties with anger control or substance misuse are referred for treatment. A therapist who has adequate general training and a good range of skills does not necessarily have the specific expertise to competently treat inadequately controlled

238. Greenberg & Shuman, *supra* note 215; Robb, *supra* note 215.

anger or substance abuse. Also, for court-involved cases, it is very important for therapists to have a solid foundation in knowing how to interact with the court system; familiarity with relevant professional guidelines[239] is very helpful in this regard.

Mental health treatment is usually carried out in a manner that assumes the client is honest and motivated to change, and it is almost always protected by confidentiality for the client. In some instances, these features may work out well in terms of desired improvement in the court-involved adult client. However, in other cases, the assumptions of client honesty and motivation for change are not true for parents involved in the family law system. For example, a client referred for anger management may not believe that he or she has any problem at all. Another client referred for alcohol treatment may think that her or his drinking habits are normal, and that the other parent has lied about them to gain an advantage in court. Under the protection of client confidentiality, either of these clients could participate in therapy and not disclose the court involvement or even that they were referred for anger management or substance abuse treatment. Such clients could be mainly motivated to talk about how stressful they find it is to interact with the other parent or any of a variety of other topics. If needed, either of these clients could obtain accurate documentation from their therapists that they had attended a reasonable number of sessions and were perceived as having successfully completed treatment.

Unfortunately, this potential problem is not entirely solved by a court order for therapy, having the court identify priority goals for treatment, or a provision that the therapist needs to supply the court with progress reports regarding such goals. In some cases, especially when there is a risk of danger, such treatment requirements make sense. However, the reality is that therapy carried out under the shadow of court involvement is quite difficult, with the therapeutic process for the client often accompanied by worry that self-disclosure might have a negative legal consequence.

There is no easy answer for this dilemma. Each case needs careful consideration as to whether to require court-related information be sent directly to a therapist or that therapy status reports need to be sent to the court. It is extremely important that legal professionals and others be aware that such complications can and do exist at times, and

239. AFCC, *supra* note 216.

that they provide a barrier to legal case management, improved parental functioning, and child well-being.

At the same time, as described earlier in this chapter, it cannot be assumed that evidence of an adult mental health problem alone means that there must be a negative impact on the children. There are numerous parents whose love for their children motivates them to routinely engage in positive, beneficial parenting despite suffering from a psychological disorder.

Regarding the possible impact of adult mental health difficulties on children, and the relevance for parenting plans, central considerations include the following:

- Often, concerns that a parent has significant mental health problems are voiced by the other parent.
- Significant problems with parental mental health need to be distinguished from transient stress reactions associated with the separation or divorce.
- In some cases, it is difficult to disentangle comparatively serious and long-term parental mental health problems from acute stress responses because both are present.
- A crucial consideration is that, to focus appropriately on child well-being, there needs to be a determination about whether alleged adult mental health problems significantly affect parent–child relationships, and if so, in what ways.
- Well-trained and experienced mental health professionals are required in order to assess the possible presence of mental health problems and the impact on parent–child relationships.
- Useful information can often be gained from treatment records that were made at the time of service and that include clinically relevant information on the parent's mental health status, history, and progress.
- However, considerable caution is needed in relying on the input of parents' therapists in parenting plans because few therapists have had the training and experience to adequately understand the crucial differences between the therapeutic and forensic roles, and many believe it is an appropriate priority to act as advocates for their clients, regardless of the potential impact on the children.

- Parenting plans need to consider the entire configuration of relevant facts and circumstances for each family, including the possible presence of mental health disorders and the extent to which they may have an impact on parent–child relationships.
- Although referring a parent for mental health treatment can be productive, the court-related nature of such cases includes risks of referrals to inadequately skilled therapists and client manipulations that avoid sincere therapeutic involvement and efforts at change, thereby interfering with efforts to facilitate child well-being.

CHAPTER 10
PARENTAL ALIENATION AND GATEKEEPING

One of the most challenging and controversial areas regarding children of divorce pertains to child resistance to spend time with a parent. A frequently contentious issue is whether one parent has contributed to a child's resistance or refusal to spend time with the other parent or whether the child has come to that position entirely independently. In some cases, parental action clearly has an influence on the frequency or extent of child contact with the other parent, though the child is not necessarily resistant to involvement with that parent.

In this chapter, I first summarize essential information about parental alienation. Second, I address questions and controversies about parental alienation primarily through an explanation of relevant research—both what is known about the phenomenon and the difficult areas in which much remains unknown, requiring further inquiry. Third, I address efforts to intervene when a child is resistant to see a parent. I include a number of summaries of published reports of intervention efforts specifically aimed at reconciling a child with a parent. Fourth, I describe allegations regarding gatekeeping and associated efforts to promote positive parent–child relationships. Fifth, I focus on parenting plan applications.

Overview of Parental Alienation

In general, the term parental alienation refers to a parent turning a child against the other parent or attempting to do so. Even though this thumbnail definition may seem clear, there is a great deal that is controversial and not clear about parental alienation.

Before turning to the more substantive and controversial matters, brief descriptions of commonly used terms are warranted. When a parent appears to be in an alliance or coalition with the child, with elements of opposition to the other parent, that individual is frequently described as the aligned, favored, or alienating parent. The parent who is the recipient of the resistance or refusal to visit is often referred to as the alienated, rejected, or target parent.

Parental alienation was brought into major focus in the field by a psychiatrist, Richard Gardner, who maintained that it was a distinctive disorder. His view of what he described as the parental alienation syndrome was that a child displayed an exceptionally negative disposition toward a target parent. It included an extremely critical attitude and denigrating actions toward the rejected parent and was not justified by inappropriate behavior by that parent. Gardner maintained that the alienation resulted primarily from brainwashing by the aligned parent.[240]

Responses to this perspective on parental alienation tended to diverge, in part, along gender lines. Because mothers characteristically have been the primary caregivers, the rejected parents have most often been fathers, and mothers are target parents less frequently. Fathers' rights groups tended to take a favorable view of Gardner's assertions about parental alienation, often associated with their assertion that the legal system favored mothers. In a number of cases, women's rights organizations contended that allegations of parental alienation served as attempts to try to hide abusive, violent, or other extremely negative actions that were actually carried out by fathers. There had been debates about whether the parental alienation syndrome should be considered a diagnosis for inclusion in the most recent revision of the diagnostic manual published by the American Psychiatric Association. Parental alienation was not included as a disorder in that publication.

On a case-by-case basis, there can be many complications involved in considering whether any type of parental alienation may be at work. A first step is to consider whether a child has or has not demonstrated a very negative attitude, rejection, or resistance to see one parent while having become aligned with the other parent. A second consideration is whether either or both parents have engaged in any statements or actions that would potentially interfere with the child's engagement with the other parent. A third, crucial matter for deliberation is to what extent there may be sound reasons for a child to have a negative attitude and to manifest resistance toward the rejected parent.

240. Richard A. Gardner, The Parental Alienation Syndrome: A Guidebook for Mental Health and Legal Professionals (1992).

There are parents who engage in child abuse, neglect, domestic violence, and otherwise poor parenting. Similarly, other parents may manifest other serious individual problems. In such unfortunate cases, children need to be protected, which might need to include limiting parental contact.

Although it was generally acknowledged in the field that, in a number of cases, parental alienation had occurred in a manner that fit Gardner's description, his conceptualization was overly limited. There was too little focus on understanding these matters from the child's perspective. There was inadequate acknowledgment of possible deficits in the alienated parent as well as other more complex family matters. In that regard, an influential reformulation of the parental alienation concept was carried out by Joan Kelly and Janet Johnston, both highly respected authorities. The main points of their reformulation[241] are summarized here.

Kelly and Johnston described that there are multiple reasons that can lead a child to resist or avoid spending time with a parent, not limited to an actively alienating parent brainwashing a child and carrying out manipulations that interfere with parent–child engagement. For example, a child might be distressed about a parent's new spouse or significant other. Very young children may experience separation anxiety. Even apart from separation anxiety, many young children manifest difficulties with the transitions between parents.

In certain cases, both parents see a child being very upset during a transition, and each parent, based on her or his own experiences with the child, develops very different worries about the reasons for the child distress. When a parent who is in the process of bringing the child to an exchange observes a child cry and fuss, that adult might develop a belief that the other parent is mistreating the child in some way. A parent on the receiving end of the transition may see the child being initially very upset but then quickly becoming calm and content when the transition has been accomplished. That receiving parent might conclude that the other parent is purposely trying to make the child upset to have a reason for the transition not to occur, or at least is failing to reassure the child and support the parent–child relationship.

In other cases, a child might perceive that a parent is very upset about the prospects that the child will be leaving for a period of time

241. Joan B. Kelly & Janet R. Johnston, *The Alienated Child: A Reformulation of the Parental Alienation Syndrome*, 39 FAM. CT. REV. 266 (2001).

to visit with the other parent. Under the extremely emotionally challenging circumstances of separation and divorce, a parent may come to emotionally rely on the presence of the child and the positive interactions with him or her.

In addition, as described earlier, children can show positive motivation to avoid and resist spending time with a parent who has engaged in highly adverse parenting. Under such circumstances, the child's resistance is categorized as estrangement and not alienation.

Accordingly, the Kelly and Johnston reformulation has the child, and not the parents, as the central focus. In that regard, relationships between the child and each parent are most productively conceptualized as existing on a continuum. On the healthiest end of that continuum, there are positive relationships between the child and each parent. A slight degree away from that most optimal circumstance involves a child who feels an affinity primarily for one parent but wishes to have routine contact with both. A next step away from the healthiest end of the continuum is a child who has an alliance with one parent and prefers to have only limited contact with the other, associated with ambivalent feelings about him or her. In certain of these cases there are good reasons for estrangement from the non-preferred parent—that individual may have displayed abusive, aggressive, or otherwise inadequate parenting; in other instances, such individuals may manifest problems such as substance misuse. The alienated child is found at the least healthy end of the continuum. He or she manifests extremely entrenched negative attitudes and behaviors toward the target parent and may refuse any contact.

The authors of the alienated child reformulation described a number of individual and circumstantial factors that can influence the reality of each case presentation. For example, developmental factors can have an effect on a child's response to a parent. Although a child can become alienated from a parent at almost any age, it is relatively rare to see unrelenting alienation in someone who is less than about seven years of age. This phenomenon may be related to the fact that young children tend to have somewhat changing internal representations of parents that are influenced by recent and current experiences, and more entrenched, permanent perceptions are characteristic of older children.

As noted earlier, extremely negative behavior by a parent can lead to a child understandably withdrawing and becoming estranged from that individual. However, there can be other, less egregious behaviors by a rejected parent that inadvertently contribute toward a child's feelings of estrangement or alienation. For example, a rejected parent may have a history of relative passivity and withdrawal in the face of significant conflict with the aligned parent. As a result, the rejected parent may have had very limited opportunities for positive interactions with the child. In some cases, an alienated parent may respond in a rather hostile manner by carrying out retaliatory rejection toward the child. If an alienated parent has been accused of sexual abuse, there may be very limited opportunities for that individual to spend time with the child and for them to have positive experiences together, which potentially can contribute to a child feeling rejected. Other rejected parents may have manifested relatively moderate problems in parenting such as limited empathy, excessive criticism, self-centeredness, or rigidity.

Parents who are aligned with an alienated child may also manifest major parenting limitations. In a number of cases, such parents voice a belief that the alienated parent does not deserve to be in the child's life. Similarly, certain aligned parents insist that the rejected parent never loved the child, and that there is no harm to the child of having an absent parent. A number of aligned parents have significant psychological problems that contribute to not upholding appropriate personal boundaries with the child. In such instances, a child might fear that by voicing any positive attitude about the rejected parent, he or she would betray the aligned parent.

A number of circumstantial factors can contribute toward the risk that a child becomes alienated from a parent. Such factors include the presence of strong marital conflict, often associated with high-conflict litigation. At times, the aligned parent has experienced severe embarrassment associated with the divorce process. Other individuals, such as extended family and friends, new romantic partners, or misguided professionals, may inadvertently contribute toward the alienation process.

Research

It is essential to examine research on parental alienation in order to try to obtain the most well-founded understanding of it. At the same time, characteristics of parental alienation make it particularly difficult to research.

At a very basic level, there is frequently vehement conflict between each parent, aided by their respective attorneys, as to whether any parental alienation has actually taken place. Therefore, it makes it challenging to ascertain what families should or should not be included in a research project. Associated with this reality, it is difficult to collect adequate numbers of cases that would allow for good-quality statistical comparisons. Research projects that have limitations of small numbers of cases have a drawback of allowing little generalization beyond the specific sample that was used.

In many clinical research projects, participants are recruited to volunteer, and they need to identify themselves as suffering from a condition under study, such as anxiety or diabetes. However, parents do not volunteer to come forward for research studies and identify that they have carried out campaigns to try to have their children reject and refuse to see the other parent. Consequently, in order to objectively identify cases in which parental alienation may have occurred, it is often necessary to closely examine many potential cases. In certain instances, the sources of such cases are limited to those with court involvement who have been referred or ordered to obtain counseling or other services.

As a result, there are significant methodological limitations in much of the research that has been conducted. At the same time, a number of those limitations are perhaps inevitable. A recent high-quality review of the parental alienation research,[242] relied upon in this chapter, covered 58 studies and described both methodological limitations and study findings. Common limitations included small sample sizes, the lack of comparison or control groups, non-random samples, methods that did not allow for testing of causality, and insufficient statistical power. However, on the whole, the productive information on parental alienation that can be derived from this body of research is a vast improvement over reliance on case anecdotes and informal observation.

The overall research evidence suggests that there are numerous factors contributing to the phenomena of alienated and estranged children. These factors include high levels of interparental conflict, ongoing custody litigation, parent–child relationship factors, personality features of individual family members, living circumstances, and attitudes of siblings. Therefore, it is most useful to conceptualize alienation as a problem in family relationships, and not any type of individual child or parental psychopathology. At the same time, while

242. Michael Saini et al., *Empirical Studies of Alienation*, *in* PARENTING PLAN EVALUATIONS: APPLIED RESEARCH FOR THE FAMILY COURT, 2d ed. 374 (Leslie Drozd et al. eds., 2016).

both parents may engage in behavior that potentially alienates the child from the other parent, there are cases in which one parent is primarily responsible for contributing toward the child's unreasonably negative disposition toward the other parent.

Perhaps associated at least in part with the reality that mothers are characteristically the primary caregivers, when there is litigation over child custody and the child becomes alienated or estranged, the father is more likely than the mother to be the rejected parent. Adolescents are more likely than younger children to manifest an entrenched, crystallized negative disposition toward a rejected parent.

When it has been determined that a parent has engaged in behavior likely to alienate a child from the other parent, there is consistency across research studies regarding the types of parental statements and actions that are likely to lead to the alienation. There can be a wide variety of negative statements made by the alienating parent to the child about the rejected parent, though common themes include allegations that the target parent is dangerous and/or does not love the child. Alienating behaviors frequently include severely limiting contact with the alienated parent, persuading the child to reject that parent, and limiting the child from even mentioning him or her. Certain alienating parents adopt a peer-like role with the child, including confiding inappropriate information and at least indirectly conveying that love will be withdrawn if the child shows any positive regard for the target parent.

In many other respects, the available research findings are mixed and inconsistent. The methodological limitations previously described likely contribute to that current state of the field. A number of research studies have focused on efforts to intervene in ways that have an objective of establishing more positive relationships between alienated children and rejected parents. Although all these studies are small and limited, in keeping with the nature of the parental alienation phenomena, a number of consistencies emerge across the different reports. Because there is understandably frequent concern about how to try to improve matters when there has been a ruptured parent–child relationship, a number of the main published intervention studies are summarized here.

Intervention Research

Reports on the results of interventions to improve relationships between alienated children and rejected parents routinely describe limitations in their findings and emphasize that they should be considered preliminary. In particular, the reports note that the very small sample sizes limit the extent to which conclusions can be generalized to other children and families, especially those that may be substantially different in important ways from the research participants. In addition, many of the research intervention reports describe results in a narrative format, as the generally small numbers are inadequate for statistical calculations.

One study described the results of family counseling from two separate sources. The first source was a follow-up study of young adults who had been children in the midst of highly conflictual custody disputes 15 to 20 years earlier; the second source was the authors' therapy records from 42 children who had been resisting or refusing visitation during lengthy custody disputes.[243] The young adults represented in the first source of data mostly reported having experienced strongly negative attitudes toward one parent, primarily fathers, during their teenage years. Of that group, only about 25 percent recalled having had strongly negative feelings toward one parent during their elementary school years.

A large proportion of the youths who had refused or resisted visitation later initiated reconciliation with the alienated parent during their late teens or early twenties. For the most part, they reported that they had done so without the help of a counselor. In addition, it was generally reported that receiving supportive counseling with a long-term therapist was experienced as beneficial. In contrast, a number of individuals who had been alienated children and were forced by court orders to see a number of different therapists for reunification counseling expressed disdain for the court and/or the rejected parent for having made such a requirement.

When parents manifested relatively severe problems, the long-term outcomes were generally worse. When a child had understandable, reality-based concerns about a parent, and when there was more chronic family dysfunction, there tended to be more enduring rejection of the parent. When such children had grown to be adults who sought out and attempted to reconcile with parents, such efforts tended not to be successful, often associated with continuing serious problems manifested by the parents.

243. Janet R. Johnston & Judith Roth Goldman, *Outcomes of Family Counseling Interventions with Children Who Resist Visitation: An Addendum to Friedlander and Walters (2010)*, 48 FAM. CT. REV. 112 (2010).

When the aligned parents were found to have significant psychopathology and sabotaged legal and therapeutic efforts to reconcile a child with an alienated parent, relevant parent–child relationships tended to improve only with strong court action. In such cases, custody was changed either to the better functioning parent or to someone other than a legal parent who could provide a healthy family upbringing.

An intensive intervention experience, called Overcoming Barriers Family Camp, was created by a number of professionals for families with a child who resisted or refused contact with a parent.[244] Participants were ten families who took part in it in 2008 or 2009. All the families except for one were court ordered to participate over the objections of the aligned parent. The families tended to have been highly involved in ongoing family litigation over the course of years. In general, all the aligned parents asserted that the rejected parents had engaged in poor parenting, abuse, neglect, or domestic violence. Accordingly, the aligned parents maintained that the rejected parents had caused the child and family problems. The rejected parents asserted that the other parent was alienating the children from them, and that they actually had previously been actively and positively engaged with the children. All the families had previously been involved in traditional mental health services that did not have any positive impact.

A significant portion of the families came to this intervention program after a neutral evaluation had taken place and the court had determined that the child's refusal to visit was largely a result of alienating behavior on the part of the aligned parent. The referral to this program took place by court order, and it was considered a last step prior to an order placing the child in the sole custody of one parent or under the care of neither parent.

The intervention program included all family members. It took place over a number of consecutive days in a secluded family camp in Vermont. The clinical program was run by a number of experienced clinical psychologists, aided by administrative staff and camp counselors who were described by the study authors as extremely competent. The program had exclusive use of the extensive campsite. It included intensive clinical intervention, psychoeducation, and multiple enjoyable camp experiences. The authors were able to collect follow-up information about the 2008 participants over a period of

244. Matthew J. Sullivan et al., *Overcoming Barriers Family Camp: A Program for High-Conflict Divorce Families Where a Child Is Resisting Contact with a Parent*, 48 FAM. CT. REV. 116 (2010).

six to nine months after that camp had concluded. Of the five families who participated in 2008, two reported generally positive family interactions, including regular contact between the alienated child and the formerly rejected parent. In a separate family, the target parent was still estranged from the children and was no longer pursuing contact. In two other families, children were visiting the target parent, though they manifested a degree of resistance in doing so.

There had been limited opportunity to obtain follow-up information on the families who participated in 2009. However, three of the five 2009 families were reported to have followed up by obtaining the services of a parenting coordinator or other therapeutic access coordinator, which was one of the goals of the program.

A separate intensive intervention program, called Family Bridges, was also the subject of a research report.[245] It was a workshop for a rejected parent and severely alienated children to participate in together as one family. It was not designed as a multiple family experience, and there were other exclusionary criteria.

The workshop explicitly was not designed for children who rejected contact with a parent for good reasons, such as abusive behavior, domestic violence, or substance misuse. It was also not appropriate for families in which the court had made a determination that it was best for the child to remain with the favored parent. Similarly, Family Bridges was not designed for families where the child would be with the rejected parent for only a brief period before returning to live with the aligned parent.

The report on Family Bridges involved 23 children in 12 families. In eight of those families, with 14 children, the program started directly after trials in which the court awarded custody to the alienated parent. The other children and families had somewhat different backgrounds, including three children who previously had been abducted and two young adult children who had been disdainful toward a parent but who nonetheless volunteered to participate in the workshop. All families previously had counseling experiences that were not successful.

In contrast to the Overcoming Barriers Family Camp, the Family Bridges workshop did not include the aligned parent in the same interventions as the other family members. However, in some cases, there was separate work done with the aligned parent.

---

245. Richard A. Warshak, *Family Bridges: Using Insights from Social Science to Reconnect Parents and Alienated Children*, 48 Fam. Ct. Rev. 48 (2010).

It was reported that, at the end of the program, 22 of the 23 children had restored a positive relationship with the formerly alienated parent. For 19 of the children, the follow-up information was collected between two years and four years after the end of the workshop. Of the 22 children who appeared to have improved as a result of the workshop, four (three of whom belonged to the same family) later returned to an alienated stance after the court gave them permission to re-establish contact with the favored parent. A more recent report about efforts to follow up on the outcomes of a larger sample of children who have gone through the Family Bridges program described similarly positive results.[246]

A therapy program carried out in Israel was aimed at children who had refused to visit the alienated parent for at least four months. In contrast to the intensive workshop approach taken by two of the reports just described, this therapy program involved 16 group sessions of 90 minutes each that occurred on a weekly basis. There were parallel therapy groups such that children and parents met in separate groups. Both favored and rejected parents were involved in the groups. The results of this parallel group therapy program were compared at a 12-month follow-up to a control group that had received standard community treatment.[247]

At that follow-up, those who participated in the parallel group therapy program were rated as showing better cooperation between parents than the families who had received standard community care. Levels of child anxiety and depression were measured only for those who participated in the parallel group therapy program, and there were significant improvements between the start of the program and the end.

A more recent study reported on the results of a four-day intensive treatment, called the Family Reflections Reunification Program, focused on reconciling alienated children and rejected parents.[248] It involved 12 families, including 22 children, six rejected mothers, and six rejected fathers.

---

246. Richard Warshak, *Parental Alienation: Overview, Management, Intervention, and Practice Tips*, 28 J. Am. Acad. Matrimonial Law. 181 (2015), at 238.

247. Paz Toren et al., *Sixteen-Session Group Treatment for Children and Adolescents with Parental Alienation and Their Parents*, 41 Am. J. Fam. Therapy 187 (2013).

248. Kathleen M. Reay, *Family Reflections: A Promising Therapeutic Program Designed to Treat Severely Alienated Children and Their Family System*, 43 Am. J. Fam. Therapy 197 (2015).

Follow-up information reportedly was collected at three-month intervals, between three and 12 months after the intervention had concluded. It was reported that all but one child re-established a relationship with the formerly alienated parent by the end of the intervention. That conclusion was based on information from children, parents, and the observations of the multidisciplinary intervention team.

A number of other therapeutic approaches have been put into effect with a main goal of improving the relationship between an alienated child and the rejected parent. Outpatient approaches include a modification of the Overcoming Barriers Family Camp and efforts that have a strong focus on attempting to provide positive family experiences,[249] though at this time there appears to be no outcome data available.

Gatekeeping

The concept of gatekeeping pertains to the attitudes and behaviors of one parent regarding the other parent's involvement with the child or children. To a considerable extent, it overlaps with the concept of coparenting. Restrictive gatekeeping relies on the metaphor of a closed gate that blocks interactions between a child and a parent. Facilitative gatekeeping refers to a metaphorical open gate in which contact between the child and the other parent is promoted. Perhaps obviously, there is overlap between aspects of gatekeeping and parental alienation. Restrictive gatekeeping, in significantly limiting or blocking parent–child involvement, is very similar to the actions of an alienating parent who works to avoid or eliminate contact between the child and the other parent.[250]

Although the concept of gatekeeping tends not to be mentioned in relevant state statutes, a number of statutes include friendly parent

---

249. Barbara J. Fidler et al., *Translating the Overcoming Barriers Approach to Outpatient Settings*, *in* OVERCOMING PARENT-CHILD CONTACT PROBLEMS: FAMILY-BASED INTERVENTIONS FOR RESISTANCE, REJECTION, AND ALIENATION 243 (Abigail M. Judge & Robin M. Deutsch eds., 2017); Abigail M. Judge & Rebecca Bailey, *More Than Words: The Use of Experiential Therapies in the Treatment of Families with Parent-Child Contact Problems and Parental Alienation*, *in* OVERCOMING PARENT-CHILD CONTACT PROBLEMS: FAMILY-BASED INTERVENTIONS FOR RESISTANCE, REJECTION, AND ALIENATION 91 (Abigail M. Judge & Robin M. Deutsch eds., 2017).

250. William G. Austin et al., *Parental Gatekeeping and the Child Custody/Child Access Evaluations, Part I: Conceptual Framework, Research, and Application*, 51 FAM. CT. REV. 485 (2013); Marsha Kline Pruett et al., *The Hand That Rocks the Cradle: Maternal Gatekeeping after Divorce*, 27 PACE L. REV. 709 (2007).

provisions, which consider the extent to which each parent facilitates a positive relationship between the child and the other parent. In that regard, such statutes include considerations regarding gatekeeping and coparenting.

Gatekeeping is best considered as existing on a continuum, varying between highly restrictive on one end and highly facilitative on the other end. In that regard, coparenting is also most productively conceptualized as being on a continuum.

As there is overlap between the concepts of gatekeeping and parental alienation, it is important to keep in mind that there can be multiple factors that contribute toward a child being resistant to see a parent, as well as one parent wishing to limit the child's contact with the other parent. For example, a parent might be inclined to engage in restrictive gatekeeping because of a sincere belief or worry that the actions of the other parent would be negative for the child.

If gatekeeping is occurring, it tends to be by mothers because they are the parents who characteristically primarily care for the children. Although there is evidence, described previously, that children raised by single mothers and those raised by single fathers have about equally positive life adjustments, there are stylistic differences in how parents interact with children. With infants and other very young children, mothers tend to be calming and soothing, whereas fathers tend to stimulate and are more encouraging of exploration. Accordingly, the patterns of mother–child and father–child interactions tend to be somewhat different, and these differences at time can lead a mother to view the father as doing things wrong in parenting, thereby contributing to a belief that she needs to restrict his interactions with the child in order to protect her or him.[251]

Of course, there are cases of children actually needing protection from inappropriate parenting. However, restrictive maternal gatekeeping can also be influenced by the mother's unhappiness with how the father treated her during the marriage. Also, at times, it is associated with maternal deficits in self-esteem, and it can be carried out without insight that it is occurring.[252]

As described previously in this book, women and men have overlapping yet somewhat distinct stylistic contributions to the parenting endeavor. It is important to be cognizant that when fathers are actively

251. Pruett et al., *supra* note 115.
252. *Id.* at 131.

engaged with children, even when they do not live with them, there are generally positive benefits emotionally, cognitively, socially, educationally, and behaviorally.[253]

Multifaceted gatekeeping treatment efforts have been carried out with the goal of enhancing positive father involvement, primarily with very young children. Because the treatment participants were almost all married or cohabiting, and without histories of domestic violence, mental health, or substance abuse, the findings have limited generalization to separated and divorced individuals. However, the treatment methods were generally positive for both individual mothers and fathers, as well as for families.[254]

Parenting Plan Applications

Children who resist seeing a parent clearly present difficult and complex issues—how does one make productive use of all of the information presented in this chapter for purposes of parenting plans? Any sound parenting plan needs to be based on a foundation of a thorough assessment of what is contributing to the child resistance.

In such cases, one of the few clear facts is that there is a child who is avoiding or even refusing contact with a parent. A practical reality is that there is very seldom direct evidence or agreement about other matters. If a parent has, in fact, made highly negative, demeaning comments about the other parent to the child, there is often no objective source of information that such statements have actually been made. An alienating parent is extremely unlikely to say such things to the child in front of any legal or mental health professional, and it is very improbable that he or she will admit to having done so. A child who is alienated and closely aligned with an alienating parent is extremely unlikely to report that parent to have made inaccurate and denigrating statements about the rejected parent. If a child makes any relevant statement at all, it is likely to be that the alienated parent has engaged in extensive wrongdoing, and that the aligned parent told him or her about it only for purposes of safety and protection.

Similarly, in many cases, there is an absence of readily available objective evidence that an alienating parent has been the sole initiator of barriers to contact between the child and the target parent. Characteristically, especially if the child is older, both the child and the

253. *Id.* at 134.
254. *Id.* at 143.

alienating parent insist that the child has come to a reasonable decision to avoid the rejected parent, based on the allegedly egregious behavior by that parent. In cases with a younger child, she or he is less likely to have a consistently strong resistance to see the target parent, but the favored parent tends to assert that the child needs to be protected from the allegedly dangerous or otherwise inappropriate behavior of the alienated parent. Alienated children of any age and aligned parents very rarely convey that they are united with one another against the other parent unless it pertains to child safety, protection, and well-being.

Children and parental alienation cases often enter into the court system when resistance to visit a parent has intensified to the point of refusal. A number of the intensive treatment approaches described earlier in this chapter indicated that participants previously had gone through more typical outpatient counseling that was not effective. The limited research on parental alienation has also raised questions about whether outpatient counseling between a refusing child and alienated parent, at times called reunification therapy, is useful or counterproductive.[255] A number of therapists have commented that such outpatient treatment has routinely been ineffective when a child has reached an entrenched stance of alienation from the target parent.

An alternative approach has emphasized identifying child problems related to visitation resistance well before negative child attitudes harden against the parent. Therapeutic objectives might primarily focus, at least initially, on separate but related problems, such as significant lags in child development, school problems, or identifying ways for the child and parent to engage in activities together that are rewarding. Instead of mainly exploring emotions and thoughts, there are numerous methods used to improve child coping, parenting practices, and related family behaviors. This treatment approach is informed by scientific findings on children of divorce,[256] though there appear to be no child or family outcome data available at this point.

Many parental alienation and serious gatekeeping cases persist for years in the legal system. Accordingly, there may be records that include many pleadings, orders, counseling reports, and other materials. A number of the allegations made by parents may pertain to

255. Saini et al., *supra* note 242.

256. Lyn R. Greenberg et al., *Catching Them Before Too Much Damage Is Done: Early Intervention with Resistance-Refusal Dynamics,* 54 FAM. CT. REV. 548 (2016).

interactions from years ago, which makes it more difficult to ascertain what is true.

For example, it is common for an aligned parent to insist that she or he has never said anything negative to the child about the other parent, whereas the rejected parent states that he or she has witnessed communication such as a statement or text by the other parent instructing the child not to obey directions. A rejected parent, in a court pleading, might identify specific dates when court-ordered visits did not actually occur. In turn, the other parent simply replies that the visits did actually take place, and it is very difficult to ascertain which report is accurate. Other "he said–she said" types of communications frequently involve whether or not an aligned parent purposely scheduled a child activity at a time when visitation with the other parent was supposed to take place, whether or not the favored parent (versus the child) contacted the police about alleged misbehavior by the target parent, and whether or not an alienating parent encouraged the child to engage in behavior toward the other parent that was noxious, oppositional, or abusive.

Through this dense fog of years of vehement discord and disputed parental and child assertions, there needs to be a process carried out by those involved in creating possible parenting plans to assess the preponderance of evidence in terms of what is best for the child. As described earlier in this book, it is necessary to use one or more methods designed to promote careful deliberation over reliance on intuition. Productive use of deliberative methods can also help guard against professionals feeling overwhelmed and ineffective, and just throwing up their hands to get something done so they can move along to another case.

Specifically, the use of forms that separately identify the main assertions of each parent and each relevant child, and that record evidence that supports or is contrary to each assertion, is among the most productively deliberative processes available. Regarding each relevant assertion, it is crucial to highlight the evidence that is relatively objective, considering the credibility of the sources.

Also, those involved in parenting planning need to consider possibilities or hypotheses other than those presented by each of the family members. For example, especially for a very young child, consideration needs to be given to whether there is separation anxiety or transient distress associated with the transition between parents. For older children and teens, there needs to be an assessment of whether there may be a particular affinity for one parent based on common interests or other factors instead of a blanket dislike of the other parent. Alternately, or perhaps in combination, there also needs to be thought given to the degree to which an older child or teen resists visiting the target parent largely because of a strong preference to spend time with peers near the main residence or due to a favored scheduled activity.

Other hypotheses for consideration may focus on the parents. A child resisting visits may worry that the favored parent will be upset if visitation takes place with the other parent. Somewhat similarly, a rejected parent may have moderate interpersonal skill deficits and consequently a rather distant relationship with the child, with few shared interests. In many cases, there may be numerous factors that are relatively nuanced instead of a relatively straightforward choice of whether there is an abusive parent or an alienating one. Perhaps obviously, professionals with suitable training and experience are needed to assess these matters.

In addition, in the midst of these multiple, often complex factors, it is possible for basic considerations to be overlooked. It is essential to keep in mind that parents who have lengthy histories of extreme conflict with one another are highly unlikely to coparent successfully.

Regarding the contents of this chapter, crucial considerations include

- An early conceptualization of parental alienation involved the following:
  - a parent essentially brainwashing a child to hold extremely negative beliefs about the other parent,
  - the child consequently resisting seeing the target parent,
  - the child being psychologically aligned with the alienating parent,
  - an absence of inappropriate behavior by the rejected parent that would justify the extreme negativity of the child toward him or her.
- A conceptual reformulation of alienation changed the main focus to the child's perspective and emphasized that resistance or rejection of a parent by a child could take place for a number of reasons, including (but not limited to)
  - dangerous or other negative actions by a parent that understandably lead a child to want to avoid that parent,

- child worry that a parent will be upset and lonely when visits occur with the other parent,
- child distress over a parent's new spouse or significant other,
- child fear that he or she would be seen as betraying the aligned parent by making any positive statement or action about the target parent,
- separation anxiety in very young children,
- difficulties in transitions between parents,
- limited opportunity for a rejected parent to have positive interactions with the child,
- and a parent's active effort to persuade the child to reject the other parent, who generally has carried out positive parenting.

- Child development factors can influence a child's attitude and behavior toward a parent.
- Circumstantial factors can heighten the risk of a child becoming alienated, including (but not limited to)
  - high-conflict family litigation,
  - intense marital conflict,
  - the input of family, friends, new romantic partners, and/or inadequately educated professionals.
- Although research on parental alienation is difficult to conduct, relevant findings can help legal and mental health professionals improve their understanding of it.
- Research evidence indicates there are multiple factors that can contribute to child resistance to see a parent, including
  - ongoing custody litigation,
  - high levels of interparental conflict,
  - parent–child relationship difficulties,
  - sibling attitudes,
  - individual personality characteristics of family members,
  - and residential circumstances.
- Fathers are more likely than mothers to be alienated parents; mothers are more likely than fathers to carry out restrictive gatekeeping.

- Adolescents are more likely than young children to develop entrenched negative attitudes toward the rejected parents.
- When there have been cases of clear alienation carried out by a parent, there are frequent parental statements and actions that contribute toward the rejection of the other parent, including
  - a broad variety of statements by the alienating parent about the other parent,
  - statements by the alienating parent that the rejected parent never loved the child,
  - statements that the rejected parent is dangerous,
  - the alienating parent limiting child contact with the target parent,
  - restricting the child from even mentioning the other parent,
  - the alienating parent not maintaining adequate boundaries with the child,
  - confiding inappropriate information to the child,
  - communicating to the child in statement or action that love will be withdrawn if the child shows a positive attitude toward the rejected parent.
- A number of research reports have found positive results of specialized, intensive interventions aimed at reconciling children and alienated parents, though the studies have had significant methodological limitations.
- The reportedly positive outcomes tended to have a number of features in common, including:
  - very small sample sizes that limit the ability to generalize to other potential participants,
  - court orders for children to change residential custody to the alienated parent with limitations on contact with the aligned parent,
  - intensive interventions.
- Outpatient therapy developed for use with young children who resist visits but do not show entrenched alienation may be more promising than outpatient reunification therapy involving an alienated child and a rejected parent, but there is no data apparently available at this time about effectiveness.

- Restrictive gatekeeping, which involves one parent limiting or blocking child involvement with the other parent, is similar conceptually to parental alienation.
- Facilitative and restrictive gatekeeping overlap a good deal with the concepts of positive and negative coparenting.
- Children generally benefit from active involvement with both parents.
- Parents with consistent patterns of vehement disputes with one another are extremely unlikely to successfully cooperate with one another.
- Methods need to be used to promote deliberation about the complex array of parental assertions and other possible causal factors, including
  - lists for each parental assertion that describe information consistent with and contrary to each such contention, with relatively objective evidence highlighted, and
  - lists for each hypothesis or consideration that originates from professionals, including indications consistent with and contrary to each one, with relatively objective evidence highlighted.

CHAPTER 11
RELOCATION

Relocation cases create extremely difficult parenting plan obstacles. They typically involve the primary residential parent wanting to move with the children to a location far away and the other parent opposing the move. There is hardly ever a compromise solution—often the only choices are yes or no regarding the move. Almost all other parenting plan disputes allow greater room for potential solutions through negotiation and compromise.

The vast majority of parents who wish to relocate are mothers who have the majority of parenting time, and fathers tend to be the parents who oppose the move. Consequently, in this chapter, the potentially moving parent is often referred to as the mother and the non-moving one as the father; similarly, the relevant gender pronouns are used.

Why are relocation cases so contentious, resistant to compromise, and difficult to settle? The main reasons include firm convictions by a mother that a potential move will substantially benefit both her and the children, often accompanied by a sense that life in their current location is needlessly stressful and isolated, and fear and worry by a father that the relationships with the moving children will be damaged and might even eventually disappear.

In this chapter, I first summarize information about relocation factors that need to be considered on a case-by-case basis. Second, I describe a number of important general factors about residential moves involving children. Third, I summarize relevant research. Fourth, I focus on a number of additional parenting plan considerations.

Relocation Factors

Perhaps obviously, it is an absolute necessity that those involved in developing parenting plans have a solid grasp of relocation legal criteria in the state where they work. Most states enumerate statutory factors that need to be considered in relocation cases. Also, there are multiple factors that have been identified in the academic and professional literature that are crucial to consider, and they overlap to some extent with many states' legal criteria. Although there are generally very sound, rational basis for these criteria, the reality that there are so many factors can be a practical challenge. An article from a judicial perspective identified 36 different factors that had been considered in relocation cases and statutes.[257] Also, there are global factors. For example, the Illinois relocation statute enumerates ten specific factors and includes a final one, "any other relevant factors bearing on the child's best interests,"[258] and Alabama has 16 specific relocation factors, plus a final global one that states "any other factor that in the opinion of the court is material to the general issue or otherwise provided by law."[259]

These types of global factors result in a necessity to consider an almost unrestricted range of facts and circumstances, depending upon what is considered relevant by the various participants. Therefore, it is a major challenge in each case to try to ascertain which are the relatively more and less central legal and psychosocial criteria to consider.

A number of custody evaluators, primarily working in private practice settings, identified multiple relocation factors as being highly important. They include the ability of the moving parent to support the relationship between the child and the other parent; the degree of involvement with the child by the non-moving parent; child age; the history of compliance with past court orders; the strengths, resources, and vulnerabilities of the moving parent; the presence of domestic violence; the child's strengths and vulnerabilities; parenting effectiveness by both parents; the degree of gatekeeping by the moving parent; and the geographical distance of the proposed move. Numerous other factors were also rated as important, though slightly less so than the ones specified here.[260]

---

257. W. Dennis Duggan, *Rock-paper-scissors: Playing the Odds with the Law of Child Relocation*, 45 FAM. CT. REV. 193 (2007).

258. 750 ILL. COMP. STAT. 5 § 609.2 (P.A. 99-90, eff. Jan. 1, 2016).

259. Jeff Atkinson, *The Law of Relocation of Children*, 28 BEHAV. SCI. & L. 563 (2010).

260. William A. Austin et al., *Relocation Issues in Child Custody Evaluations: A Survey of Professionals*, 54 FAM. CT. REV. 477 (2016).

When a child has special needs, health challenges, or even just a difficult temperament, such realities need to be included in the considerations about possible relocation. Under such circumstances, there may be a need for an especially close focus on the relationship between the child and the non-moving parent, both in terms of the emotional ties present between them and the types of actions historically carried out by that parent. For example, it is essential to closely assess the extent to which the non-moving parent has been involved in the child's health care and education. A number of non-residential parents, by virtue of their personal strengths and motivation, may have contributed substantially to the quality of life of a child with health problems or special needs. However, other non-residential parents may have had very limited emotional involvement with the child and/or have not facilitated or even been a barrier to the provision of needed child services.

A number of states have presumptions in favor of or against relocation. Similarly, certain states specify a burden of proof on the party seeking relocation, whereas others have a burden of proof on the party opposing it. A number of statutes explicitly identify an equal burden of proof or indicate that there is no presumption. Also, a few states describe a presumption in favor of relocation if there is a primary residential custodian, but that presumption is not applicable if there is approximately equally shared parenting time.[261] It is very useful for those involved in developing parenting plans to be cognizant of what is generally considered important in relocation cases, though it is essential to know the local statutory factors, presumptions, and burdens of proof.

Practicalities of Residential Moves

In the United States, there historically has been a good deal of residential mobility. A large proportion of adults who separate or divorce move residences, and relatively young parents tend to have higher than average rates of moving.

Although the percentage of Americans who move has been dropping in recent decades, there was still a substantial proportion—11 percent—who moved in 2016. U.S. Census Bureau data indicated that 42 percent of all individuals who moved stated that they did so to

261. Atkinson, *supra* note 259.

improve their housing. The other most common reasons for moving related to family (27 percent) and employment (20 percent).[262]

For individuals with and without children, most who move do so within the same county. Households with young children move more frequently than those with older children. When children in the household were five years of age and younger, 20 percent moved from 2015 to 2016. In contrast, when the children were ages six through 17 (a much larger number than the five and under group), only 10 percent moved in that same time frame.[263]

This U.S. Census Bureau data is not specific to families of separation or divorce or to parents who never lived with one another. Also, there is no universally agreed-upon distinction between what constitutes relocation versus a shorter-distance, local move. For example, a number of states identify 100 miles and over as the definition of relocation, certain others describe it as a move out of state, and others have more specific definitions. For example, Illinois law defines relocation as a move of 25 miles or more if the initial residence is located within one of the counties that are part of the greater Chicago metropolitan area, and 50 miles if it is in any other part of the state.[264]

Because a tremendous amount of the opposition to relocation has a foundation in the fear and worry of the non-moving parent that his relationship with the child or children will be damaged, it is both emotionally and practically important for those involved in parenting planning to determine if a schedule and other arrangements can be put into effect to protect and facilitate those relationships if the move does take place. Typically, an initial step in this process is to develop feasible options for when quality parenting time can take place for the non-moving parent. For the school-age child, summer, winter, and spring breaks provide opportunities for blocks of consecutive days. Usually, there are a number of long weekends during the school calendar as a result of certain holidays and school institute or staff training days. Regular weekends also need to be considered.

---

262. Press Release, U.S. Census Bureau, Americans Moving at Historically Low Rates (Nov. 16, 2016), http://www.census.gov/newsroom/press-releases/2016/cb16-189.html.

263. U.S. Census Bureau, Table 8. General Mobility of Family Householders, by Type of Household and Presence and Age of Own Children Under 18: 2015 to 2016, http://www.census.gov/data/tables/2016/demo/geographic-mobility/cps-2016.html.

264. 750 Ill. Comp. Stat. 5 § 600(g) (P.A. 99-90, eff. Jan. 1, 2016); William G. Austin, *Relocation, Research, and Forensic Evaluation, Part I: Effects of Residential Mobility on Children of Divorce*, 46 Fam. Ct. Rev. 137 (2008).

Costs, in terms of dollars, time, and child and parent wear and tear, all associated with the transportation required to carry out visits between the child and the non-moving parent, need to be carefully considered. Clearly, the greater the distance, the higher the costs are likely to be. There need to be steps taken to obtain specific estimates of major costs such as airfare or other transportation, hotels, food, gasoline, parent–child activities, and other expenses that may arise. In a number of cases, one or both parents may be able to obtain and develop such estimates. If not, professionals involved in developing a potential parenting plan need to do so to help determine the feasibility of such long-distance parenting options.

It is not useful to devise a relocation parenting plan that ignores the feasibility of costs. However, it is important not to overlook that costs can be shared between the parents, in terms of money, which parent travels, and who transports the child or children. For instance, at times, especially for shorter trips, the father may travel to the area of the relocated residence and visit there. In other instances, the mother can bring the child to the father; during shorter trips, that parent may stay in the area and bring the child back home when the visit is over. Perhaps obviously, the transportation costs can also be divided between parents for longer visits, such as during summer vacation.

Therefore, if circumstances permit, it may be possible to create a schedule in which the child and the father are together for a significant proportion of time. Such a schedule will almost inevitably need to rely on the child spending a lot of their summer vacation with the father. Assuming he is employed, he would need to have secure and supportive child care and/or activities available for when he is working.

For example, it may be possible to create a parenting plan, if there are reasonably cooperative parents and adequate resources, that involves a relocated child and the non-moving parent being together about 110 calendar days, or 30 percent of the time. Such a schedule would rely on the child spending most of the summer with the father (for example, approximately 60 days). The child potentially would be with him about half of the winter and spring school breaks (10 days), and for half of the long weekends created by federal holidays when school is in session (11 days). During the approximately nine months that school tends to be in session, there would be a monthly visit that would involve close to two full days of parenting time on each such occasion (18 days). Many public schools have teacher institute days adjacent to weekends a number of times per year, and if visits were scheduled on three or four such weekends, the final total would approximate 110 days. In addition, there might be periodic opportunities for either parent to take vacation days, travel with or to the relocated child, and provide time for the non-resident parent to be with her or him after school and/or on weekends.

This type of schedule involves considerable travel, and such expenses can be a hurdle and even a barrier to maintaining an active, positive relationship between the child and the non-moving parent. As a result, many parents look into the possibility that travel costs can be diminished by having a child travel unaccompanied, especially by airplane. There are also anecdotes from the past about children even traveling unaccompanied on trains or buses, although that appears to occur far less frequently. There are no clear rules about unaccompanied child airline travel, though there are many personal and circumstantial factors that need to be considered, and due to safety factors, there appears to be extremely little thought currently given to possible unaccompanied travel by train or bus.

Among the many important practical matters to consider is that airlines generally require a child to be at least five years of age to travel unaccompanied, and there are significant fees for an unaccompanied child—most of the major airlines charge in the range of $100 to $150. Other factors of both practical and emotional importance include the risks of significant delays in flight departures and arrivals; the very small but frightening possibility that the arrival airport could be changed; possibly inadequate monitoring of the child by airline staff; child maturity; the necessity of parental diligence in communicating with the other parent, the airline, and preparing the child; and the need for both the departure parent and the arrival parent to be at the airport gates well in advance of the official times. For further information on airplane travel for unaccompanied children, see Appendix B.

Although electronic communication between a child and parent can be relevant for all cases of separation or divorce, it can be especially important when a relocation has caused a decreased frequency and amount of visitation. Parents and children have found parent–child communication with the use of tools such as Skype or FaceTime to be positive and more engaging than simply using the telephone, though parents reportedly tend not to use such methods to communicate with one another. Direct, in-person communication is superior to any type of electronic communication. Electronic communication can be useful to augment in-person parent–child contact but should not be considered as any type of replacement for it.[265]

Research

Across all types of family structures, there is evidence that residential moves are associated with such negative child outcomes as poor academic performance, school dropout, behavioral problems, and substance misuse. In particular, when considering families who have both gone through a separation or divorce and have moved, there is evidence of negative educational outcomes.

In general, these negative effects of moving are attributed to a loss of social capital. The concept of social capital refers to non-financial resources and support available to children from numerous sources. Those sources include immediate and extended family, schools, community organizations, other role models, peer relationships, social networks, and shared values. Human relationships play a central role in social capital, and those relationships that are left behind when a family moves contribute to the loss of social capital and, it is theorized, to the negative effects of moving described earlier.[266]

However, the research that shows such negative effects as a result of residential moves generally combines a number of different types of changes in residential circumstances. Most research tends not to distinguish between the much more common, local area moves and the more long-distance ones that legally are considered relocations. Also, that body of research includes both intact families and separated/divorced ones. Questions have been raised about whether research on the effects of general residential moves are applicable for relocations in separated and divorced families.[267]

Important yet limited relocation research specific to divorced families demonstrates the risk of deteriorated relationships between children and non-moving parents. In one study, when parents moved one hour or more away from one another, the children, when young

265. Richard Wolman & Richard Pomerance, *Telepresence Technology in Divorce and Separation*, 4 Open Access J. Forensic Psychol. 51 (2012).

266. Austin, *supra* note 264.

267. Michael Saini et al., *A Critical Review of Relocation Research Specific to Separation and Divorce*, 56 J. Divorce & Remarriage 388 (2015); Philip M. Stahl, *Emerging Issues in Relocation Cases*, 25 J. Am. Ass'n Matrimonial Law. 425 (2013).

adults, reported that they had experienced higher levels of emotional distress, less parental emotional support, and lower levels of financial support. In a separate study, when a parent moved 75 miles or more away, there was a significant risk of the child's active relationship with the geographically distant parent eventually coming to an end.[268]

It is important to recognize that the negative effects regarding residential moves described earlier may not actually be a result of having moved. For example, it is possible that parents and households with lower levels of individual and interpersonal stability tend both to have more negative child outcomes (though studies generally have not measured pre-move child functioning) and to move more frequently. Similarly, the associations between moving and poorer child adjustment may be mediated by factors such as employment stability or living in neighborhoods with high levels of crime or poverty.[269] In addition, even though a disproportionate number of residential moves take place by families with very young children, there are no outcome data specific to the effects of relocation on that age group.[270] However, the negative effects of residential mobility on child outcomes have been found even when controlling for family incomes.[271]

The limitations in this body of research are likely due at least in part to the reality that relocation cases, while challenging and complex, are not very numerous compared to most other parenting plan disputes. As a result, it is difficult to find suitably large numbers of cases, especially to allow methodological features such as random sampling or assignment to good-quality control or comparison groups. Similarly, it is extremely challenging to track relevant households longitudinally. In that regard, it is crucial to maintain a balanced perspective that such research can be productively informative for the parenting plan process, and yet it also has substantial limitations.

Relatively small-scale, yet informative, qualitative research studies have taken place in Australia, New Zealand, and the United

268. Sanford L. Braver et al., *Relocation of Children after Divorce and Children's Best Interest: New Evidence and Legal Considerations*, 17 J. FAM. PSYCHOL. 206 (2003); MAVIS HETHERINGTON & JOHN KELLY, FOR BETTER OR FOR WORSE 134 (2003).

269. Saini et al., *supra* note 267, at 390.

270. Joan B. Kelly & Michael E. Lamb, *Developmental Issues in Relocation Cases Involving Young Children: When, Whether, and How?* 17 J. FAM. PSYCHOL. 193 (2003), at 193.

271. Austin, *supra* note 264, at 140.

Kingdom. The areas of focus have generally been to obtain information about child and parental perspectives regarding their experiences in relocation disputes and residential moves. That research found that the most common reasons a mother wanted to move was a wish to be near extended family or to be involved in a new romantic relationship. In a number of cases, mothers described that they wished to move at least in part in order to obtain less expensive housing. The extent to which mothers voiced a wish to move partially because of domestic violence or abuse varied a good deal between specific studies. When cases completed trials with judicial decisions, not surprisingly, there was considerable expense for each participant. The cost represented over 100 percent of the average after-tax income at the time of the trial, and a number of participants consequently lost their homes.[272]

Across a number of these studies, when relocation took place, contact between the child, father, and his extended family tended to decrease over time. Parent–child contact diminished because of travel costs, the stresses of travel for children, interparental conflict, or a maternal belief that it was not safe for the child to have contact with the father. In a number of cases, contact between the child and the father ended entirely. In such cases, there tended to be very challenged father–child relationships prior to the relocation, associated with substantial conflicts between the parents. For example, there had been allegations of child abuse or parental alienation. Children who were interviewed tended to vary considerably in their feelings and thoughts about the move, though they generally made good adjustments to the new location. However, a considerable number of children described that they wished to have more extensive relationships with their fathers.[273]

Additional Parenting Plan Considerations

As indicated in a number of statutes, it is important to consider the reasons a parent wishes to move, as well as the reasons the other parent opposes it. An element of such considerations is the potentially moving parent's degree of flexibility and choice. For example, a mother with a good-quality job may need to move in order to maintain her employment position. In such a case, it would be important to examine

272. Patrick Parkinson et al., *Relocation, Research, and Child Custody Disputes*, *in* Parenting Plan Evaluations: Applied Research for the Family Court, 2d ed. 431 (Leslie Drozd et al. eds., 2016).

273. *Id.*

whether she might be able to obtain an equally positive or even better position in the same geographical area, especially if there had been an active and beneficial relationship between the child and the father. In a number of cases, parents have maintained that they need to move in order to be with a new spouse or fiancé. In such an instance, especially if there has been a positive relationship between the child and the father, there needs to be scrutiny into whether the spouse or fiancé may be able to move to the location of the mother. At other times, the mother indicates that a main reason for the move is to be able to be near supportive extended family. However, in a number of such instances, some helpful and sympathetic extended family may be present in the mother's current geographical area, and that possibility should be investigated.

Although it appears not to happen very often, there are cases in which the father moves to the geographical area of the relocated mother and children.[274] There should be deliberation about whether such a move is a viable option in order to promote the benefits of the children having regular contact with both parents.

In some cases, financial and other socioeconomic considerations are central. A potentially moving parent may argue that the reportedly improved income that would accompany the move would benefit the children. In a number of cases, that assertion may be very accurate. However, a close look at such matters is important. For example, a new job with better income might be located in a more densely populated area where housing and other living expenses are generally higher. Consequently, if there were to be a move, it might result in no change in disposable income or even a decrease in it.

In a number of potential relocations, there are disputes about the relative merits and drawbacks of the schools the child would attend in each geographical area. In such a case, a parent might argue that higher standardized test scores or lower teacher–student ratios in the preferred school represent a superior educational opportunity. Similarly, a parent might contend that the preferred school is better because it offers a greater number of gifted or advanced placement classes. In a number of cases, those assertions might be true. However, in some instances, differences in characteristics such as average school test scores, numbers of advanced classes, and teacher–student ratios are not meaningful.

274. *Id.*

For example, a parent might assert that his or her preferred school has only an average of 20 students per class, whereas the one preferred by the other parent has 24. Similarly, a parent might contend that her or his preferred high school is superior because it offers 25 different advanced placement courses, compared to ten by the one favored by the other parent. However, research findings indicate that a difference between 20 and 24 students per classroom does not have a significant impact on student achievement, and only about one-third of high school students take even one advanced placement exam.[275]

In a number of cases, there may be statistically significant differences between schools in outcomes such as average achievement scores. For instance, on the ACT, taken by many high school students for college admission, an average score of 23 is statistically higher than 21, although it is a small effect size.[276] However, when considering how an individual student is likely to fare educationally in one school versus another, it is unlikely that such a difference in average ACT scores is going to make a meaningful difference. Schools that have very high and low average achievement scores tend to have students from families that are relatively wealthy and impoverished, respectively.

One of the most important circumstances to closely examine what a school has to offer is when a child has special educational needs. See Chapter 8 for more detail. Also, in many cases that include a child with very strong academic abilities, parents wish to closely investigate a school's relevant educational offerings. Overall, however, there needs to be an individualized assessment of each child's needs and attitudes, not only in terms of academics but also related matters such as school socioeconomic characteristics and extracurricular activities.

In general, regardless of each student's level of academic ability and achievement, there needs to be individualized assessment and deliberation about each relevant relocation factor and consideration. For good reasons, a number of relocation factors may hold more

---

275. Center for Public Education, *Class Size and Student Achievement: Research Review*, http://www.centerforpubliceducation.org/Main-Menu/Organizing-a-school/Class-size-and-student-achievement-At-a-glance/Class-size-and-student-achievement-Research-review.html; College Board, *10 Years of Advanced Placement Exam Data Show Significant Gains in Access and Success; Areas for Improvement*, https://www.collegeboard.org/releases/2014/class-2013-advanced-placement-results-announced.

276. Jacob Cohen, *A Power Primer*, 112 PSYCHOL. BULL. 155 (1992), at 157.

weight than others, even if they are not given any formal legal priority. For example, if it has been established that the non-resident parent has carried out domestic violence or child abuse, it is sound reasoning that the potentially moving parent would want to avoid and minimize the chances of future dangerous behaviors. Alternately, if it has been established that the potentially moving parent has engaged in significant negative gatekeeping or efforts to alienate the child from the other parent, there is a rational basis for a great deal of concern that a move would damage the relationship between the child and the non-moving parent, and thereby risk the child's well-being. It is reasonable to give a great deal of consideration to the quality of the pre-move relationships between the child and both of the parents, as it is to the likelihood of establishing a realistic and feasible parenting plan that would promote the relationship between the child and the non-moving parent. In particular, especially with very young children, in a potential relocation there needs to be considerable deliberation about whether a move would interfere with the attachment process between the child and the non-moving parent. In such cases, having a solid grasp of facts about marital conflict and domestic violence (Chapters 6 and 7) and regarding very young children (Chapter 5) assists the parenting plan process.

As described earlier, individuals involved in parenting planning need to consider all relevant factors. Though no one can predict the future, especially in light of major circumstantial changes such as a possible relocation, it is essential to closely deliberate about each such factor regarding the likely positive and negative effects on the child. These deliberations need to include close examinations of each parental assertion. Those involved in parenting planning need to include thorough consideration of relevant factors beyond those brought up by the parents, also. This judgment process needs to closely weigh the credibility of each source and to highlight the relatively objective available information.

Crucial factors to consider regarding parenting plans in relocation cases include the following:

- It is necessary to know the local statutory and case law factors, including any presumptions or burdens of proof—have lists of them directly available.
- It is useful to know relocation factors identified in research as important.

- Residential moves occur regularly in families with children, though most are local.
- An important parenting plan consideration is whether a schedule can be put in effect that facilitates a positive relationship between the child and the non-moving parent. In that regard
  - the child's relationship history with both parents needs to be considered, and
  - costs of travel between parents, both in terms of money and time, need to be strongly considered in order to make a parenting plan feasible.
- It may be possible to put in effect a schedule that has a relocated child with the non-resident parent about 30 percent of the time if circumstances permit.
- Electronic parent–child communication should not replace in-person contact but can productively supplement it.
- Research suggests that child residential moves contribute to negative outcomes such as academic, behavioral, and substance misuse problems.
  - However, it may be that preexisting factors, such as parental personal instability, or mediating factors, such as neighborhood quality, contribute to the negative outcomes for children who have experienced residential moves.
  - Other research limitations about child residential moves include a lack of distinctions between long-distance and local moves and between child age groups.
- Children who relocate are at risk of having diminished relationships with the non-moving parent, often due to
  - travel costs,
  - stresses of travel for the child,
  - interparental conflict, and/or
  - the mother's belief that it is dangerous for the child to see the father.
- In a minority of cases, child relocation results in the eventual ending of contact with the non-moving parent, though usually there had been pre-move relationship difficulties.

- Know the relevant general facts and case-specific ones about each area of dispute or concern.
- Include specific steps in the parenting plan process to promote adequate deliberation about relevant parental assertions and relocation factors.

CHAPTER 12
NONTRADITIONAL FAMILIES

The legalization of gay and lesbian marriage in the United States has contributed to an increased focus on the children of these marriages. Gay and lesbian couples with children have had diverse pathways to parenthood. For example, female couples at times rely on sperm donors. Male couples sometimes rely on a surrogate in order to have a child. Other same-sex couples choose to adopt. In addition, in certain cases, the children of same-sex parents were born into heterosexual relationships, including marriages, that dissolved and a parent later entered into a gay or lesbian relationship.[277]

Furthermore, recent decades have brought huge increases in the proportion of individuals in the United States who cohabit but never marry, and many cohabiting adults have children. There are a number of different categories of cohabiting parents. For example, two biological parents may live together instead of getting married. Alternately, either a mother or a father may cohabit with a live-in parent. Parents in some cohabiting families may maintain that type of union long-term, whereas others eventually marry. Live-in parents might have a biological child or children of their own, leading to relatively complex family structures.

For purposes of this chapter, nontraditional families include same-sex parents and never-married parents. Although there are other categories of nontraditional parentage, such as transgender and bisexual, there has been very limited scientific or professional knowledge developed regarding those groups.

---

277. Suzanne M. Johnson et al., *Gay and Lesbian Parents and Their Children*, *in* Parenting Plan Evaluations: Applied Research for the Family Court, 2d ed. 514 (Leslie Drozd et al. eds., 2016).

In this chapter, I first summarize research on children of same-sex parents. Second, I focus on research regarding children of never-married parents. There is an emphasis on psychosocial adjustment both for children of same-sex parents and never-married parents. Third, I describe relevant parenting plan considerations.

Gay and Lesbian Parents

Research on children from lesbian and gay marriages is relatively recent. Much of the research relies on small samples, and multiple studies are limited by a lack of comparison groups. Also, a solid majority of relevant research has been done regarding families headed by lesbian parents. The methodologically superior studies have been able to gather life adjustment data from comparison groups of children from heterosexual marriages.

In general, the research has found a consistent trend that there are no substantial differences in adjustment between children growing up in homes with same-sex parents versus those who have heterosexual parents. For example, no differences have been found in terms of psychological adjustment or school performance.[278] In a study that focused in large part on gay adoptive fathers, children from those families were found to demonstrate less externalizing behavior (e.g., impulsiveness, hyperactivity, aggressiveness) than those from heterosexual adoptive families.[279] There has been very little research conducted on children of families with lesbian or gay parents who have split up. However, one such study found that, when there had been a dissolution of a lesbian relationship, there were no differences in child psychological adjustment between those whose parents did or did not share custody. Similarly, there were no differences in adjustment regardless of whether or not the non-biological parent had adopted the child.[280]

---

278. Hanny Bos et al., *Child Adjustment and Parenting in Planned Lesbian-Parent Families*, 77 AM. J. ORTHOPSYCHIATRY 38 (2007); Jennifer L. Wainwright et al., *Psychological Adjustment, School Outcomes, and Romantic Relationships of Adolescents with Same-Sex Parents*, 75 CHILD DEV. 1886 (2004).

279. Susan Golombok et al., *Adoptive Gay Father Families: Parent-Child Relationships and Children's Psychological Adjustment*, 85 CHILD DEV. 456 (2014).

280. Nanette Gartrell et al., *Family Characteristics, Custody Arrangements, and Adolescent Psychological Well-Being after Lesbian Mothers Break Up*, 60 FAM. REL. 572 (2011).

Never-Married Parents

Cohabiting couples tend to go through multiple family transitions, and there is consistent evidence that children exposed to numerous family changes have, in a number of ways, poorer outcomes than individuals who grow up in households with two biological parents who are married to one another.[281] Cohabiting unions in the United States last for an average of only 18 months. Only about one-third of children born to cohabiting parents remain in stable families through the age of 12, as compared to about three-fourths of those born to married parents. Accordingly, children born to cohabiting parents are about three times more likely to experience a family transition than those born to married parents.[282]

As compared to biological, married parents, cohabiting parents tend to be younger, have lower levels of education, and are about two or three times as likely to be at or below the poverty level. Similarly, cohabiting parents are much less likely to own a home.[283] Unfortunately, there is very little information about never-married parents who also have never resided together.

Associated with the fact that cohabiting parents generally have lower levels of income than do married parents, it is likely that they are among the greatly increased proportion of litigants who are representing themselves. A solid majority of family law cases have at least one pro se litigant.[284]

The stark reality of such a large proportion of self-represented litigants has placed a great deal of stress on the family court system. In about half the family law cases, both parents are representing themselves. Court systems have become increasingly focused on trying to make it easier for pro se litigants to effectively represent themselves, in part through making numerous legal forms and other resources readily

---

281. Edward R. Anderson & Shannon M. Greene, *Beyond Divorce: Research on Children in Repartnered and Remarried Families*, 51 FAM. CT. REV. 119 (2013); Wendy D. Manning, *Cohabitation and Child Well-Being*, 25 FUTURE CHILD. 51 (Fall 2015), https://futureofchildren.princeton.edu/sites/futureofchildren/files/media/marriage_and_child_wellbeing_revisited_25_2_full_journal.pdf.

282. Manning, *supra* note 281, at 54.

283. *Id.*

284. Madelynn Herman, National Center for State Courts, State Court Pro Se Statistics (June 21, 2006), https://www.nacmnet.org/sites/default/files/04Greacen_ProSeStatisticsSummary.pdf.

available.[285] Though such resources can have a clearly beneficial effect, the reality in court is frequently difficult. A presiding domestic relations judge informally noted that pro se litigants often ask him or the opposing attorney, while in court, for assistance in correctly completing legal forms. The challenge of coping with self-represented litigants is particularly high in the numerous cases that include allegations such as domestic violence, other relationship conflict, child abuse, mental health problems, and substance misuse.[286]

Returning to the differences in child outcomes when comparing married to cohabiting parents, they are particularly striking when considering the relationship status at a child's birth. Children born to cohabiting parents exhibit lower levels of physical health, psychological/social health, and cognitive functioning than those born to married parents. These differences between the children of married and cohabiting parents are found in essentially all age groups, through adolescence, though the differences between married stepparents and cohabiting stepparents extend just until adolescence.[287]

Family stability is the central feature of the differences in child adjustment between households with two married parents and other households.[288] However, there are questions about whether the variations in stability cause the differences in child outcomes or whether they are due to other factors.[289]

For example, it may be that individuals who have low levels of personal stability enter into relatively short-lasting relationships, and that

---

285. Nat'l Center for State Courts, *Self-Representation: Resource Guide*, http://www.ncsc.org/Topics/Access-and-Fairness/Self-Representation/Resource-Guide.aspx.

286. Karen S. Adams & Stacy N. Brady, *Fifty Years of Judging in Family Law: The Cleavers Have Left the Building*, 51 FAM. CT. REV. 28 (2013).

287. Manning, *supra* note 281, at 57.

288. Susan L. Brown, *Marriage and the Child Well-Being: Research and Policy Perspectives*, 72 J. MARRIAGE & FAM. 1059 (2010); Paula Fomby & Andrew J. Cherlin, *Family Instability and Child Well-Being*, 72 AM. SOC. REV. 181 (2007); Dohoon Lee & Sara McLanahan, *Family Structure Transitions and Child Development: Instability, Selection, and Population Heterogeneity*, 80 AM. SOC. REV. 738 (2015); Manning, *supra* note 281.

289. Susan L. Brown, *Marriage and the Child Well-Being: Research and Policy Perspectives*, 72 J. MARRIAGE & FAM. 1059 (2010); Paula Fomby & Andrew J. Cherlin, *Family Instability and Child Well-Being*, 72 AM. SOC. REV. 181 (2007); Dohoon Lee & Sara McLanahan, *Family Structure Transitions and Child Development: Instability, Selection, and Population Heterogeneity*, 80 AM. SOC. REV. 738 (2015); Manning, *supra* note 281.

their parenting tends to be flawed, contributing to the decreased child well-being. In addition, as previously noted, cohabiting individuals tend to be younger and are at lower levels of socioeconomic status as compared to married, biological parents. Of course, there may also be a combination of individual, familial, socioeconomic, and other factors that are related to one another and emerge over time in such a way that inhibit positive child development.

In this body of research (which often has focused on lower income families), the theory that the family transitions themselves lead to negative child outcomes is referred to as the instability perspective or hypothesis. The contrasting theory argues that individuals who are healthier, happier, and have more resources make choices to get married and stay with their spouses, leading both to a relative absence of family transitions and children with better life outcomes. This theory is referred to as the selection perspective or hypothesis.

However, there is other scientific evidence that helps explain the reasons that family instability contributes to lower levels of child functioning. As described earlier in this book, research on effective parenting generally shows that it involves a combination of parental affection and support while parents maintain an executive role that includes rules, monitoring, and moderate discipline. Children also benefit from parents who cooperate well with one another, without exposure to significant conflict or dysfunctional parental behavior. Parents who are in a stable marriage with one another are likely to have the resources and motivation to carry out such positive authoritative parenting while simultaneously acting in a reasonably healthy way and not exposing the children to excessive discord. In contrast, high levels of parental conflict, individual distress, and difficulties functioning in the parental role are more likely to be associated with relationship dissolutions and transitions in family structure.[290]

Similarly, the presence of both the mother and the father in the home promotes positive child well-being. Because fathers are less likely to be the primary residential parent in a single-parent family structure, it has been methodologically easier to measure their impact on child functioning, and it has been found to be particularly positive when fathers are residing with children. Also, when two parents live together, there are more financial resources available for the entire family. Many of those financial resources have a direct positive impact

290. Brown, *supra* note 288.

on the children, and they tend to facilitate generally healthy family functioning. In married families with two biological parents, the rate of child poverty is in the single digits, whereas it approaches 50 percent in single-mother families.[291]

Children who grow up in families with two married biological parents manifest the most positive average outcomes. Interestingly, such families have better child outcomes than those with two biological cohabiting parents; similarly, they show better child adjustment than do married stepfamilies.[292]

Family transitions are associated with worse child adjustment, but there are important differences based on race, gender, and the type of transition. For example, the negative impact of family instability is larger for Caucasian families than for other racial and ethnic groups. Although available scientific evidence does not yield a clear reason for this difference, a number of possible explanations have been developed. The larger proportion of racial and ethnic minority families who manifest household instability, compared to Caucasian families, may have contributed toward the creation and greater reliance on extended kinship networks. These networks may help to cushion the negative impact of nuclear family transitions on child well-being. Also, racial and ethnic minority families tend to experience more socioeconomic disadvantage that contributes to worse child outcomes. Such a preexisting disadvantage may decrease the extent to which child adjustment worsens in minorities when a family transition takes place.[293]

Family instability also tends to have a larger effect on boys than girls. The main explanation for this finding is that fathers are much more likely than mothers to move in or out of the family residence. It is assumed that fathers generally are more influential role models for boys than girls, and accordingly, there may be stronger emotional bonds between fathers and male children than female ones. As a result, boys may suffer more stress than girls when a father leaves a residence.[294]

In addition, the effects of family transitions differ depending upon the type of transition. The transitions examined by research are at the parental level and any shifts of children in or out of the residence are not focused upon. In general, perhaps not surprisingly, a transition of

291. *Id.*

292. *Id.*

293. Lee & McLanahan, *supra* note 288.

294. *Id.*

a parent (whether biological, step- or live-in parent) out of a residence has more of a negative impact on child outcome than a transition into a residence. However, it is noteworthy that there is evidence of modestly worsened child adjustment, associated with a parent or parental figure moving into the residence.[295]

In a number of post-decree cases with disputes about parenting time and/or other areas of parental responsibility, a parent who is in a serious romantic relationship considers whether it might help if he or she got married to their partner. Often, in such circumstances, marriage has already been considered and discussed, and it is a matter of whether to get married more quickly. The assumption by that parent, often encouraged by family, friends, and/or the attorney, is that the marriage will make for a more happy and stable family unit and therefore benefit the children. However, in general, there is no evidence that forming such a stepfamily will benefit the children. Most studies have found that children in stepfamilies do not function better than those in single-parent families. The most compelling explanation for this phenomenon is that the addition of a stepparent creates stress for everyone in the family for a period of time. There are numerous adjustments that need to be made, especially as the newlyweds need to focus primarily on their adult relationship in order to make it work successfully, and consequently they may decrease their support or focus on the children. It also commonly occurs that stepparents and stepchildren experience conflict as multiple, emotionally important adjustments are made in the family.[296]

As described earlier, while the negative effects of family instability on children are clear, it can be challenging to try to disentangle the extent to which the family transitions themselves lead to worsened child outcomes, versus how much they might be due to pre-existing characteristics such as the superior personal stability, health, and financial resources of individuals who choose to get married and have children. A research project that made use of two sets of longitudinal data was able to provide useful clarification. The first data set provided information about the parents, though a number of measurements took

---

295. *Id.*; James H. Bray & E. Mavis Hetherington, *Families in Transition: Introduction and Overview*, 7 J. FAM. PSYCHOL. 3 (1993); William H. Jeynes, *The Impact of Parental Remarriage on Children: A Meta-Analysis*, 40 MARRIAGE & FAM. REV. 75 (2007).

296. Lee & McLanahan, *supra* note 288; Fomby & Cherlin, *supra* note 288.

place only of mothers. The second data set had information about the children of those mothers.

For all children, the study looked at cognitive outcomes as measured by academic achievement scores and externalizing behavior such as conduct disorder, hyperactivity, and disobedience. For children ten years of age and older, the study also measured delinquent behaviors. The results found that selection factors, based on the mother's characteristics before having had children, and family transitions after the children were born both had an impact on child outcomes. Family instability led to worse child outcomes. The patterns were somewhat different for African American and Caucasian families. When Caucasian child externalizing problems were examined, higher levels of preexisting maternal self-esteem and education were associated with fewer problems; in contrast, more child behavior problems were associated with the mother having a history of giving birth as a teenager and the number of cohabitation or marital transitions prior to the birth of the child. For African Americans, family instability did not have a significant effect on externalizing problems. When there was a focus on Caucasian child cognitive outcomes, the number of family transitions had essentially no impact, and maternal education and aptitude were positively associated with higher child functioning. In African American children, family instability was largely unrelated to child cognitive outcomes after accounting for preexisting maternal characteristics.[297]

When delinquent behaviors in older children were focused upon, among Caucasian children, there was a significant association between the number of family transitions and more severe problems whether or not maternal preexisting attributes were considered. For example, each added transition was associated with an approximately 12 percent increase in the average level of delinquent behavior. However, among African American children, there was no impact of the number of family transitions on the extent of delinquent behavior.[298]

In addition, the study looked at family structure aside from instability in the family structure. That is, family structures such as cohabitation or single-parent can remain consistent over time or go through transitions. In particular, being raised in mother-only households was associated with worse behavioral and cognitive achievement scores for both African American and Caucasian families, though the effects

297. Fomby & Cherlin, *supra* note 288.

298. *Id.*

were stronger for the current family structure in African American families and early family structure (through age four) in Caucasian families.[299]

Implications for Parenting Plans

For gay and lesbian parents, the main implications for parenting plans pertain to possible changes in sexual preferences and the beliefs of others about same-sex versus heterosexual parentage. For example, even in the United States and numerous other nations where same-sex marriage is legal, there may be individual differences in perspectives regarding whether there are any advantages or disadvantages for children of same-sex versus heterosexual parentage. In certain cases, a parent may be leaving a heterosexual marriage to enter into a gay or lesbian one. In other instances, there may be a breakup of a same-sex marriage, and one of the partners decides to enter into a heterosexual one.

Regardless of the direction of the change, the consistent research findings that there are no general differences in child adjustment between heterosexual marriages and same-sex ones is relevant and important. At the same time, those between-group empirical findings need to be considered in the context of the individual facts and circumstances of each separate case.

The general findings about never-married parents can also be very informative. In particular, the histories of each parent in terms of stability in adult romantic relationships, especially married and cohabiting ones, need to figure strongly in the parenting plan considerations. The reported expectations of each parent regarding future marriage or cohabitation should be additional areas of parenting plan focus.

A history of individual and family stability provides a relatively solid foundation for optimism regarding future child adjustment. In brief, if the relevant histories of both parents appear to be about equal in terms of stability, this realm of concern probably does not need to be focused on at length by those involved in creating a parenting plan. Otherwise, if there is a significant difference between the parents in terms of relationship stability, that difference needs to be strongly considered within the overall configuration of relevant family information.

Because single parents and cohabiting parents tend to have fewer financial resources than married ones, they may be less likely to have

299. *Id.*

an attorney and therefore more likely to be representing themselves. Any attorney who has a pro se adversary has multiple challenges, a number of which pertain to the parenting plan process. A pro se parent is at significant risk of not knowing how to carry out the mechanics of successfully representing oneself, including knowing what forms to use and when, and not having an understanding of the mechanics of submitting and responding to legal pleadings. A number of self-represented litigants appear not to know how to act, or are not motivated to act, in a reasonably respectful and civil manner in court.

Associated with the greatly expanded tendency toward self-representation in recent decades, bar associations and legal news sources have published articles and recommendations for attorneys about the trials of interacting with pro se litigants. In particular, attorneys in small firm and solo general practices who have domestic relations clients in their caseloads are heavily burdened with the frustrations that frequently accompany dealing with self-represented litigants. It is widely acknowledged that the court strives to be flexible with pro se individuals, to the point that many attorneys experience the court as being excessively lenient with them and therefore biased against an attorney who represents a client. In part, although attorneys are expected to follow rules of professional conduct, no such expectation is placed on pro se litigants, including the many who have mainly emotional arguments to make in court. At times, those emotional arguments include directly berating the other parent who is represented by an attorney. Negotiations with pro se litigants are frequently very contentious, especially with an individual who is distrustful of attorneys. However, it can be both productive and reasonably self-protective for an attorney to give a pro se litigant legal information (as opposed to advice), such as relevant statutes, child support guidelines, and court rules. In addition, it can be both productive for the case and self-protective to have a pro se litigant sign a statement of understanding that he or she is clearly aware who the attorney represents and that no legal advice was given by the attorney.[300]

A number of attorneys have recommended a carefully proactive approach in dealing with pro se litigants. It includes sending a letter to the self-represented individual very early in the case that is

---

300. Paula J. Frederick, *Learning to Live with Pro Se Opponents*, GPSolo Magazine (Oct./Nov. 2005), http://www.americanbar.org/content/newsletter/publications/gp_solo_magazine_home/gp_solo_magazine_index/proseopponents.html.

both cordial and professionally informative. That information would include how to find relevant legal sources such as statutes and procedural rules, accompanied by an explanation that the rules must be followed or there is a risk the case may be dismissed. The information to the pro se litigant would also include contact information for the court clerk so that individual knows where to go with questions. In the letter, the attorney would emphasize that she or he is strictly representing her or his own client, and that any and all signs of attorney civility or cordiality should not be interpreted as sympathy toward the pro se litigant's case. In light of the reality that judges routinely need to offer greater flexibility to self-represented individuals, if a complaint arises from such an individual about the attorney, clear indications that such information was sent early in the case can demonstrate that the attorney acted reasonably and did not try to unfairly dominate someone burdened with a lack of background and experience in the law.[301]

Professionals in other roles, such as mediators, evaluators, counselors, and parenting coordinators more routinely interact directly with parents instead of with another professional and are much less frequently in the courtroom. At the same time, for such professionals, it can be a difficult mix that a parent is both a client and is acting as one's own legal representative. Understandably, many pro se litigants seek out information that may be relevant for their cases, and they can direct many questions to professionals who are not attorneys. At times, those questions can, in essence, be requests for legal advice though it may not be entirely clear to the professional on the receiving end of the inquiry. It is always best for such professionals to make sure that they are not giving any type of legal advice. It is both wise and reasonably self-protective to recommend that the pro se litigant get an attorney, if possible to do so, and document in writing that such a recommendation was given.

Central points in this chapter to focus upon include the following:

- Children of same-sex parents generally show no differences in life functioning from those of heterosexual parents.
- Families with two biological parents who are married to one another tend to have good levels of stability and children who function well.

301. Erin Marie Daly, *How to Handle a Pro Se Litigant*, Law360 (Sept. 29, 2010), https://www.law360.com/articles/167015/how-to-handle-a-pro-se-litigant.

- Cohabiting and single-mother families generally show less family stability and less positive child functioning than families with two married biological parents.
- The effects of family stability on child outcomes is partially due to parental characteristics that were present before the child was born, such as
  - psychological health,
  - education level, and
  - socioeconomic status.
- A history of positive personal and family stability provides a more solid foundation for optimism about future child outcomes than does a pattern of past family instability.
- After a remarriage, children often have a significant period of adjustment that may include a decrease in academic achievement.
- Each case must be considered on an individual basis according to multiple individual, family, and circumstantial factors, including comparing histories of family and individual stability.
- Because single and cohabiting parents tend to be of lower socioeconomic status, they may be less able to afford an attorney and are more likely to be self-represented, therefore providing multiple challenges for the legal system.
- Attorneys who have pro se adversaries face multiple challenges during the parenting plan process and may benefit from educating them regarding where and how they may find relevant legal information.
- All professionals must avoid giving self-represented litigants legal advice.

CHAPTER 13

CHILD ABUSE AND NEGLECT

It is self-evident that child abuse and neglect are bad for children. In addition, there is abundant evidence that child abuse and neglect have multiple negative effects on health, including on brain structure, physiological functioning, and psychological well-being.[302] There are no ongoing controversies about the negative effects. So why is there even a need to consider child abuse and neglect in parenting plans?

The answer is that there are a number of content areas pertaining to child abuse and neglect that are not entirely clear and that need to be considered in the parenting plan process. Accordingly, this chapter first briefly summarizes factual information about abuse and neglect. Second, it describes ongoing challenges in determining whether child abuse has actually occurred. Third, considerations about different levels of abuse and neglect are described. Fourth, I review information about recidivism and related material about possible rehabilitation. Finally, I summarize methods designed to keep children safe from harm while also considering the possible benefits of ongoing parental contact.

Rates of child abuse and neglect are generally comparable across the world. Self-reported prevalence rates are much higher than those reported by informant sources such as child protective services agencies. For example, the global prevalence rates based on self-report

---

302. Linda L. Carpenter et al., *Effect of Childhood Emotional Abuse and Age on Cortisol Responsivity in Adulthood*, 66 Biological Psychiatry 69 (2009); Anne-Laura van Harmelen et al., *Reduced Medial Prefrontal Cortex Volume in Adults Reporting Childhood Emotional Maltreatment*, 68 Biological Psychiatry 832 (2010); Philip Yanos et al., *A Prospective Examination of Service Use by Abused and Neglected Children Followed Up into Adulthood*, 61 Psychiatric Services 796 (2010).

were 13 percent for sexual abuse (boys 8 percent, girls 18 percent), 23 percent for physical abuse, 36 percent for emotional abuse, 16 percent for physical neglect, and 18 percent for emotional neglect. In contrast, studies that relied on informant information reported an average prevalence of 0.4 percent for sexual abuse, 0.3 percent for physical abuse, and 0.3 percent for emotional abuse. In part, the much higher prevalence rates in self-reports may reflect that only a small proportion of child maltreatment comes to the attention of relevant authorities, and only a proportion of reported cases are substantiated. At the same time, some of the difference in prevalence rates is due to different measurement time frames. For example, self-report studies characteristically ask individuals if they have ever been the victim of maltreatment at any time during their childhoods, whereas data collected from child protection services and other informants often ask if there had been any such incidents within the past year.[303]

These statistics provide a useful context about child maltreatment generally, but it is important to note that they do not represent incidents that take place only within families, which has the most relevance regarding parenting plans. There appears to be very limited information on maltreatment that is specific to the nuclear family or adult perpetrators residing with the child. Research data collected on intrafamilial abuse includes uncles or brothers as perpetrators (males are by far the most frequent abusers), and the great majority of all such research is focused on sexual abuse. Available reports indicate that about half the sexual abuse of girls and about 10 to 20 percent of boys occurs within families. In approximately one-third of sexual abuse cases, the perpetrator is a minor. In a female sample, 16 percent reported having been the victim of intrafamilial sexual abuse.[304]

There are questions frequently raised about allegations and reports of child abuse and neglect within the context of custody or parenting plan disputes. Research based on Canadian child maltreatment investigations indicated that 13 percent of cases involving a child custody

---

303. Marije Stoltenborgh et al., *The Prevalence of Child Maltreatment across the Globe: Review of a Series of Meta-Analyses*, 24 CHILD ABUSE REV. 37 (2014); Saskia Euser et al., *The Prevalence of Child Maltreatment in the Netherlands over a 5-Year Period*, 37 CHILD ABUSE & NEGLECT 841 (2013).

304. David Finkelhor, *Child Sexual Abuse: Challenges Facing Child Protection and Mental Health Professionals*, *in* CHILDHOOD AND TRAUMA: SEPARATION, ABUSE, WAR 101, 104 (Elizabeth Ullmans & Werner Hilweg eds., 1997).

dispute were found to be unsubstantiated due to a malicious referral as compared to 4 percent of cases without a conflict over child custody. Malicious referrals were "made by disputing parents based on exaggerations fueled by the anger of the parents."[305] At the same time, there was little difference between the two types of cases in terms of the percentages that were substantiated. Specifically, when there was no child custody dispute, 49 percent were substantiated versus 45 percent in cases that included a child custody dispute. In cases that included a child custody dispute, the most common referral sources regarding alleged maltreatment were the custodial parent (24 percent) and the noncustodial parent (19 percent). In contrast, in cases that did not involve a child custody dispute, the custodial parent initiated the referral in 6 percent of cases and the noncustodial parent in 1 percent of the cases. For the most part, there were only relatively modest differences between the two groups in terms of the types of alleged maltreatment. In cases that included child custody conflict, 32 percent focused on possible physical abuse versus 28 percent in cases without custody disputes. There was essentially no difference between the groups (5 versus 6 percent) in terms of an investigative focus on sexual abuse. A smaller proportion of cases was focused on neglect when a child custody dispute was present (23 percent) rather than absent (35 percent).[306] There are no known U.S. child abuse and neglect data that provides comparisons between cases with and without child custody disputes.

Again, this general statistical data is useful, but it is essential to consider each child individually. If child abuse is suspected, there is characteristically a referral to the child protective services agency that decides whether or not to conduct an investigation, perhaps in coordination with the police.

Child Abuse Investigations

A central procedure in child abuse investigations is the child interview. It is characteristically carried out by the child protective services agency and is video recorded. Because of the controversy associated with repeated interviewer errors in past cases that drew considerable media

305. Michael A. Saini et al., *Child Custody Disputes within the Context of Child Protection Investigations: Secondary Analysis of the Canadian Incident Study of Reported Child Abuse and Neglect*, 92 CHILD WELFARE 118 (2013).

306. *Id.* at 115.

attention, there has been considerable focus on understanding the child abuse interview process and what contributed to those mistakes.[307]

Also, there has been a great deal of research with a main goal of developing scientifically based interview techniques that maximize the likelihood of children giving accurate and thorough answers. It culminated in an investigative interview protocol developed through the U.S. National Institute of Child Health and Human Development.[308] There are a number of important interview procedures, including, but not limited to, steps to encourage relatively thorough child responses, an emphasis on asking open questions, and not asking suggestive and yes/no types of questions.

Characteristically, investigative interviewers go through intensive classroom training in such methods and demonstrate that they have acquired relevant knowledge, including improvements in carrying out appropriate procedures in mock training interviews. However, research has repeatedly found that, after a relatively brief time, these trained interviewers tend not to carry out the correct procedures in their fieldwork. Frequent errors included very low proportions of open-ended questions and excessive reliance on yes/no types of questions. Also, an unfortunately high proportion of questions were suggestive. As a result of these findings, further research on training interviewers was conducted.[309]

Those studies found that interviewers, in order to maintain interview quality that increases the likelihood of accurate and thorough answers, need repeated and relatively frequent opportunities to obtain individualized feedback on the quality of their work. The reviews could be from supervisors or colleagues, and there were improvements in interview quality even when the practitioners were focusing on child investigative interviews carried out by others. Because such training can be expensive and agencies often have limited resources, computer-assisted training was focused upon by a number of studies and was found to be productive when there were multiple modules that focused on relevant interview procedures.[310]

---

307. *E.g.*, STEPHEN J. CECI & MAGGIE BRUCK, JEOPARDY IN THE COURTROOM: A SCIENTIFIC ANALYSIS OF CHILDREN'S TESTIMONY (1995).

308. MICHAEL E. LAMB ET AL., TELL ME WHAT HAPPENED (2008).

309. Michael E. Lamb, *Difficulties Translating Research on Forensic Interview Practices to Practitioners: Finding Water, Leading Horses, But Can We Get Them to Drink?* 71 AM. PSYCHOLOGIST 710 (2016).

310. *Id.*

At this point, the reader might wonder about the relevance of investigative training information for parenting plans. Unfortunately, the relevance is that investigative interviews regarding possible child abuse or neglect appear not to be reliably carried out in an effective manner. Often, professionals involved in developing parenting plans look to the local child protective services agency to provide an answer regarding whether abuse or neglect did or did not take place. It can be disappointing and distressing to be burdened with significant doubts about the accuracy of such an answer, but it is better to be aware of this very substantial problem. Interested individuals can determine whether there are any steps they can take, perhaps in conjunction with their colleagues, to facilitate investigative child interviewers having adequate training, in the interests of providing safety and assistance to highly vulnerable children and their families.

Heterogeneity of Abuse and Neglect, Recidivism, and Rehabilitation

There are wide ranges in the severities and frequencies of child abuse and neglect. Substantiated child physical abuse might range in severity from a spanking that was considered excessive to a child having been beaten to death. Neglect might range from a parent having left a child home alone a bit too long during a quick trip to the store to a child suffering from malnutrition or even dying as a result of having been fed inadequately. On the very severe end of the spectrum, sexual abuse can include multiple perpetrator aggressions that are tremendously unwanted, painful, and traumatic both physically and emotionally. On the least severe end of the spectrum, there can be questions about what should be categorized as sexual abuse versus a negative though perhaps less intensive classification, such as harassment. For example, as described by prominent researchers "as a society . . . , we need to decide whether we wish to count an unwanted touch on the buttocks as . . . sexual crime,"[311] such as sexual abuse. At the same time, given that the focus of this book is on what takes place in families, even if such an action were not officially categorized as sexual

311. Andrew J.R. Harris & R. Karl Hanson, Public Safety and Emergency Preparedness Canada, *Sex Offender Recidivism: A Simple Question* (last modified Dec. 15, 2015), https://www.publicsafety.gc.ca/cnt/rsrcs/pblctns/sx-ffndr-rcdvsm/index-en.aspx#a01.

abuse, depending upon circumstantial factors, it could be accurately classified as emotional abuse.

In efforts to create appropriate parenting plans, there are many individual, interpersonal, familial, and circumstantial elements to consider in each case of alleged or actual abuse or neglect. It may not be possible to derive a finite list of such factors and different combinations of them. However, one clearly important dimension is the frequency of abusive or neglectful acts. Perhaps obviously, the more frequent the inappropriate action, the greater the reason for concern for a child's safety and well-being. To some extent, frequency can overlap with other related considerations. For example, a significant proportion of parents who carry out child abuse have also been domestically violent toward their romantic partners,[312] and some of those parents have been also aggressive outside the family. The presence of multiple acts of aggression against numerous people needs to be considered in a light very different from a single instance of having slapped a child. The more physically abusive behavior has been repeated, forceful, coercive, and resulted in injury, the greater the likelihood of future dangerousness and safety risks for children.

As described earlier, there has been much more research information collected about sexual abuse than physical abuse. Accordingly, there is research data available on incest perpetrator recidivism. All the perpetrators were convicted, and the majority were incarcerated; a minority were sentenced to probation or community service. The incest perpetrators had a recidivism rate, based primarily on convictions, of 6 percent over five years. The cumulative recidivism rate over ten and 15 years was 9 and 13 percent, respectively. These rates indicate that if recidivism occurred, it was most likely to have occurred within a few years, and if it did not occur in the first few years, the likelihood of it taking place in later years decreased somewhat. The recidivism rates for incest perpetrators were lower than for other types of sexual offenders, such as extrafamilial child molesters and rapists. Across the different types of sex offenders, there were much higher recidivism rates for individuals who had more than one conviction than for those who had just one (though this comparison was not made specific to incest perpetrators). There were also higher recidivism rates for relatively younger perpetrators and in cases where the victims were male.[313]

312. Appel & Holden, *supra* note 162.
313. Harris & Hanson, *supra* note 311.

There is limited data available regarding child physical abuse recidivism. Available estimates range from 30 to 50 percent.[314]

Of course, all reported recidivism rates depend on relevant authorities knowing about the recurrence of the abusive behavior. Therefore, especially considering the huge differences in prevalence between self-reported abuse and official statistics, the reported recidivism rates may be significant underestimates.

Treatment research has been carried out regarding sex offenders, but there are no known treatment efficacy data specific to incest perpetrators. For sex offenders generally, meta-analyses indicate that treatment, which primarily has involved cognitive behavioral interventions, resulted in modestly decreased recidivism rates. The reported recidivism rates for treated sex offenders have ranged from 10 to 12 percent, and the rates for individuals who did not receive such treatment ranged from 14 to 17 percent.[315]

Also, for persistent sex offenders, generally, who had been incarcerated, and not specific to incest perpetrators, a number of factors were found in a meta-analysis to be statistical predictors of such offenses. Those factors include sexual preoccupation, any deviant sexual interest, general self-regulation problems, and antisocial personality features. A number of perpetrator characteristics frequently focused upon in treatment programs, including treatment motivation, psychological distress, and empathy for victims, were found not to be associated with later recidivism.[316]

In some child maltreatment cases associated with involvement by child protective services, there may be an individual therapist or case manager. A number of such interventions are directed to minors who are sex offenders. However, there are no known studies regarding the

314. Sharon E. Agar, *Manual for the Child Abuse Risk Evaluation (CARE): Professional Guidelines for Assessing Risk of Physical Child Abuse and Neglect*, http://sifer.no/files/CARE_Manual.pdf; Michael S. Wald & Maria Woolverton, *Risk Assessment: The Emperor's New Clothes?*, 69 Child Welfare 483 (1990).

315. R. Karl Hanson et al., *First Report of the Collaborative Outcome Data Project on the Effectiveness of Psychological Treatment for Sex Offenders*, 14 Sexual Abuse: J. Res. & Treatment 169 (2002); Martin Schmucker & Friedrich Losel, *The Effects of Sexual Offender Treatment on Recidivism: An International Meta-Analysis of Sound Quality Evaluations*, 11 J. Experimental Criminology 597 (2015).

316. R. Karl Hanson & Kelly E. Morton-Bourgon, *The Characteristics of Persistent Sexual Offenders: A Meta-Analysis of Recidivism Studies*, 71 J. Consulting & Clinical Psychol. 1154 (2005).

outcomes of individual therapy efforts for adult or minor offenders. It may be that individual therapy for abusers, including approaches such as anger management, are frequently too limited in scope, and broader interventions are needed, as described later.

When abuse or neglect has come to the attention of child protective services, intervention tends to be multifaceted, with a great deal of focus on overall family functioning. Primary goals include improving parent–child interactions and preventing further abuse or neglect. Effective program interventions have included family-level areas of focus such as enhancing supportive parent–child interactions, increasing the use of effective discipline methods, reducing family conflict and social isolation, helping families reduce poverty, and promoting positive social connections and use of community resources. Successful interventions have also entailed improving parental coping and stress management, while also working to reduce parent and child mental and physical health problems.[317]

Multifaceted intervention programs, when directed toward families in which child maltreatment has already taken place, are often called tertiary prevention programs instead of treatment programs. In a number of evaluation studies, tertiary interventions are integrated with secondary prevention programs that are directed toward at-risk populations that have not manifested child maltreatment already.

Two main types of child abuse and neglect prevention programs involve parent education and home visiting. Parent education programs characteristically teach parents child development information, behavior management approaches, healthy coping skills, and problem solving. They are thought to assist families and decrease the risk of maltreatment by increasing relevant knowledge and decreasing parental stress. Home visiting programs tend to work with prenatal women and children up through two years of age as aspects of early intervention efforts. The home visits tend to focus on expanding parenting knowledge and skills, the development of social supports, and fostering healthy parent–child interactions. Home visiting programs generally have fewer efforts

317. U.S. Dep't of Health & Human Services, Administration for Children and Families, Administration on Children, Youth and Families, Children's Bureau, Office on Abuse and Neglect, *Emerging Practices in the Prevention of Child Abuse and Neglect*, https://www.childwelfare.gov/pubPDFs/emerging_practices_report.pdf.

aimed at tertiary prevention as compared to the parent education programs.[318]

There have been two main types of measures used in program evaluations. Impact evaluations assess whether parents appear to have improved their skills consistent with the goals of the program and tend to measure parental knowledge or skill. Outcome evaluations are more directly aimed at trying to measure whether a program reduces the rate of child maltreatment. In general, impact measures are easier to collect and are found more frequently than outcome measures.[319]

A review of parent education programs in North America and Australia found generally positive results. Although only a small number of the programs directly measured child maltreatment, the overall finding was that there were fewer incidents of abuse and neglect in families who had gone through the parent education program that were examined. In terms of the impact measures, there were general improvements in parental knowledge and competency, including the use of appropriate discipline. Effective programs tended to be multifaceted, intensive, and had relatively longer durations, in excess of four to six weeks. Shorter programs and those with a narrower focus were generally less successful.[320]

In carrying out such field research, there is often a trade-off between the elegance of the research design and the applicability of the study to those in the divorce field. For example, there has been particularly well-designed research about the Triple P—Positive Parenting Program, with good evidence of its effectiveness regarding the goals of parenting competency and good parent–job relationships. However, that research has not included the prevention or reduction in child maltreatment as an outcome measure.[321]

A review of established home-visiting programs found positive results in the few cases where child maltreatment outcomes were evaluated. The home-visiting programs also manifested at least partial

---

318. Prue Holzer et al., *The Effectiveness of Parent Education and Home Visiting Child Maltreatment Prevention Programs*, Australian Institute of Family Studies, NCPC No. 24 (Autumn 2006). https://aifs.gov.au/cfca/sites/default/files/publication-documents/issues24.pdf.

319. *Id.*

320. *Id.*

321. *Id.*; Rae Thomas & Melanie J. Zimmer-Gembeck, *Behavioral Outcomes of Parent-Child Interaction Therapy and Triple P—Positive Parenting Program: A Review and Meta-Analysis*, 35 J. Abnormal Child Psychol. 475 (2007).

effectiveness in impact measures such as parental knowledge and skill, and connecting parents to relevant health care services.[322]

Parenting Plan Applications

Individuals who are involved in developing parenting plans generally are not going to be conducting child abuse or neglect evaluations on parenting plan cases. Instead, if there are serious concerns about abuse or neglect, they are likely to make a referral to child protective services. Alternately, that agency might already be involved in an investigation or coordination of services.

At the same time, professionals involved in the parenting plan process might have cases in which there is considerable uncertainty about whether abuse or neglect has taken place. In many such cases, an adequate assessment and services plan may not have been completed, and therefore, there may be very challenging questions about devising a parenting plan that protects a child's safety and well-being while at the same time considers potential child contact with the parent who is under suspicion.

Consequently, it can be very helpful to be aware of the main risk factors that are characteristically considered in child abuse and neglect. A significant proportion of abusive parents carry out more than one type of abuse; therefore, the risk factors to be assessed are generally relevant for both physically and sexually abusive actions. The presence of any or all of these risk factors by no means is proof that an individual has engaged in child abuse or neglect. However, the more these risk factors are present, the greater the reason there is for concern that highly inappropriate and even damaging behavior toward a child may take place. Under circumstances of significant concern and uncertainty about the child, professionals involved in parenting planning would do well to seriously consider these parental, family, child, and social/community factors in their deliberations.

Risk factors regarding individual parents include a history of abusive or neglectful behavior toward a child, a history of having carried out domestic violence, significant limits in parenting competency, a troubled relationship with the child, parental attitudes that justify child maltreatment, serious mental health problems, substance abuse or dependence, suicidal or violent ideation, and a history of child abuse and/or neglect in the family of origin. The risks are also somewhat

322. Holzer, *supra* note 318.

higher for demographic characteristics such as younger age, low level of education, low income, single parenthood, and a large number of dependent children.[323]

Children three years of age and younger have the highest rates of victimization, and the greatest risk is for those less than one year of age. In addition, particularly vulnerable children who may have a developmental disability, mental health problem, or serious medical condition are at increased risk for victimization.[324]

At the family level, risk factors include high levels of stress associated with parenting, intimate partner violence, family disorganization, and having a non-relative (e.g., mother's male partner) reside in the home. Social/community risk factors include social isolation, high rates of violence, and characteristics of economic disadvantage such as high levels of unemployment and poverty.[325]

For any professional involved in developing a parenting plan when there is ongoing uncertainty about whether abuse or neglect has occurred, the focus is likely to include devising at least an interim parenting plan that can effectively protect the child while also fostering positive, safe interactions with the parents. The risk factors described previously should be seriously considered—the higher the number of risk factors that are present, the greater the need for caution about child safety.

Each individual involved in parenting plan development will need to learn where child maltreatment prevention and related parenting programs are available in their local areas. Sources of information about such programs include the local child protective services office, social service agencies, and community mental health centers. Efforts should be made to determine whether local programs have a demonstrated level of effectiveness.

A number of options may need to be considered. Efforts to focus on child safety frequently consider methods such as visitation supervision, restriction of the amount of parenting time, and depending upon

323. Centers for Disease Control and Prevention, *Child Abuse and Neglect: Risk and Protective Factors* (last updated Apr. 18, 2017), https://www.cdc.gov/violenceprevention/childmaltreatment/riskprotectivefactors.html; U.S. Dep't of Health & Human Services, Administration for Children and Families, Administration on Children, Youth, and Families, Youth and Families, Children's Bureau, *Child Maltreatment 2014*, https://www.acf.hhs.gov/sites/default/files/cb/cm2014.pdf.

324. *Id.*

325. *Id.*

the circumstances, consideration of no parent–child contact, at least for a period of time. Higher levels of concern about child safety and well-being necessitate strong consideration given to more stringent means of restricting visits.

Supervision, perhaps the most common tool to restrict parenting time, can take a number of forms. In many cases, a family member or friend is designated as the visitation supervisor, at times because of financial constraints. In order to seriously consider relying on a family member or friend, there needs to be sound reasons for trust that the supervised parent and the supervisor will fully cooperate with the requirements, which need to be specified. Other supervision options include private agencies or individuals who carry out the service for a fee. A number of jurisdictions have a supervised visitation center with experienced supervisory staff who complete reports for each visit.

Perhaps obviously, suspension of visits should occur only when there is no better option. It might be necessary if a child appears very frightened or perhaps even traumatized by the prospects of spending time directly with the allegedly abusive or neglectful parent. It might also be necessary if a parent has demonstrated a serious lack of cooperation with supervised visits, such that there is reason to worry that the child might be endangered if visits continue.

Often, a requirement for supervision by itself will restrict the amount of time the child can spend with the supervised parent. There are often significant limitations in the supervisor's available time, and a requirement for fee payment has a tendency to significantly limit the number of hours that visitation can take place.

Depending upon the circumstances, electronic methods such as FaceTime, Skype, or even regular telephone can increase the amount of contact between the child and the supervised parent. In such cases, that electronic communication is characteristically supervised by the parent with whom the child is residing.

In certain cases that have allegations of child abuse or neglect, there is a search for options other than supervised visitation or suspended visits. However, while factors such as the extent, frequency, and recency of abuse/neglect need to be considered, child safety must be a priority, and options that do not clearly protect the child have to be considered with a great deal of caution.

When there has been child neglect but no abuse, depending upon the specifics of the neglect that has taken place, unsupervised visits between the child and the parent who carried out the neglect may be appropriate. For example, if a parent was identified as having been neglectful because of a severely substandard residence but otherwise shows adequate parental judgment and impulse control, and the parent–child relationship is positive, frequent unsupervised visits can be considered. The visits likely can be augmented by unsupervised electronic communication. In contrast, if the neglect included inadequate provisions of safety, such as a parent not monitoring young children closely enough to prevent them from dangerous actions such as running out into the street, supervision of visits is needed.

In certain abuse cases, questions have been raised about possibly unsupervised electronic communication. In some circumstances, such as a parent having been found to engage in physical abuse because of instances of excessive physical discipline, while concurrently, the overall parent–child relationship primarily has been positive, it has been argued that unsupervised electronic communication poses no risk at all because the parent cannot possibly carry out any inappropriate physical action during such communication. At the same time, consideration needs to be given to whether the child might experience fear or any other negative emotional reaction under such circumstances. In such cases, there needs to be thorough collection of relevant information and careful deliberation about the potential risks and benefits for the child, with safety as a priority.

Supervision carried out by a professional agency is likely to be more consistently structured and controlled, including clear rules, than when it is carried out by a family member or friend. When parenting plan professionals arrange for supervision by family or a friend, it is wise to have such supervisors sign an agreement that spells out certain behavioral requirements. For example, that agreement would specify the reasons the court was requiring supervision, and it would list rules for the supervisee and the supervisor. Rules for the supervised parent characteristically include that there would be no communication between the child and parent that cannot be observed by the supervisor, no alcohol consumption during the visit or 24 hours prior to it, and no corporal punishment. Rules for the supervisor would include that he or she maintain close direct contact with the child and parent; that there is no discussion regarding any court-related matter, regarding the other parent, or about anything having to do with the other household; and that designated visitation start and stop times be followed. Other specific provisions for the supervised parent or the supervisor might need to be added depending upon the specifics of the case.[326]

Of course, though child abuse and neglect do take place in a number of parenting plan disputes, in other cases a parent might make a false accusation. Certain false accusations might be purposeful, malicious, and made in the interests of a parent trying to obtain an advantage in court proceedings. Other false accusations can be mistakes, in which a parent might fully believe his or her allegations that the other parent has been abusive or neglectful.

Individuals involved in parenting planning under such conditions of uncertainty need to consider multiple possibilities; for example, that a parent accused of abuse actually carried out such action, that the accusing parent was sincere but mistaken in her or his allegations, and that the accusing parent intentionally invented false allegations. There needs to be careful deliberation about each of these possibilities, including a diligent search of available case information that provides indications for and against relevant, multiple hypotheses. Recording such information on forms that use a pro–con format can be very productive, along with highlighting relatively objective evidence. This deliberative process can contribute a great deal toward a well-considered, rational parenting plan developed under extremely challenging circumstances.

If such a parenting plan needs to be an interim one, greater clarity about the case may emerge through an official investigation. Of course, if no agreement can be worked out, there will likely need to be an eventual judicial ruling about the parenting plan.

Central points about the material in this chapter include the following:

- It is important for professionals involved in parenting plans to be aware of basic facts about child abuse and neglect.
- In order for child abuse/neglect investigative interviews to be effective, they require frequent, repeated training focused on interviewers receiving individualized feedback about their work quality.

326. *E.g.*, Tarrant County (TX) Domestic Relations Office, *Non-professional Supervisor's Statement of Responsibility*, http://www.texascounseling.org/Forms/DRO-form.pdf.

- Because interviewers very seldom receive the training just described, there are major questions about how often such interviews obtain correct information, and therefore considerable reason for doubt about the accuracy of the conclusions of many investigations.
- There is a good deal of heterogeneity in child abuse/neglect intensities, frequencies, types, and circumstances.
- Risk factors for child abuse and neglect include parents having
  - a history of child abuse or neglect;
  - a history of having carried out domestic violence;
  - serious mental health problems;
  - substance abuse or dependence;
  - suicidal or violent ideation;
  - attitudes that justify child maltreatment;
  - serious limits in parenting ability;
  - a difficult relationship with the child;
  - child abuse/neglect in the family of origin;
  - social isolation;
  - high levels of stress associated with parenting;
  - demographic characteristics such as
    - relatively young age,
    - a large number of dependent children,
    - single parenthood, and/or
    - lower socioeconomic status;
  - community characteristics such as
    - a high rate of violence and/or
    - high levels of poverty and unemployment.
- When there is uncertainty about whether abuse/neglect has occurred and professionals need to develop a parenting plan, it is essential to be cognizant that risk factors do not prove the presence or absence of abuse or neglect, but they should be carefully considered because each factor is statistically associated with increased risk.

- Individuals involved in the parenting plan process need to have a primary goal of balancing the safety and well-being of the child with the promotion of healthy parent–child interactions.
- Those involved in parenting plan development may need to consider treatment or tertiary prevention programs—efforts should be made to find local ones that have empirical support.

CHAPTER 14
PRACTICAL CONSIDERATIONS

This chapter focuses on practical matters that pertain to parenting plans. However, the contents also have a great deal of relevance for family emotional and physical functioning. The factors described here pertain to many day-to-day realities for families, professionals, or both.

Multiple content areas are described in this chapter. Topics that are most closely related to time-sharing schedules are covered in Chapter 15.

This chapter covers a larger number of content areas than the prior ones. Initially, there are relatively brief sections on reported parental histories, remarriage, decision making, and child safety and health. The next relatively long section pertains to concerns about children's transitions. Afterward, there are sections on child-focused calendars, interparental communication, judicial interviewing of children, court-involved therapy, and parenting plan contents.

Reports of Parenting History

The majority of state statutes that pertain to the best interest of the child include a factor that describes the degree to which each parent has provided care to the child in the past. A number of states include similar considerations about past decision making. These factors are usually accompanied by other multiple criteria.

It is important to be aware that many parents do not agree on what has been the past history of taking care of the children. Multiple sources of research, from both divorcing and intact marriages, indicate that wives and husbands give generally divergent reports about their past patterns of child caretaking, decision making, and other household matters. In one study of couples in custody disputes that used broad, presumably easy to reach criteria of agreement about child caretaking activity, only 9 percent of the parents were in agreement with one another. It may be that this phenomenon is due both to each parent having honestly different perspectives and, at least in some cases, active efforts to place oneself in a more positive light than the other parent. There are other independent studies that consistently show married couples giving very different reports about involvement with children and household tasks.[327]

Reliance on reports of past caretaking, at least in some instances, appears to have had a negative effect on many cases with parenting plan disputes. For example, there is evidence that parental awareness of the legal system looking at past caretaking behaviors has led to increased competition about involvement with the children and, consequently, heightened conflict. The increased conflict has occurred in multiple areas, such as parental attempts to change the time and/or activities with the children, resulting in open conflict. There also had been an increase in parents having called the police about altercations.[328] Furthermore, a separate study indicated that attorneys had given frequent advice to divorce litigants to arrange circumstances so that their interactions with the children were especially likely to be observed by others or recorded in a publicly available document.[329]

The basic relevance of this information for parenting plans is that parental reports of past caretaking and decision making may be quite flawed. Professionals involved in receiving and assessing such reports of past behavior may wish to try to gain more objective views in each case, if possible. It is also important to remain cognizant that the amount of time a parent spends with the child is not determinative of the emotional security of that relationship, as described in more detail in Chapter 5. While professionals need to consider statutory factors that include past caretaking and/or decision making, they also need to deliberate about the reliability of parental reports.

Remarriage

When there are disagreements about parenting time or decision making in post-decree cases, and one of the parents is in a serious romantic

327. EVALUATION, *supra* note 1, at 23.

328. *Id.* at 31.

329. Gaia Bernstein & Zvi Triger, *Over-Parenting*, 44 U.C. DAVIS L. REV. 1221 (2010), at 1245.

relationship, there are instances in which serious consideration is given to getting remarried. Of course, in some post-decree cases a parent has already gotten remarried. Often, parents and attorneys believe that the remarriage offers a higher quality family setting than that of a single parent. In certain cases, a parent or attorney expects that an advantage in court may be gained in a parenting plan dispute if a remarriage takes place prior to the final resolution of the case in that it will create an impression of a solid and stable family.

However, there is consistent research data that indicates that children experience decreases in well-being after their parents remarry. Much of the research has been focused on approximately two years after the remarriage has occurred.

More specifically, in stepfamilies, relationships between parents and children tend to be less positive than in first-marriage families, particularly in terms of being conflicted and emotionally distant. Those negative characteristics tend to be more prominent for stepparent–child interactions than the relationships between biological parents and child, though they can occur for both.

In addition, children in stepfamilies were found to manifest mildly lower levels of academic achievement than those from intact families and single-parent families. Similarly, children from stepfamilies had slightly lower levels of psychological adjustment than children from intact families.[330]

In general, the lower levels of functioning by children in stepfamilies is attributed to emotional and practical challenges faced especially by parents in the early years after a remarriage. There is a strong need for remarried adults to focus a great deal on their relationship with one another in order to make the marriage work satisfactorily. Consequently, there may be considerably less attention directed to the children during those early years, including decreased levels of child management. In addition, the need for each parent to attend to the interactions with the new spouse can detract from the quality of the emotional tie with the biological children, and there are frequent conflicts about both supportive and authoritative actions by parents toward their stepchildren.

There is much more to be learned about the psychological and interpersonal lives within stepfamilies. However, it would clearly be a

330. Bray & Hetherington, *supra* note 295; Jeynes, *supra* note 295; Lee & McLanahan, *supra* note 288.

mistake for individuals involved in the parenting plan process to assume that a remarriage is going to supply the children with a more emotionally stable and secure family environment. As with other important family features, professionals involved in parenting planning need to look closely at the characteristics of each parent and child. For example, certain remarried parents may have a history of general relationship stability, whereas there is greater reason for caution about parents who may have had multiple prior marriages or cohabitation relationships.

Decision Making

Although parenting time often takes up most of the attention in the parenting plan process, decision making is also of the utmost importance. As noted previously, the main decision-making categories generally include education, health care, religion, and extracurricular activities. When looking to devise a parenting plan with appropriate decision making that fits well for each couple and family, it is helpful to first consider whether it is the initial time a decision-making format is being developed, or whether there has been one in place and there have been difficulties associated with it, leading to considerations about possible revisions. Of course, no one is able to make accurate predictions about the future, but there are a number of factors to examine to try to determine if shared decision making is likely to be successful.

When parenting plan efforts examine decision making for the first time, an initial step is to closely examine the couple's decision-making history about the children, to the extent it can be reliably determined. As noted earlier, parents may have very different reports about their history together, and a number of parents may have purposely changed their behaviors related to decision making in anticipation of a probable divorce and related litigation. Therefore, as part of the assessment to collect information regarding an eventual parenting plan, it is necessary to try to ascertain what had been the long-term decision-making history over a number of years. Also, it is important to try to establish the extent to which the couple engaged in cooperation versus conflict in the decision-making process. Even beyond the realm of decisions about the children, the ability of the couple to generally communicate well and cooperate with one another is relevant.

Though both parents can make substantial contributions to a pattern of high conflict and poor communication, in a number of high-conflict cases one parent has been the main cause of it. The individual who initiated most of the discord created a serious risk of a harmful emotional impact on children who were exposed to it. That reality needs to be strongly considered in the parenting plan development.

In numerous cases, shared decision making had previously been established as part of the parenting plan, but the parents had recurring problems making decisions together. These problems can occur for a number of reasons, including that shared decision making was initially decided upon largely to get the couple to arrive at an agreement and to end the case. In other cases, situational factors may have contributed to increased anger and decreased cooperation between divorced parents. For example, one of the parents may have decided to get remarried or to live with a romantic partner, which caused the other parent emotional challenges and painful memories, and consequently the previous pattern of good cooperation deteriorated. Alternately, circumstances pertaining to the child, such as academic problems, may have led the parents to vigorous disagreements regarding what to do about them, and they veer into a general pattern of energetic conflict and lessened cooperation.

When there has been regression from a previously adequate history of cooperation, problem-solving interventions may be able to help the couple get back on the track of working with one another reasonably well. Parent coordination, mediation, or counseling should be considered. A change to communication by e-mail or text only, at least temporarily, may help to improve the emotional tone of interactions and promote parents being cognizant of the necessity of civility and a businesslike focus on what is best for the child. Somewhat similarly, problem-solving interventions may help the parents engage in productive negotiations with one another, such as each proposing a number of potential options to address their difficulties and sharing opinions about the pluses and minuses of each one.

In certain cases, depending upon the specific family circumstances and dynamics, it may be useful to consider giving one parent sole decision-making ability over one or more of the major areas while the other parent has sole decision-making responsibility over the other areas. It is possible that, for some decision-making categories, parents may be able to successfully share the responsibility, whereas for other areas, one parent may have sole authority. Such an arrangement may be especially worth considering when a parent has demonstrated particular strength or weakness in a decision-making realm.

In those cases in which parents have successfully carried out shared parenting for a period of time only to later backtrack into inadequately cooperating with one another, it is essential to investigate the reasons for that regression. If it is determined that one parent is primarily responsible for the heightened conflict and deteriorated collaboration, that assessment needs to inform a revised parenting plan in which the other parent will need to be very strongly considered for having sole decision making responsibility.

As described earlier, parents need to have histories of positive coparenting, mutual trust, and productive ways of dealing with conflict in order to have shared decision making be successful. When it is unsuccessful, it provides a platform for potentially exposing children to interparental conflict, thereby placing their emotional health at risk. When decision making responsibility is shared, it is simply not possible for parents to disengage from one another in instances when decisions must be made, unless one parent simply abdicates that responsibility, which rarely occurs. The higher the levels of interparental conflict and the longer its duration, the more likely it is that the parenting plan will need to rely on sole decision making.

It is important for all professionals involved in parenting plans to be aware that a decision for sole decision making does not need to be accompanied by a low proportion of parenting time for the individual who does not obtain legal decision-making responsibility. Children benefit from regular contact with both parents. Numerous parents have not been able to cooperate consistently and effectively with one another, which makes them at risk of not being able to share decision-making successfully, yet they are each able to engage in stable parallel parenting without excessively exposing the children to conflict.

In order to arrive at reasoned judgments about decision making, individuals involved in parenting plan creation need to deliberate carefully about competing parental assertions and available objective evidence. The use of pro–con lists as described in Chapter 3, informed by the contents on conflictual couples in Chapters 6 and 7, is a productive method of carrying it out.

Child Safety

A number of factors related to safety and physical health have been described in prior chapters, such as the importance of examining whether a parent can provide safe and competent care for a child and the negative impact of smoking on child physical health. There are also other safety factors that need to be considered in parenting plans that promote the child's best interest.

A leading cause of death in young children is unintentional injury. The leading causes of injury deaths for very young children are suffocation and drowning. Most injuries that result in death for older children are the consequence of motor vehicle accidents. A number of structural and environmental interventions by parents can greatly decrease the risk of death or serious injury. For example, child car seats, bicycle helmets, and smoke alarms are effective preventive measures.[331]

Parents also need to carry out reasonable diligence in monitoring young children. Infants through preschoolers require essentially constant monitoring and supervision during waking hours. Early elementary school children require very close supervision, and the need is high for risky situations such as being in close proximity to a street, as young children are generally unable to adequately make judgments about traffic.[332]

A large proportion of divorcing families have very young children who require car seats. Excellent information about car seat requirements, installation, and usage is provided by the American Academy of Pediatrics.[333] Of course, it is easiest if each parent can simply buy and correctly install their own car seats, as well as ensuring that each child is safely buckled in for each ride. However, many young couples who have split up are short on money, and they need to share a car seat for use in both their vehicles. The car seat can become one of many topics for conflict.

Professionals involved in the development of parenting plans need to consider safety factors for each separate case. For example, if a parent has a history of multiple motor vehicle accidents, especially if any have taken place with a child in the car, the relative risks between parents for future child injury need to be closely considered. In certain

---

331. Daniel J. Hynan, *Child Health and Safety Factors in Custody Evaluations*, 2 J. FORENSIC PSYCHOL. PRAC. 73 (2002).

332. Lawrence Peterson et al., *Judgment Regarding Appropriate Child Supervision to Prevent Injury: The Role of Environmental Risk and Child Age*. 64 CHILD DEV. 934 (1993).

333. American Academy of Pediatrics, *Car Seats: Information for Families* (Feb. 7, 2017), https://www.healthychildren.org/English/safety-prevention/on-the-go/Pages/Car-Safety-Seats-Information-for-Families.aspx.

cases, routine professional procedures may need to be altered to gain relevant information. For example, at times, worry is expressed about a firearm or other type of weapon that reportedly is in a residence, whether or not it is adequately secured, and the consequent risk for children. Regarding very young children, parents at times assert that the other parent does not have adequate childproofing in the home. If physical safety in one or both of the home environments is raised as a cause for concern, for any of a variety of reasons, home visits are likely necessary, at times with specific areas of particular focus.

Concerns are often expressed that when a home visit is scheduled at a specific date and time, it simply gives a parent an opportunity to arrange the residence in a way that is expected to meet with approval. However, on occasion, professionals have had parents supply them with information about when they are generally available at home, and then tell parents that an unscheduled visit is likely to occur.

A broad range of other safety-oriented matters can also emerge as causes for concern and argument. Information about many safety procedures can be found on the Safe Kids Worldwide website.[334]

In most cases, safety matters do not play a major role in the planning process. However, in a considerable proportion of high-conflict couples, disputes about safety matters are prominent. When they occur, there needs to be a section of the parenting plan that covers how relevant safety concerns are to be managed by the parents. For example, if there have been significant conflicts about childproofing one or both residences, the relevant parenting plan section would describe that each parent needs to have present in the residence child safety apparatuses in accordance with recommendations of the American Academy of Pediatrics[335] or the Safe Kids Worldwide organization.[336] Similarly, if there had been conflict about one or more firearms in the residences, there would be a parenting plan provision that any firearm needs to be kept locked in accordance with the recommendations of the Law Center to Prevent Gun Violence.[337] The parenting plan might also need to include a provision that, if a violation of safety provisions were found, it would be considered adequate legal grounds for the

334. Safe Kids Worldwide, *Safety Tips* (2016), https://www.safekids.org/safetytips.

335. American Academy of Pediatrics, *supra*, note 333.

336. Safe Kids Worldwide, *supra*, note 334.

337. Law Center to Prevent Gun Violence, *Safe Storage* (2017), http://smartgunlaws.org/gun-laws/policy-areas/child-consumer-safety/safe-storage/.

aggrieved parent to pursue modification of the allocation of parental responsibility.

Children Going between Households

In addition to the safety concerns described previously, parents often have worries about the physical and emotional health of their children when they are with the other parent. In many cases, there are concerns about child exchanges and children's emotional reactions to them.

Many overwhelming parental concerns pertain to infants and other very young children. In many cases, the parents have had their firstborn and are experiencing both the wonder and worries associated with that emotionally and physically challenging new world. Reality can be at times overwhelming for new parents, even when they have had a very good relationship with one another and their marriage is intact. When a couple has had a child together and separated, or perhaps never even lived together, the practical and emotional challenges are greatly magnified.

As described at more length in Chapter 5, the primary goal is that infants are safe and well cared for when with either parent or another caregiver. If both parents have had a good amount of experience competently caring for an infant, and each parent recognizes the other's ability to provide consistently positive care, there is not likely to be any concern or controversy. In contrast, if one of the parents is not experienced and clearly competent, that individual needs to learn through coaching and supervision. A grandparent or other relative often fills the role of coach and supervisor.

The younger the child, the greater is the necessary focus on basic physical needs. For infants, it is paramount that each parent be competent in feeding, diapering, soothing, bathing, and being able to follow a routine that includes the sleep cycle. Any parenting supervision for an infant is most likely to focus on one or all of those functions. If one parent is the primary caregiver, it is most likely to be the mother, and she will need to provide the father and his coach/supervisor, if there is one, with a schedule of the infant's routine. Both parents of infants should keep a record of feeding, elimination, sleeping, bathing, and any new developments, and give it to the other parent upon the child's return. The primary care parent should be able to receive basic information from the supervisor about the other parent's progress. Parenting plans should build in record-keeping exchanges as required provisions for this age group.

Child exchanges are extremely important, not only logistically but emotionally. It is often stressful for children and parents for the children to go back and forth between households, and a substantial proportion of interparental disputes include matters associated with transitions. Children generally suffer from exposure to conflict between the parents more than any other divorce-related factor.

When children have acquired adequate verbal skills, it is important for parents to prepare them for transitions. Steps include letting the children know that the transition is soon to occur, talking about the other parent in positive terms, and giving children a reminder that telephone or FaceTime communication can occur while they are with the other parent. Also, the parent can remind the children that they will return in a fairly short time and provide transitional objects such as favorite stuffed animals or toys to bring to the other household.

In addition to having children in a positive state of mind about the transition, the parent who is getting them ready needs to provide an appropriate activity. If the parent has children carrying out a favorite activity at the time the exchange is scheduled to occur, it can interfere with their willingness to go with the other parent. In a number of cases, a parent who has had difficulty getting the children to accompany him or her has accused the other parent of purposely setting up an activity that the children resist leaving in order to create a barrier to the transition. At the same time, it does not help to just have children look out the window waiting for the other parent to arrive, as very young children have not developed an adequate sense of time and tend to have very limited stores of patience. An activity that is mildly interesting for the children may provide optimal circumstances for waiting for the other parent to arrive, while at the same time setting the stage for a willing departure.

In some cases, parents get into conflict about the timing of exchanges, especially if one perceives the other to be frequently late, either in having the child ready or in picking up. There can also be controversy over the child's belongings. Therefore, in addition to directly preparing a child psychologically for the exchange, a parent needs to prepare logistically, with a focus on numerous details, including being on time. Older, experienced children should be able to help to some extent in these preparations; very young children may succeed only in getting in the way and slowing things down.

There should be a parenting plan provision for what materials accompany the child from one residence to the other if there has been prior conflict or controversy about it.[338] It can be very useful to have a designated bag that accompanies the child during any exchange to make it easy for the receiving parent to find whatever belongings might be needed. For infants, diapers, clothing, and expressed breast milk or formula are items that routinely are packed in such a bag. For older children, designated exchange bags may include items such as phones, phone chargers, sports equipment, clothing, paperwork for the other parent to read or sign, medication, and/or orthodontic retainers. Athough a parent should not have a child convey personal notes or any material of a potentially contentious nature to the other parent, if both agree, it can be fine for the designated transition bag to include written communications that pertain to the business of coordinating between households. Often, for school-age children, it is easiest for them to also bring their school backpacks between households.

For children who are undergoing toilet training, going back and forth between two households can be a unique challenge, and it can be very helpful for parents to communicate routinely with one another about their efforts and the child's response. Also, it may be useful for a child to have the same type of potty chair in each home.[339]

After children have been transported to the home of the parent who is starting a period of parenting time, a wind down or reentry time when the child may be alone or otherwise engaging in relaxing activity often helps with the adjustment. It may take periods of observation and conversations with the child to determine a successful wind down routine, and it may need to change as the child gets older. It may be essential for some children and unnecessary for others, depending in part on temperament and prior experiences.

Many young children experience a degree of distress during transitions that can be of concern to both parents. In many such cases, each parent blames the other for the child being upset. If a parent perceives that the child is distressed before and during the time that the child is being handed over to the other parent, there may be an assumption that the receiving parent is incompetent or perhaps even abusive or neglectful. If the receiving parent views the child as being upset when he or she is receiving the child, there is frequently an

338. RICCI, *supra* note 3, at 191.

339. JOHN HARTSON & BRENDA PAYNE, CREATING EFFECTIVE PARENTING PLANS: A DEVELOPMENTAL APPROACH FOR LAWYERS AND DIVORCE PROFESSIONALS 53 (2006).

assumption that the other parent is doing something wrong, such as trying to turn the child against the receiving parent. In the majority of these cases, the child rather quickly becomes calm and content a very short while after the transition has been completed. In a number of instances, the receiving parent can provide reassurance to the other parent that the child is fine soon after the exchange by taking a photo or brief video and sending it by text. It is also important to keep in mind that infants, around the middle of their first year, normally manifest anxiety about separations and regarding strangers.

However, there are children who appear to regress or develop problems, and either parent or both parents might wonder if such difficulties are a result of the separation or whether an aspect of the time-sharing routine does not allow for adequate security and stability. It is often difficult to assess whether or not a child is experiencing a real problem. It is important to rely on appropriate medical or mental health professionals in this regard, though an element of uncertainty can persist even after such consultations have taken place.

Separated parents often disagree about the child's condition. Especially when parents have had substantial conflict with one another, there have been many cases in which one parent asserts that the child is not functioning well, especially after a return from the home of the other parent. Characteristically, that other parent maintains that the child has been perfectly fine when with him or her. In addition, children can differ from one another in temperament, which needs to be considered as part of the assessment of possible child dysfunction.

To further complicate matters, young children can go through phases in which they appear upset or display increased problems, such as crying or tantrums, only to have those behaviors dissipate a relatively short time later for no apparent reason. Also, child behavior problems can occur in all families, whether or not there has been a divorce and regardless of any parenting time schedule.

However, it is important to stay attentive to whether a child may be experiencing difficulties associated with elements of the parenting plan, while remaining cognizant that there is no list of behaviors or symptoms that proves a child is having problems caused by the divorce or parenting plan. The types of behavioral problems manifested by a child can differ to some extent depending upon age and stage of development. In very young children, including infants, there may be regression from their characteristic eating, sleeping, or elimination routines. A child may show signs of distress such as tearfulness or irritability. Toddlers may manifest sluggishness, regression in their play, aggression toward others or oneself, increased oppositional behavior and a number of the behaviors described about infants.[340]

Young children beyond the toddler years can manifest a number of the behaviors described earlier, as well as other features such as clinging, physical complaints, and fearfulness. In older, school-age children, psychological distress can show itself in academic problems, difficulties with peers, withdrawal, anger, or aggression. Anger clearly directed toward parents is more likely to occur as children get older. In the preteen years, children have a greater likelihood of difficulties with self-esteem, peer relationships, depression, and impulsive behaviors such as substance misuse and sexual experimentation.

The potential extent and intensity of problems expands when children become teenagers. The likelihood of serious problems heightens, such as experiencing depression, self-injury, aggression, substance abuse, difficulty maintaining healthy peer relationships, and worry about the future. From early through later childhood, children may experience significant worries and fears about matters such as abandonment and the likelihood of finding consistently rewarding interpersonal relationships. They are much more likely to have self-awareness about these concerns as they grow older, though even as insight increases, many children are reluctant to talk about these worries. Regardless of the child's age, it can be useful to consider the extent to which such child health difficulties also occur in families that have not been in the divorce process, and to keep in mind that no list of child problem behaviors can accurately demonstrate that they are due to parental divorce or transitions between households.[341]

In addition, regardless of child and parent characteristics and circumstantial factors, it is crucial for there to be complete clarity about who is providing the transportation for each exchange. Especially when transitions are occurring directly between households, a simple and effective rule can be that the parent who is receiving the child provides the transportation. In other instances, such as when a child is dropped off at a daycare or school and picked up at the end of it, a similar arrangement can be easy to remember. Specifically, whichever parent the child has been with previously does the drop off and whoever is bringing the child home from that location does the pickup.

---

340. McIntosh et al., *supra* note 130.
341. Ricci, *supra* note 3, at 149.

In general, the parents should provide the transportation, but there may be numerous instances when someone else needs to do so. For example, the child care arrangements may require a babysitter, stepparent, or grandparent to provide the transportation some of the time; if so, the parent who has the substitute driver needs to clearly communicate those arrangements to the other parent in advance. Any changes from a child transportation routine should also be communicated in advance of the exchange. Efforts should be made to evenly divide the transportation responsibilities so that the time burden, vehicle wear and tear, and costs are essentially the same for both parents.

When children reach an age, frequently in early elementary school, that extracurricular activities begin, exchanges can quickly become more complicated, and therefore parents need to devote more time and attention to clearly communicate with one another about transportation needs. With the reality of possibly numerous extracurricular activities, multiple children who are engaged in them, and both parents having work schedules, it becomes very easy to overlook important details of transportation times and locations.[342] Errors about such details occur frequently in intact families, and it clearly requires greater diligence when there are two separate households. Although an online calendar (e.g., Google or Our Family Wizard) may assist with these matters, there is no simple answer, and there may be no parenting plan provision that can always successfully address this challenge.

In less complicated child transitions, when the child goes directly from one home to the other, verbal communication between the parents should usually be limited to brief pleasantries and exchanges of information relevant to the child. For young children, the transition should normally take place at the front door of the home. For older children, a drop-off at the driveway or curb can be acceptable, depending upon the weather, condition of the neighborhood, and other circumstances.

When there has been a great deal of conflict between parents, exchanges often occur at neutral, public places. A parent who expresses fear of potential harm from the other parent frequently feels safer in a public place because potential witnesses are present. Also, a parent who states there is reason to be afraid that the other parent may make a false claim of maltreatment often prefers a public place for the child

342. Ricci, *supra* note 4, at 145.

transition so that there can be witnesses that nothing inappropriate ever took place. An informal neutral exchange site could be a parking lot, fast food restaurant, large retail outlet or other location where people are frequently present. In certain cases, police stations have been identified as locations for child transitions, but they generally should be avoided because of possible exposure to the circumstances of people who are filing crime complaints or others who have been arrested.

Certain jurisdictions might have a supervised exchange site, often associated with supervised visitation services. A supervised exchange location is often an excellent solution for high conflict couples who have not been able to make productive use of an informal neutral site. Characteristically, supervisory staff interact with each of the parents, so the parents need to interact with one another.

Regardless of the parenting time schedule, the parenting plan should indicate that both parents are able to attend public events related to the children, whether they take place at school, church, or elsewhere in the community. If there have been problems with both parents or their respective family members having been present at the same public event, there may be a need for mediation or parenting coordination to work out a solution that would have a lessened risk of any difficulty occurring. There might also need to be consideration of parenting plan provisions for dividing parental attendance at such events.

Child-Focused Calendars

A sense of time develops gradually in children. Until approximately age seven, children do not have much functional comprehension of time, and it further develops for a number of years afterward. A well-designed calendar can be helpful for children of all ages to have an idea of what to expect in terms of going back and forth between two residences. Similarly, it potentially provides a sense of order and security, which is especially important for young children living in two households.

In a number of cases, professionals have focused on devising parenting plan schedules that have very basic, predictable formats. The goal has been to assist the family by making the time-sharing routine consistent and easy to remember. However, such formats have a risk of disregarding crucial elements such as having children maximize spending time with parents who are available to do so. Also, very young children who have not yet developed an adequate comprehension of time cannot make use of the intended predictability of a schedule without the assistance of a visual display such as a calendar.

Any calendar for children needs to be easily accessible and readable. Preferably, the same type of calendar would be present in both households. It would clearly need to convey basic information about where the children would be residing that day, with indications about when transitions occur. Young children may not fully comprehend all aspects of the calendar. A primary purpose is to let them know which parent they will be with on the following day or days. To help young children keep track, crossing off each day as it ends is important to help the calendar be understandable and can assist in preparing for transitions to the other household. Including extracurricular activities on the calendar can also be very useful.

For young children, there is a trade-off between how easy such a calendar is to understand and how much detail is on it. On a practical basis, it can help if the calendar is large, with enough space for indications about households, transitions, and extracurricular activities. Some families have found that they need to create such a calendar on a large white board where it can be easily seen. In the midst of busy, often hectic lives, it can be very easy to forget to update it regularly, but the time and effort is worthwhile because it can be a very useful tool and an investment in family structure and security.

Communication between Parents

When parents are in the process of separating or have recently accomplished it, they are often in a highly stressful phase of life where negative emotions are all too present. It is easy for the animosity that is routinely present between parents to affect their communication about the children. Of course, there are major differences between couples in how well they are able to be civil and effective in discussing child-related matters. Most parents do fairly well at discussing such topics productively, especially after they have made acceptable adjustments to their separate living circumstances. However, adult animosities persist for many others. In such cases, there is a great risk that ongoing mutual hostility spills over to continued conflict about the children, and a number of parents regularly expose children to the negative feelings and turmoil, whether purposely or inadvertently.

Protecting children from exposure to interparental conflict needs to be a primary goal for parenting plans, especially when children have already been subjected to it. Under such circumstances, there may need to be a provision or order for parenting coordination, mediation, or coparenting counseling.

Regardless of whether any of these interventions occur, parents need to actively work on developing a habit of communicating with one another in a civil, businesslike manner that will both protect the children from having to witness conflict and foster productive exchanges of information with one another. Crucial steps for high-conflict couples include reducing or eliminating in-person or telephone discussions and replacing them with reliance on texts and/or e-mails. An additional necessary procedure is to work in advance to create a brief, non-hostile text or e-mail that clearly conveys information focused on the child (or other relevant topic) and leaves out any material that could be considered provocative or inappropriate by the receiving parent. In addition to these communication focused steps, each parent needs to work on developing enhanced understanding of his or her own emotions, thoughts, and reactions that can be used to guide more productive and appropriate interactions with the other parent (see Chapter 5 for more detail).[343]

Interviewing Children

In some cases, judges find it necessary to conduct an in-camera interview of a child. Characteristically, such interviews occur when there is at least a substantial probability that there will be a hearing or trial focused on matters pertaining to the child. There are arguments for and against the in-camera interview, and in a number of areas there is considerable debate about it. In regions where it occurs relatively frequently, the general attitudes about it tend to be positive, whereas they tend to be more negative where it seldom takes place.

The positions in favor of in-camera interviews generally emphasize the rights of children and that their views should be heard, including in cases that include parenting disputes. Some authorities assert that such interviews are helpful emotionally for children, and though there may be anxiety prior to meeting the judge, afterward most are happy they had the opportunity to talk with him or her. Arguments against

---

343 Ricci, *supra* note 4.

such interviews include contentions that they can be very stressful for children and highlight the importance of protecting them. Opinions against in-camera interviews point out concerns that a child may be coached by a parent about what to say, and that a judge might not be an effective child interviewer.

There are assertions that the purpose of the in-camera interview is not to collect evidence. However, other authorities voice an opinion that, because the in-camera interview is believed to be less stressful and intimidating than having to testify on the stand, it is a more effective way of collecting relevant case information.[344]

Regardless of the stated purpose of an in-camera interview, discussions of the topic tend not to include the challenging realities of obtaining accurate interview information from children, especially young ones. For example, as described in Chapter 13, considerable research has found that children need to first undergo a practice interview to help establish a pattern of giving relatively comprehensive responses to open-ended questions, because that type of question and response contributes to a better likelihood of receiving an accurate answer from a child. In contrast, option-posing questions, including yes–no inquiries, have a higher likelihood of resulting in incorrect responses.[345] In addition, there needs to be a great deal of care taken to use language and concepts with younger children that can be easily understood. For example, for purposes of clarity, it is much better for an interviewer to repeatedly use a clearly descriptive term, such as "the man in the schoolyard," instead of the pronouns "he" or "him."[346]

Therefore, even though there are likely to be a limited number of cases in which in-camera interviews take place and have an influence on parenting plans, members of the judiciary who conduct them need to be aware of the limitations of a number of the types of questions that tend to be asked. In order to increase the probability of obtaining accurate understandings of the lives of children of divorce, who are twice as likely as the average child to experience significant problems

---

344. Laureen A. D'Ambra, *The Importance of Conducting In-Camera Testimony of Child Witnesses and Court Proceedings: A Comparative Legal Analysis of Relevant Domestic Relations, Juvenile Justice and Criminal Cases*, 19 Roger Williams U. L. Rev. 323 (2014); Nicholas Bala et al., *Children's Voices in Family Court: Guidelines for Judges Meeting Children*, 47 Fam. L.Q. 379 (2013).

345. Lamb et al., *supra* note 309.

346. Anne Graffam Walker, Handbook on Questioning Children: A Linguistic Perspective, 3d ed. (2013).

in life functioning, judges who do in-camera interviews should go through relevant, ongoing training.

Individual and Family Therapy

A parent, child, or family may be referred for therapy by an attorney or mental health professional, or therapy might be required by the court. At times, there are very sound reasons for the referral or requirement, with clear reasons for the therapy, identified objectives that are relevant to the child's best interest, and a recommendation for one of a number of specified providers who are highly competent clinically and adept at working with complicated, court-involved cases. At other times, when an attorney, judge, or other referral source believes an individual or family displays a problem that may have a negative impact on the child, a general recommendation for therapy is made without serious consideration of reasons or objectives. Such a referral is likely to be made without specific thought given to the potential therapist, much less the practitioner's expertise or ability to work with court-related cases.

Depending in part on the circumstances described earlier, legal and mental health professionals need to be aware that therapy may be very productive, but it can also make things worse. There are a number of ways the child and family functioning can worsen, or at least not improve at all, associated with being in therapy. For example, in some cases, a parent has gone to a therapist and described problems and goals that have nothing to do with the reasons for the referral, and thus the court-related professionals have a completely mistaken impression of the therapeutic process. In an unfortunately large proportion of cases, a therapist develops an alliance with just one parent and accepts the validity of that individual's complaints about the other without having carried out an adequate assessment. Also, a large proportion of therapists are not aware of the important difference between being in a therapeutic role and a forensic one, and they can be drawn into making recommendations for a child or family without having a sound basis for doing so.

Therefore, in parenting plan cases, when there is consideration given to establishing a referral or requirement for therapy, these factors and others (see Chapter 8 for more detail) need to be targets for deliberation.[347] Also, professional guidelines about court-involved

347. Greenberg et al., *supra* note 215; Warshak, *supra* note 246, at 246.

therapy can be very helpful in the decision-making process about possible referrals or requirements.[348]

Parenting Plan Components

Depending on the needs and circumstances, there may be differences between family parenting plans. For example, if there is a special needs child, a history of strong parental conflict and little cooperation, concerns about abuse, or circumstances requiring complicated transportation arrangements, parenting plans should include relevant sections to foster the child's well-being. However, otherwise, parenting plans routinely include the following elements.

Perhaps most clearly, a parenting plan should describe a clear parenting time schedule. All parenting plans can potentially benefit from a great deal of specificity in dates and start/stop times, though they are especially important when the parents have had a history of substantial conflict and not being able to consistently cooperate well with one another. It is best to have a graphic representation such as a calendar at least for the most routine, weekly or monthly portion of the parenting time schedule. Calendars tend to make it easier to quickly grasp the main gist of a proposed or current schedule.

There should also be a clear description of parental decision making, at least about the major areas of education, health care, and religion. At times, there will need to be a decision-making category of extracurricular activities. If there is shared decision making about health care, a provision is needed about who sets up routine appointments with medical, dental, or mental health providers. It is important to make clear that, aside from the major decision-making categories that are covered by the parenting plan, more minor, day-to-day decisions are made by the parent who is in charge at that time. If there is a health care emergency, the parent in charge at the moment must take immediate steps to get the proper care. Each parent has the responsibility to notify the other parent at the first possible opportunity about such emergencies.

The parenting plan should also lay out a procedure for instances in which the parents potentially would change a parenting time due to specific circumstances. For example, the children may need to attend a family wedding or funeral. Relatively cooperative parents may be able

348. AFCC, *supra* note 216.

to quickly agree about the children's attendance and what makeup time, if any, will occur. However, it may be necessary to include a provision that a parent can put into effect a minor scheduling change under very limited circumstances even if the other parent disagrees. The provision would need to include makeup time at the earliest opportunity—of course, it is optimal that the parents come to an agreement about the specifics. If they are not able to do so, the parent who has had to give up parenting time would be able to choose the specific makeup time.

Periodically, unpredictable circumstances occur that impact the parenting schedule. For example, children will occasionally get sick and be unable to go to school. It is preferable that parents think through in advance what they will do in terms of taking care of the child in such instances, and at least tentative provisions need to be included in the overall parenting plan.

Parenting plans can benefit from including general provisions about goals for the children, including positive relationships with both parents and other family members, promotion of good peer relationships, successful school experiences, child care considerations, and extracurricular activities. There may be a section that specifically covers child opinions or preferences about matters such as the parenting time schedule, schools, and extracurricular activities, and how parents will consider them. However, while it is important for parents to consider child preferences, parents need to clearly remain in the authoritative, executive roles within the family.

In general, parenting plans identify that both parents have equal access to records from schools and all health care providers. In limited circumstances, such as when there has been domestic violence or abuse, there may be a decision that only one parent should have access to those records.

At times, a parent who has had the child for a period of time tells the other parent that an exchange is not going to occur. In these instances, any of a number of alleged reasons are given, including that the child has a routine illness, the child does not wish to go with the receiving parent, the receiving parent has not paid bills or child support, and the receiving parent previously held back the child from an exchange. All such reasons are invalid and should be considered violations of the parenting plan.

A parenting plan may have built-in consequences for parental violation of the plan. When there are potential questions about the meanings of parenting plan provisions, the use of examples may be productive. Also, there should be provisions for updating or revising parenting plans as circumstances require, such as children growing older and their needs, interests, and activities having changed.[349] When parents have not been able to successfully work out significant differences on their own, parenting coordination, mediation, or coparenting counseling may be necessary, and parenting plans should have built-in requirements in that regard.

In a number of parenting plans, there are provisions for child-related financial matters. These include topics such as a statement or schedule regarding which parent gets to declare the child as a dependent on federal taxes; responsibility for health insurance coverage (and automobile, if applicable) and payment of premiums, deductibles, and co-pays; and funds specified for college or other future educational expenses.[350]

Crucial elements of this chapter include the following:

- Parental reported histories of child caretaking and decision making may be inaccurate.
- Parenting plan considerations regarding decision making need to include an examination of multiple factors, including but not limited to
  - history of cooperative decision making regarding children,
  - history of general interparental cooperation,
  - history of interparental conflict,
  - mutual trust between the parents,
  - parental track records of successful problem-solving about disagreements,
  - whether a parent has a particular strength or weakness regarding a category of decision making, and
  - whether it is the initial establishment of a decision-making format or a plan revision.
- Child physical health and safety factors may need to be considered in the parenting plan, including, but not limited to
  - risk of unintentional injury,

349. Ricci, *supra* note 3, at 231.

350. *E.g.*, Alaska Court System, *Model Parenting Agreement*, http://courtrecords.alaska.gov/webdocs/forms/dr-475.pdf.

  - exposure to secondhand or thirdhand smoke, and
  - possible child vulnerability.
- Children need to be cared for by competent, motivated adults who plan well for child transitions.
- It is difficult to distinguish child physiological, emotional, and behavioral problems associated with a separation or particular parenting plan from difficulties that often occur in intact families.
- Although parents need to be attentive to signs of possible excessive distress in children, there is no symptom or behavior pattern that proves such problems are a result of the divorce or the structure of the parenting plan.
- Parents can assist their children by maintaining a clearly available calendar that identifies when they will be with each parent and other relevant basic details.
- It is essential that parents maintain communication with one another that is consistently civil and businesslike.
- Judges who conduct in-camera interviews should participate in ongoing training about procedures designed to maximize the likelihood of accurate child responses.
- Any referrals or requirements for individual and/or family therapy should identify the main therapeutic objectives and direct the service recipients to providers who clearly have the necessary clinical competency as well as expertise in court-involved cases.

CHAPTER 15
SCHEDULE-FOCUSED PRACTICAL CONSIDERATIONS

If the main goal of the parenting plan schedule is to facilitate the best interests of the children, it follows that the characteristics of each child and family should be focused upon first. These characteristics include broad areas such as strengths, problems, and circumstances.

A number of the prior chapters in this book delve into frequent, serious problems for divorcing families, such as domestic violence, mental health concerns, child abuse, and parental alienation. Other chapters examine difficult circumstantial factors that often arise, such as having very young children and relocation. Almost all families have areas of significant strength, and parenting plans need to consider, for each separate family, the integration and balance of those problems, strengths, and circumstances. A particularly important circumstantial factor is the importance of parents and children being able to spend a reasonable amount of good quality time together. This factor, and the practical reality of when each parent and each child is available to spend quality time together, is often an excellent starting point.

This chapter focuses on practical yet emotionally relevant matters that are closely aligned with the parenting schedule. First, I discuss the possible use of preexisting schedule prototypes. Second, the focus is on common family circumstances that need to be considered in parenting time schedules. Third, there is a discussion of factors to be considered in deciding the extent of parental time sharing that takes place and how to schedule child exchanges. Fourth, I summarize possible parenting plan provisions when restrictions are needed on one individual's parenting time. Fifth, I examine the need for parenting plans to clarify time sharing when there are conflicts between the routine schedule, holidays, or vacations. Finally, I describe competing points of view about including parenting plan provisions that try to anticipate future family changes.

Prepared Schedule Templates

There have been a number of very helpful parenting schedule prototypes developed.[351] They offer multiple choices of possible schedules and focus on aligning them with child ages. These schedules can be especially helpful if parents or others involved in devising parenting plans experience difficulty in getting started with the process; that is, looking at prepared schedule options can potentially help individuals recognize time-sharing patterns that may work for them, at least in part. Reviewing such schedules can also help individuals identify calendar options that would not work well for them and thereby narrow the focus to other alternatives that are more likely to be successful.

Most of the packages of schedules cited here include important explanations that these time-sharing calendars are not the only ones that might work well, and that the characteristics of each family need to be carefully considered. For example, most emphasize that multiple family factors in addition to children's ages need to be considered, including ones covered in the earlier chapters of this book, such as children's needs, parenting competencies, parent–child relationships, the degrees of interparental cooperation and conflict, parental mental health that has an influence on parenting, and possible abuse or neglect.

In general, the prepared time-sharing schedules consider age clusters and offer a number of different options for each of them. The options presented for very young children appropriately consider whether both parents have sufficient competency and experience with infants to safely allow overnight stays in both households.

351. *E.g.*, American Academy of Matrimonial Lawyers (AAML), *Child Centered Residential Guidelines* (2015), http://aaml.org/sites/default/files/CCRG-Digital-Book.pdf; AFCC, *Planning Shared Parenting: A Guide for Parents Living Apart* (2010), https://www.mass.gov/files/documents/2017/09/01/afccsharedparenting.pdf; Arizona Supreme Court, *Planning for Parenting Time: Arizona's Guide for Parents Living Apart* (2009), http://www.azcourts.gov/portals/31/parentingTime/PPWguidelines.pdf; Indiana Rules of Court, *Indiana Parenting Time Guidelines* (2017), http://www.in.gov/judiciary/rules/parenting/.

Family Circumstances

A central practical consideration with vast emotional impact is parental availability. It usually varies in accordance with parental employment schedules, including time in transit to and from work. A very large proportion of both unmarried mothers and fathers with one or more children in the household are employed: 72 percent of mothers and 83 percent of fathers.[352] Therefore, most parenting plans need to deal with the reality of work-related time limitations on the part of both the mother and the father. Consequently, a good proportion of families will need to have periods of time in which the child is cared for by someone other than a parent. In that regard, if both parents can agree on the child care providers, it can aid in the parenting plan development.

Another very important practical matter is when the child or children are available. Most children attend a school outside the home, and many have periodic extracurricular activities. The time that children spend going back and forth between school and activities needs to be considered, just as the parental work transportation time does. The busy lives led by children tend to be accentuated by the routines of going back and forth between households. Especially within the context of these moving parts, children often benefit from relatively calm periods of time in a household in which they can engage in good quality interactions with a parent.

Of course, children also need adequate sleep. The realities of busy lives, associated with living in separate households, can place a strain on children getting enough sleep to promote healthy development. The specific time-sharing schedule put into effect at times has a substantial impact on sleep.

For example, a hypothetical eight-year-old child needs to wake up at 6:55 a.m. in the home of Parent A in order to get to school on time. In contrast, the wake-up time needs to be 5 a.m. in the home of Parent B, given that individual's employment and commuting requirements. That difference in available sleep needs to be given serious consideration in a parenting plan, especially since eight-year-olds are recommended to have 9 to 12 hours of sleep per night.

---

352. Press Release, U.S. Dep't of Labor, Bureau of Labor Statistics, *Employment Characteristics of Families—2016* (Apr. 20, 2017), https://www.bls.gov/news.release/pdf/famee.pdf (data excludes parents with a spouse in the household and includes widowed parents).

Very young children need sufficient good quality time in order to establish positive relationships with both parents. A hypothetical infant may have only a number of two- to three-hour visits with the father per week. Some of these visits take place on workdays. When considering the father's work and commuting time, the child's sleep schedule, and the father's understandable concern about getting to the mother's home on time, the hurrying, tension, and worry associated with such visits can undermine the development of adequate attachment and bonding.[353] Therefore, even though the multiple brief visits during the week may make sense from the standpoint of the father's limited experience caring for an infant, a parenting plan needs to consider other options that better fit the child's best interest, including overnights initially with the presence of a monitor/supervisor or a lengthening of the allowed time of each visit.

In a number of families, there are siblings of quite different ages and stages of life. A schedule that seemed like a good fit for a four-year-old may not work well for a 12-year-old. Often, in such cases, there needs to be deliberation about maintaining at least a portion of the schedule that allows them to regularly interact with one another, preferably in both homes.

It can be easy to overlook circumstantial factors that can have an abundant impact on children's best interests, such as transportation and traffic. There can be moves even within the same metropolitan area that have a serious impact on family routines and parent–child relationships. If a parenting plan was put into effect when the parents lived a ten-minute drive from one another, a number of its provisions are no longer feasible if one parent moves one hour away from the other, and they will need revision.

In that regard, a research study found that when one or both divorced parents moved an hour or more away from one another, their young adult children reported higher levels of psychological distress, less parental emotional support, and lower levels of parental financial support. In a separate research program, when a parent moved 75 miles or more away, there was a significant risk of the child's active relationship with that parent eventually coming to an end.[354] Therefore, significant moves of lesser time and distance also have a risk of creating a negative impact on the child, especially in the relationship

353. Ludolph, *supra* note 121.

354. Braver et al., supra note 268; HETHERINGTON & KELLY, *supra* note 268.

with the parent who moves further away, and this possibility needs to be considered in parenting planning.

How Much to Share and Exchange Children

Although there is no scientific evidence for one parenting plan being better than any other one, reasoning indicates that accumulated knowledge from research and professional experience should be relied upon to address questions about the extent of shared parenting and the frequency of child transitions. It has been frequently observed that parents who cooperate well with one another and who live a close distance from one another have a good likelihood of being able to successfully share considerable parenting time. Also, parents who have similar rules, family routines, and parenting styles are good candidates for successfully sharing a good deal of parenting time. Parents who perform relatively poorly in the parenting qualities mentioned here tend not to be good candidates for extensive amounts of shared parenting. Regardless of the extent of shared parenting, unless there is a good deal of concern about parenting competency, it is best for both parents to have opportunities to carry out the full range of parenting behaviors with the children.

As described in Chapter 5, infants and other very young children generally require frequent transitions to assist in the formation of secure attachments with both parents. Because such very young children have not yet been able to develop the capacities to maintain stable, positive internal representations of each parent, if they do not see a parent for a considerable period of time it is as if that individual does not exist, and there is no sense of comfort drawn from those parents. As children grow older, they develop the ability to maintain memories of parents and positive interactions with them. Consequently, older children are able to tolerate well somewhat longer periods of time without seeing the parent, and therefore they require fewer transitions. However, older children might also miss the parent who is not at their residence at the time, and the parenting plan can be structured to try to minimize such distress.

In addition, parenting plans need to consider the right of first refusal. In most circumstances, especially with reasonably cooperative parents, it is a positive feature of the parenting plan. However, for parents with frequent conflicts with one another, especially about the children, the right of first refusal can be counterproductive because it provides yet another potential forum for argument and discord. For example, high-conflict couples can be at risk of developing a pattern of mutual accusations that the other parent has been inappropriately withholding the child instead of adhering to the right of first refusal provision. Therefore, instead of routinely including such a provision, individuals involved in the creation of the parenting plan need to strongly consider relevant aspects of the history of interactions between the parents.

Restrictions on Parenting Time

Parenting time restrictions are usually considered or put into effect when there is an allegation that a parent's actions present a danger of harm to the child or there is evidence that such behaviors have actually occurred. A central consideration is whether or not a child would be endangered if unrestricted parenting time were permitted. Many times, there is a dispute over whether or not such a danger exists, and an evaluation needs to take place to shed light on the potential for risk to the child.[355]

When a parenting time restriction is put in place, it usually involves supervision for the parent. However, there are other options as well. See Chapter 13 for more detail.

Integrating Basic, Holiday, and Vacation Schedules

Although the basic schedule draws most of the attention in deriving a parenting plan, holidays and vacations can also provide a challenge, especially regarding how they interface with the basic schedule and with one another. Families can differ in terms of which holidays they celebrate, and it is important for the parenting plan that each family identify the ones they wish to recognize and include in the eventual time-sharing schedule. For practical purposes, dates such as Mother's Day, Father's Day, and children's and parents' birthdays are considered the equivalent of holidays for the parenting schedule.

In general, holidays tend to be evenly divided between parents over the course of the year. Many families alternate this division, such that certain holidays are designated to be with one parent in even-numbered

---

355. *E.g.*, EVALUATION, *supra* note 1, at 67.

years and the other parent in odd-numbered years. Because of preference or tradition, some families may divide up certain holidays so that one parent always has them. At times, holidays that always fall adjacent to weekends, such as Memorial Day and Labor Day, may not be separately identified in the schedule because parents agree to have them allocated according to which parent has that relevant weekend.

In many cases, parenting plans can provide helpful clarity by specifying that holidays take precedence over the routine schedule. In some instances, holidays are a significant portion of school breaks, such as Christmas Eve, Christmas Day, New Year's Eve, and New Year's Day. During this period of time, it can be particularly important to be sensitive to each family's history and traditions and to try to protect and promote the most positive, meaningful aspects of the holidays for the children. It is similarly important to be cognizant of such matters for other religious holidays that families might celebrate.

Family vacations need to be identified as far in advance as possible. One month is often the timeline for minimal advance notification of a potential vacation. Characteristically, a parenting plan identifies a maximum amount of vacation time that a parent can take with the children. For families who generally are able to arrive at agreements about such matters, there is often a provision for the parent who wishes to take the children on vacation to notify the other parent to obtain agreement. If it seems unlikely that certain parents would be able to arrive at an agreement, the parenting plan needs to build in parameters for parents to simply provide advance information of upcoming vacations with the children, though there may be prohibitions about vacations that include holidays without the agreement of the other parents.

When there are very young children, there often needs to be consideration about how much vacation time a child can be away from another parent. Just as a sound routine schedule for an infant would generally allow a gap of no more than three consecutive days without contact with a parent, vacations with infants may need to be similarly short. Gradually, as a child gets older, the duration of vacation time away from the other parent generally can increase. The number of consecutive vacation days away from a parent would depend on an integration of children's ages and the relationships they have with each parent. In general, as children get older, they are better able to maintain positive internal representations of parents and can tolerate longer absences. Because of schedule differences, some children may not have experienced more than short periods away from certain parents, where others have been accustomed to it without experiencing undue distress. These factors need to be considered on an individual basis for each child and family.

For longer vacations, such as those that include two weekends, there periodically are conflicts with an alternating weekend parenting time schedule. For example, a hypothetical father wishes to begin his summer vacation with the children on the Friday that begins his regular weekend. He plans to return on Sunday of the following weekend, and that weekend routinely would be the mother's parenting time. The weekend following that one would again be his routine parenting time, and consequently, if his plan was put into effect, he would have three consecutive weekends. Many parents might object to missing three consecutive weekends. Also, due to a holiday schedule, a parent at times may receive two consecutive weekends and therefore have three weekends in a row.

Without a parental agreement about this matter, different options need to be examined to find a possible solution. For example, while the Indiana Parenting Time Guidelines generally recommend flexibility and cooperation, the default rule is that if a parent has two consecutive weekends due to a holiday, that individual also receives the third weekend (assuming the parents alternate weekends).[356] Alternately, in the potential vacation scenario described in the preceding paragraph, the parents could come to a compromise that involves the father returning two days earlier, on a Friday, so that the mother can have her usual weekend time.

Perhaps obviously, there are potentially many effective solutions to such quandaries, and parental agreement is the key. In general, it is advisable to have the specifics of the vacation or holiday arrangement laid out as clearly as possible. If the parents have a history of having battled a great deal with one another, it is essential to have a clearly written document describing the specific vacation or holiday arrangements, preferably requiring statements from each parent that they have read it and agree to it.

Provisions for Future Parenting Plans

As described earlier, parenting plans usually acknowledge that there may be a need for future revision. In many instances, there is a provision

356. *Supra* note 351, at 15.

that the plan needs to be reviewed at a future time, often when the child reaches a certain age or school grade.

A parenting plan characteristically identifies potential problem-solving avenues if the parents develop significant disagreements or conflicts. Characteristically, that provision identifies that mediation would occur, and plans frequently identify who would be the mediator. Alternately, parenting coordination or counseling might be required under such circumstances.

At times, there are assertions that parenting plans should build in automatic future changes in the time-sharing schedule, associated with a child reaching an identified age or level of education. Individuals who argue in favor of establishing parenting plans with automatic future changes point out that they can save future major costs and stresses of having to revisit the legal system.

However, others maintain that it is impossible to accurately anticipate relevant future circumstances, and therefore it is counterproductive to try to establish automatic future changes in parenting plans. Individuals who hold that position assert that there are frequent situational shifts in families' worlds, such as job changes, residential moves, remarriages, new health problems, and alterations in parent–child relationships that cannot be anticipated in advance, and consequently, automatic parenting plan changes are just as likely to make family circumstances worse as they are to make things better.

Central points in this chapter are

- Preexisting schedule templates can be very useful in the recognition of calendars that may be applicable for a case at hand, though time-sharing schedules need to be well informed by the relevant characteristics of each child and family, including
  - child age and stage of development,
  - parent–child relationships,
  - child needs and characteristics,
  - parenting competencies,
  - levels of interparental cooperation and conflict,
  - parental mental health that affects parenting,
  - possible abuse or neglect.
- Parenting time schedules should have a priority focus on children being able to spend time directly with each parent, including both enjoyment- and task-oriented activities.

- Sibling relationships should be fostered in time-sharing schedules.
- Consistently high levels of parental cooperation, reasonable geographical proximity, and similar parenting styles often provide a foundation for extensively shared parenting time to have a good chance of being successful.
- Younger children generally require more frequent child exchanges to facilitate the development of positive relationships with both parents.
- Older children require fewer transitions than younger ones.
- Parenting plans need to consider individual differences between children regarding how well they carry out transition-related behaviors such as bringing school materials between households and being on time.
- A right of first refusal needs to be included in parenting plans, except when interparental cooperation is so low that it would likely be counterproductive.
- Significant restrictions on parenting time need to occur if there is a danger to the child under conditions of unrestricted parenting time.
- There are competing points of view about whether to build future, automatic changes into parenting time or decision making as a child grows older.

CHAPTER 16
AGE-APPROPRIATE PARENTING SCHEDULES

In developing parenting schedules, it is best to start with human beings—the children and families who are going through divorce and need schedules that will promote children's well-being and healthy development. Because parenting calendars display who has the children on specific dates and times, they demonstrate a great deal about which parent is in control at any particular moment. Although both time sharing and decision making represent realms of parental control, the time-sharing element more frequently is the focus of a potential court clash. As a result, there is often abundant emotion wrapped up in the formation of the parenting time schedule.

Preexisting parenting calendars and related general recommendations for creating them[357] can be very useful. However, it may be impossible to simultaneously identify general schedule options that might be productive while at the same time considering the widely disparate characteristics of individual children and families. Especially when there is conflict about the time-sharing schedule, there can be a great deal of emotion, energy, and time spent in its development. In the midst of such difficulties, without anyone realizing it, it is easy to start with relatively concrete entities like prepared schedules and argue or negotiate about them without adequate consideration of family members' needs and characteristics.

The starting point in a negotiation or argument serves as a cognitive anchor that establishes a foundation for ongoing negotiations and tends to have a major impact on the final outcome.[358] Therefore, because the goal of a parenting plan is to promote what is best for

357. *Supra* note 351.
358. THINKING, *supra* note 10.

children and families, their needs, characteristics, and circumstances should be the starting point. If a preset calendar is the starting point, there is a risk of devoting too little attention to the important human factors.

In this chapter, first there are descriptions of factors related to child age, developmental level, and other characteristics insofar as they affect the creation of parenting schedules. Second, there are examples of time-sharing calendars that are devised in accordance with child age, family characteristics, and relevant circumstances. The examples make use of hypothetical cases and cover child ages from a few months through later teenage years.

Child Age, Development, and Individual Factors

Children obviously go through a profound extent of development from infancy through the verge of adulthood. For parents who have teenagers or grown children, and yet who can also remember attending to the seemingly never-ending demands of very young children, the old saying "the days are long, but the years are short" rings extremely true. From the perspective of having an older teen or young adult, the speed of development is rapid.

There are multiple aspects of child development. Relevant theories and accumulated scientific findings include areas such as physiological, cognitive, psychosexual, psychosocial, language, and emotional development. There are many descriptions of child development, from very short to very long. Very brief summaries can be found in materials about parenting plans primarily aimed at legal professionals,[359] and highly extensive, detailed coverage can be found in textbooks.[360]

Temperament is a related behavioral framework that integrates multiple types of development. Based in part on a longitudinal study that lasted approximately 30 years, a number of temperamental factors were identified that are believed to be evident starting in infancy and continuing, depending upon environmental factors, through adulthood. These factors include features such as activity level, adaptability, approach–withdrawal tendencies, quality of mood, and distractibility. The authors maintained that the goodness of fit between parenting

359. *E.g.*, Hartson & Payne, *supra* note 339, at 9; *supra* note 351.

360. *E.g.*, David R. Shaffer & Katherine Kipp, Developmental Psychology: Childhood & Adolescence, 9th ed. (2014).

style and child temperament is an important factor in facilitating development.[361] In practice, child temperament is considered an important factor generally, especially when emotional or behavioral difficulties are present. However, there appears to be no scientifically supported method of assessing the goodness of fit between parenting behaviors and child temperament factors. Therefore, considerations about child temperament in parenting plans primarily rely on subjective impressions by parents and mental health professionals.

These facets of child development overlap with one another and can influence each other in important ways. Consequently, different children manifest their developmental achievements in ways that are widely divergent from one another, and each must be considered individually in parenting plan considerations. In that regard, in the creation of parenting plans, it is necessary to consider the specific reality of each child's attributes, needs, and family relationships. Such an approach is far more productive than a general focus on temperament or multiple stages of development.

As described previously in this book, decades of scientific research and professional knowledge have identified a number of child experiences that are associated with positive or negative life outcomes. Although such experiences pertain to multiple age groups, not surprisingly, the most vulnerable, youngest age group has drawn the most attention. There is consistent agreement that a primary goal for the youngest children is for there to be safe and secure parenting that promotes healthy development. The main controversy about the youngest children pertains to overnight visits and the effects they have on development, especially secure attachment to one or both parents.

In that regard, individuals involved in parenting plan development for this age group need to closely examine factors including parenting competency, the degree to which the child has a safe and secure relationship with each parent, the histories of interparental cooperation and conflict, parental availability, and any child or parent health or related problem that might be present (see Chapters 5, 7, and 8). Also, a great deal of thought needs to be devoted to creating a parenting plan that does not lead to excessive family stresses that would have the potential to interfere with the development of healthy parent–child relationships.

---

361. Alexander Thomas & Stella Chess, Temperament & Development (1977).

As parenting schedule options are considered, it is important to remain cognizant that there are inevitable trade-offs. A prominent trade-off involves the extent to which children are able to see each parent frequently and the degree to which a schedule is stable. When children are able to see each parent frequently, it inevitably means there are numerous exchanges and the children go back and forth between households a great deal, resulting in a low level of residential stability. When there is a high level of residential stability, children stay at the same household for relatively long periods of time, which increases the risk of children missing the parent whom they have not seen for a while.

Parenting Schedule Examples

Very Young Children

The examples of parenting calendars throughout this book are structured in a Monday through Sunday format that makes it somewhat easier to conceptualize schedule details. Relevant initials are used for Mother and Father. When a calendar day shows a time listed, it indicates the start of parenting time for that individual—until that time, the other parent would have had the child. For example, if a Wednesday reads "F 5 P.M.," it indicates that the mother would have had the child until the father took over at 5 P.M. for the rest of that day. Similarly, if a day reads "M 7–11 A.M.," it means that the mother had the child during that time, and the father had parenting time the rest of that day.

Many of the basic, routine aspects of parenting schedules (not inclusive of holidays or vacations) operate on a two-week cycle. Most others operate on a four-week cycle. Accordingly, most of these calendars display two weeks. When needed, they show four weeks.

All the examples here are hypothetical and are not representative of any actual families. However, all examples are thoroughly informed by real-life family challenges, strengths, and circumstances.

In the first example, the parents had been married for five years, have a ten-month-old daughter, and recently separated. Despite their differences, both parents had been fully involved in all aspects of caring for their infant. Each parent was confident that the other parent was able to care for their daughter competently. Both were attuned to her schedule. The parents had no substantive disagreements about the child's needs or how to carry out relevant parenting tasks. The mother was still breast-feeding, and the couple had coordinated well in having the mother express breast milk that the father routinely fed to their daughter. The parents agreed they would continue to do so. Both parents were employed and had relied on family members to care for their daughter when neither of them were able to do so. The parents felt that arrangement was a good one and agreed to continue it. The parents and caregivers carried out child exchanges smoothly and collectively had a good track record of communicating with one another about the child's condition, eating, sleeping, and other relevant activities. On weekdays, the exchanges often involved a family member taking care of the child. That individual would come to the home of whichever parent had the child on that day. Typically, much of the care took place in the home. The basic calendar is shown here.

Monday	Tuesday	Wednesday	Thursday	Friday	Saturday	Sunday
M	M	F	F	M	M	F
M	M	F	F	M	F	F

The parents had learned that a very young child should not experience lengthy periods of time without contact with a parent. Therefore, the schedule is structured so that, at most, there are two consecutive days of no contact with a parent.

In a different hypothetical case, the parents dated for a few months but had never married nor lived with one another. Neither had prior experience as a parent. Soon after the birth of their child, the mother permitted the father to come to her home for a few brief visits. However, the parents had numerous arguments with one another and those visits ended. A few months later, when the child was eight months old, the father was able to obtain an order for visits outside the mother's home, though *his* mother needed to be present at all times as a supervisor and parenting coach. She was employed as a waitress and had work hours that often changed day-to-day but tended to be fairly consistent each week. The order stipulated that the paternal grandmother was to model and otherwise teach parenting skills to the father during the visits. In the calendar for this case, the grandmother was present during all the father's time blocks.

Monday	Tuesday	Wednesday	Thursday	Friday	Saturday	Sunday
F 8–11 A.M.	F 12–4 P.M.	M	M	F 12–4 P.M.	F 10–2 P.M.	M
F 8–10 A.M.	F 12–5 P.M.	M	M	F 12–4 P.M.	F 10–2 P.M.	M

The goal was that the father would acquire adequate parenting competency over a number of weeks, and then the grandmother's supervision and training role would be phased out. The schedule represented here shows the initial visitation calendar. It was structured in accordance with the grandmother's availability and in an effort to provide the infant with reasonably frequent contact with both parents. Therefore, there were no more than two consecutive days with no father–child contact. Most of the time blocks were four hours in length, which allowed adequate time for father–child interaction, the grandmother's coaching, and travel from and back to the mother's residence. When the schedule was put into effect, the matter was to be revisited within 60 days in order to assess the extent of the father's progress and consider schedule alterations.

In a separate hypothetical case, there was an order for the mother, who was employed full-time, to have only supervised visits. The order had been set up when the child, a boy, was three years old, and it had been in effect for over a year. Previously, before the order, there were allegations that the mother had been verbally and at times physically aggressive toward the child. The father, who worked part-time, had initiated these allegations, and there had been considerable concern voiced by a family therapist and by daycare providers that the boy's emotional reactions and impulsivity were considerably stronger than that of most three-year-olds. An evaluation regarding time sharing and possible restrictions on the mother's parenting time had been ordered when the child was three, though he was resistant to participate directly. Therefore, the main sources of information were the perspectives of both parents and the concerns expressed by the therapist and daycare staff. The father had expressed worry about the son's alleged statements about the mother and voiced an impression that his rather poorly controlled behavior was representative of having been abused. The mother insisted that her parenting was very good, and that she had never done anything wrong toward the child. Child protective services had not completed an investigation by the time the initial evaluation report was issued. That report had recommended the parenting time restrictions in the form of limited and supervised visitation, and noted that while the issue of abuse had not been entirely clarified, the safety of the child was paramount.

The parents could not agree on any family member or friend to carry out the supervisory duties for free. Therefore, a supervisor was hired through an agency. The extensive time restrictions in the mother's visitation schedule were due both to her own limited ability to pay for a supervisor and the times that both she and a supervisor could be present. The basic schedule consequently included only 9 to 11 A.M. each Saturday and 1 to 3 P.M. on alternate Sundays.

After the supervised visits had been taking place for over a year, the mother was able to obtain an order for a new evaluation. The child had made improvements in self-control and took part in the evaluation, having participated in parent–child observation sessions and individual interviews.

The evaluator concluded that the mother had not carried out abusive behavior or any other type of substantively negative parenting, though she had periodically yelled at the son when frustrated and on a few occasions needed to briefly restrain him by holding him when he had been hitting and trying to kick her. Child protective services had come to essentially the same conclusion by the time the evaluator had finished his work. The evaluator recommended a schedule in which the supervisory requirement and time limitations would be phased out in stages. The attorneys for the parents took those recommendations under advisement and came to a negotiated agreement for a parenting schedule. Both parents stated that there were elements of it that each of them disliked, but they approved the proposed agreement largely because they wanted to move forward and were pessimistic that they would find a different schedule about which they would both have greater enthusiasm.

In order to put into effect a gradual transition that potentially might benefit the child, the supervisor remained present for half the time for the first two weeks of the revised parenting time schedule. The parenting plan specifically stated that the presence of the supervisor did not represent or suggest that the mother's parenting was incompetent in any way, but it was included to ease the child's adjustment to a very different parenting time arrangement. In this first step of the transition, the times that the supervisor was present with the mother and child are represented by S in the calendar.

Monday	Tuesday	Wednesday	Thursday	Friday	Saturday	Sunday
F	F	F	F	F	S 2–3 P.M. M 3–4 P.M.	S 1–2 P.M. M 2–3 P.M.
F	F	S 5–6 P.M. M 6–7 P.M.	F	F	S 2–3 P.M. M 3–4 P.M.	S 1–2 P.M. M 2–3 P.M.

This two-week schedule included parenting time on both Sundays and a Wednesday evening, which was an initial step to increase the frequency of contact. The supervisor was present for the first hour and then departed, allowing the child and mother to spend an hour alone together. That mother–child, one-on-one time both reflected the practical reality of phasing out the supervisor and was a potential step toward the initial enhancement of their reciprocal emotional connection.

The supervisor was no longer present after the first two weeks. Subsequently, for a period of four weeks, the mother had parenting time for six hours each Saturday and an alternating two or three hours each Sunday. Also, there was a two-hour visit each Wednesday.

Monday	Tuesday	Wednesday	Thursday	Friday	Saturday	Sunday
F	F	M 6–8 P.M.	F	F	M 1–7 P.M.	M 2–4 P.M.
F	F	M 6–8 P.M.	F	F	M 1–7 P.M.	M 1–4 P.M.

The third step of the schedule was identified as continuing long-term. The mother had parenting time alternate weekends, an overnight every Wednesday, and an overnight on alternate Mondays. Also, on alternate Fridays, she had a two-hour dinner visit.

Monday	Tuesday	Wednesday	Thursday	Friday	Saturday	Sunday
F	F	M 5 P.M.	F 8 A.M.	M 5–7 P.M.	F	F
M 5 P.M.	F 8 A.M.	M 5 P.M.	F 8 A.M.	M 5 P.M.	M	F 7 P.M.

Consequently, overall the schedule represents an integration of a number of developmentally important factors. It provides the very young child with regular contact with both parents, providing opportunities for a full range of parent–child interactions. Also, this basic schedule is structured so that the duration of time with no in-person contact with either parent is always less than three days.

Middle Childhood

When the Johnsons divorced, the mother went back to her prior career in marketing and the father continued in his full-time management work. They had two children, a ten-year-old daughter named Wanda and a seven-year-old boy named Clay. Their parenting time schedule reflected both the differences in parental availability and their histories of taking care of the children. The children took the bus to school from the mother's home, though the father drove them to school because he did not live near a bus route. The father's parenting time included alternate weekends through Sunday night and one weekday overnight, alternating between Wednesday and Thursday.

Monday	Tuesday	Wednesday	Thursday	Friday	Saturday	Sunday
M	M	F 6 P.M.	M	F 6 P.M.	F	F
M 3 P.M.	M	M	F 6 P.M.	M 3 P.M.	M	M

After about a year, the father obtained a new job that required him to leave for work at 5:30 A.M. For the first few months with his new employer, when the children had their weekday overnight, he got them up very early and dropped them at their mother's home on his way to work. However, on those days, the children were extremely tired by late afternoon, and it affected their mood, schoolwork, and participation in extracurricular activities. For example, although Wanda had consistently loved soccer in the past, she repeatedly complained about going to practice and spent increased time lying in bed while looking through her phone. Clay started to insist that his homework was too difficult and often did not complete it. As a result, both parents agreed that the father would change his weekday parenting time from an overnight to a return to the home of the mother by 9 P.M. They also agreed that every other Tuesday he would have the children for a shorter dinner visit.

Monday	Tuesday	Wednesday	Thursday	Friday	Saturday	Sunday
M	M	F 6–9 P.M.	M	F 6 P.M.	F	M 8 P.M.
M	F 6–8 P.M.	M	F 6–9 P.M.	M	M	M

Even though these changes led to decreased parenting time for the father, this basic schedule still allowed the children to spend considerable time with him. Because the parents had an equal number of holidays and vacation days, the percentage across the entire year was actually somewhat higher. The father had parenting time on well over 40 percent of the days during the calendar year.

This calendar reflects the fact that, as children get older, they generally are better able to maintain internal psychological representations of each parent and thus have improved abilities to tolerate somewhat longer periods of time without direct contact. In addition, this family scenario manifests the central role that school and activities play in the lives of children in this age group.

The Garcias divorced when their daughter, Sofia, was in fourth grade and their son, Santiago, was in second grade. Both parents worked in the local schools. The mother was a high school principal and the father a middle school teacher. Consequently, they had similar work schedules.

In general, the parents cooperated well with one another and viewed the other's parenting as very competent. The parents also thought it best for the children that there be equally shared parenting. They created the following schedule, which is sometimes called a 2–2–3 calendar.

Monday	Tuesday	Wednesday	Thursday	Friday	Saturday	Sunday
F 6 P.M.	F	M 6 P.M.	M	F 6 P.M.	F	F
M 6 P.M.	M	F 6 P.M.	F	M 6 P.M.	M	M

When Santiago was in fourth grade, he began to consistently display serious problems with attention, focus, and organization. For example, he routinely forgot books and related supplies at school, requiring a parent to drive back with him to the school to get those materials. On a number of occasions, after they returned home, they realized that Santiago had forgotten additional school material that he had not earlier identified. As a result, there needed to be a second trip back to the school to gather up the twice-forgotten school belongings. The boy was very inconsistent in writing down assignments given in class and turning in homework and projects on time. Similarly, he regularly forgot school supplies, clothing, and other belongings when going from one household to the other, despite numerous prompts and lists made by both parents. As these problems continued, the family consulted with a psychologist who had relevant training and experience, and the boy was diagnosed as suffering from an Attention Deficit Hyperactivity Disorder (ADHD).

During fourth grade, as Santiago's problems persisted, both parents made efforts to help the child and coordinate with the school. Over time, it became clear that the mother was better able than the father to diligently focus on assisting Santiago in core executive functions such as identifying and organizing school assignments. Also, she communicated with relevant school personnel to facilitate Santiago's academic progress more frequently than did the father.

Although medication and therapy moderated the extent of Santiago's ADHD symptoms, it became clear that his related problems were going to continue. Both parents had the impression that they might need to change the parenting time schedule, though they had very different ideas about how it would be best to do so. As a result, they sought assistance from a parenting coordinator.

Eventually, they agreed upon a revised schedule that reduced the number of transitions and had the children reside with the mother most of the time. The father still had three overnights and three evening visits in a 14-day block of time. Because there were characteristically no after school homework assignments on Fridays, one of the evening visits occurred on the Friday that was not the father's routine weekend.

The father acknowledged that fewer transitions and greater reliance on the mother's assistance with executive functions could help Santiago, but he also feared that their son might be harmed by substantially less time spent with him. The parents were able to come to their final agreement only after the parenting coordinator proposed that the basic schedule essentially be reversed during summer vacations. Specifically, when school was out of session during the summer, the father would have parenting time on ten overnights during a 14-day block of time, except for when either parent had the children for vacation. That adjustment to the summer parenting time schedule partially yet significantly offset the increased number of days both children were with the mother while school was in session. The revised parenting time schedule for a typical week when school was in session is shown here.

Monday	Tuesday	Wednesday	Thursday	Friday	Saturday	Sunday
M	F 6–9 P.M.	M	M	F 6 P.M.	F	F
M	F 5–7 P.M.	M	M	F 6–9 P.M.	M	M

The parents initially discussed establishing a partially different parenting time schedule for Sofia, as she did not manifest any ADHD problem behaviors. However, they decided not to do so because having the same schedule for both children would facilitate the positive relationship they had with one another. Also, it seemed daunting to both parents to try to simultaneously manage two somewhat different parenting calendars.

Therefore, this schedule represents a balance of factors, focused on a need to make a significant parenting time change as a result of a chronic mental health disorder that developed during childhood. The specific changes made in this case included the necessity of maximizing the child's time with the parent most able to assist in crucial areas of his functioning, while simultaneously maintaining positive, frequent interactions with both parents and his sibling.

The Thompsons divorced when their daughter, Jada, was 8 years old. Both parents continued to be very active with her following the divorce. Three years later, the mother, who had the majority of parenting time, wanted to move from the Dallas area to Boston, both to live closer to her family of origin and because she had obtained a better job there.

The father knew her family was mainly in the Boston area and could see that the new employment position was an advancement. However, he initially was very reluctant to have his daughter move further away, much less the great distance between those two metropolitan areas. Although their relationship had been consistently positive, he feared that they would grow increasingly emotionally distant if she were living so far away, especially as her interest in peers and social interactions would likely expand as she entered her preteen and teen years. He considered going to court to try to block the potential relocation, but he and his former wife decided to attempt mediation.

In mediation, he was readily able to identify his worries and fears about the possible loss of a good relationship with Jada. A number of options were examined to protect and foster the parent–child relationship while also permitting the distant relocation. The calendar that follows represents post-relocation parenting time during a typical month that school would be in session. It shows both in-person contact as well as communication by Skype, FaceTime, or telephone (represented by T) with the father. Although it was agreed that electronic communication could potentially occur at any time, the father preferred to also have designated dates and times as a routine.

The father thought a great deal about the possibility that Jada might eventually be inclined not to travel back to Dallas to spend most of the summer with him. Therefore, the mediation included a substantial focus on how both parents could encourage her to regularly spend time with the father. The mother was very aware that if they were able to develop a parenting plan that would maximize the odds of an ongoing positive father–daughter relationship, it would increase the likelihood of the father agreeing to the relocation.

A main element in establishing a positive routine for Jada, which she presumably would want to continue, focused on peer interactions.

Therefore, the mediation agreement included a provision that both parents would encourage Jada to have regular electronic communication with her friends, both those who lived in Dallas and future ones in Boston. They set up a specific plan to help her set up a group chat with friends in Dallas. The strategy was to facilitate electronic communication with friends in Dallas, within reasonable limits, so that she would likely maintain a good deal of contact with them when she moved to Boston. Then, when it was time to spend the vast majority of summer with her father, it would probably be easy to reconnect with her Dallas area peers in person. Similarly, when Jada was in Dallas, she would be able to maintain regular contact with Boston friends and would not miss them as much. Also, the parents agreed that the summer experience for the daughter would be facilitated by having her come back to Boston at least for a few days. The father would travel to Boston with her and she would stay with him at least part of that time, though there was an agreement that she would then be able to spend substantial time with her local peers.

During the school year, the father agreed that he would travel to the Boston area for all visits, though the parents agreed to consider a modification of that routine when Jada reached 14 years of age. In the following October calendar, the mother has parenting time on all dates other than those indicating that the father is with Jada. Specific times are not listed due to the uncertainty associated with airplane flight schedules.

Monday	Tuesday	Wednesday	Thursday	Friday	Saturday	Sunday
T 8 P.M.		T 8 P.M.			F	F
T 8 P.M.		T 8 P.M.			T noon	
T 8 P.M.		T 8 P.M.			T noon	
T 8 P.M.		T 8 P.M.			T noon	

The Thompson's parenting schedule over the course of 12 months had Jada with the father almost one-third of the time, including most of the summer. The vast majority of the time that the father and daughter were together during the summer vacation, she was staying with him at his Dallas home. However, as noted earlier, there were limited times during the summer when the father visited in Boston. Also, the mother flew to visit in Dallas. Both are indicated by asterisks in the following July calendar.

Monday	Tuesday	Wednesday	Thursday	Friday	Saturday	Sunday
F	F	F	F	F	F	F
F	F	F	F	F	M*	M*
F	F	F	F	F	F	F
F	M	M	M	F*	F*	F*

The scenario of the Thompson family represents a combination of strongly considering the expanding social interests of a child approaching preteen years and the realities of trying to promote active and loving parent–child relationships across a very large expanse of the country. It also highlights the role of mediation or a similar negotiation that focuses on finding solutions through an integration of addressing the human needs and interests of all family members.

Adolescents

The Desmond parents had a rocky marriage for number of years but had stayed together. They had one child, a 14-year-old daughter named Melissa. The parents intermittently got into very heated arguments with one another. On one occasion, the police were called. They were able to get the parents to calm down and stay in separate parts of the house until the next day. Over the years, the couple had gone through two marital separations but reconciled both times.

Later, well after their second reconciliation, the parents returned from a Saturday night party and got into a loud argument with one another on the upper level of their home, near the top of the stairs. Melissa said she could generally hear the yelling but otherwise did not observe the interaction and did not hear most of what her parents said. The mother maintained that the father had shoved her and wanted to push her down the stairs, but she was able to physically maneuver away from him. The father reported that she shoved him, and he merely tried to deflect her hands away from him. She called the police, and the father was arrested and charged with domestic battery. He was able to be bailed out of jail after spending overnight there.

The next day, the mother completed a petition for an emergency order of protection and included both Melissa and herself as protected individuals. In that pleading, the mother stated that she was afraid that the father might attempt to retaliate against her by acting in an aggressive manner toward their daughter. The mother also maintained that the father had a history of making negative comments about her to Melissa, and she feared that the father would try to alienate their daughter from her by claiming that she had maliciously invented false accusations of domestic violence in order to get him removed from the home.

The emergency order of protection was granted and a hearing on the matter was set up for a few days later. After the hearing, the judge ruled that an interim order of protection would be granted. He stated that while there was uncertainty about what had actually taken place between the parents, he wanted to provide for adequate safety for both the mother and the daughter. He added that the attorneys for the parties could work to see if they could establish an agreement about the matter, but if that did not take place, there would be a future hearing about a possible plenary order of protection that could be in effect for up to two years. An interim parenting plan was also established that required all contact between the father and the daughter to be supervised.

The only individual about whom the parents could agree regarding the father's supervision had very limited availability. The father also had designated telephone, FaceTime, or Skype (shown on the calendar as T) contact with Melissa, though because no one else was able to supervise it, the mother needed to do so. In the following calendar, only the father's time with Melissa is shown, and all of it was supervised.

Monday	Tuesday	Wednesday	Thursday	Friday	Saturday	Sunday
T 7 P.M.		T 6 P.M.		F 5–7 P.M.		F 1–3 P.M.
T 7 P.M.		T 6 P.M.		F 5–7 P.M.		

The second hearing was brief and focused largely on whether Melissa should remain a protected person in the order of protection. She described that her father had never been aggressive toward her in any way and she was not afraid of him at all. She acknowledged that she had heard her parents yelling at one another on a number of occasions and indicated that both had made critical comments to her about the other parent, at about an equal frequency. The daughter stated that she found her mother's supervision of electronic communication with the father to be unnecessary and intrusive.

In addition, the father's attorney explained that he had spoken with the local facility that provided a limited number of supervision times for parental visits, and they had a time slot available. The judge decided to continue to have Melissa identified as a protected person though he lifted the requirement that electronic communication be supervised.

He extended the order of protection for three months, at which time there would be a more extensive hearing if the parties had not come to an agreement about the matter. The revised calendar is shown here.

Monday	Tuesday	Wednesday	Thursday	Friday	Saturday	Sunday
T 7 P.M.	F 4–5 P.M.	T 6 P.M.		F 5–7 P.M.		F 1–3 P.M.
T 7 P.M.	F 4–5 P.M.	T 6 P.M.		F 5–7 P.M.		

The Desmond case, in part, represents the challenging uncertainties of disputed allegations regarding domestic violence. It also reflects the reality that older children, including those in their teens, often have opinions about parenting matters that frequently are seriously considered by the court.

The Hernandez parents had been divorced for six years and had 16-year-old twins, Jimena and Matteo. Each parent recognized that their former spouse functioned very competently as a parent, and they were consistently cooperative with one another. Both parents had positive relationships with both of the children. Also, each of them agreed that they should have an approximately equal amount of time with the children.

Both children had strong track records of taking initiative and reliably completing tasks in a timely way. They had consistently good academic records and both were reasonably active in extracurriculars. In both homes, they showed that they were reliably able to carry out duties such as getting up in the morning and getting out of the house to catch the school bus on time.

The mother was employed as a trader of international currencies and had an unusual work schedule of Monday through Friday, 10 P.M. through 6 A.M. Recently, the father had changed jobs and became a fireman, which required that he work a 24-hour shift, starting at 6 A.M., followed by being off for 48 consecutive hours. Periodically, he also worked as a handyman and painter.

In order to integrate their agreement for equally shared parenting with the realities of their work schedules, they repeatedly had to plot on a calendar (not shown) their respective availabilities to be with their teenagers. Although the mother's schedule was consistent week to week, the father's changed, though the pattern repeated itself every three weeks.

When there was a transition on a school day, it was scheduled to occur after school and is listed on the calendar as 3 P.M., though it could be later depending upon after-school activities. The parents and teenagers together decided on 1 P.M. as a weekend transition time to allow for possibly sleeping in late.

The following calendar shows a representative four-week schedule. Because it was impossible to know when the father would have additional handyman or painting work, the calendar does not include his side jobs.

Monday	Tuesday	Wednesday	Thursday	Friday	Saturday	Sunday
M 3 P.M.	F 3 P.M.	F	M 3 P.M.	M	M	M
F 3 P.M.	F	M 3 P.M.	F 3 P.M.	F	M 1 P.M.	F 1 P.M.
F	M 3 P.M.	F 3 P.M.	M 3 P.M.	M	M	M
M	F 3 P.M.	F	M 3 P.M.	F 3 P.M.	F	M 1 P.M.

The consistent cooperation between the Hernandez parents was a major factor in having this parenting schedule run effectively. Its success also relied on the ability of the teenagers to manage their time and duties well. The schedule represents that many different types of calendars can work for older children, especially when they and their parents all function well.

The Bridgemans had two daughters, Sara and Claire, who were 16 and 17 years of age, respectively. Both girls were involved in school activities. Sara was on the swim team. She practiced daily from 5:30 A.M. to 7:30 A.M. Claire was on the speech team, and her practices occurred Monday, Wednesday, and Thursday after school until 5 P.M. Both Bridgeman parents were employed and worked routine daytime hours. When they divorced two years ago, they decided to alternate weeks with the children.

Monday	Tuesday	Wednesday	Thursday	Friday	Saturday	Sunday
M 5 P.M.	M	M	M	M	M	M
F 5 P.M.	F	F	F	F	F	F

The parents lived about a mile apart from one another, and the father lived within two blocks of the high school. As a result, when it was swim season, Sara preferred to stay overnight at the father's home, regardless of the parenting schedule, to make it easy to get to school very early in the morning for practice. Claire had a friend on her speech team who lived near the mother's residence, and therefore she sometimes chose to get a ride there instead of staying at the father's home. The girls started these routines a few weeks after the parental separation. After discussions with the girls, both parents approved these routines as long as the girls gave adequate advance notice. However, in order for the girls to spend time together and be with each parent about the same amount of time, all family members agreed that the daughters would follow the official parenting time schedule on weekends.

As described earlier in the book, a number of research studies described that, after a time-sharing schedule has been put in effect, there are frequently changes from it in actual practice. Also, extracurricular activities can be especially difficult to incorporate into parenting schedules as dates and times frequently change. This hypothetical example of the Bridgeman family represents circumstances in which the actual parenting time bears only modest similarity to the official schedule. In cases with good levels of cooperation and minimal conflict, such arrangements can work out successfully.

The main points from this chapter include the following:

- The creation of parenting time schedules should begin with close consideration of child and family needs, characteristics, and circumstances.
- Preexisting parental schedules can be productive in stimulating thought and discussion about possibly useful calendars for individual families.
- Child development and temperament factors can helpfully inform parenting schedule considerations.
- Because each child manifests combinations of developmental and temperamental characteristics in unique ways, especially when combined with environmental and situational influences, each child and family must be considered individually in parenting time schedule efforts.
- There are inevitable trade-offs in timesharing schedules between temporal stability and how frequently a child is able to see each parent.
- Parenting time schedules routinely need to balance multiple child, family, and circumstantial elements.

APPENDIX A

Assertion/Information Worksheet

Assertion/Information Worksheet

Case Name ____

Statement by Mo ____ Fa ____ Other ____ Own hypo ____

Assertion:

SUPPORTIVE	**CONTRADICTORY**

Consider: Docs ____ Collateral Info ____ Legal Info ____
Pa Int ____ Child Int ____ Obs ____ Other ____

Highlight/Circle Relatively Objective Information Collect Other Info:

APPENDIX B

Airplane Travel for Unaccompanied Children

The following are information resources, including travel and safety tips. There is no assurance that all the information is correct or fully up to date. No endorsement is made or implied.

Newspaper Article

https://www.usatoday.com/story/travel/columnist/mcgee/2016/02/03/unaccompanied-minors/79703136/

Safety Tips

http://www.airsafe.com/kidsafe/kidsolo.htm

A Number of Airline Policies

https://www.learnvest.com/knowledge-center/the-best-and-cheapest-airlines-to-let-your-kid-fly-alone/

U.S. Department of Transportation Brochure "When Kids Fly Alone"

https://www.transportation.gov/sites/dot.dev/files/docs/Kids_Fly_Alone.pdf

APPENDIX C

Parenting Plan Legal Criteria

There is no guarantee that these criteria are the most recent or complete. Readers are advised to check official state sources. If relevant criteria are covered by copyright or are lengthy, the website location is given.

Alabama

Section 30-3-153

Implementation; required provisions; plan set by court.

(a) In order to implement joint custody, the court shall require the parents to submit, as part of their agreement, provisions covering matters relevant to the care and custody of the child, including, but not limited to, all of the following:

   (1) The care and education of the child.

   (2) The medical and dental care of the child.

   (3) Holidays and vacations.

   (4) Child support.

   (5) Other necessary factors that affect the physical or emotional health and well-being of the child.

   (6) Designating the parent possessing primary authority and responsibility regarding involvement of the minor child in academic, religious, civic, cultural, athletic, and other activities, and in medical and dental care if the parents are unable to agree on these decisions. The exercise of this primary authority is not intended to negate the responsibility of the parties to notify and communicate with each other as provided in this article.

(b) If the parties are unable to reach an agreement as to the provisions in subsection (a), the court shall set the plan.

(Acts 1996, No. 96-520, p. 666, § 4)

Arizona

25-403.02. Parenting plans

A. If the child's parents cannot agree on a plan for legal decision-making or parenting time, each parent must submit a proposed parenting plan.

B. Consistent with the child's best interests in section 25-403 and sections 25-403.03, 25-403.04 and 25-403.05, the court shall adopt a parenting plan that provides for both parents to share legal decision-making regarding their child and that maximizes their respective parenting time. The court shall not prefer a parent's proposed plan because of the parent's or child's gender.

C. Parenting plans shall include at least the following:

   1. A designation of the legal decision-making as joint or sole as defined in section 25-401.
   2. Each parent's rights and responsibilities for the personal care of the child and for decisions in areas such as education, health care and religious training.
   3. A practical schedule of parenting time for the child, including holidays and school vacations.
   4. A procedure for the exchanges of the child, including location and responsibility for transportation.
   5. A procedure by which proposed changes, relocation of where a child resides with either parent pursuant to section 25-408, disputes and alleged breaches may be mediated or resolved, which may include the use of conciliation services or private counseling.
   6. A procedure for periodic review of the plan's terms by the parents.
   7. A procedure for communicating with each other about the child, including methods and frequency.
   8. A statement that each party has read, understands and will abide by the notification requirements of section 25-403.05, subsection B.

D. If the parents are unable to agree on any element to be included in a parenting plan, the court shall determine that element. The court may determine other factors that are necessary to promote and protect the emotional and physical health of the child.

E. Shared legal decision-making does not necessarily mean equal parenting time.

Separately, there are nonmandatory parenting time guidelines: http://www.azcourts.gov/portals/31/parentingTime/PPWguidelines.pdf.

California

California Family Code Section 3020.

(a) The Legislature finds and declares that it is the public policy of this state to assure that the health, safety, and welfare of children shall be the court's primary concern in determining the best interest of children when making any orders regarding the physical or legal custody or visitation of children. The Legislature further finds and declares that the perpetration of child abuse or domestic violence in a household where a child resides is detrimental to the child.

(b) The Legislature finds and declares that it is the public policy of this state to assure that children have frequent and continuing contact with both parents after the parents have separated or dissolved their marriage, or ended their relationship, and to encourage parents to share the rights and responsibilities of child rearing in order to effect this policy, except where the contact would not be in the best interest of the child, as provided in Section 3011.

(c) Where the policies set forth in subdivisions (a) and (b) of this section are in conflict, any court's order regarding physical or legal custody or visitation shall be made in a manner that ensures the health, safety, and welfare of the child and the safety of all family members.

Section 3040

(a) Custody should be granted in the following order of preference according to the best interest of the child as provided in Sections 3011 and 3020:

   (1) To both parents jointly pursuant to Chapter 4 (commencing with Section 3080) or to either parent. In making an order

granting custody to either parent, the court shall consider, among other factors, which parent is more likely to allow the child frequent and continuing contact with the noncustodial parent, consistent with Sections 3011 and 3020, and shall not prefer a parent as custodian because of that parent's sex. The court, in its discretion, may require the parents to submit to the court a plan for the implementation of the custody order.

(2) If to neither parent, to the person or persons in whose home the child has been living in a wholesome and stable environment.

(3) To any other person or persons deemed by the court to be suitable and able to provide adequate and proper care and guidance for the child.

(b) The immigration status of a parent, legal guardian, or relative shall not disqualify the parent, legal guardian, or relative from receiving custody under subdivision (a).

(c) This section establishes neither a preference nor a presumption for or against joint legal custody, joint physical custody, or sole custody, but allows the court and the family the widest discretion to choose a parenting plan that is in the best interest of the child.

(d) In cases where a child has more than two parents, the court shall allocate custody and visitation among the parents based on the best interest of the child, including, but not limited to, addressing the child's need for continuity and stability by preserving established patterns of care and emotional bonds. The court may order that not all parents share legal or physical custody of the child if the court finds that it would not be in the best interest of the child as provided in Sections 3011 and 3020.

Section 3080

There is a presumption, affecting the burden of proof, that joint custody is in the best interest of a minor child, subject to Section 3011, where the parents have agreed to joint custody or so agree in open court at a hearing for the purpose of determining the custody of the minor child.

Colorado

Revised Statutes Section 14-10-124

(1.5) Allocation of parental responsibilities. The court shall determine the allocation of parental responsibilities, including parenting time and decision-making responsibilities, in accordance with the best interests of the child giving paramount consideration to the child's safety and the physical, mental, and emotional conditions and needs of the child as follows:

(a) Determination of parenting time. The court, upon the motion of either party or upon its own motion, may make provisions for parenting time that the court finds are in the child's best interests unless the court finds, after a hearing, that parenting time by the party would endanger the child's physical health or significantly impair the child's emotional development. In addition to a finding that parenting time would endanger the child's physical health or significantly impair the child's emotional development, in any order imposing or continuing a parenting time restriction, the court shall enumerate the specific factual findings supporting the restriction and may enumerate the conditions that the restricted party could fulfill in order to seek modification in the parenting plan. When a claim of child abuse or neglect, domestic violence, or sexual assault where there is also a claim that the child was conceived as a result of the sexual assault has been made to the court, or the court has reason to believe that a party has committed child abuse or neglect, domestic violence, or sexual assault where there is also a claim that the child was conceived as a result of the sexual assault, prior to determining parenting time, the court shall follow the provisions of subsection (4) of this section. In determining the best interests of the child for purposes of parenting time, the court shall consider all relevant factors, including:

   (I) The wishes of the child's parents as to parenting time;

   (II) The wishes of the child if he or she is sufficiently mature to express reasoned and independent preferences as to the parenting time schedule;

   (III) The interaction and interrelationship of the child with his or her parents, his or her siblings, and any other person who may significantly affect the child's best interests;

(IV) The child's adjustment to his or her home, school, and community;

(V) The mental and physical health of all individuals involved, except that a disability alone shall not be a basis to deny or restrict parenting time;

(VI) The ability of the parties to encourage the sharing of love, affection, and contact between the child and the other party; except that, if the court determines that a party is acting to protect the child from witnessing domestic violence or from being a victim of child abuse or neglect or domestic violence, the party's protective actions shall not be considered with respect to this factor;

(VII) Whether the past pattern of involvement of the parties with the child reflects a system of values, time commitment, and mutual support;

(VIII) The physical proximity of the parties to each other as this relates to the practical considerations of parenting time;

(IX) and (X) Repealed.

(XI) The ability of each party to place the needs of the child ahead of his or her own needs.

(b) Allocation of decision-making responsibility. The court, upon the motion of either party or its own motion, shall allocate the decision-making responsibilities between the parties based upon the best interests of the child. In determining decision-making responsibility, the court may allocate the decision-making responsibility with respect to each issue affecting the child mutually between both parties or individually to one or the other party or any combination thereof. When a claim of child abuse or neglect or domestic violence has been made to the court, or the court has reason to believe that a party has committed child abuse or neglect, domestic violence, or sexual assault where there is also a claim that the child in question was conceived as a result of the sexual assault, prior to allocating decision-making responsibility, the court shall follow the provisions of subsection (4) of this section. In determining the best interests of the child for purposes of allocating decision-making responsibilities, the court shall consider, in addition to the factors set forth in paragraph (a) of this subsection (1.5), all relevant factors including:

(I) Credible evidence of the ability of the parties to cooperate and to make decisions jointly;

(II) Whether the past pattern of involvement of the parties with the child reflects a system of values, time commitment, and mutual support that would indicate an ability as mutual decision makers to provide a positive and nourishing relationship with the child;

(III) Whether an allocation of mutual decision-making responsibility on any one or a number of issues will promote more frequent or continuing contact between the child and each of the parties.

(IV) and (V) Repealed.

(1.7) Pursuant to section 14-10-123.4, children have the right to have the determination of matters relating to parental responsibilities based upon the best interests of the child. In contested hearings on final orders regarding the allocation of parental responsibilities, the court shall make findings on the record concerning the factors the court considered and the reasons why the allocation of parental responsibilities is in the best interests of the child.

(2) The court shall not consider conduct of a party that does not affect that party's relationship to the child.

(3) In determining parenting time or decision-making responsibilities, the court shall not presume that any person is better able to serve the best interests of the child because of that person's sex.

(3.5) A request by either party for genetic testing shall not prejudice the requesting party in the allocation of parental responsibilities pursuant to subsection (1.5) of this section. (4) (a) When a claim of child abuse or neglect, domestic violence, or sexual assault where there is also a claim that the child was conceived as a result of the sexual assault has been made to the court, or the court has reason to believe that a party has committed child abuse or neglect, domestic violence, or sexual assault that resulted in the conception of the child, prior to allocating parental responsibilities, including parenting time and decision-making responsibility, and prior to considering the factors set forth in paragraphs (a) and (b) of subsection (1.5) of this section, the court shall consider the following actors:

(I) Whether one of the parties has committed an act of child abuse or neglect as defined in section 18-6-401, C.R.S., or as defined under the law of any state, which factor must be supported by a preponderance of the evidence. If the court finds that one of the parties has committed child abuse or neglect, then it shall not be in the best interests of the child to allocate mutual decision making with respect to any issue over the objection of the other party or the legal representative of the child.

(II) Whether one of the parties has committed an act of domestic violence, has engaged in a pattern of domestic violence, or has a history of domestic violence, which factor must be supported by a preponderance of the evidence. If the court finds by a preponderance of the evidence that one of the parties has committed domestic violence: (A) It shall not be in the best interests of the child to allocate mutual decision-making responsibility over the objection of the other party or the legal representative of the child, unless the court finds that there is credible evidence of the ability of the parties to make decisions cooperatively in the best interest of the child in a manner that is safe for the abused party and the child; and (B) The court shall not appoint a parenting coordinator solely to ensure that mutual decision making can be accomplished.

(III) Whether one of the parties has committed an act of sexual assault resulting in the conception of the child, which factor must be supported by a preponderance of the evidence. If the court finds by a preponderance of the evidence that one of the parties has committed sexual assault and the child was conceived as a result of the sexual assault, there is a rebuttable presumption that it is not in the best interests of the child to allocate sole or split decision-making authority to the party found to have committed sexual assault or to allocate mutual decision-making between a party found to have committed sexual assault and the party who was sexually assaulted with respect to any issue.

(IV) If one of the parties is found by a preponderance of the evidence to have committed sexual assault resulting in the conception of the child, whether it is in the best interests of the child to prohibit or limit the parenting time of that party with the child.

(b) The court shall consider the additional factors set forth in paragraphs (a) and (b) of subsection (1.5) of this section in light of any finding of child abuse or neglect, domestic violence, or sexual assault resulting in the conception of a child pursuant to this subsection (4).

(c) If a party is absent or leaves home because of an act or threatened act of domestic violence committed by the other party, such absence or leaving shall not be a factor in determining the best interests of the child.

(d) When the court finds by a preponderance of the evidence that one of the parties has committed child abuse or neglect, domestic violence, or sexual assault resulting in the conception of the child, the court shall consider, as the primary concern, the safety and well-being of the child and the abused party.

(e) When the court finds by a preponderance of the evidence that one of the parties has committed child abuse or neglect, domestic violence, or sexual assault resulting in the conception of the child, in formulating or approving a parenting plan, the court shall consider conditions on parenting time that ensure the safety of the child and of the abused party. In addition to any provisions set forth in subsection (7) of this section that are appropriate, the parenting plan in these cases may include, but is not limited to, the following provisions:

(I) An order limiting contact between the parties to contact that the court deems is safe and that minimizes unnecessary communication between the parties;

(II) An order that requires the exchange of the child for parenting time to occur in a protected setting determined by the court;

(III) An order for supervised parenting time;

(IV) An order restricting overnight parenting time;

(V) An order that restricts the party who has committed domestic violence, sexual assault resulting in the conception of the child, or child abuse or neglect from possessing or consuming alcohol or controlled substances during parenting time or for twenty-four hours prior to the commencement of parenting time;

(VI) An order directing that the address of the child or of any party remain confidential;

(VII) An order that imposes any other condition on one or more parties that the court determines is necessary to protect the child, another party, or any other family or household member of a party; and

(VIII) An order that requires child support payments to be made through the child support registry to avoid the need for any related contact between the parties and an order that the payments be treated as a nondisclosure of information case.

(f) When the court finds by a preponderance of the evidence that one of the parties has committed domestic violence, the court may order the party to submit to a domestic violence evaluation. If the court determines, based upon the results of the evaluation, that treatment is appropriate, the court may order the party to participate in domestic violence treatment. At any time, the court may require a subsequent evaluation to determine whether additional treatment is necessary. If the court awards parenting time to a party who has been ordered to participate in domestic violence treatment, the court may order the party to obtain a report from the treatment provider concerning the party's progress in treatment and addressing any ongoing safety concerns regarding the party's parenting time. The court may order the party who has committed domestic violence to pay the costs of the domestic violence evaluations and treatment.

(5) Repealed.

(6) In the event of a medical emergency, either party shall be allowed to obtain necessary medical treatment for the minor child or children without being in violation of the order allocating decision-making responsibility or in contempt of court.

(7) In order to implement an order allocating parental responsibilities, both parties may submit a parenting plan or plans for the court's approval that shall address both parenting time and the allocation of decision-making responsibilities. If no parenting plan is submitted or if the court does not approve a submitted parenting plan, the court, on its own motion, shall formulate a parenting plan that

shall address parenting time and the allocation of decision-making responsibilities. When issues relating to parenting time are contested, and in other cases where appropriate, the parenting plan must be as specific as possible to clearly address the needs of the family as well as the current and future needs of the aging child. In general, the parenting plan may include, but is not limited to, the following provisions:

(a) A designation of the type of decision-making awarded;

(b) A practical schedule of parenting time for the child, including holidays and school vacations;

(c) A procedure for the exchanges of the child for parenting time, including the location of the exchanges and the party or parties responsible for the child's transportation;

(d) A procedure for communicating with each other about the child, including methods for communicating and frequency of communication;

(e) A procedure for communication between a parent and the child outside of that parent's parenting time, including methods for communicating and frequency of communication; and

(f) Any other orders in the best interests of the child.

(8) The court may order mediation, pursuant to section 13-22-311, C.R.S., to assist the parties in formulating or modifying a parenting plan or in implementing a parenting plan specified in subsection (7) of this section and may allocate the cost of said mediation between the parties.

Connecticut

General Statutes Section 46b-56a

(d) In any proceeding before the Superior Court involving a dispute between the parents of a minor child with respect to the custody, care, education and upbringing of such child, the parents shall file with the court, at such time and in such form as provided by rule of court, a proposed parental responsibility plan that shall include, at a minimum, the following: (1) A schedule of the physical residence of the child during the year; (2) provisions allocating decision-making authority to one or both parents regarding the child's health, education and religious upbringing; (3) provisions for the resolution of future disputes between the parents, including, where appropriate, the involvement of a mental health professional or other parties to assist the parents in reaching a developmentally appropriate resolution to such disputes; (4) provisions for dealing with the parents' failure to honor their responsibilities under the plan; (5) provisions for dealing with the child's changing needs as the child grows and matures; and (6) provisions for minimizing the child's exposure to harmful parental conflict, encouraging the parents in appropriate circumstances to meet their responsibilities through agreements, and protecting the best interests of the child.

Delaware

http://courts.delaware.gov/family/visitation/visitation.aspx

District of Columbia

Section 16-914(c)

(c) In any custody proceeding under this chapter, the Court may order each parent to submit a detailed parenting plan which shall delineate each parent's position with respect to the scheduling and allocation of rights and responsibilities that will best serve the interest of the minor child or children. The parenting plan may include, but shall not be limited to, provisions for:

(1) the residence of the child or children;

(2) the financial support based on the needs of the child and the actual resources of the parent;

(3) visitation;

(4) holidays, birthdays, and vacation visitation;

(5) transportation of the child between the residences;

(6) education;

(7) religious training, if any;

(8) access to the child's educational, medical, psychiatric, and dental treatment records;

(9) except in emergencies, the responsibility for medical, psychiatric, and dental treatment decisions;

(10) communication between the child and the parents; and

(11) the resolution of conflict, such as a recognized family counseling or mediation service, before application to the Court to resolve a conflict.

Florida

http://www.leg.state.fl.us/statutes/index.cfm?App_mode=Display_Statute&URL=0000-0099/0061/Sections/0061.13.html

Georgia

Sec. 19-9-1. Parenting plans; requirements for plan

(a) Except when a parent seeks emergency relief for family violence pursuant to Code Section 19-13-3 or 19-13-4, in all cases in which the custody of any child is at issue between the parents, each parent shall prepare a parenting plan or the parties may jointly submit a parenting plan. It shall be in the court's discretion as to when a party shall be required to submit a parenting plan to the court. A parenting plan shall be required for permanent custody and modification actions and in the court's discretion may be required for temporary hearings. The final order in any legal action involving the custody of a child, including modification actions, shall incorporate a permanent parenting plan as further set forth in this Code section; provided, however, that unless otherwise ordered by the court, a separate court order exclusively devoted to a parenting plan shall not be required.

(b) (1) Unless otherwise ordered by the court, a parenting plan shall include the following:

(A) A recognition that a close and continuing parent-child relationship and continuity in the child's life will be in the child's best interest;

(B) A recognition that the child's needs will change and grow as the child matures and demonstrate that the parents will make an effort to parent that takes this issue into account so that future modifications to the parenting plan are minimized;

(C) A recognition that a parent with physical custody will make day-to-day decisions and emergency decisions while the child is residing with such parent; and

(D) That both parents will have access to all of the child's records and information, including, but not limited to, education, health, health insurance, extracurricular activities, and religious communications.

(2) Unless otherwise ordered by the court, or agreed upon by the parties, a parenting plan shall include, but not be limited to:

(A) Where and when a child will be in each parent's physical care, designating where the child will spend each day of the year;

(B) How holidays, birthdays, vacations, school breaks, and other special occasions will be spent with each parent including the time of day that each event will begin and end;

(C) Transportation arrangements including how the child will be exchanged between the parents, the location of the exchange, how the transportation costs will be paid, and any other matter relating to the child spending time with each parent;

(D) Whether supervision will be needed for any parenting time and, if so, the particulars of the supervision;

(E) An allocation of decision-making authority to one or both of the parents with regard to the child's education, health, extracurricular activities, and religious upbringing, and if the parents agree the matters should be jointly decided, how to resolve a situation in which the parents disagree on resolution;

(F) What, if any, limitations will exist while one parent has physical custody of the child in terms of the other parent contacting the child and the other parent's right to access education, health, extracurricular activity, and religious information regarding the child; and

(G) If a military parent is a party in the case:

(i) How to manage the child's transition into temporary physical custody to a nondeploying parent if a military parent is deployed;

(ii) The manner in which the child will maintain continuing contact with a deployed parent;

(iii) How a deployed parent's parenting time may be delegated to his or her extended family;

(iv) How the parenting plan will be resumed once the deployed parent returns from deployment; and

(v) How divisions (i) through (iv) of this subparagraph serve the best interest of the child.

(c) If the parties cannot reach agreement on a permanent parenting plan, each party shall file and serve a proposed parenting plan on or before the date set by the court. Failure to comply with filing a parenting plan may result in the court adopting the plan of the opposing party if the judge finds such plan to be in the best interests of the child.

Idaho

https://legislature.idaho.gov/statutesrules/idstat/title32/t32ch7/sect32-717/

Illinois

(750 ILCS 5/602.5)

Sec. 602.5. Allocation of parental responsibilities: decision-making.

(a) Generally. The court shall allocate decision-making responsibilities according to the child's best interests. Nothing in this Act requires that each parent be allocated decision-making responsibilities.

(b) Allocation of significant decision-making responsibilities. Unless the parents otherwise agree in writing on an allocation of significant decision-making responsibilities, or the issue of the allocation of parental responsibilities has been reserved under Section 401, the court shall make the determination. The court shall allocate to one or both of the parents the significant decision-making responsibility for each significant issue affecting the child. Those significant issues shall include, without limitation, the following:

(1) Education, including the choice of schools and tutors.

(2) Health, including all decisions relating to the medical, dental, and psychological needs of the child and to the treatments arising or resulting from those needs.

(3) Religion, subject to the following provisions:

(A) The court shall allocate decision-making responsibility for the child's religious upbringing in accordance with any express or implied agreement between the parents.

(B) The court shall consider evidence of the parents' past conduct as to the child's religious upbringing in allocating decision-making responsibilities consistent with demonstrated past conduct in the absence of an express or implied agreement between the parents.

(C) The court shall not allocate any aspect of the child's religious upbringing if it determines that the parents do not or did not have an express or implied agreement for such religious upbringing or that there is insufficient evidence to demonstrate a course of conduct regarding the child's religious upbringing that could serve as a basis for any such order.

(4) Extracurricular activities.

(c) Determination of child's best interests. In determining the child's best interests for purposes of allocating significant decision-making responsibilities, the court shall consider all relevant factors, including, without limitation, the following:

(1) the wishes of the child, taking into account the child's maturity and ability to express reasoned and independent preferences as to decision-making;

(2) the child's adjustment to his or her home, school, and community;

(3) the mental and physical health of all individuals involved;

(4) the ability of the parents to cooperate to make decisions, or the level of conflict between the parties that may affect their ability to share decision-making;

(5) the level of each parent's participation in past significant decision-making with

(6) any prior agreement or course of conduct between the parents relating to decision-making with respect to the child;

(7) the wishes of the parents;

(8) the child's needs;

(9) the distance between the parents' residences, the cost and difficulty of transporting the child, each parent's and the child's daily schedules, and the ability of the parents to cooperate in the arrangement;

(10) whether a restriction on decision-making is appropriate under Section 603.10;

(11) the willingness and ability of each parent to facilitate and encourage a close and continuing relationship between the other parent and the child;

(12) the physical violence or threat of physical violence by the child's parent directed against the child;

(13) the occurrence of abuse against the child or other member of the child's household;

(14) whether one of the parents is a sex offender, and if so, the exact nature of the offense and what, if any, treatment in which the parent has successfully participated; and

(15) any other factor that the court expressly finds to be relevant.

(d) A parent shall have sole responsibility for making routine decisions with respect to the child and for emergency decisions affecting the child's health and safety during that parent's parenting time.

(e) In allocating significant decision-making responsibilities, the court shall not consider conduct of a parent that does not affect that parent's relationship to the child.

Sec. 602.7. Allocation of parental responsibilities: parenting time.

(a) Best interests. The court shall allocate parenting time according to the child's best interests.

(b) Allocation of parenting time. Unless the parents present a mutually agreed written parenting plan and that plan is approved by the court, the court shall allocate parenting time. It is presumed both parents are fit and the court shall not place any restrictions on parenting time as defined in Section 600 and described in Section 603.10, unless it finds by a preponderance of the evidence that a parent's exercise of parenting time would seriously endanger the child's physical, mental, moral, or emotional health.

In determining the child's best interests for purposes of allocating parenting time, the court shall consider all relevant factors, including, without limitation, the following:

(1) the wishes of each parent seeking parenting time;

(2) the wishes of the child, taking into account the child's maturity and ability to express reasoned and independent preferences as to parenting time;

(3) the amount of time each parent spent performing caretaking functions with respect to the child in the 24 months preceding the filing of any petition for allocation of parental responsibilities or, if the child is under 2 years of age, since the child's birth;

(4) any prior agreement or course of conduct between the parents relating to caretaking functions with respect to the child;

(5) the interaction and interrelationship of the child with his or her parents and siblings and with any other person who may significantly affect the child's best interests;

(6) the child's adjustment to his or her home, school, and community;

(7) the mental and physical health of all individuals involved;

(8) the child's needs;

(9) the distance between the parents' residences, the cost and difficulty of transporting the child, each parent's and the child's daily schedules, and the ability of the parents to cooperate in the arrangement;

(10) whether a restriction on parenting time is appropriate;

(11) the physical violence or threat of physical violence by the child's parent directed against the child or other member of the child's household;

(12) the willingness and ability of each parent to place the needs of the child ahead of his or her own needs;

(13) the willingness and ability of each parent to facilitate and encourage a close and continuing relationship between the other parent and the child;

(14) the occurrence of abuse against the child or other member of the child's household;

(15) whether one of the parents is a convicted sex offender or lives with a convicted sex offender and, if so, the exact nature of the offense and what if any treatment the offender has successfully participated in; the parties are entitled to a hearing on the issues raised in this paragraph (15);

(16) the terms of a parent's military family-care plan that a parent must complete before deployment if a parent is a member of the United States Armed Forces who is being deployed; and

(17) any other factor that the court expressly finds to be relevant.

(c) In allocating parenting time, the court shall not consider conduct of a parent that does not affect that parent's relationship to the child.

(d) Upon motion, the court may allow a parent who is deployed or who has orders to be deployed as a member of the United States Armed Forces to designate a person known to the child to exercise reasonable substitute visitation on behalf of the deployed parent, if the court determines that substitute visitation is in the best interests of the child. In determining whether substitute visitation is in the best interests of the child, the court shall consider all of the relevant factors listed in subsection (b) of this Section and apply those factors to the person designated as a substitute for the deployed parent for visitation purposes. Visitation orders entered under this subsection are subject to subsections (e) and (f) of Section 602.9 and subsections (c) and (d) of Section 603.10.

(e) If the street address of a parent is not identified pursuant to Section 708 of this Act, the court shall require the parties to identify reasonable alternative arrangements for parenting time by the other parent including, but not limited to, parenting time of the minor child at the residence of another person or at a local public or private facility.

(750 ILCS 5/602.8)

Sec. 602.8. Parenting time by parents not allocated significant decision-making responsibilities.

(a) A parent who has established parentage under the laws of this State and who is not granted significant decision-making responsibilities for a child is entitled to reasonable parenting time with the child, subject to subsections (d) and (e) of Section 603.10 of this

Act, unless the court finds, after a hearing, that the parenting time would seriously endanger the child's mental, moral, or physical health or significantly impair the child's emotional development. The order setting forth parenting time shall be in the child's best interests pursuant to the factors set forth in subsection (b) of Section 602.7 of this Act.

(b) The court may modify an order granting or denying parenting time pursuant to Section 610.5 of this Act. The court may restrict parenting time, and modify an order restricting parenting time, pursuant to Section 603.10 of this Act.

(c) If the street address of the parent allocated parental responsibilities is not identified, pursuant to Section 708 of this Act, the court shall require the parties to identify reasonable alternative arrangements for parenting time by a parent not allocated parental responsibilities, including but not limited to parenting time of the minor child at the residence of another person or at a local public or private facility.

Sec. 602.10. Parenting plan.

(a) Filing of parenting plan. All parents, within 120 days after service or filing of any petition for allocation of parental responsibilities, must file with the court, either jointly or separately, a proposed parenting plan. The time period for filing a parenting plan may be extended by the court for good cause shown. If no appearance has been filed by the respondent, no parenting plan is required unless ordered by the court.

(b) No parenting plan filed. In the absence of filing of one or more parenting plans, the court must conduct an evidentiary hearing to allocate parental responsibilities.

(c) Mediation. The court shall order mediation to assist the parents in formulating or modifying a parenting plan or in implementing a parenting plan unless the court determines that impediments to mediation exist. Costs under this subsection shall be allocated between the parties pursuant to the applicable statute or Supreme Court Rule.

(d) Parents' agreement on parenting plan. The parenting plan must be in writing and signed by both parents. The parents must submit the parenting plan to the court for approval within 120 days after service of a petition for allocation of parental responsibilities or the filing of an appearance, except for good cause shown. Notwithstanding the provisions above, the parents may agree upon and submit a parenting plan at any time after the commencement of a proceeding until prior to the entry of a judgment of dissolution of marriage. The agreement is binding upon the court unless it finds, after considering the circumstances of the parties and any other relevant evidence produced by the parties, that the agreement is not in the best interests of the child. If the court does not approve the parenting plan, the court shall make express findings of the reason or reasons for its refusal to approve the plan. The court, on its own motion, may conduct an evidentiary hearing to determine whether the parenting plan is in the child's best interests.

(e) Parents cannot agree on parenting plan. When parents fail to submit an agreed parenting plan, each parent must file and submit a written, signed parenting plan to the court within 120 days after the filing of an appearance, except for good cause shown. The court's determination of parenting time should be based on the child's best interests. The filing of the plan may be excused by the court if:

(1) the parties have commenced mediation for the purpose of formulating a parenting plan; or

(2) the parents have agreed in writing to extend the time for filing a proposed plan and the court has approved such an extension; or

(3) the court orders otherwise for good cause shown.

(f) Parenting plan contents. At a minimum, a parenting plan must set forth the following:

(1) an allocation of significant decision-making responsibilities;

(2) provisions for the child's living arrangements and for each parent's parenting time, including either:

(A) a schedule that designates in which parent's home the minor child will reside on given days; or

(B) a formula or method for determining such a schedule in sufficient detail to be enforced in a subsequent proceeding;

(3) a mediation provision addressing any proposed reallocation of parenting time or regarding the terms of allocation of parental responsibilities, except that this provision is not required

if one parent is allocated all significant decision-making responsibilities;

(4) each parent's right of access to medical, dental, and psychological records (subject to the Health and Developmental Disabilities Confidentiality Act), child care records, and school and extracurricular records, reports, and schedules, unless expressly denied by a court Mental order or denied under Section 602.11;

(5) a designation of the parent who will be denominated as the parent with the majority of parenting time for purposes of Section 606.10;

(6) the child's residential address for school enrollment purposes only;

(7) each parent's residence address and phone number, and each parent's place of employment and employment address and phone number;

(8) a requirement that a parent changing his or her residence provide at least 60 days prior written notice of the change to any other parent under the parenting plan or allocation judgment, unless such notice is impracticable or unless otherwise ordered by the court. If such notice is impracticable, written notice shall be given at the earliest date practicable. At a minimum, the notice shall set forth the following:

(A) the intended date of the change of residence; and

(B) the address of the new residence;

(9) provisions requiring each parent to notify the other of emergencies, health care, travel plans, or other significant child-related issues;

(10) transportation arrangements between the parents;

(11) provisions for communications, including electronic communications, with the child during the other parent's parenting time;

(12) provisions for resolving issues arising from a parent's future relocation, if applicable;

(13) provisions for future modifications of the parenting plan, if specified events occur;

(14) provisions for the exercise of the right of first refusal, if so desired, that are consistent with the best interests of the

minor child; provisions in the plan for the exercise of the right of first refusal must include:

(i) the length and kind of child-care requirements invoking the right of first refusal;

(ii) notification to the other parent and for his or her response;

(iii) transportation requirements; and

(iv) any other provision related to the exercise of the right of first refusal necessary to protect and promote the best interests of the minor child; and

(15) any other provision that addresses the child's best interests or that will otherwise facilitate cooperation between the parents.

The personal information under items (6), (7), and (8) of this subsection is not required if there is evidence of or the parenting plan states that there is a history of domestic violence or abuse, or it is shown that the release of the information is not in the child's or parent's best interests.

(g) The court shall conduct a trial or hearing to determine a plan which maximizes the child's relationship and access to both parents and shall ensure that the access and the overall plan are in the best interests of the child. The court shall take the parenting plans into consideration when determining parenting time and responsibilities at trial or hearing.

(h) The court may consider, consistent with the best interests of the child as defined in Section 602.7 of this Act, whether to award to one or both of the parties the right of first refusal in accordance with Section 602.3 of this Act.

Indiana

Indiana Rules of Court Parenting Time Guidelines (2017): http://www.in.gov/judiciary/rules/parenting/

Iowa

598.41 Custody of children. 1. a. The court may provide for joint custody of the child by the parties. The court, insofar as is reasonable and in the best interest of the child, shall order the custody award, including liberal visitation rights where appropriate, which will assure the child the opportunity for the maximum continuing physical and emotional contact with both parents after the parent shall have separated or dissolved the marriage, and which will encourage parents to share the rights and responsibilities of raising the child unless direct physical harm or significant emotional harm to the child, other children, or a parent is likely to result from such contact with one parent. b. Notwithstanding paragraph "a", if the court finds that a history of domestic abuse exists, a rebuttable presumption against the awarding of joint custody exists. c. The court shall consider the denial by one parent of the child's opportunity for maximum continuing contact with the other parent, without just cause, a significant factor in determining the proper custody arrangement. Just cause may include a determination by the court pursuant to subsection 3, paragraph "j", that a history of domestic abuse exists between the parents. d. If a history of domestic abuse exists as determined by a court pursuant to subsection 3, paragraph "j", and if a parent who is a victim of such domestic abuse relocates or is absent from the home based upon the fear of or actual acts or threats of domestic abuse perpetrated by the other parent, the court shall not consider the relocation or absence of that parent as a factor against that parent in the awarding of custody or visitation. e. Unless otherwise ordered by the court in the custody decree, both parents shall have legal access to information concerning the child, including but not limited to medical, educational and law enforcement records. 2. a. On the application of either parent, the court shall consider granting joint custody in cases where the parents do not agree to joint custody. b. If the court does not grant joint custody under this subsection, the court shall cite clear and convincing evidence, pursuant to the factors in subsection 3, that joint custody is unreasonable and not in the best interest of the child to the extent that the legal custodial relationship between the child and a parent should be severed. c. A finding by the court that a history of domestic abuse exists, as specified in subsection 3, paragraph "j", which is not rebutted, shall outweigh consideration of any other factor specified in subsection 3 in the determination of the awarding of custody under this subsection. d. Before ruling upon the joint custody petition in these cases, unless the court determines that a history of domestic abuse exists as specified in subsection 3, paragraph "j", or unless the court determines that direct physical harm or significant emotional harm to the child, other children, or a parent is likely to result, the court may require the parties to participate in custody mediation to determine whether joint custody is in the best interest of the child. The court may require the child's participation in the mediation insofar as the court determines the child's participation is advisable. e. The costs of custody mediation shall be paid in full or in part by the parties and taxed as court costs. 3. In considering what custody arrangement under subsection 2 is in the best interest of the minor child, the court shall consider the following factors: a. Whether each parent would be a suitable custodian for the child. b. Whether the psychological and emotional needs and development of the child will suffer due to lack of active contact with and attention from both parents. c. Whether the parents can communicate with each other regarding the child's needs. d. Whether both parents have actively cared for the child before and since the separation. e. Whether each parent can support the other parent's relationship with the child. f. Whether the custody arrangement is in accord with the child's wishes or whether the child has strong opposition, taking into consideration the child's age and maturity. g. Whether one or both the parents agree or are opposed to joint custody. h. The geographic proximity of the parents. i. Whether the safety of the child, other children, or the other parent will be jeopardized by the awarding of joint custody or by unsupervised or unrestricted visitation. j. Whether a history of domestic abuse, as defined in section 236.2, exists. In determining whether a history of domestic abuse exists, the court's consideration shall include but is not limited to commencement of an action pursuant to section 236.3, the issuance of a protective order against the parent or the issuance of a court order or consent agreement pursuant to section 236.5, the issuance of an emergency order pursuant to section 236.6, the holding of a parent in contempt pursuant to section 664A.7, the response of a peace officer to the scene of alleged domestic abuse or the arrest of a parent following response to a report of alleged domestic abuse, or a conviction for domestic abuse assault pursuant to section 708.2A. k. Whether a parent has allowed a person custody or control of, or unsupervised access to a child after knowing the person is required to register or is on the sex offender registry as a sex offender under chapter 692A. 4. Subsection 3 shall not apply when parents agree to joint custody. 5. a. If joint legal custody is awarded to both parents, the court may award joint physical care to both joint custodial parents upon the request of either parent. Prior to ruling on the request for the award of joint physical care, the court may require the parents to submit, either individually or jointly, a proposed joint physical care parenting plan. A proposed joint physical care parenting plan shall address how the parents will make decisions affecting the child, how the parents will provide a home for the child, how the child's time will be divided between the parents and how each parent will facilitate the child's time with the other parent, arrangements in addition to court-ordered child support for the child's expenses, how the parents will resolve major changes or disagreements affecting the child including changes that arise due to the child's age and developmental needs, and any other issues the court may require. If the court denies the request for joint physical care, the determination shall be accompanied by specific findings of fact and conclusions of law that the awarding of joint physical care is not in the best interest of the child. b. If joint physical care is not awarded under paragraph "a", and only one joint custodial parent is awarded physical care, the parent responsible for providing physical care shall support the other parent's relationship with the child. Physical care awarded to one parent does not affect the other parent's rights and responsibilities as a joint legal custodian of the child. Rights and responsibilities as joint legal custodian of the child include but are not limited to equal participation in decisions affecting the child's legal status, medical care, education, extracurricular activities, and religious instruction. 6. If the parties have more than one minor child, and the court awards each party the physical custody of one or more of the children, upon application by either party, and if it is reasonable and in the best interest of the children, the court shall include a provision in the custody order directing the parties to allow visitation between the children in each party's custody. 7. When a parent awarded legal custody or physical care of a child cannot act as custodian or caretaker because the parent has died or has been judicially adjudged incompetent, the court shall award legal custody including physical care of the child to the surviving parent unless the court finds that such an award is not in the child's best interest. 8. If an application for modification of a decree or a petition for modification of an order is filed, based upon differences between the parents regarding the custody arrangement established under the decree or order, unless the court determines that a history of domestic abuse exists as specified in subsection 3, paragraph "j", or unless the court determines that direct physical harm or significant emotional harm to the child, other children, or a parent is likely to result, the court may require the parents to participate in mediation to attempt to resolve the differences between the parents. 9. All orders relating to custody of a child are subject to chapter 598B.

Kansas

http://www.ksrevisor.org/statutes/chapters/ch23/023_032_0013.html

Kentucky

403.130 Rules of Civil Procedure to apply.

(d) The court shall develop a permanent parenting plan, which may include such detailed provisions as the court deems appropriate, when:

(1) So requested by either parent; or

(2) the parent or parents are unable to develop a parenting plan.

FCRPP IX. Appendix A

Model Time-Sharing/Visitation Guidelines

The following schedules are suggested as guidelines for the parents and the court in establishing time-sharing/visitation schedules. Each case will present unique facts or circumstances which shall be considered by the court in establishing a time-sharing/visitation schedule and the final schedule established by the court or agreed to by the parents may or may not be what these guidelines suggest.

1. The time-sharing/visitation schedule set by the court for holidays, school breaks and summer break should control over regularly scheduled time-sharing/visitation time, even if this allows successive time-sharing/visitation periods.
2. The parent exercising time-sharing/visitation should be responsible for timely picking up the child(ren) at the beginning of the time-sharing/visitation period and returning the child(ren) in a timely manner at the end of the time-sharing/visitation period.
3. Times in a time-sharing/visitation schedule should be set in the time zone where the child primarily resides.
4. For time-sharing/visitation times pertaining to school holidays, whether in a formal school or homeschooled, the school holidays where the child(ren) primarily resides should apply.
5. Each parent should provide to the other parent contact numbers and addresses (unless a domestic violence order is in effect) where

the child(ren) can be located during their scheduled timesharing/visitation time.

6. The parent exercising time-sharing/visitation should be given a minimum of every other weekend as time-sharing/visitation time with the child(ren) and one midweek overnight time-sharing/visitation. The parent having such time-sharing/visitation should be responsible for delivering the child(ren) to school, child care, or the other parent's home as specifically ordered by the court or agreed to by the parents.

7. Holidays.

   a. If a holiday is celebrated on a Monday following a parent's regularly scheduled timesharing/visitation, then that parent should be permitted to extend parenting time until 6:00 P.M. on the holiday, unless the parents agree otherwise.

   b. Other holidays.

(i) Parent exercising time-sharing/visitation.

   1) During the first full year after divorce/custody proceedings have been filed, the non-residential parent should have time-sharing/visitation scheduled as follows:

      a) New Year's Day and July 4th from 8:00 A.M. until 6:00 P.M.

   b) Thanksgiving, beginning at 6:00 P.M. the day school ends until 3:00 p. m. Thanksgiving Day.

   c) Christmas/Winter Break, beginning at 6:00 P.M. the day school ends until noon on December 25.

   d) Holidays not listed that are of special interest to the family should be assigned to the non-residential parent in time amounts similar to those in a), b) and c) above.

2) Holiday time not scheduled above to the parent exercising time-sharing/visitation should be with the other parent.

3) Mother's Day and Father's Day, regardless of any conflict with the above proposed schedule, should be spent with the appropriate parent from 8:00 A.M. until 6:00 P.M.

4) Fall Break or Spring Break, as allowed by the child(ren)'s school calendar, should be scheduled for the parent with whom the child(ren) primarily resides in the first full year after the divorce/custody proceedings are filed from 6:00 P.M. the day school ends

until 6:00 P.M. the following Friday. If school breaks are longer than one week due to the school schedule, the parent with whom the child(ren) primarily resides should be scheduled for the first half of the break and the other parent should be scheduled for the last half.

5) Summer Break should be scheduled to allow the parent exercising timesharing/visitation a minimum of two periods of two consecutive weeks during the Summer Break. Each parent should provide the time periods he or she desires to the other parent before the end of the school year, or at least 60 days in advance of the requested time. If a child(ren) must attend summer school in order to pass to the next grade, summer time-sharing/visitation should not prevent school time.

6) Birthdays: Unless the birthday falls on a regularly scheduled time-sharing/visitation day, the parent exercising time-sharing/visitation should be scheduled for birthday time from 5:00 P.M. until 8:00 P.M. If it is a regular day of the parent exercising timesharing/visitation where the child(ren) does not primarily reside, the other parent should have birthday time from 5:00 P.M. until 8:00 P.M.

   (ii) Alternating years: For each year thereafter, the time-sharing/visitation set out above should alternate between the parent with whom the child(ren) primarily resides and the parent exercising time-sharing/visitation.

8. Waiting/Tardiness/Cancellations.

   a. In the event either parent will be more than 30 minutes late, due to reasonable unforeseen circumstances, to pick up the child(ren), he or she should provide direct notice to the other parent or a designated third party and make suitable arrangements for exchange of the child(ren).

   b. If time-sharing/visitation is missed through no fault of the parent, and reasonable notice has been given, that time should be made up, if reasonable to do so.

   c. If the child(ren) is ill, the parent who has the child should give 24-hour notice, if possible, to allow for appropriate plans to be made.

9. Transportation: The parents should transport the child(ren) in a safe manner, which includes utilizing the appropriate child restraint systems and not driving under the influence of intoxicants.

Louisiana

335. Joint custody decree and implementation order

A. (1) In a proceeding in which joint custody is decreed, the court shall render a joint custody implementation order except for good cause shown.

(2) (a) The implementation order shall allocate the time periods during which each parent shall have physical custody of the child so that the child is assured of frequent and continuing contact with both parents.

(b) To the extent it is feasible and in the best interest of the child, physical custody of the children should be shared equally.

(3) The implementation order shall allocate the legal authority and responsibility of the parents.

B. (1) In a decree of joint custody the court shall designate a domiciliary parent except when there is an implementation order to the contrary or for other good cause shown.

(2) The domiciliary parent is the parent with whom the child shall primarily reside, but the other parent shall have physical custody during time periods that assure that the child has frequent and continuing contact with both parents.

(3) The domiciliary parent shall have authority to make all decisions affecting the child unless an implementation order provides otherwise. All major decisions made by the domiciliary parent concerning the child shall be subject to review by the court upon motion of the other parent. It shall be presumed that all major decisions made by the domiciliary parent are in the best interest of the child.

C. If a domiciliary parent is not designated in the joint custody decree and an implementation order does not provide otherwise, joint custody confers upon the parents the same rights and responsibilities as are conferred on them by the provisions of Title VII of Book I of the Civil Code.

Maine

§1653. Parental rights and responsibilities

1. Legislative findings and purpose. The Legislature makes the following findings concerning relationships among family members in determining what is in the best interest of children.
   A. The Legislature finds and declares as public policy that encouraging mediated resolutions of disputes between parents is in the best interest of minor children. [1995, c. 694, Pt. B, §2 (NEW); 1995, c. 694, Pt. E, §2 (AFF).]
   B. The Legislature finds that domestic abuse is a serious crime against the individual and society, producing an unhealthy and dangerous family environment, resulting in a pattern of escalating abuse, including violence, that frequently culminates in intrafamily homicide and creating an atmosphere that is not conducive to healthy childhood development. [1995, c. 694, Pt. B, §2 (NEW); 1995, c. 694, Pt. E, §2 (AFF).]
   C. The Legislature finds and declares that, except when a court determines that the best interest of a child would not be served, it is the public policy of this State to assure minor children of frequent and continuing contact with both parents after the parents have separated or dissolved their marriage and to encourage parents to share the rights and responsibilities of child rearing in order to effect this policy. [2009, c. 593, §1 (AMD).]
2. Parental rights and responsibilities; order. This subsection governs parental rights and responsibilities and court orders for parental rights and responsibilities.
   A. When the parents have agreed to an award of shared parental rights and responsibilities or so agree in open court, the court shall make that award unless there is substantial evidence that it should not be ordered. The court shall state in its decision the reasons for not ordering a shared parental rights and responsibilities award agreed to by the parents. [1995, c. 694, Pt. B, §2 (NEW); 1995, c. 694, Pt. E, §2 (AFF).]
   B. The court may award reasonable rights of contact with a minor child to a 3rd person. [1995, c. 694, Pt. B, §2 (NEW); 1995, c. 694, Pt. E, §2 (AFF).]

C. The court may award parental rights and responsibilities with respect to the child to a 3rd person, a suitable society or institution for the care and protection of children or the department, upon a finding that awarding parental rights and responsibilities to either or both parents will place the child in jeopardy as defined in Title 22, section 4002, subsection 6. [1995, c. 694, Pt. B, §2 (NEW); 1995, c. 694, Pt. E, §2 (AFF).]

D. The order of the court awarding parental rights and responsibilities must include the following:

(1) Allocated parental rights and responsibilities, shared parental rights and responsibilities or sole parental rights and responsibilities, according to the best interest of the child as provided in subsection 3. An award of shared parental rights and responsibilities may include either an allocation of the child's primary residential care to one parent and rights of parent-child contact to the other parent, or a sharing of the child's primary residential care by both parents. If either or both parents request an award of shared primary residential care and the court does not award shared primary residential care of the child, the court shall state in its decision the reasons why shared primary residential care is not in the best interest of the child;

(2) Conditions of parent-child contact in cases involving domestic abuse as provided in subsection 6;

(3) A provision for child support as provided in subsection 8 or a statement of the reasons for not ordering child support;

(4) A statement that each parent must have access to records and information pertaining to a minor child, including, but not limited to, medical, dental and school records and other information on school activities, whether or not the child resides with the parent, unless that access is found not to be in the best interest of the child or that access is found to be sought for the purpose of causing detriment to the other parent. If that access is not ordered, the court shall state in the order its reasons for denying that access;

(5) A statement that violation of the order may result in a finding of contempt and imposition of sanctions as provided in subsection 7; and

(6) A statement of the definition of shared parental rights and responsibilities contained in section 1501, subsection 5, if the order of the court awards shared parental rights and responsibilities.

An order modifying a previous order is not required to include provisions of the previous order that are not modified. [2015, c. 494, Pt. A, §11 (AMD).]

E. The order of the court may not include a requirement that the State pay for the defendant to attend a batterers' intervention program unless the program is certified under section 4014.

3. Best interest of child. The court, in making an award of parental rights and responsibilities with respect to a child, shall apply the standard of the best interest of the child. In making decisions regarding the child's residence and parent-child contact, the court shall consider as primary the safety and well-being of the child. In applying this standard, the court shall consider the following factors:

A. The age of the child; [1995, c. 694, Pt. B, §2 (NEW); 1995, c. 694, Pt. E, §2 (AFF).

B. The relationship of the child with the child's parents and any other persons who may significantly affect the child's welfare; [1995, c. 694, Pt. B, §2 (NEW); 1995, c. 694, Pt. E, §2 (AFF).

C. The preference of the child, if old enough to express a meaningful preference; [1995, c. 694, Pt. B, §2 (NEW); 1995, c. 694, Pt. E, §2 (AFF).]

D. The duration and adequacy of the child's current living arrangements and the desirability of maintaining continuity; [1995, c. 694, Pt. B, §2 (NEW); 1995, c. 694, Pt. E, §2 (AFF).]

E. The stability of any proposed living arrangements for the child; [1995, c. 694, Pt. B, §2 (NEW); 1995, c. 694, Pt. E, §2 (AFF).]

F. The motivation of the parties involved and their capacities to give the child love, affection and guidance; [1995, c. 694, Pt. B, §2 (NEW); 1995, c. 694, Pt. E, §2 (AFF).]

G. The child's adjustment to the child's present home, school and community; [1995, c. 694, Pt. B, §2 (NEW); 1995, c. 694, Pt. E, §2 (AFF).]

H. The capacity of each parent to allow and encourage frequent and continuing contact between the child and the other parent, including physical access; [1995, c. 694, Pt. B, §2 (NEW); 1995, c. 694, Pt. E, §2 (AFF).]

I. The capacity of each parent to cooperate or to learn to cooperate in child care; [1995, c. 694, Pt. B, §2 (NEW); 1995, c. 694, Pt. E, §2 (AFF).]

J. Methods for assisting parental cooperation and resolving disputes and each parent's willingness to use those methods; [1995, c. 694, Pt. B, §2 (NEW); 1995, c. 694, Pt. E, §2 (AFF).]

K. The effect on the child if one parent has sole authority over the child's upbringing; [1995, c. 694, Pt. B, §2 (NEW); 1995, c. 694, Pt. E, §2 (AFF).]

L. The existence of domestic abuse between the parents, in the past or currently, and how that abuse affects:

   (1) The child emotionally;

   (2) The safety of the child; and

   (3) The other factors listed in this subsection, which must be considered in light of the presence of past or current domestic abuse; [2009, c. 593, §2 (AMD).]

M. The existence of any history of child abuse by a parent; [1997, c. 187, §3 (AMD); 1997, c. 187, §5 (AFF).]

N. All other factors having a reasonable bearing on the physical and psychological well-being of the child; [1999, c. 702, §1 (AMD).]

O. A parent's prior willful misuse of the protection from abuse process in chapter 101 in order to gain tactical advantage in a proceeding involving the determination of parental rights and responsibilities of a minor child. Such willful misuse may only be considered if established by clear and convincing evidence, and if it is further found by clear and convincing evidence that in the particular circumstances of the parents and child, that willful misuse tends to show that the acting parent will in the future have a lessened ability and willingness to cooperate and work with the other parent in their shared responsibilities for the child. The court shall articulate findings of fact whenever relying upon this factor as part of its determination of a child's best interest. The voluntary dismissal of a protection from abuse petition may not, taken alone, be treated as evidence of the willful misuse of the protection from abuse process; [2001, c. 665, §1 (AMD).]

P. If the child is under one year of age, whether the child is being breast-fed; [2005, c. 567, §1 (AMD).]

Q. The existence of a parent's conviction for a sex offense or a sexually violent offense as those terms are defined in Title 34-A, section 11203; [2009, c. 593, §3 (AMD).]

R. If there is a person residing with a parent, whether that person:

(1) Has been convicted of a crime under Title 17-A, chapter 11 or 12 or a comparable crime in another jurisdiction;

(2) Has been adjudicated of a juvenile offense that, if the person had been an adult at the time of the offense, would have been a violation of Title 17-A, chapter 11 or 12; or

(3) Has been adjudicated in a proceeding, in which the person was a party, under Title 22, chapter 1071 as having committed a sexual offense; and [2009, c. 593, §4 (AMD).]

S. Whether allocation of some or all parental rights and responsibilities would best support the child's safety and well-being. [2009, c. 593, §5 (NEW).]

4. Equal consideration of parents. The court may not apply a preference for one parent over the other in determining parental rights and responsibilities because of the parent's gender or the child's age or gender. [1995, c. 694, Pt. B, §2 (NEW); 1995, c. 694, Pt. E, §2 (AFF).]

5. Departure from family residence. The court may not consider departure from the family residence as a factor in determining parental rights and responsibilities with respect to a minor child when the departing parent has been physically harmed or seriously threatened with physical harm by the other parent and that harm or threat of harm was causally related to the departure, or when one parent has left the family residence by mutual agreement or at the request or insistence of the other parent. [1995, c. 694, Pt. B, §2 (NEW); 1995, c. 694, Pt. E, §2 (AFF).]

5 A. Effect of protective order. Although the court shall consider the fact that a protective order was issued under chapter 101, the court shall determine the proper award of parental rights and responsibilities and award of rights of contact de novo

and may not use as precedent the award of parental rights and responsibilities and rights of contact included in the protective order. [2001, c. 273, §1 (NEW).]

6. Conditions of parent-child contact in cases involving domestic abuse. The court shall establish conditions of parent-child contact in cases involving domestic abuse as follows.
   A. A court may award primary residence of a minor child or parent-child contact with a minor child to a parent who has committed domestic abuse only if the court finds that contact between the parent and child is in the best interest of the child and that adequate provision for the safety of the child and the parent who is a victim of domestic abuse can be made. [1995, c. 694, Pt. B, §2 (NEW); 1995, c. 694, Pt. E, §2 (AFF).]
   B. In an order of parental rights and responsibilities, a court may:
      (1) Order an exchange of a child to occur in a protected setting;
      (2) Order contact to be supervised by another person or agency;
      (3) Order the parent who has committed domestic abuse to attend and complete to the satisfaction of the court a domestic abuse intervention program or other designated counseling as a condition of the contact;
      (4) Order either parent to abstain from possession or consumption of alcohol or controlled substances, or both, during the visitation and for 24 hours preceding the contact;
      (5) Order the parent who has committed domestic abuse to pay a fee to defray the costs of supervised contact;
      (6) Prohibit overnight parent-child contact; and
      (7) Impose any other condition that is determined necessary to provide for the safety of the child, the victim of domestic abuse or any other family or household member. [1995, c. 694, Pt. B, §2 (NEW); 1995, c. 694, Pt. E, §2 (AFF).]
   C. The court may require security from the parent who has committed domestic abuse for the return and safety of the child. [1995, c. 694, Pt. B, §2 (NEW); 1995, c. 694, Pt. E, §2 (AFF).]

D. The court may order the address of the child and the victim to be kept confidential. [1995, c. 694, Pt. B, §2 (NEW); 1995, c. 694, Pt. E, §2 (AFF).]

E. The court may not order a victim of domestic abuse to attend counseling with the parent who has committed domestic abuse. [1995, c. 694, Pt. B, §2 (NEW); 1995, c. 694, Pt. E, §2 (AFF).]

F. If a court allows a family or household member to supervise parent-child contact, the court shall establish conditions to be followed during that contact. Conditions include but are not limited to:

(1) Minimizing circumstances when the family of the parent who has committed domestic abuse would be supervising visits;

(2) Ensuring that contact does not damage the relationship with the parent with whom the child has primary physical residence;

(3) Ensuring the safety and well-being of the child; and

(4) Requiring that supervision is provided by a person who is physically and mentally capable of supervising a visit and who does not have a criminal history or history of abuse or neglect. [1995, c. 694, Pt. B, §2 (NEW); 1995, c. 694, Pt. E, §2 (AFF).]

G. Fees set forth in this subsection incurred by the parent who has committed domestic abuse may not be considered as a mitigating factor reducing that parent's child support obligation. [1995, c. 694, Pt. B, §2 (NEW); 1995, c. 694, Pt. E, §2 (AFF).]

6-A. Custody and contact limited; convictions for sexual offenses. The award of primary residence and parent-child contact with a person who has been convicted of a child-related sexual offense is governed by this subsection.

A. For the purposes of this section, "child-related sexual offense" means the following sexual offenses if, at the time of the commission of the offense, the victim was under 18 years of age or the victim was a student enrolled in a private or public elementary, secondary or special education school, facility or institution and the person was a teacher, employee or other official having instructional, supervisory or disciplinary authority over the student:

(1) Sexual exploitation of a minor, under Title 17-A, section 282;

(2) Gross sexual assault, under Title 17-A, section 253;

(3) Sexual abuse of a minor, under Title 17-A, section 254;

(4) Unlawful sexual contact, under Title 17-A, section 255-A or former section 255;

(5) Visual sexual aggression against a child, under Title 17-A, section 256;

(6) Sexual misconduct with a child under 14 years of age, under Title 17-A, section 258;

(6-A) Solicitation of a child to commit a prohibited act, under Title 17-A, section 259-A; or

(7) An offense in another jurisdiction that involves conduct that is substantially similar to that contained in subparagraph (1), (2), (3), (4), (5), (6) or (6-A). For purposes of this subparagraph, "another jurisdiction" means the Federal Government, the United States military, the District of Columbia, the Commonwealth of Puerto Rico, the Commonwealth of the Northern Mariana Islands, the United States Virgin Islands, Guam, American Samoa and each of the several states except Maine. "Another jurisdiction" also means the Passamaquoddy Tribe when that tribe has acted pursuant to Title 30, section 6209-A, subsection 1, paragraph A or B and the Penobscot Nation when that tribe has acted pursuant to Title 30, section 6209-B, subsection 1, paragraph A or B. [2015, c. 509, §4 (AMD).]

B. A court may award primary residence of a minor child or parent-child contact with a minor child to a parent who has been convicted of a child-related sexual offense only if the court finds that contact between the parent and child is in the best interest of the child and that adequate provision for the safety of the child can be made. [2001, c. 665, §4 (NEW).]

C. In an order of parental rights and responsibilities, a court may require that parent-child contact between a minor child and a person convicted of a child-related sexual offense may occur only if there is another person or agency present to supervise the contact. If the court allows a family or household member to supervise parent-child contact, the court shall establish conditions to be followed during that contact. Conditions include, but are not limited to, those that:

(1) Minimize circumstances when the family of the parent who is a sex offender or sexually violent predator would be supervising visits;

(2) Ensure that contact does not damage the relationship with the parent with whom the child has primary physical residence;

(3) Ensure the safety and well-being of the child; and

(4) Require that supervision be provided by a person who is physically and mentally capable of supervising a visit and who does not have a criminal history or history of abuse or neglect. [2001, c. 665, §4 (NEW).][2015, c. 509, §4 (AMD) .]

6-B. Conviction or adjudication for certain sex offenses; presumption. There is a rebuttable presumption that the petitioner would create a situation of jeopardy for the child if any contact were to be permitted and that any contact is not in the best interests of the child if the court finds that the person seeking primary residence or contact with the child:

A. Has been convicted of an offense listed in subsection 6-A, paragraph A in which the victim was a minor at the time of the offense and the person was at least 5 years older than the minor at the time of the offense except that, if the offense was gross sexual assault under Title 17-A, section 253, subsection 1, paragraph B or C, or an offense in another jurisdiction that involves conduct that is substantially similar to that contained in Title 17-A, section 253, subsection 1, paragraph B or C, and the minor victim submitted as a result of compulsion, the presumption applies regardless of the ages of the person and the minor victim at the time of the offense; or [2007, c. 513, §3 (AMD).]

B. Has been adjudicated in an action under Title 22, chapter 1071 of sexually abusing a person who was a minor at the time of the abuse. [2005, c. 366, §3 (NEW).]

The person seeking primary residence or contact with the child may present evidence to rebut the presumption. [2007, c. 513, §3 (AMD) .]

7. Violation of order concerning parental rights and responsibilities and contact. Either parent may petition the court for a hearing on the issue of noncompliance with the order issued under subsection 2. If the court finds that a parent has violated a part of the order, the court may find that parent in contempt and may:
   A. Require additional or more specific terms and conditions consistent with the order; [1995, c. 694, Pt. B, §2 (NEW); 1995, c. 694, Pt. E, §2 (AFF).]
   B. Order that additional visitation be provided for a parent to take the place of visitation that was wrongfully denied; or [1995, c. 694, Pt. B, §2 (NEW); 1995, c. 694, Pt. E, §2 (AFF).]
   C. Order a parent found in contempt to pay a forfeiture of at least $100.

Massachusetts

https://malegislature.gov/Laws/GeneralLaws/PartII/TitleIII/Chapter208/Section31

Separately, there is a nonmandatory model parenting plan: http://www.mass.gov/courts/docs/courts-and-judges/courts/probate-and-family-court/parentingplan.pdf

Michigan

http://www.legislature.mi.gov/(S(d23z5cpw4c5gx4v310hmjcgj))/mileg.aspx?page=getobject&objectname=mcl-722-27a

Separately, there are parenting time guidelines: http://courts.mi.gov/administration/scao/resources/documents/publications/manuals/focb/pt_gdlns.pdf

Minnesota

https://www.revisor.leg.state.mn.us/statutes/?id=518.1705

Missouri

http://www.moga.mo.gov/mostatutes/stathtml/45200003751.HTML

Montana

40-4-234. Final parenting plan criteria.

(1) In every dissolution proceeding, proceeding for declaration of invalidity of marriage, parenting plan proceeding, or legal separation proceeding that involves a child, each parent or both parents jointly shall submit to the court, in good faith, a proposed final plan for parenting the child, which may include the allocation of parenting functions. A final parenting plan must be incorporated into any final decree or amended decree, including cases of dissolution by default. As used in this section, parenting functions means those aspects of the parent-child relationship in which the parent makes decisions and performs functions necessary for the care and growth of the child, which may include:

(a) maintaining a loving, stable, consistent, and nurturing relationship with the child;

(b) attending to the daily needs of the child, such as feeding, physical care, development, and grooming, supervision, spiritual growth and development, health care, day care, and engaging in other activities that are appropriate to the developmental level of the child and that are within the social and economic circumstances of the particular family;

(c) attending to adequate education for the child, including remedial or other education essential to the best interest of the child;

(d) ensuring the interactions and interrelationship of the child with the child's parents and siblings and with any other person who significantly affects the child's best interest; and

(e) exercising appropriate judgment regarding the child's welfare, consistent with the child's developmental level and the family's social and economic circumstances.

(2) Based on the best interest of the child, a final parenting plan may include, at a minimum, provisions for:

(a) designation of a parent as custodian of the child, solely for the purposes of all other state and federal statutes that require a designation or determination of custody, but the designation may not affect either parent's rights and responsibilities under the parenting plan;

(b) designation of the legal residence of both parents and the child, except as provided in 40-4-217;

(c) a residential schedule specifying the periods of time during which the child will reside with each parent, including provisions for holidays, birthdays of family members, vacations, and other special occasions;

(d) finances to provide for the child's needs;

(e) any other factors affecting the physical and emotional health and well-being of the child;

(f) periodic review of the parenting plan when requested by either parent or the child or when circumstances arise that are foreseen by the parents as triggering a need for review, such as attainment by the child of a certain age or if a change in the child's residence is necessitated;

(g) sanctions that will apply if a parent fails to follow the terms of the parenting plan, including contempt of court;

(h) allocation of parental decisionmaking authority regarding the child's:

 (i) education;

 (ii) spiritual development; and

 (iii) health care and physical growth;

(i) the method by which future disputes concerning the child will be resolved between the parents, other than court action; and

(j) the unique circumstances of the child or the family situation that the parents agree will facilitate a meaningful, ongoing relationship between the child and parents.

(3) In approving a final parenting plan for a child of a parent in military service, the court may not disapprove the plan only because of the parent's military service.

(4) The court may in its discretion order the parties to participate in a dispute resolution process to assist in resolving any conflicts

between the parties regarding adoption of the parenting plan. The dispute resolution process may include counseling or mediation by a specified person or agency or court action.

(5) Each parent may make decisions regarding the day-to-day care and control of the child while the child is residing with that parent, and either parent may make emergency decisions affecting the child's safety or health. When mutual decision making is designated in the parenting plan but cannot be achieved regarding a particular issue, the parents shall make a good faith effort to resolve the issue through any dispute resolution process provided for in the final parenting plan.

(6) If a parent fails to comply with a provision of the parenting plan, the other parent's obligations under the parenting plan are not affected.

(7) At the request of either parent or appropriate party, the court shall order that the parenting plan be sealed except for access by the parents, guardian, or other person having custody of the child.

Nebraska

http://nebraskalegislature.gov/laws/statutes.php?statute=43-2929

New Hampshire

461-A:4 Parenting Plans; Contents.

I. In any proceeding to establish or modify a judgment providing for parenting time with a child, except for matters filed under RSA 173-B, the parents shall develop and file with the court a parenting plan to be included in the court's decree. If the parents are unable to develop a parenting plan, the court may develop it. In developing a parenting plan under this section, the court shall consider only the best interests of the child as provided under RSA 461-A:6 and the safety of the parties.

II. A parenting plan may include provisions relative to:

(a) Decision-making responsibility and residential responsibility.

(b) Information sharing and access, including telephone and electronic access.

(c) Legal residence of a child for school attendance.

(d) Parenting schedule, including:

(1) Holiday, birthday, and vacation planning.

(2) Weekends, including holidays, and school in-service days preceding or following weekends.

(e) Transportation and exchange of the child.

(f) Relocation of parents.

(g) Procedure for review and adjustment of the plan.

(h) Methods for resolving disputes.

III. If the parties are insured and the parenting plan directs the parties to participate in counseling, the court shall give due consideration to selecting a counselor who accepts direct payment from the parties' health insurance carrier.

IV. If the parents have joint decision-making responsibility under RSA 461-A:5, the parenting plan shall include the legal residence of each parent unless the court finds that there is a history of domestic abuse or stalking or that including such information would not be in the best interest of the child. If the parenting plan includes a parent's residence, the parent shall be responsible for promptly notifying the court and the other parent of any change in residence. The failure to provide such information may result in a finding of contempt of court.

V. If the court orders supervised visitation, it may order that such visitation shall take place only at a visitation center that uses a metal detection device and has trained security personnel on-site.

Source. 2005, 273:1, eff. Oct. 1, 2005. 2011, 106:3, eff. July 30, 2011; 176:1, eff. Jan. 1, 2012. 2014, 107:3, eff. June 11, 2014.

Section 461-A:4-a

461-A:4-a Judicial Enforcement of Parenting Plan.—Any motion for contempt or enforcement of an order regarding an approved parenting plan under this chapter, if filed by a parent, shall be reviewed by the court within 30 days.

New Jersey

Rule 5:8-5. Custody and Parenting Time/Visitation Plans, Recital in Judgment or Order § (a) In any family action in which the parties cannot agree to a custody or parenting time/visitation arrangement, the parties must each submit a Custody and Parenting Time/Visitation Plan to the court no later than seventy-five (75) days after the last responsive pleading, which the court shall consider in awarding custody and fixing a parenting time or visitation schedule. Contents of Plan. The Custody and Parenting Time/Visitation Plan shall include but shall not be limited to the following factors: (1) Address of the parties. (2) Employment of the parties. (3) Type of custody requested with the reasons for selecting the type of custody. (a) Joint legal custody with one parent having primary residential care. (b) Joint physical custody. (c) Sole custody to one parent, parenting time/visitation to the other. (d) Other custodial arrangement. (4) Specific schedule as to parenting time/visitation including, but not limited to, weeknights, weekends, vacations, legal holidays, religious holidays, school vacations, birthdays and special occasions (family outings, extracurricular activities and religious services). (5) Access to medical school records. (6) Impact if there is to be a contemplated change of residence by a parent. (7) Participation in making decisions regarding the child(ren). (8) Any other pertinent information. (b) The court shall set out in its order or judgment fully and specifically all terms and conditions relating to the award of custody and proper support for the children. (c) Failure to comply with the provisions of the Custody and Parenting Time/Visitation Plan may result in the dismissal of the non-complying party's pleadings or the imposition of other sanctions, or both. Dismissed pleadings shall be subject to reinstatement upon such conditions as the court may order.

New Mexico

40-4-9.1. Joint custody; standards for determination; parenting plan.

A. There shall be a presumption that joint custody is in the best interests of a child in an initial custody determination. An award of joint custody does not imply an equal division of financial responsibility for the child. Joint custody shall not be awarded as a substitute for an existing custody arrangement unless there has been a substantial and material change in circumstances since the entry of the prior custody order or decree, which change affects the welfare of the child such that joint custody is presently in the best interests of the child. With respect to any proceeding in which it is proposed that joint custody be terminated, the court shall not terminate joint custody unless there has been a substantial and material change in circumstances affecting the welfare of the child, since entry of the joint custody order, such that joint custody is no longer in the best interests of the child.

B. In determining whether a joint custody order is in the best interests of the child, in addition to the factors provided in Section 40-4-9 NMSA 1978, the court shall consider the following factors:

(1) whether the child has established a close relationship with each parent;

(2) whether each parent is capable of providing adequate care for the child throughout each period of responsibility, including arranging for the child's care by others as needed;

(3) whether each parent is willing to accept all responsibilities of parenting, including a willingness to accept care of the child at specified times and to relinquish care to the other parent at specified times;

(4) whether the child can best maintain and strengthen a relationship with both parents through predictable, frequent contact and whether the child's development will profit from such involvement and influence from both parents;

(5) whether each parent is able to allow the other to provide care without intrusion, that is, to respect the other's parental rights and responsibilities and right to privacy;

(6) the suitability of a parenting plan for the implementation of joint custody, preferably, although not necessarily, one arrived at through parental agreement;

(7) geographic distance between the parents' residences;

(8) willingness or ability of the parents to communicate, cooperate or agree on issues regarding the child's needs; and

(9) whether a judicial adjudication has been made in a prior or the present proceeding that either parent or other person seeking custody has engaged in one or more acts of domestic abuse against the child, a parent of the child or other household member. If a determination is made that domestic abuse has

occurred, the court shall set forth findings that the custody or visitation ordered by the court adequately protects the child, the abused parent or other household member.

C. In any proceeding in which the custody of a child is at issue, the court shall not prefer one parent as a custodian solely because of gender.

D. In any case in which the parents agree to a form of custody, the court should award custody consistent with the agreement unless the court determines that such agreement is not in the best interests of the child.

E. In making an order of joint custody, the court may specify the circumstances, if any, under which the consent of both legal custodians is required to be obtained in order to exercise legal control of the child and the consequences of the failure to obtain mutual consent.

F. When joint custody is awarded, the court shall approve a parenting plan for the implementation of the prospective custody arrangement prior to the award of joint custody. The parenting plan shall include a division of a child's time and care into periods of responsibility for each parent. It may also include:

(1) statements regarding the child's religion, education, child care, recreational activities and medical and dental care;

(2) designation of specific decision-making responsibilities;

(3) methods of communicating information about the child, transporting the child, exchanging care for the child and maintaining telephone and mail contact between parent and child;

(4) procedures for future decision making, including procedures for dispute resolution; and

(5) other statements regarding the welfare of the child or designed to clarify and facilitate parenting under joint custody arrangements.

In a case where joint custody is not agreed to or necessary aspects of the parenting plan are contested, the parties shall each submit parenting plans. The court may accept the plan proposed by either party or it may combine or revise these plans as it deems necessary in the child's best interests. The time of filing of parenting plans shall be set by local rule. A plan adopted by the court shall be entered as an order of the court.

G. Where custody is contested, the court shall refer that issue to mediation if feasible. The court may also use auxiliary services such as professional evaluation by application of Rule 706 [Rule 11-706 NMRA] of the New Mexico Rules of Evidence or Rule 53 [Rule 1-053 NMRA] of the Rules of Civil Procedure for the District Courts.

H. Notwithstanding any other provisions of law, access to records and information pertaining to a minor child, including medical, dental and school records, shall not be denied to a parent because that parent is not the child's physical custodial parent or because that parent is not a joint custodial parent.

I. Whenever a request for joint custody is granted or denied, the court shall state in its decision its basis for granting or denying the request for joint custody. A statement that joint custody is or is not in the best interests of the child is not sufficient to meet the requirements of this subsection.

J. An award of joint custody means that:

(1) each parent shall have significant, well-defined periods of responsibility for the child;

(2) each parent shall have, and be allowed and expected to carry out, responsibility for the child's financial, physical, emotional and developmental needs during that parent's periods of responsibility;

(3) the parents shall consult with each other on major decisions involving the child before implementing those decisions; that is, neither parent shall make a decision or take an action which results in a major change in a child's life until the matter has been discussed with the other parent and the parents agree. If the parents, after discussion, cannot agree and if one parent wishes to effect a major change while the other does not wish the major change to occur, then no change shall occur until the issue has been resolved as provided in this subsection;

(4) the following guidelines apply to major changes in a child's life:

(a) if either parent plans to change his home city or state of residence, he shall provide to the other parent thirty days' notice in writing stating the date and destination of move;

(b) the religious denomination and religious activities, or lack thereof, which were being practiced during the marriage should not be changed unless the parties agree or it has been otherwise resolved as provided in this subsection;

(c) both parents shall have access to school records, teachers and activities. The type of education, public or private, which was in place during the marriage should continue, whenever possible, and school districts should not be changed unless the parties agree or it has been otherwise resolved as provided in this subsection;

(d) both parents shall have access to medical and dental treatment providers and records. Each parent has authority to make emergency medical decisions. Neither parent may contract for major elective medical or dental treatment unless both parents agree or it has been otherwise resolved as provided in this subsection; and

(e) both parents may attend the child's public activities and both parents should know the necessary schedules. Whatever recreational activities the child participated in during the marriage should continue with the child's agreement, regardless of which of the parents has physical custody. Also, neither parent may enroll the child in a new recreational activity unless the parties agree or it has been otherwise resolved as provided in this subsection; and

(5) decisions regarding major changes in a child's life may be decided by:

(a) agreement between the joint custodial parents;

(b) requiring that the parents seek family counseling, conciliation or mediation service to assist in resolving their differences;

(c) agreement by the parents to submit the dispute to binding arbitration;

(d) allocating ultimate responsibility for a particular major decision area to one legal custodian;

(e) terminating joint custody and awarding sole custody to one person;

(f) reference to a master pursuant to Rule 53 [Rule 1-053 NMRA] of the Rules of Civil Procedure for the District Courts; or

(g) the district court.

K. When any person other than a natural or adoptive parent seeks custody of a child, no such person shall be awarded custody absent a showing of unfitness of the natural or adoptive parent.

L. As used in this section:

(1) "child" means a person under the age of eighteen;

(2) "custody" means the authority and responsibility to make major decisions in a child's best interests in the areas of residence, medical and dental treatment, education or child care, religion and recreation;

(3) "domestic abuse" means any incident by a household member against another household member resulting in:

(a) physical harm;

(b) severe emotional distress;

(c) a threat causing imminent fear of physical harm by any household member;

(d) criminal trespass;

(e) criminal damage to property;

(f) stalking or aggravated stalking, as provided in Sections 30-3A-3 and 30-3A-3.1 NMSA 1978; or

(g) harassment, as provided in Section 30-3A-2 NMSA 1978;

(4) "joint custody" means an order of the court awarding custody of a child to two parents. Joint custody does not imply an equal division of the child's time between the parents or an equal division of financial responsibility for the child;

(5) "parent" means a natural parent, adoptive parent or person who is acting as a parent who has or shares legal custody of a child or who claims a right to have or share legal custody;

(6) "parenting plan" means a document submitted for approval of the court setting forth the responsibilities of each parent individually and the parents jointly in a joint custody arrangement;

(7) "period of responsibility" means a specified period of time during which a parent is responsible for providing for a child's physical, developmental and emotional needs, including the decision making required in daily living. Specified periods of responsibility shall not be changed in an instance or more permanently except by the methods of decision making described under Subsection L [sic] of this section;

(8) "sole custody" means an order of the court awarding custody of a child to one parent; and

(9) "visitation" means a period of time available to a noncustodial parent, under a sole custody arrangement, during which a child resides with or is under the care and control of the noncustodial parent.

North Dakota

1. In any proceeding to establish or modify a judgment providing for parenting time with a child, the parents shall develop and file with the court a parenting plan to be included in the court's decree. If the parents are unable to agree on a parenting plan, the court shall issue a parenting plan considering the best interests of the child.

2. A parenting plan must include, at a minimum, provisions regarding the following or an explanation as to why a provision is not included:

   a. Decision making responsibility relative to:

      (1) Routine or day-to-day decisions; and

      (2) Major decisions such as education, health care, and spiritual development;

   b. Information sharing and access, including telephone and electronic access;

   c. Legal residence of a child for school attendance;

   d. Residential responsibility, parenting time, and parenting schedule, including:

      (1) Holidays and days off from school, birthday, and vacation planning;

      (2) Weekends and weekdays; and

      (3) Summers;

e. Transportation and exchange of the child, considering the safety of the parties;

f. Procedure for review and adjustment of the plan; and g. Methods for resolving disputes.

Ohio

3109.04 Allocating parental rights and responsibilities for care of children—shared parenting.

(A) In any divorce, legal separation, or annulment proceeding and in any proceeding pertaining to the allocation of parental rights and responsibilities for the care of a child, upon hearing the testimony of either or both parents and considering any mediation report filed pursuant to section 3109.052 of the Revised Code and in accordance with sections 3127.01 to 3127.53 of the Revised Code, the court shall allocate the parental rights and responsibilities for the care of the minor children of the marriage. Subject to division (D)(2) of this section, the court may allocate the parental rights and responsibilities for the care of the children in either of the following ways:

(1) If neither parent files a pleading or motion in accordance with division (G) of this section, if at least one parent files a pleading or motion under that division but no parent who filed a pleading or motion under that division also files a plan for shared parenting, or if at least one parent files both a pleading or motion and a shared parenting plan under that division but no plan for shared parenting is in the best interest of the children, the court, in a manner consistent with the best interest of the children, shall allocate the parental rights and responsibilities for the care of the children primarily to one of the parents, designate that parent as the residential parent and the legal custodian of the child, and divide between the parents the other rights and responsibilities for the care of the children, including, but not limited to, the responsibility to provide support for the children and the right of the parent who is not the residential parent to have continuing contact with the children.

(2) If at least one parent files a pleading or motion in accordance with division (G) of this section and a plan for shared parenting pursuant to that division and if a plan for shared parenting

is in the best interest of the children and is approved by the court in accordance with division (D)(1) of this section, the court may allocate the parental rights and responsibilities for the care of the children to both parents and issue a shared parenting order requiring the parents to share all or some of the aspects of the physical and legal care of the children in accordance with the approved plan for shared parenting. If the court issues a shared parenting order under this division and it is necessary for the purpose of receiving public assistance, the court shall designate which one of the parents' residences is to serve as the child's home. The child support obligations of the parents under a shared parenting order issued under this division shall be determined in accordance with Chapters 3119., 3121., 3123., and 3125. of the Revised Code.

(B) (1) When making the allocation of the parental rights and responsibilities for the care of the children under this section in an original proceeding or in any proceeding for modification of a prior order of the court making the allocation, the court shall take into account that which would be in the best interest of the children. In determining the child's best interest for purposes of making its allocation of the parental rights and responsibilities for the care of the child and for purposes of resolving any issues related to the making of that allocation, the court, in its discretion, may and, upon the request of either party, shall interview in chambers any or all of the involved children regarding their wishes and concerns with respect to the allocation.

(2) If the court interviews any child pursuant to division (B)(1) of this section, all of the following apply:

(a) The court, in its discretion, may and, upon the motion of either parent, shall appoint a guardian ad litem for the child.

(b) The court first shall determine the reasoning ability of the child. If the court determines that the child does not have sufficient reasoning ability to express the child's wishes and concern with respect to the allocation of parental rights and responsibilities for the care of the child, it shall not determine the child's wishes and concerns with respect to the allocation. If the court determines that the child has sufficient reasoning ability to express the child's wishes or concerns with respect to the allocation, it then shall determine whether, because of special circumstances, it would not be in the best interest of the child to determine the child's wishes and concerns with respect to the allocation. If the court determines that, because of special circumstances, it would not be in the best interest of the child to determine the child's wishes and concerns with respect to the allocation, it shall not determine the child's wishes and concerns with respect to the allocation and shall enter its written findings of fact and opinion in the journal. If the court determines that it would be in the best interests of the child to determine the child's wishes and concerns with respect to the allocation, it shall proceed to make that determination.

(c) The interview shall be conducted in chambers, and no person other than the child, the child's attorney, the judge, any necessary court personnel, and, in the judge's discretion, the attorney of each parent shall be permitted to be present in the chambers during the interview.

(3) No person shall obtain or attempt to obtain from a child a written or recorded statement or affidavit setting forth the child's wishes and concerns regarding the allocation of parental rights and responsibilities concerning the child. No court, in determining the child's best interest for purposes of making its allocation of the parental rights and responsibilities for the care of the child or for purposes of resolving any issues related to the making of that allocation, shall accept or consider a written or recorded statement or affidavit that purports to set forth the child's wishes and concerns regarding those matters.

(C) Prior to trial, the court may cause an investigation to be made as to the character, family relations, past conduct, earning ability, and financial worth of each parent and may order the parents and their minor children to submit to medical, psychological, and psychiatric examinations. The report of the investigation and examinations shall be made available to either parent or the parent's counsel of record not less than five days before trial, upon written request. The report shall be signed by the investigator, and the investigator shall be subject to cross-examination by either parent concerning the contents of the report. The court may tax as costs all or any part of the expenses for each investigation.

If the court determines that either parent previously has been convicted of or pleaded guilty to any criminal offense involving any act that resulted in a child being a neglected child, that either parent previously has been determined to be the perpetrator of the neglectful act that is the basis of an adjudication that a child is a neglected child, or that there is reason to believe that either parent has acted in a manner resulting in a child being a neglected child, the court shall consider that fact against naming that parent the residential parent and against granting a shared parenting decree. When the court allocates parental rights and responsibilities for the care of children or determines whether to grant shared parenting in any proceeding, it shall consider whether either parent or any member of the household of either parent has been convicted of or pleaded guilty to a violation of section 2919.25 of the Revised Code or a sexually oriented offense involving a victim who at the time of the commission of the offense was a member of the family or household that is the subject of the proceeding, has been convicted of or pleaded guilty to any sexually oriented offense or other offense involving a victim who at the time of the commission of the offense was a member of the family or household that is the subject of the proceeding and caused physical harm to the victim in the commission of the offense, or has been determined to be the perpetrator of the abusive act that is the basis of an adjudication that a child is an abused child. If the court determines that either parent has been convicted of or pleaded guilty to a violation of section 2919.25 of the Revised Code or a sexually oriented offense involving a victim who at the time of the commission of the offense was a member of the family or household that is the subject of the proceeding, has been convicted of or pleaded guilty to any sexually oriented offense or other offense involving a victim who at the time of the commission of the offense was a member of the family or household that is the subject of the proceeding and caused physical harm to the victim in the commission of the offense, or has been determined to be the perpetrator of the abusive act that is the basis of an adjudication that a child is an abused child, it may designate that parent as the residential parent and may issue a shared parenting decree or order only if it determines that it is in the best interest of the child to name that parent the residential parent or to issue a shared parenting decree or order and it makes specific written findings of fact to support its determination.

(D) (1) (a) Upon the filing of a pleading or motion by either parent or both parents, in accordance with division (G) of this section, requesting shared parenting and the filing of a shared parenting plan in accordance with that division, the court shall comply with division (D)(1)(a)(i), (ii), or (iii) of this section, whichever is applicable:

(i) If both parents jointly make the request in their pleadings or jointly file the motion and also jointly file the plan, the court shall review the parents' plan to determine if it is in the best interest of the children. If the court determines that the plan is in the best interest of the children, the court shall approve it. If the court determines that the plan or any part of the plan is not in the best interest of the children, the court shall require the parents to make appropriate changes to the plan to meet the court's objections to it. If changes to the plan are made to meet the court's objections, and if the new plan is in the best interest of the children, the court shall approve the plan. If changes to the plan are not made to meet the court's objections, or if the parents attempt to make changes to the plan to meet the court's objections, but the court determines that the new plan or any part of the new plan still is not in the best interest of the children, the court may reject the portion of the parents' pleadings or deny their motion requesting shared parenting of the children and proceed as if the request in the pleadings or the motion had not been made. The court shall not approve a plan under this division unless it determines that the plan is in the best interest of the children.

(ii) If each parent makes a request in the parent's pleadings or files a motion and each also files a separate plan, the court shall review each plan filed to determine if either is in the best interest of the children. If the court determines that one of the filed plans is in the best interest of the children, the court may approve the plan. If the court determines that neither filed plan is in the best interest of the children, the court may order each parent to submit appropriate changes to the parent's plan or both of the filed plans to meet the court's objections, or may select one of the filed plans and order each parent to submit appropriate changes to the selected plan to meet the court's objections. If changes to the plan or plans are submitted to meet the court's objections, and if any of the filed plans with the changes is in the best interest of the children, the court may approve the plan with the changes. If changes to the plan or plans are not submitted to meet the court's objections, or if the parents submit changes to the plan or plans to meet the court's objections but the court determines that none of the filed plans with the submitted changes is in the best interest of the children, the court may reject the portion of the parents' pleadings or deny their motions requesting shared parenting of the children and proceed as if the requests in the pleadings or the motions had not been made. If the court approves a plan under this division, either as originally filed or with submitted changes, or if the court rejects the portion of the parents' pleadings or denies their motions requesting shared parenting under this division and proceeds as if the requests in the pleadings or the motions had not been made, the court shall enter in the record of the case findings of fact and conclusions of law as to the reasons for the approval or the rejection or denial. Division (D)(1)(b) of this section applies in relation to the approval or disapproval of a plan under this division.

(iii) If each parent makes a request in the parent's pleadings or files a motion but only one parent files a plan, or if only one parent makes a request in the parent's pleadings or files a motion and also files a plan, the court in the best interest of the children may order the other parent to file a plan for shared parenting in accordance with division (G) of this section. The court shall review each plan filed to determine if any plan is in the best interest of the children. If the court determines that one of the filed plans is in the best interest of the children, the court may approve the plan. If the court determines that no filed plan is in the best interest of the children, the court may order each parent to submit appropriate changes to the parent's plan or both of the filed plans to meet the court's objections or may select one filed plan and order each parent to submit appropriate changes to the selected plan to meet the court's objections. If changes to the plan or plans are submitted to meet the court's objections, and if any of the filed plans with the changes is in the best interest of the children, the court may approve the plan with the changes. If changes to the plan or plans are not submitted to meet the court's objections, or if the parents submit changes to the plan or plans to meet the court's objections but the court determines that none of the filed plans with the submitted changes is in the best interest of the children, the court may reject the portion of the parents' pleadings or deny the parents' motion or reject the portion of the parents' pleadings or deny their motions requesting shared parenting of the children and proceed as if the request or requests or the motion or motions had not been made. If the court approves a plan under this division, either as originally filed or with submitted changes, or if the court rejects the portion of the pleadings or denies the motion or motions requesting shared parenting under this division and proceeds as if the request or requests or the motion or motions had not been made, the court shall enter in the record of the case findings of fact and conclusions of law as to the reasons for the approval or the rejection or denial. Division (D)(1)(b) of this section applies in relation to the approval or disapproval of a plan under this division.

(b) The approval of a plan under division (D)(1)(a)(ii) or (iii) of this section is discretionary with the court. The court shall not approve more than one plan under either division and shall not approve a plan under either division unless it determines that the plan is in the best interest of the children. If the court, under either division, does not determine that any filed plan or any filed plan with submitted changes is in the best interest of the children, the court shall not approve any plan.

(c) Whenever possible, the court shall require that a shared parenting plan approved under division (D)(1)(a)(i), (ii), or (iii) of this section ensure the opportunity for both parents to have frequent and continuing contact with the child, unless frequent and continuing contact with any parent would not be in the best interest of the child.

(d) If a court approves a shared parenting plan under division (D)(1)(a)(i), (ii), or (iii) of this section, the approved plan shall be incorporated into a final shared parenting decree granting the parents the shared parenting of the children. Any final shared parenting decree shall be issued at the same time as and shall be appended to the final decree of dissolution, divorce, annulment, or legal separation arising out of the action out of which the question of the allocation of parental rights and responsibilities for the care of the children arose.

No provisional shared parenting decree shall be issued in relation to any shared parenting plan approved under division (D)(1)(a)(i), (ii), or (iii) of this section. A final shared parenting decree issued under this division has immediate effect as a final decree on the date of its issuance, subject to modification or termination as authorized by this section.

(2) If the court finds, with respect to any child under eighteen years of age, that it is in the best interest of the child for neither parent to be designated the residential parent and legal custodian of the child, it may commit the child to a relative of the child or certify a copy of its findings, together with as much of the record and the further information, in narrative form or otherwise, that it considers necessary or as the juvenile court requests, to the juvenile court for further proceedings, and, upon the certification, the juvenile court has exclusive jurisdiction.

(E) (1) (a) The court shall not modify a prior decree allocating parental rights and responsibilities for the care of children unless it finds, based on facts that have arisen since the prior decree or that were unknown to the court at the time of the prior decree, that a change has occurred in the circumstances of the child, the child's residential parent, or either of the parents subject to a shared parenting decree, and that the modification is necessary to serve the best interest of the child. In applying these standards, the court shall retain the residential parent designated by the prior decree or the prior shared parenting decree, unless a modification is in the best interest of the child and one of the following applies:

(i) The residential parent agrees to a change in the residential parent or both parents under a shared parenting decree agree to a change in the designation of residential parent.

(ii) The child, with the consent of the residential parent or of both parents under a shared parenting decree, has been integrated into the family of the person seeking to become the residential parent.

(iii) The harm likely to be caused by a change of environment is outweighed by the advantages of the change of environment to the child.

(b) One or both of the parents under a prior decree allocating parental rights and responsibilities for the care of children that is not a shared parenting decree may file a motion requesting that the prior decree be modified to give both parents shared rights and responsibilities for the care of the children. The motion shall include both a request for modification of the prior decree and a request for a shared parenting order that complies with division (G) of this section. Upon the filing of the motion, if the court determines that a modification of the prior decree is authorized under division (E)(1)(a) of this section, the court may modify the prior decree to grant a shared parenting order, provided that the court shall not modify the prior decree to grant a shared parenting order unless the court complies with divisions (A) and (D)(1) of this section and, in accordance with those divisions, approves the submitted shared parenting plan and determines that shared parenting would be in the best interest of the children.

(2) In addition to a modification authorized under division (E)(1) of this section:

(a) Both parents under a shared parenting decree jointly may modify the terms of the plan for shared parenting approved by the court and incorporated by it into the shared parenting decree. Modifications under this division may be made at any time. The modifications to the plan shall be filed jointly by both parents with the court, and the court shall include them in the plan, unless they are not in the best interest of the children. If the modifications are not in the best interests of the children, the court, in its discretion, may reject the modifications or make modifications to the proposed modifications or the plan that are in the best interest of the children. Modifications jointly submitted by both parents under a shared parenting decree shall be effective, either as originally filed or as modified by the court, upon their inclusion by the court in the plan. Modifications to the plan made by the court shall be effective upon their inclusion by the court in the plan.

(b) The court may modify the terms of the plan for shared parenting approved by the court and incorporated by it into the shared parenting decree upon its own motion at any time if the court determines that the modifications are in the best interest of the children or upon the request of one or both of the parents under the decree. Modifications under this division may be made at any time. The court shall not make any modification to the plan under this division, unless the modification is in the best interest of the children.

(c) The court may terminate a prior final shared parenting decree that includes a shared parenting plan approved under division (D)(1)(a)(i) of this section upon the request of one or both of the parents or whenever it determines that shared parenting is not in the best interest of the children. The court may terminate a prior final shared parenting decree that includes a shared parenting plan approved under division (D)(1)(a)(ii) or (iii) of this section if it determines, upon its own motion or upon the request of one or both parents, that shared parenting is not in the best interest of the children. If modification of the terms of the plan for shared parenting approved by the court and incorporated by it into the final shared parenting decree is attempted under division (E)(2)(a) of this section and the court rejects the modifications, it may terminate the final shared parenting decree if it determines that shared parenting is not in the best interest of the children.

(d) Upon the termination of a prior final shared parenting decree under division (E)(2)(c) of this section, the court shall proceed and issue a modified decree for the allocation of parental rights and responsibilities for the care of the children under the standards applicable under divisions (A), (B), and (C) of this section as if no decree for shared parenting had been granted and as if no request for shared parenting ever had been made.

(F) (1) In determining the best interest of a child pursuant to this section, whether on an original decree allocating parental rights and responsibilities for the care of children or a modification of a decree allocating those rights and responsibilities, the court shall consider all relevant factors, including, but not limited to:

(a) The wishes of the child's parents regarding the child's care;

(b) If the court has interviewed the child in chambers pursuant to division (B) of this section regarding the child's wishes and concerns as to the allocation of parental rights and responsibilities concerning the child, the wishes and concerns of the child, as expressed to the court;

(c) The child's interaction and interrelationship with the child's parents, siblings, and any other person who may significantly affect the child's best interest;

(d) The child's adjustment to the child's home, school, and community;

(e) The mental and physical health of all persons involved in the situation;

(f) The parent more likely to honor and facilitate court-approved parenting time rights or visitation and companionship rights;

(g) Whether either parent has failed to make all child support payments, including all arrearages, that are required of that parent pursuant to a child support order under which that parent is an obligor;

(h) Whether either parent or any member of the household of either parent previously has been convicted of or pleaded guilty to any criminal offense involving any act that resulted in a child being an abused child or a neglected child; whether either parent, in a case in which a child has been adjudicated an abused child or a neglected child, previously has been determined to be the perpetrator of the abusive or neglectful act that is the basis of an adjudication; whether either parent or any member of the household of either parent previously has been convicted of or pleaded guilty to a violation of section 2919.25 of the Revised Code or a sexually oriented offense involving a victim who at the time of the commission of the offense was a member of the family or household that is the subject of the current proceeding; whether either parent or any member of the household of either parent previously has been convicted of or pleaded guilty to any offense involving a victim who at the time of the commission of the offense was a member of the family or household that is the subject of the current proceeding and caused physical harm to the victim in the commission of the offense; and whether there is reason to believe that either parent has acted in a manner resulting in a child being an abused child or a neglected child;

(i) Whether the residential parent or one of the parents subject to a shared parenting decree has continuously and willfully denied the other parent's right to parenting time in accordance with an order of the court;

(j) Whether either parent has established a residence, or is planning to establish a residence, outside this state.

(2) In determining whether shared parenting is in the best interest of the children, the court shall consider all relevant factors, including, but not limited to, the factors enumerated in division (F)(1) of this section, the factors enumerated in section 3119.23 of the Revised Code, and all of the following factors:

(a) The ability of the parents to cooperate and make decisions jointly, with respect to the children;

(b) The ability of each parent to encourage the sharing of love, affection, and contact between the child and the other parent;

(c) Any history of, or potential for, child abuse, spouse abuse, other domestic violence, or parental kidnapping by either parent;

(d) The geographic proximity of the parents to each other, as the proximity relates to the practical considerations of shared parenting;

(e) The recommendation of the guardian ad litem of the child, if the child has a guardian ad litem.

(3) When allocating parental rights and responsibilities for the care of children, the court shall not give preference to a parent because of that parent's financial status or condition.

(G) Either parent or both parents of any children may file a pleading or motion with the court requesting the court to grant both parents shared parental rights and responsibilities for the care of the children in a proceeding held pursuant to division (A) of this section. If a pleading or motion requesting shared parenting is filed, the parent or parents filing the pleading or motion also shall file with the court a plan for the exercise of shared parenting by both parents. If each parent files a pleading or motion requesting shared parenting but only one parent files a plan or if only one parent files a pleading or motion requesting shared parenting and also files a plan, the other parent as ordered by the court shall file with the court a plan for the exercise of shared parenting by both parents. The plan for shared parenting shall be filed with the petition for dissolution of marriage, if the question of parental rights and responsibilities for the care of the children arises out of an action for dissolution of marriage, or, in other cases, at a time at least thirty days prior to the hearing on the issue of the parental rights and responsibilities for the care of the children. A plan for shared parenting shall include provisions covering all factors that are relevant to the care of the children, including, but not limited to, provisions covering factors such as physical living arrangements, child support obligations, provision for the children's medical and dental care, school placement, and the parent with which the children will be physically located during legal holidays, school holidays, and other days of special importance.

(H) If an appeal is taken from a decision of a court that grants or modifies a decree allocating parental rights and responsibilities for the care of children, the court of appeals shall give the case calendar priority and handle it expeditiously.

(I) (1) Upon receipt of an order for active military service in the uniformed services, a parent who is subject to an order allocating parental rights and responsibilities or in relation to whom an action to allocate parental rights and responsibilities is pending and who is ordered for active military service shall notify the other parent who is subject to the order or in relation to whom the case is pending of the order for active military service within three days of receiving the military service order.

(2) On receipt of the notice described in division (I)(1) of this section, either parent may apply to the court for a hearing to expedite an allocation or modification proceeding so that the court can issue an order before the parent's active military service begins. The application shall include the date on which the active military service begins.

The court shall schedule a hearing upon receipt of the application and hold the hearing not later than thirty days after receipt of the application, except that the court shall give the case calendar priority and handle the case expeditiously if exigent circumstances exist in the case.

The court shall not modify a prior decree allocating parental rights and responsibilities unless the court determines that there has been a change in circumstances of the child, the child's residential parent, or either of the parents subject to a shared parenting decree, and that modification is necessary to serve the best interest of the child. The court shall not find past, present, or possible future active military service in the uniformed services to constitute a change in circumstances justifying modification of a prior decree pursuant to division (E) of this section. The court shall make specific written findings of fact to support any modification under this division.

(3) Nothing in division (I) of this section shall prevent a court from issuing a temporary order allocating or modifying parental rights and responsibilities for the duration of the parent's active military service. A temporary order shall specify whether the parent's active military service is the basis of the order and shall provide for termination of the temporary order and resumption of the prior order within ten days after receipt of notice pursuant to division (I)(5) of this section, unless the other parent demonstrates that resumption of the prior order is not in the child's best interest.

(4) At the request of a parent who is ordered for active military service in the uniformed services and who is a subject of a proceeding pertaining to a temporary order for the allocation or modification of parental rights and responsibilities, the court shall permit the parent to participate in the proceeding and present evidence by electronic means, including communication by telephone, video, or internet to the extent permitted by the rules of the supreme court of Ohio.

(5) A parent who is ordered for active military service in the uniformed services and who is a subject of a proceeding pertaining to the allocation or modification of parental rights and responsibilities shall provide written notice to the court, child support enforcement agency, and the other parent of the date of termination of the parent's active military service not later than thirty days after the date on which the service ends.

(J) As used in this section:

(1) "Abused child" has the same meaning as in section 2151.031 of the Revised Code.

(2) "Active military service" means service by a member of the uniformed services in compliance with military orders to report for combat operations, contingency operations, peacekeeping

operations, a remote tour of duty, or other active service for which the member is required to report unaccompanied by any family member, including any period of illness, recovery from injury, leave, or other lawful absence during that operation, duty, or service.

(3) "Neglected child" has the same meaning as in section 2151.03 of the Revised Code.

(4) "Sexually oriented offense" has the same meaning as in section 2950.01 of the Revised Code.

(5) "Uniformed services" means the United States armed forces, the army national guard, and the air national guard or any reserve component thereof, or the commissioned corps of the United States public health service.

(K) As used in the Revised Code, "shared parenting" means that the parents share, in the manner set forth in the plan for shared parenting that is approved by the court under division (D)(1) and described in division (L)(6) of this section, all or some of the aspects of physical and legal care of their children.

(L) For purposes of the Revised Code:

(1) A parent who is granted the care, custody, and control of a child under an order that was issued pursuant to this section prior to April 11, 1991, and that does not provide for shared parenting has "custody of the child" and "care, custody, and control of the child" under the order, and is the "residential parent," the "residential parent and legal custodian," or the "custodial parent" of the child under the order.

(2) A parent who primarily is allocated the parental rights and responsibilities for the care of a child and who is designated as the residential parent and legal custodian of the child under an order that is issued pursuant to this section on or after April 11, 1991, and that does not provide for shared parenting has "custody of the child" and "care, custody, and control of the child" under the order, and is the "residential parent," the "residential parent and legal custodian," or the "custodial parent" of the child under the order.

(3) A parent who is not granted custody of a child under an order that was issued pursuant to this section prior to April 11, 1991, and that does not provide for shared parenting is the "parent

who is not the residential parent," the "parent who is not the residential parent and legal custodian," or the "noncustodial parent" of the child under the order.

(4) A parent who is not primarily allocated the parental rights and responsibilities for the care of a child and who is not designated as the residential parent and legal custodian of the child under an order that is issued pursuant to this section on or after April 11, 1991, and that does not provide for shared parenting is the "parent who is not the residential parent," the "parent who is not the residential parent and legal custodian," or the "noncustodial parent" of the child under the order.

(5) Unless the context clearly requires otherwise, if an order is issued by a court pursuant to this section and the order provides for shared parenting of a child, both parents have "custody of the child" or "care, custody, and control of the child" under the order, to the extent and in the manner specified in the order.

(6) Unless the context clearly requires otherwise and except as otherwise provided in the order, if an order is issued by a court pursuant to this section and the order provides for shared parenting of a child, each parent, regardless of where the child is physically located or with whom the child is residing at a particular point in time, as specified in the order, is the "residential parent," the "residential parent and legal custodian," or the "custodial parent" of the child.

(7) Unless the context clearly requires otherwise and except as otherwise provided in the order, a designation in the order of a parent as the residential parent for the purpose of determining the school the child attends, as the custodial parent for purposes of claiming the child as a dependent pursuant to section 152(e) of the "Internal Revenue Code of 1986," 100 Stat. 2085, 26 U.S.C.A. 1, as amended, or as the residential parent for purposes of receiving public assistance pursuant to division (A)(2) of this section, does not affect the designation pursuant to division (L)(6) of this section of each parent as the "residential parent," the "residential parent and legal custodian," or the "custodial parent" of the child.

(M) The court shall require each parent of a child to file an affidavit attesting as to whether the parent, and the members of the parent's household, have been convicted of or pleaded guilty to any of the offenses identified in divisions (C) and (F)(1)(h) of this section.

Oklahoma

Sec. 43-111.1A

B. The standard visitation schedule should include a minimum graduated visitation schedule for children under the age of five (5) years and a minimum graduated visitation schedule for children five (5) years of age through seventeen (17) years of age. In addition, the standard visitation schedule should address:

1. Midweek and weekend time-sharing;
2. Differing geographical residences of the custodian and noncustodian of the child requesting visitation;
3. Holidays, including Friday and Monday holidays;
4. Summer vacation break;
5. Midterm school breaks;
6. Notice requirements and authorized reasons for cancellations of visitation;
7. Transportation and transportation costs, including pick up and return of the child;
8. Religious, school, and extracurricular activities;
9. Grandparent and relative contact;
10. The birthday of the child;
11. Sibling visitation schedules;
12. Special circumstances, including, but not limited to, emergencies; and
13. Any other standards deemed necessary by the Administrative Director of the Courts.

C. 1. The Administrative Director of the Courts shall develop advisory guidelines for use by the district courts when parties to any action concerning the custody of a child are unable to mutually agree upon a visitation schedule.

2. The advisory guidelines should include the following considerations at a minimum:

a. a preference for visitation schedules that are mutually agreed upon by both parents over a court-imposed solution,

b. a visitation schedule which should maximize the continuity and stability of the life of the child,

c. special considerations should be given to each parent to make the child available to attend family functions, including funerals, weddings, family reunions, religious holidays, important ceremonies, and other significant events in the life of the child or in the life of either parent which may inadvertently conflict with the visitation schedule,

d. a visitation schedule which will not interrupt the regular school hours of the child,

e. a visitation schedule should reasonably accommodate the work schedule of both parents and may increase the visitation time allowed to the noncustodial parent but should not diminish the standardized visitation schedule provided in Section 111.1 of Title 43 of the Oklahoma Statutes,

f. a visitation schedule should reasonably accommodate the distance between the parties and the expense of exercising visitation,

g. each parent should permit and encourage liberal electronic contact during reasonable hours and uncensored mail privileges with the child, and

h. each parent should be entitled to an equal division of major religious holidays celebrated by the parents, and the parent who celebrates a religious holiday that the other parent does not celebrate shall have the right to be together with the child on the religious holiday.

Oregon

ORS 107.102

(1) In any proceeding to establish or modify a judgment providing for parenting time with a child, except for matters filed under ORS 107.700 (Short title) to 107.735 (Duties of State Court

Administrator), there shall be developed and filed with the court a parenting plan to be included in the judgment. A parenting plan may be either general or detailed.

(2) A general parenting plan may include a general outline of how parental responsibilities and parenting time will be shared and may allow the parents to develop a more detailed agreement on an informal basis. However, a general parenting plan must set forth the minimum amount of parenting time and access a noncustodial parent is entitled to have.

(3) A detailed parenting plan may include, but need not be limited to, provisions relating to:

(a) Residential schedule;

(b) Holiday, birthday and vacation planning;

(c) Weekends, including holidays, and school in-service days preceding or following weekends;

(d) Decision-making and responsibility;

(e) Information sharing and access;

(f) Relocation of parents;

(g) Telephone access;

(h) Transportation; and

(I) Methods for resolving disputes.

(4) (a) The court shall develop a detailed parenting plan when:

(A) So requested by either parent; or

(B) The parent or parents are unable to develop a parenting plan.

(b) In developing a parenting plan under this subsection, the court may consider only the best interests of the child and the safety of the parties. [1997 c.707 §2]

Pennsylvania

§ 5331. Parenting plan.

(a) Purpose. In a contested custody proceeding, the court may require the parties to submit parenting plans for the care and custody of the child to aid the court in resolving the custody dispute. A parenting plan and the position of a party as set forth in that parenting plan shall not be admissible as evidence by another party.

(b) Contents. A parenting plan shall include the following:

(1) The schedule for personal care and control of the child, including parenting time, holidays and vacations.

(2) The education and religious involvement, if any, of the child.

(3) The health care of the child.

(4) Child-care arrangements.

(5) Transportation arrangements.

(6) A procedure by which proposed changes, disputes and alleged breaches of the custody order may be adjudicated or otherwise resolved through mediation, arbitration or other means.

(7) Any matter specified by the court.

(8) Any other matter that serves the best interest of the child.

South Carolina

SECTION 63-15-220. Parenting plans.

(A) At all temporary hearings where custody is contested, each parent must prepare, file, and submit to the court a parenting plan, which reflects parental preferences, the allocation of parenting time to be spent with each parent, and major decisions, including, but not limited to, the child's education, medical and dental care, extracurricular activities and religious training. However, the parties may elect to prepare, file, and submit a joint parenting plan. The court shall issue temporary and final custody orders only after considering these parenting plans; however, the failure by a party to submit a parenting plan to the court does not preclude the court from issuing a temporary or final custody order.

(B) At the final hearing, either party may file and submit an updated parenting plan for the court's consideration.

(C) The South Carolina Supreme Court shall develop rules and forms for the implementation of the parenting plan.

SECTION 63-15-230. Final custody determination; considerations.

(A) The court shall make the final custody determination in the best interest of the child based upon the evidence presented.

(B) The court may award joint custody to both parents or sole custody to either parent.

(C) If custody is contested or if either parent seeks an award of joint custody, the court shall consider all custody options, including, but not limited to, joint custody, and, in its final order, the court shall state its determination as to custody and shall state its reasoning for that decision.

(D) Notwithstanding the custody determination, the court may allocate parenting time in the best interest of the child.

SECTION 63-15-240. Contents of order for custody affecting rights and responsibilities of parents; best interests of the child.

(A) In issuing or modifying an order for custody affecting the rights and responsibilities of the parents, the order may include, but is not limited to:

(1) the approval of a parenting plan;

(2) the award of sole custody to one parent with appropriate parenting time for the noncustodial parent;

(3) the award of joint custody, in which case the order must include:

(a) residential arrangements with each parent in accordance with the needs of each child; and

(b) how consultations and communications between the parents will take place, generally and specifically, with regard to major decisions concerning the child's health, medical and dental care, education, extracurricular activities, and religious training;

(4) other custody arrangements as the court may determine to be in the best interest of the child.

(B) In issuing or modifying a custody order, the court must consider the best interest of the child, which may include, but is not limited to:

(1) the temperament and developmental needs of the child;

(2) the capacity and the disposition of the parents to understand and meet the needs of the child;

(3) the preferences of each child;

(4) the wishes of the parents as to custody;

(5) the past and current interaction and relationship of the child with each parent, the child's siblings, and any other person, including a grandparent, who may significantly affect the best interest of the child;

(6) the actions of each parent to encourage the continuing parent-child relationship between the child and the other parent, as is appropriate, including compliance with court orders;

(7) the manipulation by or coercive behavior of the parents in an effort to involve the child in the parents' dispute;

(8) any effort by one parent to disparage the other parent in front of the child;

(9) the ability of each parent to be actively involved in the life of the child;

(10) the child's adjustment to his or her home, school, and community environments;

(11) the stability of the child's existing and proposed residences;

(12) the mental and physical health of all individuals involved, except that a disability of a proposed custodial parent or other party, in and of itself, must not be determinative of custody unless the proposed custodial arrangement is not in the best interest of the child;

(13) the child's cultural and spiritual background;

(14) whether the child or a sibling of the child has been abused or neglected;

(15) whether one parent has perpetrated domestic violence or child abuse or the effect on the child of the actions of an abuser if any domestic violence has occurred between the parents or between a parent and another individual or between the parent and the child;

(16) whether one parent has relocated more than one hundred miles from the child's primary residence in the past year, unless the parent relocated for safety reasons; and

(17) other factors as the court considers necessary.

SECTION 63-15-250. Telephonic and electronic communication between minor child and parents.

In addition to all rights and duties given to parents pursuant to Section 63-5-30:

(A) when a court orders sole custody to one parent, the custodial parent, except in cases of abuse, neglect, or abandonment, should facilitate opportunities for reasonable telephonic and electronic communication between the minor child and the noncustodial parent, as appropriate, as provided for by court order if the court determines that this type of communication is in the best interest of the child; and

(B) when a court orders joint custody to both parents, each parent should facilitate opportunities for reasonable telephonic and electronic communication between the minor child and the other parent, as appropriate, as provided for by court order if the court determines that this type of communication is in the best interest of the child.

SECTION 63-15-260. Equal access to educational and medical records of child by parents.

Notwithstanding the custody arrangement and in addition to all rights and duties given to parents pursuant to Section 63-5-30, each parent has equal access and the same right to obtain all educational records and medical records of his or her minor children and the right to participate in the children's school activities and extracurricular activities that are held in public locations unless prohibited by an order of the court or State law.

South Dakota

http://sdlegislature.gov/Statutes/Codified_Laws/DisplayStatute.aspx?Type=Statute&Statute=25-4A-10

Separately, there are parenting guidelines: http://ujs.sd.gov/uploads/pubs/UJS%20302%20-%20South%20Dakota%20Visitation%20Guidelines.pdf

Tennessee

http://www.lexisnexis.com/hottopics/tncode/

Texas

Sec. 153.001. PUBLIC POLICY.

(a) The public policy of this state is to:

    (1) assure that children will have frequent and continuing contact with parents who have shown the ability to act in the best interest of the child;

    (2) provide a safe, stable, and nonviolent environment for the child; and

    (3) encourage parents to share in the rights and duties of raising their child after the parents have separated or dissolved their marriage.

(b) A court may not render an order that conditions the right of a conservator to possession of or access to a child on the payment of child support.

Sec. 153.002. BEST INTEREST OF CHILD. The best interest of the child shall always be the primary consideration of the court in determining the issues of conservatorship and possession of and access to the child.

Sec. 153.003. NO DISCRIMINATION BASED ON SEX OR MARITAL STATUS. The court shall consider the qualifications of the parties without regard to their marital status or to the sex of the party or the child in determining:

(1) which party to appoint as sole managing conservator;

(2) whether to appoint a party as joint managing conservator; and

(3) the terms and conditions of conservatorship and possession of and access to the child.

Sec. 153.004. HISTORY OF DOMESTIC VIOLENCE OR SEXUAL ABUSE.

(a) In determining whether to appoint a party as a sole or joint managing conservator, the court shall consider evidence of the intentional use of abusive physical force, or evidence of sexual abuse, by a party directed against the party's spouse, a parent of the child, or any person younger than 18 years of age committed within a two-year period preceding the filing of the suit or during the pendency of the suit.

(b) The court may not appoint joint managing conservators if credible evidence is presented of a history or pattern of past or present child neglect, or physical or sexual abuse by one parent directed against the other parent, a spouse, or a child, including a sexual assault in violation of Section 22.011 or 22.021, Penal Code, that results in the other parent becoming pregnant with the child. A history of sexual abuse includes a sexual assault that results in the other parent becoming pregnant with the child, regardless of the prior relationship of the parents. It is a rebuttable presumption that the appointment of a parent as the sole managing conservator of a child or as the conservator who has the exclusive right to determine the primary residence of a child is not in the best interest of the child if credible evidence is presented of a history or pattern of past or present child neglect, or physical or sexual abuse by that parent directed against the other parent, a spouse, or a child.

(c) The court shall consider the commission of family violence or sexual abuse in determining whether to deny, restrict, or limit the possession of a child by a parent who is appointed as a possessory conservator.

(d) The court may not allow a parent to have access to a child for whom it is shown by a preponderance of the evidence that:

  (1) there is a history or pattern of committing family violence during the two years preceding the date of the filing of the suit or during the pendency of the suit; or

  (2) the parent engaged in conduct that constitutes an offense under Section 21.02, 22.011, 22.021, or 25.02, Penal Code, and that as a direct result of the conduct, the victim of the conduct became pregnant with the parent's child.

(d-1) Notwithstanding Subsection (d), the court may allow a parent to have access to a child if the court:

  (1) finds that awarding the parent access to the child would not endanger the child's physical health or emotional welfare and would be in the best interest of the child; and

  (2) renders a possession order that is designed to protect the safety and well-being of the child and any other person who has been a victim of family violence committed by the parent and that may include a requirement that:

(A) the periods of access be continuously supervised by an entity or person chosen by the court;

(B) the exchange of possession of the child occur in a protective setting;

(C) the parent abstain from the consumption of alcohol or a controlled substance, as defined by Chapter 481, Health and Safety Code, within 12 hours prior to or during the period of access to the child; or

(D) the parent attend and complete a battering intervention and prevention program as provided by Article 42.141, Code of Criminal Procedure, or, if such a program is not available, complete a course of treatment under Section 153.010.

(e) It is a rebuttable presumption that it is not in the best interest of a child for a parent to have unsupervised visitation with the child if credible evidence is presented of a history or pattern of past or present child neglect or physical or sexual abuse by that parent directed against the other parent, a spouse, or a child.

(f) In determining under this section whether there is credible evidence of a history or pattern of past or present child neglect or physical or sexual abuse by a parent directed against the other parent, a spouse, or a child, the court shall consider whether a protective order was rendered under Chapter 85, Title 4, against the parent during the two-year period preceding the filing of the suit or during the pendency of the suit.

Sec. 153.005. APPOINTMENT OF SOLE OR JOINT MANAGING CONSERVATOR.

(a) In a suit, except as provided by Section 153.004, the court:

(1) may appoint a sole managing conservator or may appoint joint managing conservators; and

(2) if the parents are or will be separated, shall appoint at least one managing conservator.

(b) A managing conservator must be a parent, a competent adult, the Department of Family and Protective Services, or a licensed child-placing agency.

(c) In making an appointment authorized by this section, the court shall consider whether, preceding the filing of the suit or during the pendency of the suit:

(1) a party engaged in a history or pattern of family violence, as defined by Section 71.004;

(2) a party engaged in a history or pattern of child abuse or child neglect; or

(3) a final protective order was rendered against a party.

Sec. 153.006. APPOINTMENT OF POSSESSORY CONSERVATOR.

(a) If a managing conservator is appointed, the court may appoint one or more possessory conservators.

(b) The court shall specify the rights and duties of a person appointed possessory conservator.

(c) The court shall specify and expressly state in the order the times and conditions for possession of or access to the child, unless a party shows good cause why specific orders would not be in the best interest of the child.

Sec. 153.007. AGREED PARENTING PLAN.

(a) To promote the amicable settlement of disputes between the parties to a suit, the parties may enter into a written agreed parenting plan containing provisions for conservatorship and possession of the child and for modification of the parenting plan, including variations from the standard possession order.

(b) If the court finds that the agreed parenting plan is in the child's best interest, the court shall render an order in accordance with the parenting plan.

(c) Terms of the agreed parenting plan contained in the order or incorporated by reference regarding conservatorship or support of or access to a child in an order may be enforced by all remedies available for enforcement of a judgment, including contempt, but are not enforceable as a contract.

(d) If the court finds the agreed parenting plan is not in the child's best interest, the court may request the parties to submit a revised parenting plan. If the parties do not submit a revised parenting plan satisfactory to the court, the court may, after notice and hearing, order a parenting plan that the court finds to be in the best interest of the child.

Sec. 153.015. ELECTRONIC COMMUNICATION WITH CHILD BY CONSERVATOR.

(a) In this section, "electronic communication" means any communication facilitated by the use of any wired or wireless technology via the Internet or any other electronic media. The term includes communication facilitated by the use of a telephone, electronic mail, instant messaging, videoconferencing, or webcam.

(b) If a conservator of a child requests the court to order periods of electronic communication with the child under this section, the court may award the conservator reasonable periods of electronic communication with the child to supplement the conservator's periods of possession of the child. In determining whether to award electronic communication, the court shall consider:

(1) whether electronic communication is in the best interest of the child;

(2) whether equipment necessary to facilitate the electronic communication is reasonably available to all parties subject to the order; and

(3) any other factor the court considers appropriate.

(c) If a court awards a conservator periods of electronic communication with a child under this section, each conservator subject to the court's order shall:

(1) provide the other conservator with the e-mail address and other electronic communication access information of the child;

(2) notify the other conservator of any change in the e-mail address or other electronic communication access information not later than 24 hours after the date the change takes effect; and

(3) if necessary equipment is reasonably available, accommodate electronic communication with the child, with the same privacy, respect, and dignity accorded all other forms of access, at a reasonable time and for a reasonable duration subject to any limitation provided by the court in the court's order.

(d) The court may not consider the availability of electronic communication as a factor in determining child support. The availability of electronic communication under this section is not intended as a substitute for physical possession of or access to the child where otherwise appropriate.

(e) In a suit in which the court's order contains provisions related to a finding of family violence in the suit, including supervised visitation, the court may award periods of electronic communication under this section only if:

  (1) the award and terms of the award are mutually agreed to by the parties; and

  (2) the terms of the award:

    (A) are printed in the court's order in boldfaced, capitalized type; and

    (B) include any specific restrictions relating to family violence or supervised visitation, as applicable, required by other law to be included in a possession or access order.

Sec. 153.071. COURT TO SPECIFY RIGHTS AND DUTIES OF PARENT APPOINTED A CONSERVATOR. If both parents are appointed as conservators of the child, the court shall specify the rights and duties of a parent that are to be exercised:

(1) by each parent independently;

(2) by the joint agreement of the parents; and

(3) exclusively by one parent.

Sec. 153.072. WRITTEN FINDING REQUIRED TO LIMIT PARENTAL RIGHTS AND DUTIES. The court may limit the rights and duties of a parent appointed as a conservator if the court makes a written finding that the limitation is in the best interest of the child.

Sec. 153.073. RIGHTS OF PARENT AT ALL TIMES.

(a) Unless limited by court order, a parent appointed as a conservator of a child has at all times the right:

  (1) to receive information from any other conservator of the child concerning the health, education, and welfare of the child;

(2) to confer with the other parent to the extent possible before making a decision concerning the health, education, and welfare of the child;

(3) of access to medical, dental, psychological, and educational records of the child;

(4) to consult with a physician, dentist, or psychologist of the child;

(5) to consult with school officials concerning the child's welfare and educational status, including school activities;

(6) to attend school activities;

(7) to be designated on the child's records as a person to be notified in case of an emergency;

(8) to consent to medical, dental, and surgical treatment during an emergency involving an immediate danger to the health and safety of the child; and

(9) to manage the estate of the child to the extent the estate has been created by the parent or the parent's family.

(b) The court shall specify in the order the rights that a parent retains at all times.

Sec. 153.074. RIGHTS AND DUTIES DURING PERIOD OF POSSESSION. Unless limited by court order, a parent appointed as a conservator of a child has the following rights and duties during the period that the parent has possession of the child:

(1) the duty of care, control, protection, and reasonable discipline of the child;

(2) the duty to support the child, including providing the child with clothing, food, shelter, and medical and dental care not involving an invasive procedure;

(3) the right to consent for the child to medical and dental care not involving an invasive procedure; and

(4) the right to direct the moral and religious training of the child.

Sec. 153.075. DUTIES OF PARENT NOT APPOINTED CONSERVATOR. The court may order a parent not appointed as a managing or a possessory conservator to perform other parental duties, including paying child support.

Sec. 153.076. DUTY TO PROVIDE INFORMATION.

(a) The court shall order that each conservator of a child has a duty to inform the other conservator of the child in a timely manner of significant information concerning the health, education, and welfare of the child.

(b) The court shall order that each conservator of a child has the duty to inform the other conservator of the child if the conservator resides with for at least 30 days, marries, or intends to marry a person who the conservator knows:

(1) is registered as a sex offender under Chapter 62, Code of Criminal Procedure; or

(2) is currently charged with an offense for which on conviction the person would be required to register under that chapter.

(b-1) The court shall order that each conservator of a child has the duty to inform the other conservator of the child if the conservator:

(1) establishes a residence with a person who the conservator knows is the subject of a final protective order sought by an individual other than the conservator that is in effect on the date the residence with the person is established;

(2) resides with, or allows unsupervised access to a child by, a person who is the subject of a final protective order sought by the conservator after the expiration of the 60-day period following the date the final protective order is issued; or

(3) is the subject of a final protective order issued after the date of the order establishing conservatorship.

(c) The notice required to be made under Subsection (b) must be made as soon as practicable but not later than the 40th day after the date the conservator of the child begins to reside with the person or the 10th day after the date the marriage occurs, as appropriate. The notice must include a description of the offense that is the basis of the person's requirement to register as a sex offender or of the offense with which the person is charged.

(c-1) The notice required to be made under Subsection (b-1) must be made as soon as practicable but not later than:

(1) the 30th day after the date the conservator establishes residence with the person who is the subject of the final protective order, if the notice is required by Subsection (b-1)(1);

(2) the 90th day after the date the final protective order was issued, if the notice is required by Subsection (b-1)(2); or

(3) the 30th day after the date the final protective order was issued, if the notice is required by Subsection (b-1)(3).

(d) A conservator commits an offense if the conservator fails to provide notice in the manner required by Subsections (b) and (c), or Subsections (b-1) and (c-1), as applicable. An offense under this subsection is a Class C misdemeanor.

Sec. 153.131. PRESUMPTION THAT PARENT TO BE APPOINTED MANAGING CONSERVATOR.

(a) Subject to the prohibition in Section 153.004, unless the court finds that appointment of the parent or parents would not be in the best interest of the child because the appointment would significantly impair the child's physical health or emotional development, a parent shall be appointed sole managing conservator or both parents shall be appointed as joint managing conservators of the child.

(b) It is a rebuttable presumption that the appointment of the parents of a child as joint managing conservators is in the best interest of the child. A finding of a history of family violence involving the parents of a child removes the presumption under this subsection.

Sec. 153.132. RIGHTS AND DUTIES OF PARENT APPOINTED SOLE MANAGING CONSERVATOR. Unless limited by court order, a parent appointed as sole managing conservator of a child has the rights and duties provided by Subchapter B and the following exclusive rights:

(1) the right to designate the primary residence of the child;

(2) the right to consent to medical, dental, and surgical treatment involving invasive procedures;

(3) the right to consent to psychiatric and psychological treatment;

(4) the right to receive and give receipt for periodic payments for the support of the child and to hold or disburse these funds for the benefit of the child;

(5) the right to represent the child in legal action and to make other decisions of substantial legal significance concerning the child;

(6) the right to consent to marriage and to enlistment in the armed forces of the United States;

(7) the right to make decisions concerning the child's education;

(8) the right to the services and earnings of the child; and

(9) except when a guardian of the child's estate or a guardian or attorney ad litem has been appointed for the child, the right to act as an agent of the child in relation to the child's estate if the child's action is required by a state, the United States, or a foreign government.

Sec. 153.133. PARENTING PLAN FOR JOINT MANAGING CONSERVATORSHIP.

(a) If a written agreed parenting plan is filed with the court, the court shall render an order appointing the parents as joint managing conservators only if the parenting plan:

  (1) designates the conservator who has the exclusive right to designate the primary residence of the child and:

    (A) establishes, until modified by further order, the geographic area within which the conservator shall maintain the child's primary residence; or

    (B) specifies that the conservator may designate the child's primary residence without regard to geographic location;

  (2) specifies the rights and duties of each parent regarding the child's physical care, support, and education;

  (3) includes provisions to minimize disruption of the child's education, daily routine, and association with friends;

  (4) allocates between the parents, independently, jointly, or exclusively, all of the remaining rights and duties of a parent provided by Chapter 151;

(5) is voluntarily and knowingly made by each parent and has not been repudiated by either parent at the time the order is rendered; and

(6) is in the best interest of the child.

(b) The agreed parenting plan may contain an alternative dispute resolution procedure that the parties agree to use before requesting enforcement or modification of the terms and conditions of the joint conservatorship through litigation, except in an emergency.

(c) Notwithstanding Subsection (a)(1), the court shall render an order adopting the provisions of a written agreed parenting plan appointing the parents as joint managing conservators if the parenting plan:

(1) meets all the requirements of Subsections (a)(2) through (6); and

(2) provides that the child's primary residence shall be within a specified geographic area.

Sec. 153.134. COURT-ORDERED JOINT CONSERVATORSHIP.

(a) If a written agreed parenting plan is not filed with the court, the court may render an order appointing the parents joint managing conservators only if the appointment is in the best interest of the child, considering the following factors:

(1) whether the physical, psychological, or emotional needs and development of the child will benefit from the appointment of joint managing conservators;

(2) the ability of the parents to give first priority to the welfare of the child and reach shared decisions in the child's best interest;

(3) whether each parent can encourage and accept a positive relationship between the child and the other parent;

(4) whether both parents participated in child rearing before the filing of the suit;

(5) the geographical proximity of the parents' residences;

(6) if the child is 12 years of age or older, the child's preference, if any, regarding the person to have the exclusive right to designate the primary residence of the child; and

(7) any other relevant factor.

(b) In rendering an order appointing joint managing conservators, the court shall:

(1) designate the conservator who has the exclusive right to determine the primary residence of the child and:

(A) establish, until modified by further order, a geographic area within which the conservator shall maintain the child's primary residence; or

(B) specify that the conservator may determine the child's primary residence without regard to geographic location;

(2) specify the rights and duties of each parent regarding the child's physical care, support, and education;

(3) include provisions to minimize disruption of the child's education, daily routine, and association with friends;

(4) allocate between the parents, independently, jointly, or exclusively, all of the remaining rights and duties of a parent as provided by Chapter 151; and

(5) if feasible, recommend that the parties use an alternative dispute resolution method before requesting enforcement or modification of the terms and conditions of the joint conservatorship through litigation, except in an emergency.

Sec. 153.135. EQUAL POSSESSION NOT REQUIRED. Joint managing conservatorship does not require the award of equal or nearly equal periods of physical possession of and access to the child to each of the joint conservators.

Sec. 153.138. CHILD SUPPORT ORDER AFFECTING JOINT CONSERVATORS. The appointment of joint managing conservators does not impair or limit the authority of the court to order a joint managing conservator to pay child support to another joint managing conservator.

Sec. 153.191. PRESUMPTION THAT PARENT TO BE APPOINTED POSSESSORY CONSERVATOR. The court shall appoint as a possessory conservator a parent who is not appointed as a sole or joint managing conservator unless it finds that the appointment is not in the best interest of the child and that parental possession or access would endanger the physical or emotional welfare of the child.

Sec. 153.192. RIGHTS AND DUTIES OF PARENT APPOINTED POSSESSORY CONSERVATOR.

(a) Unless limited by court order, a parent appointed as possessory conservator of a child has the rights and duties provided by Subchapter B and any other right or duty expressly granted to the possessory conservator in the order.

(b) In ordering the terms and conditions for possession of a child by a parent appointed possessory conservator, the court shall be guided by the guidelines in Subchapter E.

Sec. 153.193. MINIMAL RESTRICTION ON PARENT'S POSSESSION OR ACCESS. The terms of an order that denies possession of a child to a parent or imposes restrictions or limitations on a parent's right to possession of or access to a child may not exceed those that are required to protect the best interest of the child.

Sec. 153.251. POLICY AND GENERAL APPLICATION OF GUIDELINES.

(a) The guidelines established in the standard possession order are intended to guide the courts in ordering the terms and conditions for possession of a child by a parent named as a possessory conservator or as the minimum possession for a joint managing conservator.

(b) It is the policy of this state to encourage frequent contact between a child and each parent for periods of possession that optimize the development of a close and continuing relationship between each parent and child.

(c) It is preferable for all children in a family to be together during periods of possession.

(d) The standard possession order is designed to apply to a child three years of age or older.

Sec. 153.252. REBUTTABLE PRESUMPTION. In a suit, there is a rebuttable presumption that the standard possession order in Subchapter F:

(1) provides reasonable minimum possession of a child for a parent named as a possessory conservator or joint managing conservator; and

(2) is in the best interest of the child.

Sec. 153.253. STANDARD POSSESSION ORDER INAPPROPRIATE OR UNWORKABLE. The court shall render an order that grants periods of possession of the child as similar as possible to those provided by the standard possession order if the work schedule or other special circumstances of the managing conservator, the possessory conservator, or the child, or the year-round school schedule of the child, make the standard order unworkable or inappropriate.

Sec. 153.254. CHILD LESS THAN THREE YEARS OF AGE.

(a) The court shall render an order appropriate under the circumstances for possession of a child less than three years of age. In rendering the order, the court shall consider evidence of all relevant factors, including:

(1) the caregiving provided to the child before and during the current suit;

(2) the effect on the child that may result from separation from either party;

(3) the availability of the parties as caregivers and the willingness of the parties to personally care for the child;

(4) the physical, medical, behavioral, and developmental needs of the child;

(5) the physical, medical, emotional, economic, and social conditions of the parties;

(6) the impact and influence of individuals, other than the parties, who will be present during periods of possession;

(7) the presence of siblings during periods of possession;

(8) the child's need to develop healthy attachments to both parents;

(9) the child's need for continuity of routine;

(10) the location and proximity of the residences of the parties;

(11) the need for a temporary possession schedule that incrementally shifts to the schedule provided in the prospective order under Subsection (d) based on:

(A) the age of the child; or

(B) minimal or inconsistent contact with the child by a party;

(12) the ability of the parties to share in the responsibilities, rights, and duties of parenting; and

(13) any other evidence of the best interest of the child.

(b) Notwithstanding the Texas Rules of Civil Procedure, in rendering an order under Subsection (a), the court shall make findings in support of the order if:

(1) a party files a written request with the court not later than the 10th day after the date of the hearing; or

(2) a party makes an oral request in court during the hearing on the order.

(c) The court shall make and enter the findings required by Subsection (b) not later than the 15th day after the date the party makes the request.

(d) The court shall render a prospective order to take effect on the child's third birthday, which presumptively will be the standard possession order.

Sec. 153.255. AGREEMENT. The court may render an order for periods of possession of a child that vary from the standard possession order based on the agreement of the parties.

Sec. 153.256. FACTORS FOR COURT TO CONSIDER. In ordering the terms of possession of a child under an order other than a standard possession order, the court shall be guided by the guidelines established by the standard possession order and may consider:

(1) the age, developmental status, circumstances, needs, and best interest of the child;

(2) the circumstances of the managing conservator and of the parent named as a possessory conservator; and

(3) any other relevant factor.

Sec. 153.257. MEANS OF TRAVEL. In an order providing for the terms and conditions of possession of a child, the court may restrict the means of travel of the child by a legal mode of transportation only after a showing of good cause contained in the record and a finding by the court that the restriction is in the best interest of the child. The court shall specify the duties of the conservators to provide transportation to and from the transportation facilities.

Sec. 153.258. REQUEST FOR FINDINGS WHEN ORDER VARIES FROM STANDARD ORDER. Without regard to Rules 296 through

299, Texas Rules of Civil Procedure, in all cases in which possession of a child by a parent is contested and the possession of the child varies from the standard possession order, on written request made or filed with the court not later than 10 days after the date of the hearing or on oral request made in open court during the hearing, the court shall state in the order the specific reasons for the variance from the standard order.

Sec. 153.3101. REFERENCE TO "SCHOOL" IN STANDARD POSSESSION ORDER. In a standard possession order, "school" means the elementary or secondary school in which the child is enrolled or, if the child is not enrolled in an elementary or secondary school, the public school district in which the child primarily resides.

Sec. 153.311. MUTUAL AGREEMENT OR SPECIFIED TERMS FOR POSSESSION. The court shall specify in a standard possession order that the parties may have possession of the child at times mutually agreed to in advance by the parties and, in the absence of mutual agreement, shall have possession of the child under the specified terms set out in the standard possession order.

Sec. 153.312. PARENTS WHO RESIDE 100 MILES OR LESS APART.

(a) If the possessory conservator resides 100 miles or less from the primary residence of the child, the possessory conservator shall have the right to possession of the child as follows:

   (1) on weekends throughout the year beginning at 6 P.M. on the first, third, and fifth Friday of each month and ending at 6 P.M. on the following Sunday; and

   (2) on Thursdays of each week during the regular school term beginning at 6 P.M. and ending at 8 P.M., unless the court finds that visitation under this subdivision is not in the best interest of the child.

(b) The following provisions govern possession of the child for vacations and certain specific holidays and supersede conflicting weekend or Thursday periods of possession. The possessory conservator and the managing conservator shall have rights of possession of the child as follows:

   (1) the possessory conservator shall have possession in even-numbered years, beginning at 6 P.M. on the day the child is

dismissed from school for the school's spring vacation and ending at 6 P.M. on the day before school resumes after that vacation, and the managing conservator shall have possession for the same period in odd-numbered years;

(2) if a possessory conservator:

(A) gives the managing conservator written notice by April 1 of each year specifying an extended period or periods of summer possession, the possessory conservator shall have possession of the child for 30 days beginning not earlier than the day after the child's school is dismissed for the summer vacation and ending not later than seven days before school resumes at the end of the summer vacation, to be exercised in not more than two separate periods of at least seven consecutive days each, with each period of possession beginning and ending at 6 P.M. on each applicable day; or

(B) does not give the managing conservator written notice by April 1 of each year specifying an extended period or periods of summer possession, the possessory conservator shall have possession of the child for 30 consecutive days beginning at 6 P.M. on July 1 and ending at 6 P.M. on July 31;

(3) if the managing conservator gives the possessory conservator written notice by April 15 of each year, the managing conservator shall have possession of the child on any one weekend beginning Friday at 6 P.M. and ending at 6 P.M. on the following Sunday during one period of possession by the possessory conservator under Subdivision (2), provided that the managing conservator picks up the child from the possessory conservator and returns the child to that same place; and

(4) if the managing conservator gives the possessory conservator written notice by April 15 of each year or gives the possessory conservator 14 days' written notice on or after April 16 of each year, the managing conservator may designate one weekend beginning not earlier than the day after the child's school is dismissed for the summer vacation and ending not later than seven days before school resumes at the end of the summer vacation, during which an otherwise scheduled weekend period of possession by the possessory

conservator will not take place, provided that the weekend designated does not interfere with the possessory conservator's period or periods of extended summer possession or with Father's Day if the possessory conservator is the father of the child.

Sec. 153.313. PARENTS WHO RESIDE OVER 100 MILES APART. If the possessory conservator resides more than 100 miles from the residence of the child, the possessory conservator shall have the right to possession of the child as follows:

(1) either regular weekend possession beginning on the first, third, and fifth Friday as provided under the terms applicable to parents who reside 100 miles or less apart or not more than one weekend per month of the possessory conservator's choice beginning at 6 P.M. on the day school recesses for the weekend and ending at 6 P.M. on the day before school resumes after the weekend, provided that the possessory conservator gives the managing conservator 14 days' written or telephonic notice preceding a designated weekend, and provided that the possessory conservator elects an option for this alternative period of possession by written notice given to the managing conservator within 90 days after the parties begin to reside more than 100 miles apart, as applicable;

(2) each year beginning at 6 P.M. on the day the child is dismissed from school for the school's spring vacation and ending at 6 P.M. on the day before school resumes after that vacation;

(3) if the possessory conservator:

(A) gives the managing conservator written notice by April 1 of each year specifying an extended period or periods of summer possession, the possessory conservator shall have possession of the child for 42 days beginning not earlier than the day after the child's school is dismissed for the summer vacation and ending not later than seven days before school resumes at the end of the summer vacation, to be exercised in not more than two separate periods of at least seven consecutive days each, with each period of possession beginning and ending at 6 P.M. on each applicable day; or

(B) does not give the managing conservator written notice by April 1 of each year specifying an extended period or periods of summer possession, the possessory conservator shall have possession of the child for 42 consecutive days beginning at 6 P.M. on June 15 and ending at 6 P.M. on July 27;

(4) if the managing conservator gives the possessory conservator written notice by April 15 of each year the managing conservator shall have possession of the child on one weekend beginning Friday at 6 P.M. and ending at 6 P.M. on the following Sunday during one period of possession by the possessory conservator under Subdivision (3), provided that if a period of possession by the possessory conservator exceeds 30 days, the managing conservator may have possession of the child under the terms of this subdivision on two nonconsecutive weekends during that time period, and further provided that the managing conservator picks up the child from the possessory conservator and returns the child to that same place; and

(5) if the managing conservator gives the possessory conservator written notice by April 15 of each year, the managing conservator may designate 21 days beginning not earlier than the day after the child's school is dismissed for the summer vacation and ending not later than seven days before school resumes at the end of the summer vacation, to be exercised in not more than two separate periods of at least seven consecutive days each, with each period of possession beginning and ending at 6 P.M. on each applicable day, during which the possessory conservator may not have possession of the child, provided that the period or periods so designated do not interfere with the possessory conservator's period or periods of extended summer possession or with Father's Day if the possessory conservator is the father of the child.

Sec. 153.314. HOLIDAY POSSESSION UNAFFECTED BY DISTANCE PARENTS RESIDE APART. The following provisions govern possession of the child for certain specific holidays and supersede conflicting weekend or Thursday periods of possession without regard to the distance the parents reside apart. The possessory conservator and the managing conservator shall have rights of possession of the child as follows:

(1) the possessory conservator shall have possession of the child in even-numbered years beginning at 6 P.M. on the day the child is dismissed from school for the Christmas school vacation and ending at noon on December 28, and the managing conservator shall have possession for the same period in odd-numbered years;

(2) the possessory conservator shall have possession of the child in odd-numbered years beginning at noon on December 28 and ending at 6 P.M. on the day before school resumes after that vacation, and the managing conservator shall have possession for the same period in even-numbered years;

(3) the possessory conservator shall have possession of the child in odd-numbered years, beginning at 6 P.M. on the day the child is dismissed from school before Thanksgiving and ending at 6 P.M. on the following Sunday, and the managing conservator shall have possession for the same period in even-numbered years;

(4) the parent not otherwise entitled under this standard possession order to present possession of a child on the child's birthday shall have possession of the child beginning at 6 P.M. and ending at 8 P.M. on that day, provided that the parent picks up the child from the residence of the conservator entitled to possession and returns the child to that same place;

(5) if a conservator, the father shall have possession of the child beginning at 6 P.M. on the Friday preceding Father's Day and ending on Father's Day at 6 P.M., provided that, if he is not otherwise entitled under this standard possession order to present possession of the child, he picks up the child from the residence of the conservator entitled to possession and returns the child to that same place; and

(6) if a conservator, the mother shall have possession of the child beginning at 6 P.M. on the Friday preceding Mother's Day and ending on Mother's Day at 6 P.M., provided that, if she is not otherwise entitled under this standard possession order to present possession of the child, she picks up the child from the residence of the conservator entitled to possession and returns the child to that same place.

Sec. 153.315. WEEKEND POSSESSION EXTENDED BY HOLIDAY.

(a) If a weekend period of possession of the possessory conservator coincides with a student holiday or teacher in-service day that falls on a Monday during the regular school term, as determined by the school in which the child is enrolled, or with a federal, state, or local holiday that falls on a Monday during the summer months in which school is not in session, the weekend possession shall end at 6 P.M. on Monday.

(b) If a weekend period of possession of the possessory conservator coincides with a student holiday or teacher in-service day that falls on a Friday during the regular school term, as determined by the school in which the child is enrolled, or with a federal, state, or local holiday that falls on a Friday during the summer months in which school is not in session, the weekend possession shall begin at 6 P.M. on Thursday.

Sec. 153.316. GENERAL TERMS AND CONDITIONS. The court shall order the following general terms and conditions of possession of a child to apply without regard to the distance between the residence of a parent and the child:

(1) the managing conservator shall surrender the child to the possessory conservator at the beginning of each period of the possessory conservator's possession at the residence of the managing conservator;

(2) if the possessory conservator elects to begin a period of possession at the time the child's school is regularly dismissed, the managing conservator shall surrender the child to the possessory conservator at the beginning of each period of possession at the school in which the child is enrolled;

(3) the possessory conservator shall be ordered to do one of the following:

(A) the possessory conservator shall surrender the child to the managing conservator at the end of each period of possession at the residence of the possessory conservator; or

(B) the possessory conservator shall return the child to the residence of the managing conservator at the end of each period of possession, except that the order shall provide that the possessory conservator shall surrender the child to the managing conservator at the end of each period of possession at the residence of the possessory conservator if:

(i) at the time the original order or a modification of an order establishing terms and conditions of possession or access the possessory conservator and the managing conservator lived in the same county, the possessory conservator's county of residence remains the same after the rendition of the order, and the managing conservator's county of residence changes, effective on the date of the change of residence by the managing conservator; or

(ii) the possessory conservator and managing conservator lived in the same residence at any time during a six-month period preceding the date on which a suit for dissolution of the marriage was filed and the possessory conservator's county of residence remains the same and the managing conservator's county of residence changes after they no longer live in the same residence, effective on the date the order is rendered;

(4) if the possessory conservator elects to end a period of possession at the time the child's school resumes, the possessory conservator shall surrender the child to the managing conservator at the end of each period of possession at the school in which the child is enrolled;

(5) each conservator shall return with the child the personal effects that the child brought at the beginning of the period of possession;

(6) either parent may designate a competent adult to pick up and return the child, as applicable; a parent or a designated competent adult shall be present when the child is picked up or returned;

(7) a parent shall give notice to the person in possession of the child on each occasion that the parent will be unable to exercise that parent's right of possession for a specified period;

(8) written notice, including notice provided by electronic mail or facsimile, shall be deemed to have been timely made if received or, if applicable, postmarked before or at the time that notice is due; and

(9) if a conservator's time of possession of a child ends at the time school resumes and for any reason the child is not or will not be returned to school, the conservator in possession of the child shall immediately notify the school and the other conservator that the child will not be or has not been returned to school.

Sec. 153.317. ALTERNATIVE BEGINNING AND ENDING POSSESSION TIMES.

(a) If elected by a conservator, the court shall alter the standard possession order under Sections 153.312, 153.314, and 153.315 to provide for one or more of the following alternative beginning and ending possession times for the described periods of possession, unless the court finds that the election is not in the best interest of the child:

(1) for weekend periods of possession under Section 153.312(a)(1) during the regular school term:

(A) beginning at the time the child's school is regularly dismissed;

(B) ending at the time the child's school resumes after the weekend; or

(C) beginning at the time described by Paragraph (A) and ending at the time described by Paragraph (B);

(2) for Thursday periods of possession under Section 153.312(a)(2):

(A) beginning at the time the child's school is regularly dismissed;

(B) ending at the time the child's school resumes on Friday; or

(C) beginning at the time described by Paragraph (A) and ending at the time described by Paragraph (B);

(3) for spring vacation periods of possession under Section 153.312(b)(1), beginning at the time the child's school is dismissed for those vacations;

(4) for Christmas school vacation periods of possession under Section 153.314(1), beginning at the time the child's school is dismissed for the vacation;

(5) for Thanksgiving holiday periods of possession under Section 153.314(3), beginning at the time the child's school is dismissed for the holiday;

(6) for Father's Day periods of possession under Section 153.314(5), ending at 8 A.M. on the Monday after Father's Day weekend;

(7) for Mother's Day periods of possession under Section 153.314(6):

(A) beginning at the time the child's school is regularly dismissed on the Friday preceding Mother's Day;

(B) ending at the time the child's school resumes after Mother's Day; or

(C) beginning at the time described by Paragraph (A) and ending at the time described by Paragraph (B); or

(8) for weekend periods of possession that are extended under Section 153.315(b) by a student holiday or teacher in-service day that falls on a Friday, beginning at the time the child's school is regularly dismissed on Thursday.

(b) A conservator must make an election under Subsection (a) before or at the time of the rendition of a possession order. The election may be made:

(1) in a written document filed with the court; or

(2) through an oral statement made in open court on the record.

Sec. 153.371. RIGHTS AND DUTIES OF NONPARENT APPOINTED AS SOLE MANAGING CONSERVATOR. Unless limited by court order or other provisions of this chapter, a nonparent, a licensed child-placing agency, or the Department of Family and Protective Services appointed as a managing conservator of the child has the following rights and duties:

(1) the right to have physical possession and to direct the moral and religious training of the child;

(2) the duty of care, control, protection, and reasonable discipline of the child;

(3) the duty to provide the child with clothing, food, shelter, education, and medical, psychological, and dental care;

(4) the right to consent for the child to medical, psychiatric, psychological, dental, and surgical treatment and to have access to the child's medical records;

(5) the right to receive and give receipt for payments for the support of the child and to hold or disburse funds for the benefit of the child;

(6) the right to the services and earnings of the child;

(7) the right to consent to marriage and to enlistment in the armed forces of the United States;

(8) the right to represent the child in legal action and to make other decisions of substantial legal significance concerning the child;

(9) except when a guardian of the child's estate or a guardian or attorney ad litem has been appointed for the child, the right to act as an agent of the child in relation to the child's estate if the child's action is required by a state, the United States, or a foreign government;

(10) the right to designate the primary residence of the child and to make decisions regarding the child's education; and

(11) if the parent-child relationship has been terminated with respect to the parents, or only living parent, or if there is no living parent, the right to consent to the adoption of the child and to make any other decision concerning the child that a parent could make.

Sec. 153.372. NONPARENT APPOINTED AS JOINT MANAGING CONSERVATOR.

(a) A nonparent, the Department of Family and Protective Services, or a licensed child-placing agency appointed as a joint managing conservator may serve in that capacity with either another nonparent or with a parent of the child.

(b) The procedural and substantive standards regarding an agreed or court-ordered joint managing conservatorship provided by Subchapter C apply to a nonparent joint managing conservator.

Sec. 153.3721. ACCESS TO CERTAIN RECORDS BY NONPARENT JOINT MANAGING CONSERVATOR. Unless limited by court order or other provisions of this chapter, a nonparent joint managing conservator has the right of access to the medical records of the child, without regard to whether the right is specified in the order.

Sec. 153.373. VOLUNTARY SURRENDER OF POSSESSION REBUTS PARENTAL PRESUMPTION. The presumption that a parent should be appointed or retained as managing conservator of the child is rebutted if the court finds that:

(1) the parent has voluntarily relinquished actual care, control, and possession of the child to a nonparent, a licensed child-placing agency, or the Department of Family and Protective Services for a period of one year or more, a portion of which was within 90 days preceding the date of intervention in or filing of the suit; and

(2) the appointment of the nonparent, agency, or Department of Family and Protective Services as managing conservator is in the best interest of the child.

Utah

30-3-10.9. Parenting plan — Objectives — Required provisions — Dispute resolution.

(1) The objectives of a parenting plan are to:
  (a) provide for the child's physical care;
  (b) maintain the child's emotional stability;
  (c) provide for the child's changing needs as the child grows and matures in a way that minimizes the need for future modifications to the parenting plan;
  (d) set forth the authority and responsibilities of each parent with respect to the child consistent with the definitions outlined in this chapter;
  (e) minimize the child's exposure to harmful parental conflict;
  (f) encourage the parents, where appropriate, to meet the responsibilities to their minor children through agreements in the parenting plan rather than relying on judicial intervention; and
  (g) protect the best interests of the child.

(2) The parenting plan shall contain provisions for resolution of future disputes between the parents, allocation of decision-making authority, and residential provisions for the child, and provisions addressing notice and parent-time responsibilities in the event of the relocation of either party. It may contain other provisions comparable to those in Sections 30-3-5 and 30-3-10.3 regarding the welfare of the child.

(3) A process for resolving disputes shall be provided unless precluded or limited by statute. A dispute resolution process may include:
  (a) counseling;
  (b) mediation or arbitration by a specified individual or agency; or
  (c) court action.

(4) In the dispute resolution process:

(a) preference shall be given to the provisions in the parenting plan;

(b) parents shall use the designated process to resolve disputes relating to implementation of the plan, except those related to financial support, unless an emergency exists;

(c) a written record shall be prepared of any agreement reached in counseling or mediation and provided to each party;

(d) if arbitration becomes necessary, a written record shall be prepared and a copy of the arbitration award shall be provided to each party;

(e) if the court finds that a parent has used or frustrated the dispute resolution process without good reason, the court may award attorney's fees and financial sanctions to the prevailing parent;

(f) the district court shall have the right of review from the dispute resolution process; and

(g) the provisions of this Subsection (4) shall be set forth in any final decree or order.

(5) The parenting plan shall allocate decision-making authority to one or both parties regarding the children's education, health care, and religious upbringing. The parties may incorporate an agreement related to the care and growth of the children in these specified areas or in other areas into their plan, consistent with the criteria outlined in Subsection 30-3-10.7(2) and Subsection (1). Regardless of the allocation of decision-making in the parenting plan, either parent may make emergency decisions affecting the health or safety of the child.

(6) Each parent may make decisions regarding the day-to-day care and control of the child while the child is residing with that parent.

(7) When mutual decision-making is designated but cannot be achieved, the parties shall make a good faith effort to resolve the issue through the dispute resolution process.

(8) The plan shall include a residential schedule which designates in which parent's home each minor child shall reside on given days of the year, including provisions for holidays, birthdays of family members, vacations, and other special occasions.

(9) If a parent fails to comply with a provision of the parenting plan or a child support order, the other parent's obligations under the parenting plan or the child support order are not affected. Failure to comply with a provision of the parenting plan or a child support order may result in a finding of contempt of court.

Virginia

http://law.lis.virginia.gov/vacode/title20/chapter6.1/section20-124.2/

Washington

RCW 26.09.184 Permanent parenting plan.

(1) OBJECTIVES. The objectives of the permanent parenting plan are to:

   (a) Provide for the child's physical care;

   (b) Maintain the child's emotional stability;

   (c) Provide for the child's changing needs as the child grows and matures, in a way that minimizes the need for future modifications to the permanent parenting plan;

   (d) Set forth the authority and responsibilities of each parent with respect to the child, consistent with the criteria in RCW 26.09.187 and 26.09.191;

   (e) Minimize the child's exposure to harmful parental conflict;

   (f) Encourage the parents, where appropriate under RCW 26.09.187 and 26.09.191, to meet their responsibilities to their minor children through agreements in the permanent parenting plan, rather than by relying on judicial intervention; and

   (g) To otherwise protect the best interests of the child consistent with RCW 26.09.002.

(2) CONTENTS OF THE PERMANENT PARENTING PLAN. The permanent parenting plan shall contain provisions for resolution of future disputes between the parents, allocation of decision-making authority, and residential provisions for the child.

(3) CONSIDERATION IN ESTABLISHING THE PERMANENT PARENTING PLAN. In establishing a permanent parenting plan,

the court may consider the cultural heritage and religious beliefs of a child.

(4) DISPUTE RESOLUTION. A process for resolving disputes, other than court action, shall be provided unless precluded or limited by RCW 26.09.187 or 26.09.191. A dispute resolution process may include counseling, mediation, or arbitration by a specified individual or agency, or court action. In the dispute resolution process:

(a) Preference shall be given to carrying out the parenting plan;

(b) The parents shall use the designated process to resolve disputes relating to implementation of the plan, except those related to financial support, unless an emergency exists;

(c) A written record shall be prepared of any agreement reached in counseling or mediation and of each arbitration award and shall be provided to each party;

(d) If the court finds that a parent has used or frustrated the dispute resolution process without good reason, the court shall award attorneys' fees and financial sanctions to the prevailing parent;

(e) The parties have the right of review from the dispute resolution process to the superior court; and

(f) The provisions of (a) through (e) of this subsection shall be set forth in the decree.

(5) ALLOCATION OF DECISION-MAKING AUTHORITY.

(a) The plan shall allocate decision-making authority to one or both parties regarding the children's education, health care, and religious upbringing. The parties may incorporate an agreement related to the care and growth of the child in these specified areas, or in other areas, into their plan, consistent with the criteria in RCW 26.09.187 and 26.09.191. Regardless of the allocation of decision-making in the parenting plan, either parent may make emergency decisions affecting the health or safety of the child.

(b) Each parent may make decisions regarding the day-to-day care and control of the child while the child is residing with that parent.

(c) When mutual decision making is designated but cannot be achieved, the parties shall make a good faith effort to resolve the issue through the dispute resolution process.

(6) RESIDENTIAL PROVISIONS FOR THE CHILD. The plan shall include a residential schedule which designates in which parent's home each minor child shall reside on given days of the year, including provision for holidays, birthdays of family members, vacations, and other special occasions, consistent with the criteria in RCW 26.09.187 and 26.09.191.

(7) PARENTS' OBLIGATION UNAFFECTED. If a parent fails to comply with a provision of a parenting plan or a child support order, the other parent's obligations under the parenting plan or the child support order are not affected. Failure to comply with a provision in a parenting plan or a child support order may result in a finding of contempt of court, under RCW 26.09.160.

(8) PROVISIONS TO BE SET FORTH IN PERMANENT PARENTING PLAN. The permanent parenting plan shall set forth the provisions of subsections (4)(a) through (c), (5)(b) and (c), and (7) of this section.

West Virginia

http://www.legis.state.wv.us/wvcode/chapterentire.cfm?chap=48&art=9&section=205

Wisconsin

(1) General provisions.

(a) Subject to ch. 822, the question of a child's custody may be determined as an incident of any action affecting the family or in an independent action for custody. The effect of any determination of a child's custody is not binding personally against any parent or guardian unless the parent or guardian has been made personally subject to the jurisdiction of the court in the action as provided under ch. 801 or has been notified under s. 822.08, as provided in s. 822.06. Nothing in this chapter may be construed to foreclose a person other than a parent who has physical custody of a child from proceeding under ch. 822.

(b) In rendering a judgment of annulment, divorce, legal separation, or paternity, or in rendering a judgment in an action under s. 767.001 (1) (e), 767.501, or 767.805 (3), the court shall make such provisions as it deems just and reasonable concerning the legal custody and physical placement of any minor child of the parties, as provided in this section.

(1m) Parenting plan. Unless the court orders otherwise, in an action for annulment, divorce, or legal separation, an action to determine paternity, or an action under s. 767.001 (1) (e), 767.501, or 767.805 (3), in which legal custody or physical placement is contested, a party seeking sole or joint legal custody or periods of physical placement shall file a parenting plan with the court if the court waives the requirement to attend mediation under s. 767.405 (8) (b) or if the parties attend mediation and the mediator notifies the court under s. 767.405 (12) (b) that the parties have not reached an agreement. Unless the court orders otherwise, the parenting plan shall be filed within 60 days after the court waives the mediation requirement or the mediator notifies the court that no agreement has been reached. Except for cause shown, a party required to file a parenting plan under this subsection who does not timely file a parenting plan waives the right to object to the other party's parenting plan. A parenting plan shall provide information about the following questions:

(a) What legal custody or physical placement the parent is seeking.

(b) Where the parent lives currently and where the parent intends to live during the next 2 years. If there is evidence that the other parent engaged in interspousal battery, as described under s. 940.19 or 940.20 (1m), or domestic abuse, as defined in s. 813.12 (1) (am), with respect to the parent providing the parenting plan, the parent providing the parenting plan is not required to disclose the specific address but only a general description of where he or she currently lives and intends to live during the next 2 years.

(c) Where the parent works and the hours of employment. If there is evidence that the other parent engaged in interspousal battery, as described under s. 940.19 or 940.20 (1m), or domestic abuse, as defined in s. 813.12 (1) (am), with respect to the parent providing the parenting plan, the parent providing the parenting plan is not required to disclose the specific address but only a general description of where he or she works.

(d) Who will provide any necessary child care when the parent cannot and who will pay for the child care.

(e) Where the child will go to school.

(f) What doctor or health care facility will provide medical care for the child.

(g) How the child's medical expenses will be paid.

(h) What the child's religious commitment will be, if any.

(i) Who will make decisions about the child's education, medical care, choice of child care providers and extracurricular activities.

(j) How the holidays will be divided.

(k) What the child's summer schedule will be.

(L) Whether and how the child will be able to contact the other parent when the child has physical placement with the parent providing the parenting plan, and what electronic communication, if any, the parent is seeking.

(Lm) Whether equipment for providing electronic communication is reasonably available to both parents.

(m) How the parent proposes to resolve disagreements related to matters over which the court orders joint decision making.

(n) What child support, family support, maintenance or other income transfer there will be.

(o) If there is evidence that either party engaged in interspousal battery, as described under s. 940.19 or 940.20 (1m), or domestic abuse, as defined in s. 813.12 (1) (am), with respect to the other party, how the child will be transferred between the parties for the exercise of physical placement to ensure the safety of the child and the parties.

Wyoming

20-2-201

(a) In granting a divorce, separation or annulment of a marriage or upon the establishment of paternity pursuant to W.S. 14-2-401 through 14-2-907, the court may make by decree or order any disposition of the children that appears most expedient and in the best interests of the children. In determining the best interests of the child, the court shall consider, but is not limited to, the following factors:

(i) The quality of the relationship each child has with each parent;

(ii) The ability of each parent to provide adequate care for each child throughout each period of responsibility, including arranging for each child's care by others as needed;

(iii) The relative competency and fitness of each parent;

(iv) Each parent's willingness to accept all responsibilities of parenting, including a willingness to accept care for each child at specified times and to relinquish care to the other parent at specified times;

(v) How the parents and each child can best maintain and strengthen a relationship with each other;

(vi) How the parents and each child interact and communicate with each other and how such interaction and communication may be improved;

(vii) The ability and willingness of each parent to allow the other to provide care without intrusion, respect the other parent's rights and responsibilities, including the right to privacy;

(viii) Geographic distance between the parents' residences;

(ix) The current physical and mental ability of each parent to care for each child;

(x) Any other factors the court deems necessary and relevant.

(b) In any proceeding in which the custody of a child is at issue the court shall not prefer one (1) parent as a custodian solely because of gender.

(c) The court shall consider evidence of spousal abuse or child abuse as being contrary to the best interest of the children. If the court finds that family violence has occurred, the court shall make arrangements for visitation that best protects the children and the abused spouse from further harm.

(d) The court shall order custody in well defined terms to promote understanding and compliance by the parties. Custody shall be crafted to promote the best interests of the children, and may include any combination of joint, shared or sole custody.

(e) Unless otherwise ordered by the court, the noncustodial parent shall have the same right of access as the parent awarded custody to any records relating to the child of the parties, including school records, activities, teachers and teachers' conferences as well as medical and dental treatment providers and mental health records.

(f) At any time the court may require parents to attend appropriate parenting classes, including but not limited to, parenting classes to lessen the effects of divorce on children.

(g) At any time a court is considering the custody or visitation rights of a service member, as defined by W.S. 20-2-205, the court shall comply with W.S. 20-2-205.

20-2-202

(a) The court may order visitation it deems in the best interests of each child and the court shall:

   (i) Order visitation in enough detail to promote understanding and compliance;

   (ii) Provide for the allocation of the costs of transporting each child for purposes of visitation;

   (iii) Require either parent who plans to change their home city or state of residence, to give written notice thirty (30) days prior to the move, both to the other parent and to the clerk of district court stating the date and destination of the move.

Index

absent parents. *See* dropout or absent parents
abuse. *See* child abuse and neglect; domestic violence
affect heuristics, 15
age-appropriate parenting schedules, 243–260
  for adolescents, 256–260
  developmental and individual factors for, 244–246
  examples of, 246–260
  for middle childhood, 250–256
  overview of considerations with, 243–244, 260
  for very young children, 246–250
agoraphobia, 140–141
Alabama
  parenting plan legal criteria, 265–266
  relocation statute in, 168
alcohol abuse. *See* substance use/abuse
alienation, parental. *See* parental alienation
American Academy of Pediatrics, 215, 216
American Coalition for Fathers and Children (ACFC), 9
anchoring, 16–17, 243–244
anxiety disorders
  agoraphobia as, 140–141
  childhood, 110, 111, 119–122
  parental, 19, 132, 140–141
  prevalence of, 111, 132
Arizona, parenting plan legal criteria, 266–267
assessments
  of child abuse and neglect, 195–197, 202, 206
  of children's mental health and special needs, 112–113
  for domestic violence, 78–80
  of emotional attachment, 47–48, 49–50, 53
  for marital conflict, 93
  of parental alienation, 148–149
  of parental mental health, 135–140, 142
  parenting plans based on, 4
Association of Family and Conciliation Courts, 77
attachment. *See* emotional attachment
Attachment Q Sort, 47, 53
attention deficit hyperactivity disorders (ADHD)
  childhood, 110, 114, 115–118, 252–254
  description of, 110
  parental, 117
  prevalence of, 110
Australia
  child abuse intervention outcomes in, 201
  relocation research in, 174
  shared parenting law in, 48
  very young children research in, 51–53, 54, 55
Autism Spectrum Disorders (ASD)
  childhood, 110, 111–112, 114, 123–125
  description of, 111–112, 123
  individual education plans for, 124
  prevalence of, 112
availability, parental. *See* parental availability
availability heuristics, 16

biases, 14, 19
blended families. *See* step– or blended families

California, parenting plan legal criteria, 267–268
Canada, child abuse and neglect research in, 194–195
car seats, 66, 106, 215
child abuse and neglect, 193–208
domestic violence including, 78–79, 81, 87, 203
electronic communication in cases of, 204, 205
frequency of, 198
heterogeneity of, 197–202
home visiting programs for, 200–202
interventions addressing, 199–202, 203
investigations of, 195–197, 202, 206
overview of considerations with, 193–195, 206–208
parental alienation due to, 148, 149, 151
parental mental health issues affecting, 135, 139
parent education programs for, 200–201
parenting plan consideration of, 202–206
parenting schedules and, 203–206, 248–249
prevalence of, 193–195
recidivism rates with, 198–199
relocation in cases of, 175, 178
risk factors for, 202–203
severity of, 197
sexual, 151, 194, 195, 197–198, 199–200, 202
substantiated *vs.* unsubstantiated claims of, 194–195, 206
supervised visitation with, 204, 205–206
suspended visitation with, 204
of very young children, 203
child adjustment
marital conflict affecting, 87–88, 90, 92
in nontraditional families, 182–191
parental mental health issues affecting, 133–134
remarriage affecting, 211–212
scientific evidence on, 27, 28–29, 31–35, 53, 54
shared parenting effects on, 7, 27, 91–92
child-focused calendars, 223–224
children of divorce/separation
abuse and neglect of (*see* child abuse and neglect)
mental health and special needs of (*see* children's mental health issues and special needs)
parenting plans for (*see* parenting plans)
parents of (*see* fathers; mothers; parents)
residential changes for (*see* overnight visits; relocation; residential changes; transitions)
safety of (*see* safety and health issues)
scientific evidence on (*see* scientific evidence on children of divorce)
temperament of, 60, 88, 169, 219–220, 244–245
terminology related to, 3–4
very young (*see* very young children of divorce/separation)
children's mental health issues and special needs
ADHD as, 110, 114, 115–118, 252–254
anxiety disorders as, 110, 111, 119–122
assessments of, 112–113
Autism Spectrum Disorders as, 110, 111–112, 114, 123–125
child abuse and neglect in relation to, 193, 203
conduct disorders as, 110, 111, 117, 118–119, 221
court-involved therapy for, 125–127
depressive disorders as, 90–91, 110–111, 119–122, 221
domestic violence affecting, 74

gender differences in, 110–111
interparental communication on, 114, 119, 121–122, 123
learning disorders as, 110, 111, 122–123
marital conflict affecting, 86–88, 90–92, 100–101, 120
nontraditional family effects on, 182, 184, 188
overnight visits and, 59
overview of considerations with, 109–112, 127–129
parental acknowledgment *vs.* denial of, 113, 115–116
parental competence and availability to manage, 114–115, 117, 118–119, 120–125
parental decision making on, 119, 122, 123
parenting schedules adapted for, 252–254
prevalence of, 109–112
professional competence to address, 125–127
relocation considerations with, 169
residential changes affecting, 219–221
safety and health issues with, 111, 114, 119–120, 123
substance abuse as, 40, 118, 221
transition considerations with, 117–118
very young children's, 59

cohabiting parents. *See* never-married parents

Colorado, parenting plan legal criteria, 269–275

communication. *See* electronic or written communication; interparental communication

conduct disorders
ADHD and, 117, 118
childhood, 110, 111, 117, 118–119, 221
description of, 118
parental, 83, 88, 118, 139
prevalence of, 111

conflict
interparental (*see* interparental conflict; marital conflict)
violent (*see* child abuse and neglect; domestic violence)

Connecticut, parenting plan legal criteria, 275–276

controversies, parenting plan, 5–10

cooperation, parental. *See* interparental cooperation

cultural issues
gender as, 9, 31–32, 74–76, 77–78, 110–111, 132, 186
race and ethnicity as, 19, 186, 188–189
sexual orientation as, 8, 181, 182, 189
stereotypes as, 19

decision making, parental. *See* parental decision making

Delaware, parenting plan legal criteria, 276

depressive and mood disorders
childhood, 90–91, 110–111, 119–122, 221
parental, 33, 76, 83, 86, 88, 118, 132–133, 134–135, 139
prevalence of, 110
residential changes affecting, 221
substance use and, 33, 133, 141

developmental factors
age-appropriate parenting schedules based on, 243–260
parental alienation affected by, 149, 150
very young child parenting plans considering (*see* very young children of divorce/separation)

District of Columbia, parenting plan legal criteria, 276–277

domestic violence, 73–84
assessment of and screening for, 78–80
categories of, 77–78
child abuse or neglect in, 78–79, 81, 87, 203

domestic violence *(continued)*
gender differences in, 74–76, 77–78
interparental communication and, 81
overview of considerations with, 73, 83–84
parental alienation due to, 148, 149
parental decision making challenges with, 82
parental mental health affecting, 76, 83
parenting plan consideration of, 80–83
parenting schedules affected by, 256–258
prevalence of, 74
professional competence with, 79, 83
relocation in cases of, 175, 178
shared parenting success affected by, 8, 81–82, 95–96
transition structure and, 80, 82
dropout or absent parents
prevalence of and reasons for, 8–9
scientific evidence on impact of, 32, 36–37
drug abuse. *See* substance use/abuse
Duluth model, 76

economic status. *See* socioeconomic status
electronic or written communication
interparental, 41, 65, 81, 96–99, 102, 213, 225
parenting schedules including, 172–173, 204, 205, 254–255, 257
emergencies, interparental communication in, 81, 97, 228
emotional attachment
assessment of, 47–48, 49–50, 53
with mothers *vs.* fathers, 5–6, 31, 48
parental mental health issues affecting, 133
parenting schedule allowances for, 236, 237, 245
security of, 46–47, 50, 52, 53, 59
very young children's, 5–6, 46–48, 49–50, 52, 53, 55–57, 59, 236, 237, 245
emotions
affect heuristics defined by, 15
attachment and (*see* emotional attachment)
intuition *vs.* reasoning in relation to, 12–13
equally shared parenting, 3, 7, 39, 48, 95, 169, 252, 258. *See also* shared parenting
estrangement, parental alienation *vs.*, 150

families
children in (*see* children of divorce/separation)
conflict and violence in (*see* child abuse and neglect; domestic violence; interparental conflict; marital conflict)
nontraditional, 8, 9, 181–192, 203
parents in (*see* fathers; mothers; parents)
residential changes for (*see* overnight visits; relocation; residential changes; transitions)
step– or blended, 176, 184, 186, 187, 210–212
Family Bridges, 156–157
Family Reflections Unification Program, 157–158
family therapy, 117, 227–228
fathers
dropout or absent, 9, 36–37
emotional attachment to, 6, 31, 48, 49–50, 57, 236
gatekeeping as barrier for, 58, 159–160
gender issue perceptions of, 9, 31–32
marital conflict and children's contact with, 90–92
never-married, 185–186 (*see also* never-married parents)
parental alienation with, 148, 153
parenting styles of, 31–32
relocation opposition by, 167
scientific evidence on involvement of, 31–32, 34, 36–37, 57

step-up parenting of, 67–68
very young children with, 6, 45, 48, 49–54, 57, 67–68, 160, 217, 236
financial status. *See* socioeconomic status
firearms, safety from, 216
Florida, parenting plan legal criteria, 277
foundation for good parenting plans, 11–23
biases affecting, 14, 19
checklists or decision trees for, 20–21
cognitive processes and principles applied to, 12–23
complexity addressed in, 12, 13, 20, 68
goal of, 11
halo effect avoidance for, 22
heuristics affecting, 14–17
intuition application in, 12–19, 28
lists of support and contradiction of assertions for, 21–22, 262 (*see also* pro-con lists)
personal experience as poor, 11, 17–18
premortem approach to, 21
professional competence for, 22
reasoning application in, 12–14, 16–17, 19–22, 28, 68–69, 262
time pressure affecting, 18
uncertainty addressed in, 12, 13
WYSIATI errors affecting, 18
Fragile Families and Child Wellbeing Study, 53

Gardner, Richard, 148, 149
gatekeeping
facilitative, 158–159
interventions efforts for, 160
parental alienation and, 62, 158–160, 166, 178
restrictive, 58, 62, 158–159, 178
state statutes on, 158–159
very young children's parental relations affected by, 58, 62, 160
gay/lesbian parents, 8, 181, 182, 189
gender
children's mental health differences by, 110–111
controversies over, 9
domestic violence differences by, 74–76, 77–78
never-married parents' familial instability in relation to, 186
parental mental health differences by, 132
parenting style differences by, 31–32
Georgia, parenting plan legal criteria, 277–279

halo effect, 22
heuristics, 14–17, 138
holidays, parenting schedules with, 238–239, 240
home visiting programs, 200–202
households, shifting between. *See* residential changes

Idaho, parenting plan legal criteria, 279
Illinois
parenting plan legal criteria, 279–287
relocation statute in, 168, 170
impulse disorders. *See* conduct disorders
Indiana, Parenting Time Guidelines, 240, 287
individual therapy, 227–228
interparental communication
children's mental health and special needs necessitating, 114, 119, 121–122, 123
domestic violence and, 81
electronic or written, 41, 65, 81, 96–99, 102, 213, 225
in emergencies, 81, 97, 228
marital conflict and, 96–99, 100, 102–103, 141, 224–225
parental decision making and, 213
parenting plan consideration of, 224–225
transitions necessitating, 65–66, 219–220, 222
very young child care requiring, 50, 51–52, 63–66

interparental conflict. *See also* marital conflict
child adjustment affected by, 29
controversies over affect of, 7–8
parenting schedule discord and, 104, 106–107, 237–238, 240, 241
professional competence to address, 22
scientific evidence on effects of, 29, 32, 33–34, 37, 39, 41–42
strategies to limit, 41
very young children's overnight visits affected by, 57–58, 62
interparental cooperation
parental beliefs and attitudes toward, 41
parenting schedule success with, 237, 259
patterns of, 94–95
scientific evidence on effects of, 27, 38, 41
shared parenting effectiveness and, 7
very young children's overnight visits affected by, 58, 59, 61–62, 68
interventions
ADHD, 116–117
anxiety, 120–121
Autism Spectrum Disorder, 123–124
child abuse, 199–202, 203
conduct disorder, 118–119
court-involved or court-ordered, 125–127, 143, 154–155, 227–228
depression, 120–121
domestic violence, 76
gatekeeping, 160
interparental communication, 225
learning disorder, 122
parental alienation, 153–158, 161
parental decision making, 213
parental mental health issues requiring, 142–143
parenting plan referrals for, 227–228
parenting plans as, 4 (*see also* parenting plans)
sex offender, 199–200
interviews
child, 93, 140, 195–197, 225–227
parental, 78, 139–140
intuition
biases as errors of, 14, 19
definition and description of, 12–13
foundation for good parenting plans based on, 12–19, 28
heuristics as errors of, 14–17, 138
Iowa, parenting plan legal criteria, 287–290
Israel, parental alienation intervention in, 157

Johnston, Janet, 149
joint parenting. *See* shared parenting

Kahneman, Daniel, 11–12, 14–15, 18, 20–21
Kansas, parenting plan legal criteria, 291
Kelly, Joan, 149
Kentucky, parenting plan legal criteria, 291–293

Law Center to Prevent Gun Violence, 216
LEAD (Longitudinal, Expert, All Data) criteria, 93
learning disorders
childhood, 110, 111, 122–123
description of, 111
individual education plans for, 122
prevalence of, 111
lists, pro-con. *See* pro-con lists
Longitudinal Study of Australian Children, 51–53
Louisiana, parenting plan legal criteria, 294

Maine, parenting plan legal criteria, 295–304
marital conflict, 85–108. *See also* domestic violence; interparental conflict
apologies for, 88
assessment of, 93

children negatively affected by, 86–88, 90–93, 99–101, 120, 141, 218
children's mediation of, 87, 88, 100
definition of, 85
family disintegration concerns with, 87, 88, 120
healthy parental contact with children despite, 89–96
interparental communication and, 96–99, 100, 102–103, 141, 224–225
negative comments about other parent and, 99–100, 101
overview of considerations with, 85–86, 107–108
parallel parenting with, 94, 96
parental alienation associated with, 151
parental decision making affected by, 89, 95, 96, 101–104, 106, 212–214
parental mental health factors in, 86, 88–89, 94, 133, 141
parenting plan consideration of, 96–107
parenting schedule challenges with, 104, 106–107, 237–238, 240, 241
patterns of, 94–95
problem-solving to resolve, 88, 101–103, 105
professional competence for planning with, 96–99, 103, 105–106
protecting children from, 89–96
reasons and motivations for, 93–94
shared parenting success affected by, 7–8, 89, 95–96, 103–104
transition planning with, 106–107, 141, 218, 222–223
Massachusetts, parenting plan legal criteria, 304
mental health issues. *See* children's mental health issues and special needs; parental mental health issues
Michigan, parenting plan legal criteria, 304
Minnesota, parenting plan legal criteria, 304
Missouri, parenting plan legal criteria, 305
Montana, parenting plan legal criteria, 305–307
mood disorders. *See* depressive and mood disorders
mothers
children's mental health and special needs addressed by, 113, 123–124
emotional attachment to, 5–6, 31, 48, 49–50, 52, 57
gatekeeping by, 58, 159–160
gender issue perceptions of, 9, 31–32
never-married, 185–186 (*see also* never-married parents)
parental alienation with, 148, 153
parenting styles of, 31–32
relocation by, 167
very young children with, 5–6, 45, 48, 49–54, 57, 217, 236

National Council of Juvenile and Family Court Judges, 76–77
National Institute of Child Health and Human Development, U.S., 196
National Longitudinal Study of Youth, 34
Nebraska, parenting plan legal criteria, 307
negative comments about other parent, 99–100, 101
never-married parents
child abuse and neglect by, 203
child adjustment with, 183–189
dropout or absent parents as, 9
duration of unions of, 183
family transitions *vs.* stability with, 183–189
overview of considerations with, 191–192
parenting plans for, 189–191
pathways to parenthood for, 181
prevalence of, 8

never-married parents *(continued)*
pro se litigants among, 183–184, 190–191
socioeconomic status of, 183, 185–186, 189–190
stepfamilies *vs.,* 184, 186, 187
New Hampshire, parenting plan legal criteria, 307–308
New Jersey, parenting plan legal criteria, 309
New Mexico, parenting plan legal criteria, 309–315
New Zealand, relocation research in, 174
nontraditional families, 181–192
child adjustment in, 182–191
controversies over, 8
gay/lesbian parents as, 8, 181, 182, 189
never-married parents as, 8, 9, 181, 183–192, 203
overview of considerations with, 181–182, 191–192
parenting plan considerations with, 189–191
pro se litigants among, 183–184, 190–191
socioeconomic status of, 183, 185–186, 189–190
North Dakota, parenting plan legal criteria, 315–316

Ohio, parenting plan legal criteria, 316–333
Oklahoma, parenting plan legal criteria, 333–334
Oregon, parenting plan legal criteria, 334–335
Overcoming Barriers Family Camp, 155–156, 158
overnight visits. *See also* residential changes
children's mental health and special needs considerations for, 59
marital conflict and communication about, 100–101
parental mental health considerations for, 57, 60–61
transitions for (*see* transitions)
very young children's, 5–6, 47, 48, 49–62, 68, 217–221

parallel group therapy, 157
parallel parenting, 82, 94, 96
parental alienation, 147–166
aligned parent role in, 148, 151, 153, 155, 156, 160–161, 162
assessment of, 148–149
child's perspective in, 149–151
definition of, 147
domestic violence or abuse affecting, 148, 149, 151
estrangement *vs.,* 150
gatekeeping and, 62, 158–160, 166, 178
interventions for, 153–158, 161
overview of considerations with, 147–151, 163–166
parental mental health issues and, 148, 150, 151, 155
parenting plan consideration of, 160–163
professional competence to address, 160–163
relocation and, 175, 178
research on, 151–158
terminology associated with, 147–148
transitions and, 149–150, 220
very young children's, 62, 149
parental availability
children's mental health and special needs considerations with, 114–115
parenting schedules reflecting, 235
transitions and, 80
for very young child care, 57, 62
parental decision making
on children's mental health and special needs, 119, 122, 123
domestic violence affecting, 82
marital conflict impacting, 89, 95, 96, 101–104, 106, 212–214
parenting plan consideration of, 212–214, 228

qualitative *vs.* quantitative criteria for, 6–7
sole decision making as option for, 103–104, 106, 119, 213–214
parental mental health issues, 131–145
ADHD as, 117
anxiety disorders as, 19, 132, 140–141
assessment of, 135–140, 142
child abuse and neglect tied to, 135, 139
conduct or impulse disorders as, 83, 88, 118, 139
court-ordered therapy for, 143
depressive and mood disorders as, 33, 76, 83, 86, 88, 118, 132–133, 134–135, 139
domestic violence attributed to poor, 76, 83
foundation for good parenting plans consideration of, 16, 19
gender differences in, 132
marital conflict affected by, 86, 88–89, 94, 133, 141
overview of considerations with, 131, 144–145
parental alienation and, 148, 150, 151, 155
parenting plan considerations of, 16, 19, 138–144
personality disorders as, 76, 83, 94, 135–136
post-traumatic stress disorder as, 16
prevalence of, 131–133
professional competence to address, 135, 138–144
scientific evidence on effects of, 32, 33–34, 39–40
substance use/abuse as (*see* substance use/abuse)
treatment or interventions for, 142–143
very young child care and, 57, 60–61, 67
parent education programs, 200–201
parenting plans
children in (*see* children of divorce/separation; very young children of divorce/separation)
components of, 228–230
conflict and violence considerations in (*see* child abuse and neglect; domestic violence; interparental conflict; marital conflict)
consequences for violation of, 229–230
controversies on, 5–10
families in (*see* families)
foundation for building good (*see* foundation for good parenting plans)
introduction to, 1–4
mental health considerations for (*see* children's mental health issues and special needs; parental mental health issues)
practical considerations for (*see* practical considerations)
residential change considerations for (*see* overnight visits; relocation; residential changes; transitions)
revising, provisions for, 230
schedules in (*see* parenting schedules)
scientific evidence informing (*see* scientific evidence on children of divorce)
state statutes affecting (*see* state statutes)
parenting schedules
adolescents', 256–260
age-appropriate, 243–260
availability affecting (*see* parental availability)
child abuse and domestic violence considerations for, 203–206, 248–249, 256–258
child availability and schedule affecting, 223–224, 235
children's mental health issues affecting, 252–254

parenting schedules *(continued)*
electronic communication in, 172–173, 204, 205, 254–255, 257
examples of, 246–260
family circumstances dictating, 235–237
frequency of sharing and exchanges in, 237–238
holiday schedules in, 238–239, 240
marital conflict and challenges of, 104, 106–107, 237–238, 240, 241
middle childhood, 250–256
overview of considerations with, 233–234, 241–242
parental availability awareness for, 235
parenting plans detailing, 228–229 (*see also* parenting plans)
practical considerations with, 233–242
prepared schedule templates for, 234
procedures for altering, 228–229
provisions for future changes to, 240–241, 248, 249–250
qualitative *vs.* quantitative criteria for, 6–7
relocation affecting, 170–172, 236–237, 254–256
restricted parenting time affecting, 238, 247–250
right of first refusal provision with, 237–238
shared parenting defined in relation to, 3, 5
sibling interactions and, 236, 253–254
sleep as factor in, 61, 235, 251
supervised visitation and, 204, 205–206, 238, 247–250, 257–258
transportation and traffic allowances in, 235, 236, 250–251
vacation schedules in, 239–240
very young children's, 236, 237, 245, 246–250 (*see also* overnight visits)

parenting styles
authoritarian, 29–30
authoritative, 29, 30, 31, 119, 185
child temperament and, 244–245
gender differences in, 31–32
parental mental health issues affecting, 139
permissive, 30
parents. *See also* fathers; mothers
alienation from, 62, 147–166, 175, 178, 220
communication between (*see* interparental communication)
conflict among (*see* domestic violence; interparental conflict; marital conflict)
cooperation between (*see* interparental cooperation)
decision making by (*see* parental decision making)
dropout or absent, 8–9, 32, 36–37
emotional attachment to (*see* emotional attachment)
gay/lesbian, 8, 181, 182, 189
mental health issues of (*see* parental mental health issues)
negative comments about other parent by, 99–100, 101
never-married, 8, 9, 181, 183–192, 203
parenting styles of, 29–30, 31–32, 119, 139, 185, 244–245
psychological parent, as legal term, 29
relocation of, 167–180, 236–237, 254–256, 263
Pennsylvania, parenting plan legal criteria, 335–336
perception, intuition and, 13
personality disorders
childhood experiences leading to, 133
parental, 76, 83, 94, 135–136
physical attractiveness biases, 19
Positive Parenting Program, 201
post-traumatic stress disorder, parental, 16
Power and Control Wheel, 76

practical considerations, 209–231, 233–242
child-focused calendars as, 223–224
child in-camera interviews as, 225–227
child safety as, 214–217
decision making as, 212–214
household or residential changes as, 217–223
interparental communication as, 224–225
overview of, 209, 230–231
parenting plan components as, 228–230
remarriage as, 210–212
reports of parenting history as, 209–210
schedule-focused, 233–242
pro-con lists
child abuse and neglect substantiation via, 206
foundation for good parenting plans using, 21–22, 262
marital conflict problem-solving using, 105
parental alienation assertion clarity via, 162
parental decision making determinations via, 214
sample, 262
very young children's overnight visit dispute resolution using, 68
pro se litigants, 183–184, 190–191
Protective Mothers' Alliance International (PMAI), 9
psychological parent, 29

race and ethnicity
biases based on, 19
never-married parents' familial instability in relation to, 186, 188–189
reasoning
definition and description of, 13
foundation for good parenting plans based on, 12–14, 16–17, 19–22, 28, 68–69, 262
methods to improve, 20–22, 262
scientific evidence underlying, 28
Rehabilitation Act of 1973, 122
relocation, 167–180
costs associated with, 171–172
definition of, 170
education effects of, 173, 176–177
electronic communication after, 172–173, 254–255
legal criteria and factors for, 167–169
motivations for, 175–176
overview of considerations with, 167, 178–180
parenting schedules and, 170–172, 236–237, 254–256
practicalities of, 169–173
prevalence of, 169–170
research on, 173–175
transportation issues and, 171, 172, 263
remarriage, 176, 210–212. *See also* step– or blended families
reports of parenting history, 6–7, 209–210
representativeness heuristics, 16
residential changes
children's mental health and behavior affected by, 219–221
overnight visits and (*see* overnight visits)
parenting plan consideration of, 217–223
relocation and, 167–180, 236–237, 254–256, 263
scientific evidence on effects of, 37–39, 173–175
transitions for (*see* transitions)
resistance to time with parent. *See* parental alienation
reunification therapy, 161

Safe Kids Worldwide, 216
safety and health issues
children's mental health and special needs affecting, 111, 114, 119–120, 123

safety and health issues *(continued)*
parental alienation for reasons of, 160–161
parenting plan consideration of, 214–217
for very young children, 215, 216
violence in families affecting (*see* child abuse and neglect; domestic violence)
same-sex parents, 8, 181, 182, 189
schedules. *See* parenting schedules
schizophrenia, parental, 118
scientific evidence on children of divorce, 25–44
on child adjustment, 27, 28–29, 31–35, 53, 54
on divorce-specific effects, 32–34
on dropout or absent parents, 32, 36–37
on economic strain, 32, 34
on excessive stress, 32, 39
on factors influencing well-being, 28–34
on fathers' involvement, 31–32, 34, 36–37, 57
on interparental conflict, 29, 32, 33–34, 37, 39, 41–42
overview of, 25, 42–44
on parental mental health, 32, 33–34, 39–40
parenting plan consideration of, 39–44
on parenting styles, 29–30, 31–32
research providing, 25–28, 40–41, 49–61, 173–175
on residential changes, 37–39, 173–175
on shared/joint parenting, 34–39
self-injury, childhood, 111, 120, 221
shared parenting
Australian law on, 48
domestic violence affecting success of, 8, 81–82, 95–96
equally, 3, 7, 39, 48, 95, 169, 252, 258
interparental conflict affecting success of, 7–8
interparental cooperation affecting success of, 7
marital conflict affecting, 7–8, 89, 95–96, 103–104
parallel parenting *vs.,* 82, 94, 96
schedules outlining (*see* parenting schedules)
scientific evidence on, 34–39
sole custody *vs.,* 7, 35, 38, 91–92
terminology for, 3, 5
smoking, 132, 134, 215
socioeconomic status
child abuse and neglect in relation to, 203
marital conflict legal proceedings affecting, 95
never-married parents', 183, 185–186, 189–190
relocation and, 171–172, 176, 177
scientific evidence on effect of, 32, 34
very young child's overnight visits and, 55
South Carolina, parenting plan legal criteria, 336–339
South Dakota, parenting plan legal criteria, 339
spousal abuse. *See* domestic violence
state statutes. *See also specific states*
friendly parent provisions in, 158–159
parenting plan legal criteria, 265–373
relocation factors in, 167–169, 170
reports of parenting history under, 209
Uniform Marriage and Divorce Act influencing, 33
step– or blended families
child adjustment in, 184, 186, 187, 211–212
remarriage creating, 176, 210–212
step-up parenting, 67–68
stereotypes, biases based on, 19
Strange Situation procedure, 46–47, 49
stress
children's mental health and special needs creating, 115, 125

scientific evidence on effects of, 32, 39
very young child care creating, 63
substance use/abuse
assessment or testing for, 136–138, 139–140
child or adolescent, 40, 118, 221
conduct disorders and, 118
domestic violence and, 83
marital conflict affected by, 86, 88, 133, 141
parental, 33, 57, 60, 67, 83, 86, 88, 118, 132–135, 136–138, 139–140, 141–143, 150
parental alienation due to, 150
prevalence of, 132–133
residential changes leading to, 221
scientific evidence on effects of, 33, 40
smoking as, 132, 134, 215
treatment or interventions for, 142–143
very young child care and, 57, 60, 67
suicide, childhood, 111, 119–120
supervised transitions, 223
supervised visitation, 204, 205–206, 238, 247–250, 257–258
suspended visitation, 204

temperament, 60, 88, 169, 219–220, 244–245
Tennessee, parenting plan legal criteria, 339
Texas, parenting plan legal criteria, 340–365
transitions
cancellation of, 229
child preparation for, 218
children's mental health and special needs considerations with, 117–118
designated exchange bags for, 219
domestic violence and, 80, 82
frequency of, 237–238
limited or no contact during, 66, 80, 106
marital conflict and specifics of, 106–107, 141, 218, 222–223
parental alienation and, 149–150, 220
parenting plan provisions for smooth, 217–223
supervised, 223
transition objects in, 66, 218
transportation for, 66, 106, 221–222
very young children's, 60, 65–66, 149, 218–220
transportation
airplane, for unaccompanied children, 172, 263
car seats for, 66, 106, 215
parental mental health and issues of, 140, 141
parenting schedule allowances for, 235, 236, 250–251
relocation and issues of, 171, 172, 263
for transitions, agreements on, 66, 106, 221–222
very young child parenting plan consideration of, 63, 66
Triple P-Positive Parenting Program, 201

Uniform Marriage and Divorce Act (UMDA), 33
United Kingdom, relocation research in, 174–175
Utah, parenting plan legal criteria, 365–367

vacation, parenting schedules with, 239–240
very young children of divorce/separation, 45–71
child abuse and neglect among, 203
child-parent interaction levels considered for, 57, 58–59
emotional attachment in, 5–6, 46–48, 49–50, 52, 53, 55–57, 59, 236, 237, 245
interparental communication about, 50, 51–52, 63–66

very young children of divorce/separation *(continued)*
interparental conflict affecting, 57–58, 62
interparental cooperation affecting, 58, 59, 61–62, 68
overnight visits for, 5–6, 47, 48, 49–62, 68, 217–221
overview of considerations with, 45–46, 69–71
parental alienation with, 62, 149
parental mental health affecting, 57, 60–61, 67
parenting competence with, 57, 58–59, 67, 68, 217, 245, 247–248
parenting plans for, 45–71
parenting schedules with, 236, 237, 245, 246–250 (*see also* overnight visits)
practical considerations with, 61–63
professional competence with planning for, 63–69
safety and health issues, 215, 216
step-up of involvement with, 67–68
time management considerations with, 62, 63
transitions of, 60, 65–66, 149, 218–220
violence in families. *See* child abuse and neglect; domestic violence
Virginia, parenting plan legal criteria, 367

Washington, parenting plan legal criteria, 367–369
West Virginia, parenting plan legal criteria, 369
Wingspread Conference on Domestic Violence and Family Courts, 76–77
Wisconsin, parenting plan legal criteria, 369–371
Wyoming, parenting plan legal criteria, 371–373
WYSIATI (What You See Is All There Is), 18, 89